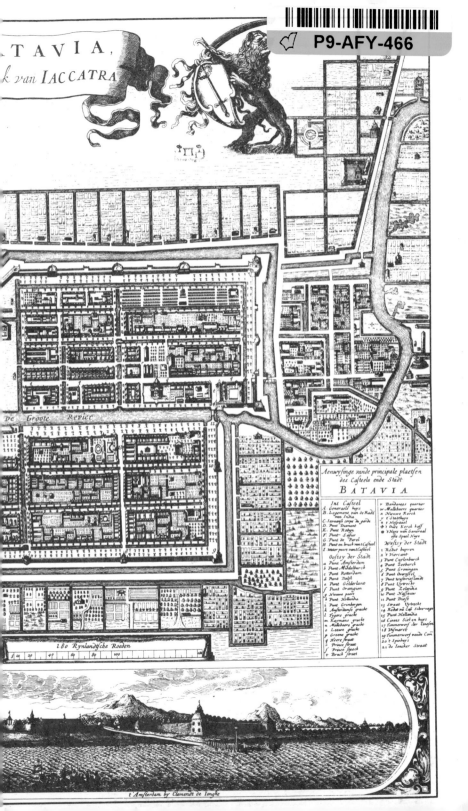

BATAVIA,
oock van IACCATRA

De Groote Revier

Aenwysinge vande principale plaetfen
des Cafteels ende Stadt
BATAVIA

Int Cafteel

A. Generaels huys
B. Logement van de Radé
C. Jans eels corpe de garde
D. Punt Diamant
E. Punt Robyn
F. Punt Safier
G. Punt de Parel
H. Punt en bruch van t Cafteel
I. Water poort van t Cafteel

Oostsy der Stadt

a. Pune Amsterdam
b. Punt Middelburch
c. Punt Rotterdam
d. Punt Delft
e. Punt Gelderlant
f. Punt Orangien
g. Nieuwe poort
h. Punt Hollanda
i. Punt Grunbergen
Amsterdamse grache
k. Tygers grache
l. Raymans grache
m. Maleborgs grache
n. Leeuw grache
o. Groene grache
p. Heere straat
q. Princi straat
r. Princi speech
s. Bruch straat

t. Bandanees quarter
v. Malebaers quarter
x. Nieuwe Kerck
y. t Stadthuys
z. t Nolspaeel
* t Oude Kerck hoff
⊙ t Huys van Generael
ofte Spoel Huys

Weftsy der Stadt

1. Redut buyren
2. t Diercant
3. Punt Coelenburch
4. Punt Zeeburch
5. Punt Groningen
6. Punt Overyssel
7. Punt Wefterwolfslant
8. Punt Utyrecht
9. Punt Zelouda
10. Punt Naffauw
11. Punt Dreft
12. Straat Uytrecht
13. Reduut na Siherwage
14. Punt Hollandia
15. Conees Siel en huys
16. t Timmerwerf der Tunefen
17. Weruert
18. Timmerwerf vande Com
19. t Spynhuys
20. de Toucher Straat

180 Rynlandsche Roeden

t'Amsterdam by Clemendt de Ionghe

JAKARTA
A HISTORY

JAKARTA
A HISTORY

Revised Edition

SUSAN ABEYASEKERE

SINGAPORE
OXFORD UNIVERSITY PRESS
OXFORD   NEW YORK

Oxford University Press

Oxford New York Toronto
Delhi Bombay Calcutta Madras Karachi
Petaling Jaya Singapore Hong Kong Tokyo
Nairobi Dar es Salaam Cape Town
Melbourne Auckland
and associated companies in
Berlin Ibadan

Oxford is a trade mark of Oxford University Press

ISBN 0 19 588947 9

The author has made every effort to trace the copyright
holders of maps and photographs but, in some instances,
without success. To these, the author and publisher
offer their apologies, trusting that they will accept
the will for the deed.

Printed in Malaysia by Peter Chong Printers Sdn. Bhd.
Published by Oxford University Press Pte. Ltd.,
Unit 221, Ubi Avenue 4, Singapore 1440

Acknowledgements

SINCE this book has been many years in the making, there are a large number of people who should be thanked.

First there is the happy band of scholars at the Centre of Southeast Asian Studies at Monash University, who have since 1969 nourished my interest in South-East Asia. Special thanks are due to Jamie Mackie and John Legge who started me off on the road of Indonesian history, and to Merle Ricklefs who offered encouragement and detailed comments on the typescript of this book.

Many librarians and archivists in Australia, Indonesia and the Netherlands have been most helpful to me over the years. For enthusiasm and friendship I must mention the late Bob Muskens of the Monash Library.

People who offered me hospitality and gave me interviews in Indonesia and the Netherlands during my stays there in 1970–1 and 1979–80 should be thanked. Although they are too many to name, I remember them most warmly, especially the Tarekats of Menteng and Els Vitringa of Leiden.

Research on this book was made possible through study leave from my place of work, Footscray Institute of Technology. I am also indebted to my students there for teaching me the need to address a more general audience rather than a narrowly academic one.

While writing this book I have received assistance from Dayal Abeyasekere, Lea Jellinek, Merle Ricklefs, John Ingleson, Robert Cribb and Tony Reid, among others. I would like to thank them all, although none of them, of course, bears any responsibility for the outcome. Patrick Miller's work on maps and figures was much appreciated.

For inspiration I thank Lea Jellinek and my friends at Community Aid Abroad.

Contents

Acknowledgements   v
Figures   x
Maps   x
Plates   xii
Introduction   xvi

PART I
The Old Masters

1 Company Town: Early Origins to 1800   3

Sunda Kalapa to Jayakarta   3
Origins of Batavia   7
An Isolated Town   12
Early Batavia   14
A Mixed Society   19
Batavia's Chinese   23
Mardijkers and Others   28
Life in Eighteenth-century Batavia   31
The Decline of Old Batavia   38
Decline of the Company   41

2 The Colonial City: Batavia in the Nineteenth Century 48

Harbour and Old Town   48
Weltevreden   54
European Society   57
Eurasians, Chinese, Arabs   60
Indonesians   64
Divisive Forces   68
Health   71
Culture and Women   75
Batavia: Growth and Role   81

3 Batavia, 1900–1942: The Colonial City under Challenge   88

Batavia in 1940   88
The Impact of Education   94
The Potential for Indonesian Nationalism in Batavia   99
Sarekat Islam, the Communist Party and the
    Aftermath   103
Arabs and Chinese   109
Europeans   114
A Forum for Urban Debate: the Municipal Council   117
Kampung Improvement   120
The Coming of War   125

PART II
Interregnum

**4 Japanese Occupation and the Struggle for
Independence, 1942–1949**   133

Japanese Reorganization of Batavia   134
Life under the Japanese   138
Jakarta and the War Effort   142
Jakarta: Kota Proklamasi   146
Jakarta in Dispute   148
Jakarta: Kota Diplomasi   151
Batavia Again   157
Transfer of Sovereignty   160

PART III
The New Masters

5 Sukarno's Jakarta: 1950–1965   167

Sukarno's Influence   167
Straining at the Seams   171
Modest Achievements   177
The Urban Economy   181
'The Foreigners'   187
A New Urban Society   191
Urban Regulation and Planning   196
Contentious Years   202
The End of Sukarno's Rule   209

6 Jakarta under Sadikin and His Successors: 1966–1985   215

Sadikin   215
Pembangunan: the Era of Development   217
Managing Population Growth   221
Land Clearance   226
Street Clearance   229
Rich and Poor   232
Politics in Abeyance   237
Sadikin's Dilemma   241
Sadikin's Successors   243
Recent Political Developments   246

Conclusion   254
Glossary   264
Select Bibliography   267
Index   285

Note on Spelling
Modern Indonesian spelling has been used except where quotations use older forms.

Figures

2.1 Ethnic Distribution of the Population of Batavia,
   *c.*1885   69

2.2 Population of Batavia by Ethnic Group, 1820–1900   73

Maps

Batavia in 1650. North is on the left. Since the fort was built, the coastline has moved beyond it. The view from the sea is shown below. (Reproduced from F. de Haan, *Oud Batavia*, Batavia, 1922)   *front endpaper*

Batavia in 1780. North is at the bottom of the page. The coastline has further lengthened. A 'Chinese quarter' has been built south of the town walls, following the massacre of 1740. (Reproduced from F. de Haan, *Oud Batavia*, Batavia, 1922)   *back endpaper*

1.1 The Bay of Jakarta (Reproduced from H. Th. Verstappen, *Djakarta Bay. A Geomorphological Study on Shoreline Development*, 's-Gravenhage, Trio, 1953)   4

1.2 Jayakarta, 1618 (Reproduced from F. de Haan, *Oud Batavia*, Batavia, 1922)   10

1.3 Batavia, 1650 (Reproduced from Abdurrachman Surjomihardjo, *Pemekaran Kota* (The Growth of Jakarta), Jakarta, Djambatan, 1977)   16

1.4 Batavia and Surroundings, 1740 (Reproduced from
Adolf Heuken, *Historical Sites of Jakarta*, Jakarta,
Cipta Loka Caraka, 1982)   32

2.1 Batavia and Environs, *c.*1885 (J. Vos, Batavia, 1887)   50–1

3.1 The Growth of Batavia to 1938 (Reproduced from
Abdurrachman Surjomihardjo, *Pemekaran Kota*
(The Growth of Jakarta), Jakarta, Djambatan, 1977)   89

4.1 Batavia in 1946 (Based on a map from J. Fabricius,
Hoe ik Indie Terugvond, Den Haag, Leopoldus,
1947)   153

5.1 Jakarta in 1965 (Reproduced from Lance Castles,
'The Ethnic Profile of Djakarta', *Indonesia*, Vol. 3,
1967)   172

6.1 Jakarta in 1977 (Based on a map from Gunther W.
Holtorf, *Falk Plan Jakarta*, Hamburg, Falk-Verlag,
1977)   218

Plates

Between pages 142 and 143

1 Inter-island boats unloading at Sunda Kelapa, the oldest port area of Jakarta.

2 Jan Pieterszoon Coen (1587–1629), founder of Batavia. (From F. de Haan, *Oud Batavia*, Batavia, G. Kolff, 1922.)

3 The oldest extant Buddhist temple in Jakarta, the Wihara Dharma Bhakti, founded in the mid-seventeenth century.

4 Town Hall of Batavia, built in 1710, now the Jakarta City Museum.

5 Mesjid Angke, a mosque built by a Chinese architect for Balinese Muslims in Batavia in 1761.

6 House of the former Governor-General Reinier de Klerk, built in 1760 and now the National Archives.

7 Tiger's Canal, sketched by Johannes Rach in the 1770s. (From F. de Haan, *Oud Batavia*, Batavia, G. Kolff, 1922.)

8 Old houses in Glodok, the 'Chinese camp' built after the massacre of 1740.

9 Auction of slaves in Batavia, early nineteenth century. (From *Tijdschrift voor Nederlandsch Indie*, Vol. 15, No. 9, 1853.)

10 Waterloo Square in Weltevreden, about 1840. (From J. J. van Braan, *Vues de Java*, Amsterdam, c.1840.)

11 A street-stall in Batavia in the mid-nineteenth century. (From *Tijdschrift voor Nederlandsch Indie*, Vol. 15, No. 7, 1853.)

12 Coolies waiting for work at a Batavia warehouse, mid-nineteenth century. (From A. van Pers, *Nederlandsch Oost-Indische Typen*, 's-Gravenhage, 1856.)

13 Woman making batik, mid-nineteenth century. (From E. Hardouin and W. L. Ritter, *Java. Tooneelen uit het Leven*, 's-Gravenhage, 1855.)

14 Chinese playing cards in Batavia, mid-nineteenth century. (From A. van Pers, *Nederlandsch Oost-Indische Typen*, 's-Gravenhage, 1856.)

15 *Kampung* on outskirts of Batavia in the nineteenth century. (From V. I. van der Wall, *Oude Hollandsche Buitenplaatsen van Batavia*, Deventer, Van Hoeve, 1943.)

16 A *nyai*, photographed in about the 1860s. (From E. Breton de Nijs, *Tempo Doeloe*, Amsterdam, Querido, 1961.)

17 The numerous Indonesian servants employed in a European house, around 1870. (From *Gambar Gambar, Nederlandsch-Indische Prenten*, Leiden, 1879.)

18 Interior of a horse-drawn tram in late nineteenth-century Batavia, illustrating the city's ethnic diversity. (From M. T. H. Perelaer, *Het Kamerlid Van Berkenstein in Nederlandsch Indie*, Leiden, 1888, illustrated by J. C. Rappard.)

19 A *ronggeng* (Indonesian dancer) with orchestra performs at a European house in the late nineteenth century. (From E. Breton de Nijs, *Tempo Doeloe*, Amsterdam, Querido, 1961.)

20 A Eurasian family in the late nineteenth century. (From E. Breton de Nijs, *Batavia, Koningin van het Oosten*, 's-Gravenhage, Thomas en Eras, 1977.)

21 The Batavia 'roads', now known as Sunda Kelapa, in the late nineteenth century. (From E. Breton de Nijs, *Batavia, Koningin van het Oosten*, 's-Gravenhage, Thomas en Eras, 1977.)

22 Said Abdullah bin Aloie bin Abdullah Alatas, a successful Arab merchant, and his house in Tanah Abang at the turn of this century. (From A. Wright and O. T. Breakspear, *Twentieth Century Impressions of Netherlands India*, London, Lloyds Greater Britain Publishing Co., 1909.)

23 Officers of the Chinese Council of Batavia at the beginning of the twentieth century. (From A. Wright and O. T. Breakspear, *Twentieth Century Impressions of Netherlands India*, London, Lloyds Greater Britain Publishing Co., 1909.)

24 *Ondel-ondel*, a form of street theatre associated with the Orang Betawi, in a *kampung* early this century. (From H. J. de Graaf, *Batavia in Oude Ansichten*, Zaltbommel, Europese Bibliotheek, 1970.)

25 Mohammad Husni Thamrin (1894–1941), a nationalist leader and the most famous Orang Betawi. (From R. M. Ali and F. Bodmer, *Djakarta Through the Ages*, Djakarta, Government of the Capital City of Djakarta, 1969.)

26 Flooding in a *kampung* in about the 1930s. (From H. J. de Graaf, *Batavia in Oude Ansichten*, Zaltbommel, Europese Bibliotheek, 1970.)

27 A street in the new European suburb of Menteng in about 1935. (From *Batavia als Handels-, Industrie- en Woonstad*, Batavia, Kolff, 1937.)

28 Pasar Baru, the main shopping centre in Weltevreden for Europeans, in about 1935. (From *Batavia als Handels-, Industrie- en Woonstad*, Batavia, Kolff, 1937.)

29 The rally of 19 August 1945 to celebrate the declaration of independence. (From *Karya Jaya: Kenang-kenangan Lima Kepala Daerah Jakarta, 1945–1966*, Jakarta, Pemerintah Daerah Khusus Ibu Kota Jakarta, 1977.)

30 Independence slogans on the Dutch monument to General van Heutsz, conqueror of Aceh, greet Allied troops arriving in Jakarta at the end of 1943. (From *Karya Jaya: Kenang-kenangan Lima Kepala Daerah Jakarta, 1945–1966*, Jakarta, Pemerintah Daerah Khusus Ibu Kota Jakarta, 1977.)

31 Jakartans enjoy a snack from a street vendor in the 1940s. (From Hein Buitenweg, *Zo Kenden Wij Batavia*, Katwijk aan Zee, Servire, 1977.)

32 One of Jakarta's last trams, typically overcrowded, passes Chinese shops on Jalan Senen Raya in the 1950s. (From J. J. A. Duparc, *De Elektrische Stadstrams op Java*, Rotterdam, Wijt en Zoonen, 1972.)

33 President Sukarno and Mayor Sudiro contemplate a pile of garbage in Jakarta in 1957. (From *Karya Jaya: Kenang-kenangan Lima Kepala Daerah Jakarta, 1945–1966*, Jakarta, Pemerintah Daerah Khusus Ibu Kota Jakarta, 1977.)

34 President Sukarno and Governor Sumarno inspect a model of the cloverleaf bridge in the Blueprint Building in 1962. (From Soedarmadji J. H. Damais, *Bung Karno dan Seni*, Jakarta, Yayasan Bung Karno, 1979.)

35 The National Monument erected in the central Independence Square.

36 Inauguration of the Welcome Monument and Hotel Indonesia, ready for the Asian Games in 1962. (From *Karya Jaya: Kenang-kenangan Lima Kepala Daerah Jakarta, 1945–1966*, Jakarta, Pemerintah Daerah Khusus Ibu Kota Jakarta, 1977.)

37 A suspected communist is arrested in Jakarta at the end of 1965. (The Bettmann Archive)

38 Ali Sadikin, Governor of Jakarta 1966–1977. (From R. M. Ali and F. Bodmer, *Djakarta Through the Ages*, Djakarta, Government of the Capital City of Djakarta, 1969.)

39 Market building at Glodok: New-style shopping centre of the 1970s.

40 Street vendor: Old-style shopping. (Courtesy Lea Jellinek)

41 Squatter housing in Jakarta in the 1970s. (Courtesy Lea Jellinek)

42 Lane in a relatively prosperous inner-city *kampung* in 1980.

43 A leafy street in spacious Kebayoran Baru.

44 New house in a recent wealthy residential suburb, 1980.

45 Scavengers recycling waste paper. (Courtesy Lea Jellinek)

46 Bamboo rafts on the River Ciliwung in southern Jakarta: A timeless scene.

47 Jalan Thamrin, the main road of modern Jakarta at the end of the 1970s. (Courtesy Lea Jellinek)

48 The inner-city *kampung* of Kebun Kacang before demolition in 1980. (Courtesy Lea Jellinek)

Introduction

JAKARTA has more than seven million people. In any big city one is aware of the distinction between the imposing structures of the central business district and the more modest areas beyond, but Jakarta divides in a peculiarly blatant way into the city of the cosmopolitan élite, with its own brash image of what Jakarta aspires to be (another international metropolis like Singapore or Hong Kong), and the barely disguised reality of most Jakartans' irrepressible urge to find a foothold, to build their own lives. The two cities overlap, footpath vendors displaying their meagre wares outside brand-new multi-storey market buildings, scavengers making good pickings in the streets of prosperous suburbs. They conflict: police round up unlicensed pedlars; they arrest pedicab drivers venturing illegally into the main streets.

Set in a swampy hot plain, its little islands and peninsulas of modern metropolis lapped by a vast sea of slums, Jakarta appears to the foreign visitor to offer few attractions. Tourists in search of the exotic flee from the capital to the refuge of Yogyakarta or Bali, leaving behind what they see merely as a wilderness of Western-style shopping complexes and garish hoardings advertising imported films. Foreign businessmen who may prefer this side of modern life are continually affronted by sudden gaps in the stage set through which they glimpse beggars lurking on overpasses and vistas of crumbling shanties. Jakarta's inhabitants, most of them born outside, sometimes regard their town ambivalently. From a million transistor radios and cassette-players the popular singer Ebiet Ade drawls, Bob Dylan style:

> Dust lies hot on streets
> Clearly empty of love and pity;
> It's not like my green village
> Here.[1]

Yet even the outsider can sense the pull of Jakarta. Like every big capital, it emanates power: it is here that important things happen in Indonesia, here you can feel part of the world scene. In a country with a censored mass media that has only very limited scope for disseminating information, Jakarta buzzes with rumours: since here you are closest to the action, surely in Jakarta you will pick up first what is really going on. And for those uninterested in politics, there is the assurance that Jakarta concentrates the widest variety of jobs and the best of all services—educational, medical, cultural—and takes the cream of foreign investment.

That could be said about almost any capital in a Third World country. What makes Jakarta specially *Indonesian*? This is a difficult question in a country of many thousands of islands which is still trying to determine what it is to be Indonesian. What can a city of some seven million have in common with a country whose population of one hundred and seventy-five million is overwhelmingly rural? As any Indonesian will tell you, Jakarta is different from the rest of the nation, a world of its own, because it is a large urban concentration, because it is the centre of government and administration, because it is exceptionally privileged in its amenities, and because it is a melting-pot of cultures. This last point has been considered a justification for regarding Jakarta as the only Indonesian town in the nation, since there people from all over the archipelago meet.[2] Jakarta is one of the very few cities where most people speak Indonesian as the normal means of communication. Elsewhere the national Bahasa Indonesia is a purely official language for school and formal occasions; the majority of Indonesians speak the local language, whether it be Sundanese, Javanese, Balinese or one of the other hundred-odd languages of the archipelago.

To a contemporary observer, it might seem that the pretentious mask which the city wears and its isolation from its region are features which emerged only recently, a result perhaps of government policy and the attractiveness of the capital to people from all over the country. Yet these features can be traced far back into Jakarta's colonial past. Starting with the port of Batavia in 1619, the population was composed of a mix of people quite different from its West Javanese environs—a unique amalgam which developed its own culture. And from colonial times onwards, governments have sought to impose an inappropriate facade on Jakarta, a facade which was unable to conceal the sprawl of the city.

For the student of Jakarta's history, tracing these continuities through the changes in the city's past has its own fascination.[3] For the student of Indonesia as a whole, the role of Jakarta within the wider scheme of things is also of interest. What kind of an impact has it had on the country at large? Surely considerable since it has long been the seat of government and a cultural trend-setter. Is Jakarta the awful culmination of the nation's past or does it in fact mirror Indonesia's future? Throughout its history its rulers have certainly intended the latter, but the real city has always taken its own perversely different path, making it to some extent a microcosm of the country at large—a forum for government policies at odds with people struggling to make a life of their own.

1. Ebiet G. Ade, 'Jakarta 1', *Album Camellia 1*, Jakarta, Jackson Record cassette, 1977.

2. Lance Castles, 'The Ethnic Profile of Djakarta', *Indonesia*, Vol. 1, April 1967, p. 153.

3. The classic work on the history of Jakarta is F. de Haan's *Oud Batavia*, Batavia, Kolff, 1922. As its name implies, the book deals only with Batavia in the seventeenth to early nineteenth centuries. Entertaining to read, this detailed study is unfortunately quite without source references: one has to trust de Haan's great scholarship. (He was the state archivist in Batavia early this century.) Indonesians are now beginning to write about Jakarta's history, but much of their work is not easily obtained. An example is S. Z. Hadisutjipto, *Sekitar 200 Tahun Sejarah Jakarta (1750–1945)*, Jakarta, Pemerintah DKI Jakarta, 1979. Very little is available in English on Jakarta's history. The most useful work is Lance Castles, op. cit., pp. 153–204. A detailed study of Batavia up to the nineteenth century can be found in P. Milone, 'Queen City of the East: the Metamorphosis of a Colonial Capital', Ph.D. dissertation, University of California, 1966. For a brief overview of Jakarta's physical growth, see Abdurrachman Surjomihardjo, *Pemekaran Kota/The Growth of Jakarta*, Jakarta, Djambatan, 1977. Adolf Heuken has written a useful guide to historical buildings: *Historical Sites of Jakarta* (Jakarta, Cipta Loka Caraka, 1982).

PART I
The Old Masters

1

Company Town: Early Origins to 1800

DUTCH and Indonesian historians present sharply differing views on the early history of Jakarta. Indonesian nationalists like to dwell on the long antecedents of the present city, tracing it back through Muslim and Hindu-Javanese kingdoms to prehistoric times, while the Dutch, writing about *their* Batavia, start the story with the conquest by Dutch East India Company forces and the building of a Dutch fort in 1619.[1] The difference of viewpoint is easy to understand. Indonesians are naturally eager to see the capital of their independent republic as the direct descendant of great centres from pre-colonial times, making Batavia just a brief aberration of foreign domination amidst centuries of Indonesian control. To the Dutch, however, the previously existing towns near the site of Batavia were historically irrelevant: not only was the last of those Indonesian ports wiped off the map forever by Dutch arms, but moreover Batavia was a completely new species of city, having nothing in common with Indonesian towns which might have happened to pre-exist there. Batavia to the Dutch was a European creation, built by them out of nothing from entirely new materials.

Today, the colonial view seems rather far-fetched since Batavia cannot be as completely divorced from its past as the Dutch might have wished. Nevertheless, the scarcity of information and material relics from Indonesian ports on the site of Jakarta would seem to excuse only a brief survey of the pre-colonial days in favour of greater attention to the 'Queen of the East', as the Dutch gloried in calling Batavia.

Sunda Kalapa to Jayakarta

The area around the mouth of the Ciliwung River in West Java, the site of present-day Jakarta, has known human settlement from prehistoric times.[2] Built up from the silt washed down from the volcanic mountain range to the south, an alluvial plain spreads out in a fan shape traversed by several rivers—the Cisadane, Angke, Ciliwung, Bekasi and Citarum. Over time the coast, a strip of low-lying swampy land fringing the alluvial plain, has been gradually extended further and further to the north by river mud. Anyone living in Jakarta is aware of the distinction between the easily flooded marshy area near the coast and the higher, fertile 'red earth' region. (See Map 1.1.)

Archaeological excavations in the greater Jakarta area have unearthed implements from the Neolithic, Bronze and Iron Ages. A rock inscription discovered near the present harbour of Tanjung Priok bears witness to irrigation works conducted in the area by orders of a King Purnawarman of the Kingdom of Tarumanegara in the mid-fifth century AD—evidence of the existence of Hindu-Javanese civilization.

Jakarta's origins as a port can be traced back to about the twelfth century, when there is mention of a town called Sunda

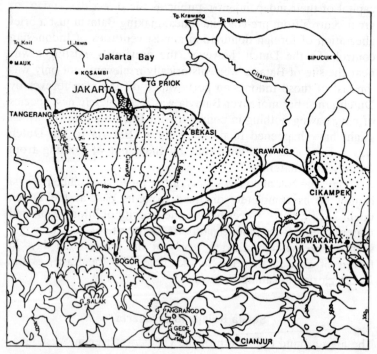

1.1 The Bay of Jakarta (Reproduced from H. Th. Verstappen, *Djakarta Bay. A Geomorphological Study on Shoreline Development*, 's-Gravenhage, Trio, 1953)

Kalapa, which appears to have been a harbour for a Hindu-Javanese kingdom called Pajajaran, the capital of which was near the present mountain resort of Bogor, south of Jakarta. This kingdom lasted until the sixteenth century. The port's name refers to the West Javanese region of Sunda, where the people speak their own language and have a culture distinct from that of Central and Eastern Java, and also to the *kelapa*, the coconut palm which thrives in this coastal area. Here, for the first time, a port on the Ciliwung emerged as an important part of the web of Indonesian trade.

With the growth in trade around and through the Indonesian archipelago, various towns along the Malacca Straits rose to prominence, since ships had to traverse these straits on their voyage between the archipelago and the west. In a time of sailing ships, these coasts were natural stopping places for travellers and sailors whose vessels sailed in this direction on one monsoon and could load and refurbish there while awaiting the change of winds which would carry their vessels back again. So ports on these straits could act as convenient provisioning harbours and entrepôts where goods were brought from all over the islands ready for transhipment elsewhere. A port which could establish its pre-eminence here could benefit from taxes and imposts on this trade. Such was the aim of several South-East Asian maritime rulers, who built up empires based on the control of international trade and who personally supervised transactions for their own aggrandizement. If the ruler's navy was strong and his terms not too onerous, traders were prepared to accept the protection of such ports, but the history of the region reflects fluctuations in the fortunes of the great port cities, as trading patterns shifted.

The importance of Sunda Kalapa was similarly affected: as the port of Malacca on the west coast of Malaya rose in power, that of Sunda Kalapa waned along with other ports in the region. However, when Malacca was conquered by the Portuguese in 1511, Sunda Kalapa benefited from increased patronage by Muslim traders who boycotted Malacca.

Trade in the archipelago brought foreigners and foreign influences. From India, Hinduism and Buddhism had already been accepted in many parts of Indonesia, adopted first by rulers who expected their subjects to follow suit. In the sixteenth century Sunda Kalapa, which had remained Hindu in religious affiliation, was caught in the mesh of rivalry between two new foreign forces—Islam and Christianity. Although it wished to benefit from the patronage of Muslim traders, the leadership of Pajajaran was anxiously aware of the inroads being made by the new religion in neighbouring Javanese ports. Adept as all the maritime leaders were at manipulating traders to their own advantage, Sunda Kalapa's rulers observed the intense hostility that existed between the Muslims and the new foreign influence on the scene—the Christian Portuguese, the first European sailors to frequent Indonesia, who had already proved their mettle by wresting Malacca from the hated infidels.[3] Hoping to gain some protection against their Muslim neighbours, in 1522 Sunda Kalapa made an agreement with the Portuguese to guarantee a certain amount of pepper annually, in return for which the Portuguese would build a fort at Sunda Kalapa. When the Portuguese returned in 1527 to build their fort, however, they found they had been forestalled by the Muslims. The rising West Javanese power, the Sultanate of Banten to the west of Sunda Kalapa, had sent a commander called Fatahillah (also known as Fadhillah Khan or, to the Portuguese, as Tagaril or Falatehan) to conquer the town, turning it into a vassal state of Banten. The Portuguese fleet was successfully turned back by Fatahillah, who renamed the port Jayakarta, or Victorious and Prosperous—the origin of the present name Jakarta. The supposed date of this event was chosen much later by the independent Indonesian administration of Jakarta as the city's anniversary: the defeat of a European power was considered a matter for yearly celebration, especially in the light of the city's subsequent history.

Jayakarta, subordinated to Banten, was a less considerable town than Sunda Kalapa. It lasted until its demolition by the Dutch in 1619. Shortly before its demise, Dutch accounts described it as a town of about ten thousand people, built on the west bank of the River Ciliwung. In keeping with Javanese town planning, the centre of the town was the masonry residence of the Prince of Jayakarta (appointed by the Sultan of Banten), located next to the town square and mosque. Jayakarta had a reputation as a provisioning port where ships could anchor in an excellent harbour and find good drinking water, local timber for repairs, and *arak* (rice wine) produced by the Chinese who had settled there. Incoming ships were controlled by customs officials near the mouth of the river. The town was surrounded by a wooden palisade, outside which lay a thinly-populated region of stagnant swamps and jungle, where the aristocracy regularly hunted tigers, rhinoceros and other game. Traders from different countries—India, China, England, Holland and the other islands of the archipelago—continued to visit the port and wait there for the change of monsoon.

Origins of Batavia

Although South-East Asians were not aware of it at the time, the appearance on the scene of the Portuguese in the fifteenth century heralded the emergence of European power in the region. The Portuguese, fired by commercial and religious motives, hoped to dominate Asia. The seeds of this ambition were laid in the territories they acquired, strung out all over Asia; in South-East Asia the pearl was of course Malacca. However, the Portuguese never mustered sufficient naval and organizational strength to achieve their aims, and they were rapidly overtaken by more advanced European rivals, notably the English and the Dutch.

The commercial interest of all the Europeans in the Indonesian archipelago in the sixteenth and seventeenth centuries focused on spices, the most lucrative long-distance product which the region could provide for Europe. The sale of spices—pepper from the western archipelago but more especially nutmeg, mace and cloves from the eastern islands—was already part of a complex trade system which knit together the archipelago and in turn linked it with the rest of Asia. West Java produced pepper; the ports of East and Central Java imported spices and sandalwood in exchange for local textiles and the surplus of rice grown in the island's interior and exchanged these items for Indian textiles and Chinese luxury goods. The entry of the Europeans onto the scene was destined to shatter the profitable trade system established in the region, for a struggle soon developed amongst them to monopolize the region's trade for their own benefit. Jayakarta was to become the centre of that struggle, and a symbol of the victory of the Dutch.

In the early seventeenth century both the Dutch and the English formed East India Companies as state monopolies to pursue trade in Asia, and both companies were immediately locked in rivalry. A chartered company run by a board of directors referred to as the 'Gentlemen Seventeen', the Dutch

East India Company was created in 1602 for national ends, and its directors were responsible to the parliament of the Netherlands. By the terms of its charter the Company, commonly known by its Dutch initials as VOC, could exercise quasi-sovereign powers from the Cape of Good Hope to the East. Since the Company was founded at a time when Holland was still struggling for its independence against Spain, the Government anticipated that through trade it would provide finances for Holland to pursue its war effort against Spain at the same time as it undermined the enemy's international position by displacing it as a commercial power. In the western Indonesian archipelago, however, the VOC soon found that its main competitor was not the Spanish and their allies the Portuguese, but rather the English, since by the seventeenth century the Iberians were clearly outclassed in shipbuilding, navigation, arms and organization by the northern Europeans.

The issue that determined Jayakarta's fate was the Dutch need for a headquarters in the Indonesian archipelago.[4] They required somewhere to build and repair ships, a resting-place and provisioning base, a store for goods, a source of local intelligence and translators, and a military and administrative centre. It was not territory which they sought, but a base for their trading operations. In 1605, the Dutch acquired Fort Victoria in Ambon, a very important gain for their trade in the Spice Islands but too far east to be suitable as a centre for overseeing wider activities. They sought a port in the perennially popular trading area of west Indonesia, near the Malacca and Sunda Straits.

The problem with existing big ports in the area was that they were already dominated by powers unfriendly to the Dutch. Malacca was Portuguese; Banten, the biggest port in West Java, was controlled by a ruler who was understandably suspicious of Dutch ambitions and wary of the troublesome rivalry between the Dutch and the English. The most that he would allow the Dutch was to build a warehouse in Banten—a privilege which he also extended to the English.

It was not long before the Dutch began turning their attention to Jayakarta—or, as they called it, Jacatra—as a possible site for a headquarters. Its advantages were, firstly, that, like Banten, it was close to the Sunda Straits which were extensively used by Dutch ships in their voyage across the Indian Ocean to and from Europe via the Cape of Good Hope; secondly, its ruler, the

Prince of Jayakarta, although a vassal of Banten, had fallen out with the latter and now sought to build up his own wealth and independence by winning away traders from Banten. In 1610 a contract was signed between the Dutch and the Prince, allowing the Company to build warehouses on the east bank of the Ciliwung River.

The man who sealed Jayakarta's doom was Jan Pieterszoon Coen, appointed Governor-General of the Dutch East India Company in 1618. In Dutch eyes, Coen was a far-sighted founder of empire; others might see him as a murderous megalomaniac. In 1614, as a young man of twenty-eight, he was already spelling out extraordinarily ambitious plans for the new company. He foresaw the Netherlands possessing a string of trading posts all over Asia which would enable it to dominate the entire trade of the region. He stressed the necessity of a locality to act as a collection point for Asian goods and as a centre for colonization, since he regarded it as essential for Dutch domination to have a pool of Dutch expertise in the area—for intra-regional trade, military activities, accounting, skilled trades, and supervision of plantation agriculture. As the man on the spot, far from the Netherlands which took months to reach by ship, Coen was in a position to take vital decisions, and being a man of ambition he exercised his power to the full, bullying the Gentlemen Seventeen in his correspondence to support him after the fact. His letters are full of eternal complaints about their tardiness in backing him up with essential supplies—ships, money and manpower.

By the time that Coen was made Governor-General in 1618 relations between the Dutch, the English and the Javanese had deteriorated badly. The only thing which preserved the Dutch then, as in the years ahead, was disunity among their enemies. The Dutch and the English were locked in an intense trading rivalry, which in West Java often exploded into naked aggression in the port of Banten. Exasperated by the behaviour of the Europeans, the ruler was increasingly hostile towards them as they fought each other and at the same time tried to force the local Javanese and Chinese traders into lowering their pepper prices. While Banten was proving increasingly dangerous for the Dutch, they had an even more powerful enemy in the ruler of Mataram, Sultan Agung, the aspiring master of East and Central Java, who resented the hindrance which the Dutch presence formed to his ambitions to conquer the whole island. If the rulers of Banten and Mataram had been able to unite with each other or with the English, the VOC would never have been able to establish a foothold on the island; but each of these powers had strong reason to distrust the other, since each was out to strengthen its own position.

In 1618 Coen decided to try to get the upper hand in Banten

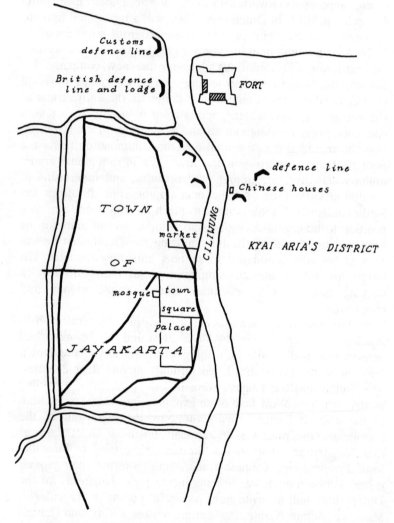

1.2 Jayakarta, 1618 (Reproduced from F. de Haan, *Oud Batavia*, Batavia, 1922)

where he believed the VOC was in imminent danger from both the English and the Bantenese. In preparation for action, he fortified the defences of the Dutch buildings in Jayakarta and increased the garrison there. (See Map 1.2.) This was naturally met on the Prince's side by an upgrading of Jayakarta's defences. The English had also set up a factory on the opposite side of the river from the Dutch. Coen was spoiling for a fight. He wrote to the Gentlemen Seventeen:

Your excellencies should please consider how nicely we are sitting here with the enmity of all the world breathing down our necks. But for all that we do not lack courage.... Therefore once again I pray you very humbly that at the first opportunity you send hither a great number of people, a great number of ships and a great sum of money, with all sorts of necessities. If this be done, everything will turn out well; if not, Your Excellencies will regret it. Do not despair, do not spare your enemies, as there is nothing in the world which can hinder or harm us, for God is with us; and be not affected by previous defeats, for great work can be done in the Indies and at the same time yearly very rich returns can be made there.[5]

The anxiety, mingled with Coen's usual ebullience, was justified, since at that time, at the end of 1618, his forces were well outnumbered by the English.

On 14 December 1618, the English fleet seized a Dutch ship at Banten in retaliation for which Coen set fire to the English lodge at Jayakarta. The English fleet of fourteen ships set sail for Jayakarta where there were a few indecisive skirmishes with the eight Dutch vessels. Being so strongly outnumbered, Coen decided he had no alternative but to sail for the Moluccas to seek reinforcements from the VOC outpost there, leaving the fort at Jayakarta very poorly defended with a critical shortage of gunpowder. Before setting off he wrote angrily to the Gentlemen Seventeen: 'I swear to you by the Almighty that the general Company has no enemies who more hinder and harm it here than the ignorance and thoughtlessness (to put it mildly) which reigns amongst Your Excellencies and defies understanding.'[6]

The 'siege' of the Jayakarta fort which then followed was a far from heroic story. The commander of the fort, Pieter van den Broecke, was such a storekeeper at heart that what concerned him most about the situation was that expensive bales of cotton and silk cloth had to be taken out of the warehouse and used for barricades. In fact, the fort proved to be in little danger for the simple reason that the English and the Javanese could not agree among themselves as to which should take the prey. The Banten ruler had sent his own fleet to the scene, determined that neither the English nor the Prince of Jayakarta should benefit from Dutch weakness and thus boost their position against Banten. After a half-hearted exchange of fire between the Dutch and the Jayakartans, hostilities were replaced on 14 January by negotiations. Despite a desperate move by the Prince of Jayakarta, who imprisoned some of the leading Dutch negotiators, the situation rapidly reached a stalemate. The Dutch realized they were safe when the English, deterred by the Bantenese presence, withdrew, and then the Prince of Jayakàrta was removed by the Bantenese. Inside the fort the Dutch lost no time in celebrating these moves. At one such feast on 12 March 1619 they christened the fort Batavia in honour of the ancestors of the Dutch nation, the Batavians. Although the name was not immediately given official recognition, it endured and was accepted by the Company in 1621.

When Coen returned in May 1619, very late due to unforeseen complications, he found the fort and its occupants quite safe, through no merit on their own part. With the superior forces now at his command, he seized the opportunity to make Jayakarta into the long desired headquarters of the Company in the Indies: on 30 May the VOC army razed the Indonesian town and court; all the inhabitants fled.

An Isolated Town

For a long time the Dutch felt insecure in Batavia. During Coen's second term as Governor-General the town fought off two sieges from Mataram, which aimed to subdue West Java.[7] In August 1628, sixty vessels came from Mataram ports, claiming to bring food for the town; Coen allowed only twenty to enter. That night men from all sixty boats launched an attack on the fort. Scarcely had they been repulsed after hard fighting than the main Javanese force of ten thousand men arrived and laid siege to Batavia. They tried unsuccessfully to deprive the town of water by damming the river; in the meantime the Javanese army itself succumbed to- hunger and disease, since the commander had failed to arrange adequate lines of supply. The Dutch watched in amazement as the retreating commander executed more than seven hundred of his own men as punishment and then marched home to meet the same fate himself.

Angered, the Sultan planned a second attempt, sending an even larger army to besiege the town. Again the Javanese were unable to provision their forces. Since the roads in the region were so poor, they had to rely on sending food by sea, and the superior naval strength of the VOC ensured that supplies never reached the Javanese army. The besiegers were forced to retire, losing three-quarters of their men through starvation on the way back to Mataram. On this occasion the Dutch did not celebrate since their leader, Jan Pieterszoon Coen, had died of a tropical disease in 1629 during the siege.

Although Batavia suffered no further attacks from Mataram, which was soon weakened irretrievably by internal rifts, it was still harried by its enemy to the west, Banten. For many years the environs were troubled by Bantenese marauders, and it was not until the Sultanate surrendered in 1684 that Batavians ventured to settle outside the walls of their town.

It was partly the fear of its neighbours which cut Batavia off from its hinterland. Javanese were not permitted to live within the town, by Company decree. But then Batavia was not intended to be the colonial capital of a large territory; it was run by a trading company which envisaged the town as a port where its ships could be serviced, as a collection point for goods and as an administrative headquarters for company activities in the region. Coen's vision rapidly materialized: in the seventeenth century Batavia became the centre of a great web of Dutch commerce in Asia, with trading posts stretching from Capetown and Persia through India, Ceylon, Burma, Thailand, Cambodia, Vietnam, Laos and Malacca through to Formosa and Deshima in Japan. And most of these places contributed to building up the population of Batavia, which was not a Javanese but a Company town.

Coen had vigorously propounded the idea of European colonization for Batavia: how better, he thought, to provide a loyal, skilled citizenry who could perform necessary services (such as accounting and ship building) for the Company as well as act as a local garrison which would save the VOC the expense of financing defence?[8] Very quickly, however, he was forced to swallow the fact that few Europeans wished to come to Batavia, and those who did were, in his view, mainly 'the scum of the earth'. In vain he pleaded with the Gentlemen Seventeen to send out respectable citizens and especially young girls. In a letter of 1620 he complained:

Everyone knows that the male sex cannot exist without women. Yet it seems that Your Excellencies wish to have a colony planted without them. To make good that lack, we have sought finance here and had many women purchased. But just as up to now you gentleman have sent me only the dregs of the earth, so it seems that here also only dregs are bought for us, for several good fellows have been poisoned by the women, for which some have had to be severely punished. Shall we, on account of these rejects, give up seeking good citizens, as it seems you people have done? Do we have to die out entirely? On this matter we request that, if Your Excellencies cannot get any honest married people, do not neglect to send under-age young girls: thus we hope to do better with them than with older women.[9]

The number of Europeans in Batavia always remained small and the number of European women infinitesimal. Most of the Europeans were Company servants. A major obstacle in attracting Europeans to the settlement was always the Company monopoly: almost no private trading was permitted to Europeans, and what else were they to do in the town? Skilled European tradesmen, outside the Company workshops, could not hope to compete with Asians who could undercut them and work harder. Even when the land surrounding the town was opened up for farming, agriculture was not of the kind to which Dutch farmers were accustomed, and the tropical conditions discouraged most settlers. After all, when it was widely believed that walking about in the tropical sun could be fatal to Europeans, how could they hope to farm the land?

So Batavia continued as it had begun, a town of people brought in from all over Asia at the convenience of the Company. Good and loyal fighters were recruited from as far afield as Japan and the Philippines for the town's garrison; Chinese were encouraged to settle as shopkeepers and as a link with the lucrative China trade, and labour was provided by slaves from anywhere but Java, whose inhabitants were too suspect. It was a society assembled by the Company exclusively for its own interests.

Early Batavia

In the middle of the jungle the Dutch re-created the streets and canals of home, undeterred by the crocodiles which occasionally ventured up those canals into the very heart of town. Their first structure was the fort, originally built out into the sea at the mouth of the River Ciliwung but soon landlocked as the coastline crept northward.[10] (See Map 1.3.) In Batavia's early years the fort *was* the Company since it housed almost all the VOC buildings: the Governor-General's residence, the workshops, treasury, garrison, armoury, counting-houses, prison, the first church, and the meeting-hall of the Council of the Indies, the governing body. Visitors wrote with deep respect of the pomp with which Company business was conducted within the fort, whose Council chambers witnessed such epoch-making events as the signing of contracts with the Sultan of Macassar in 1669. Yet the fortress was tiny, and so crowded with buildings that it must have been stifling for the wretched clerks who toiled in the counting-houses for long hours each day and were locked up in the attics at night.

Several activities conducted within the fort quickly outgrew its confines and spilled out into the walled town which had developed immediately to the south. By 1645 fortification work had been completed for the two halves of the town on the east and west banks of the Ciliwung. The Company workshops, staffed largely by slaves, were moved to the south-east corner of the town. Just south-west of the fort, on the opposite bank of the river, stood the main wharf buildings, still visible in a decrepit state today. Here Company goods were loaded and unloaded, and conveniently close were built the massive western warehouses, now the maritime museum of Jakarta, the Museum Bahari. One thick side of these warehouses formed the northern wall of this part of the town, as can be seen by the sentry-walk along the top. The huge rooms and heavily timbered lofts inside first housed nutmeg from eastern Indonesia, and later China tea and silks and local coffee, awaiting export to the Netherlands. No imports from Europe were stored here, since Holland had nothing which Asia wanted to buy except silver coins. From the loft windows one can peer out towards the nearby river where, as for hundreds of years, graceful inter-island boats lie at anchor.

From the river the Company had dug a system of channels to surround and penetrate the town, giving it a typically Dutch appearance. The river itself was straightened out to form the biggest canal of all. This was done not merely out of nostalgia but for the same utilitarian reasons as canal towns had developed in

On the western side of the river:
Bastions on the walls:
  a Buren
  b Vierkant
  c Cullenburch
  d Zeeburch
  e Groningen
  f Overrijsel
  g Friesland
  h Utrecht
  i Zeeland
  j Nassau
  k Diest
  I Chinese Hospital
  II Spinning-house (for single women)
  III Carpenters' shops of the Chinese
  IV Fish Market
  V Carpenters' shops of the East India Company
  VI Old Utrecht gate
On the eastern side of the river:
  A Castle gate
  B Amsterdam bastion
  C Middelburg bastion
  D Rotterdam bastion
  E Enkhuizen bastion
  F Gelderland bastion

G Oranje bastion
H Nieuwpoort gate (now Pintu Besar)
I Hollandia bastion
J Grimbergen bastion
1 Fort
2 Brugstraat
3 New Church
4 City Hall
5 Hospital
6 Government house
7 Old Gelderland defence works

1.3 Batavia, 1650 (Reproduced from Abdurrachman Surjomihardjo, *Pemekaran Kota* (The Growth of Jakarta), Jakarta, Djambatan, 1977)

Holland: because the land was so low-lying that unless earth was dug out to raise the level of built-up areas, the settlement would be regularly flooded. Moreover, as in Dutch towns, the canals were used for transport: boats bringing goods from the interior came downriver and out along the canals to their destinations, while ships from overseas which were too big to enter the river anchored in the roads and unloaded onto lighters, which plied the inner waterways. Chinese junks were able to sail right up the river into the canals for unloading. In what is now Jalan Blandongan Selatan, but used to be a canal street known as Bacharachtsgracht, one can still see a neat little eighteenth-century Chinese temple, Wihara Dewi Samudera, dedicated to the Goddess of the Sea. Chinese sailors could leap from their junks in front of this temple to burn incense in thanks for a successful voyage. Before its porch of red pillars, wreathed with dragons and flanked by stone lions, there were probably performances of Chinese theatre, as described in the 1720s:

When the Chinese have made a safe voyage by junk or *wangkang*, they are accustomed to give a *wayang*. This is a comic or tragic Chinese theatre such as is performed very often in Batavia.... The actors are young and impoverished boys and girls who are engaged for that purpose.... The performances, whether comedy or tragedy, begin on Mondays at three or four o'clock and last until six; after which they go and eat something and begin performing again from nine in the evening until three or four o'clock in the morning. Newly arrived Chinese meet the cost of such performances by grouping together in threes or fours; and everyone who wishes can go and watch the spectacle for nothing; and if they are people of standing, they are entertained in the house with tea, preserves and *sampsoe* (a sort of strong Chinese beer).[11]

As in Holland, people aspired to live on a canal: it was both more convenient and more fashionable. Housing conformed closely to the Dutch pattern, built with one or two storeys with shared side walls. Building regulations enforced the use of brick within the town, through fear of fire. They also prohibited the proliferation of the stalls so dear to Asian hearts, but which in the Dutch view cluttered up the streets. The Europeans liked a clear space in front of each house: since there were no front gardens, houses had a 'stoop' in front (separated from the footpath by a railing until about 1700), where citizens sat in the cool of the morning or evening to smoke a pipe or drink wine.

At first sight many of the houses looked precisely like those in

Holland, and indeed the differences were only slight. Something of the flavour of the old Dutch town can still be gained by walking through many of the streets of Kota, the northern section of modern Jakarta, especially south along what is now Kali Besar, beside the canalized river. You pass the last Dutch swinging drawbridge left in Jakarta, looking for all the world like a Rembrandt painting, and then comes a series of stately old buildings just back from the water's edge, of which the most impressive stand at the south-western end of the street. One of red brick and the other (now a bank) painted white, they exemplify the old Batavian architecture, the only concession to a tropical climate being the projection of the steeply inclined roof out over the upper storey like a porch. The facades are austere—plain walls pierced by high rectangular windows, the main ornamentation being provided by the entrances: the door surround of the red building is elegantly sculpted from stone imported as ship's ballast from the coast of India; the door of the bank is surmounted by a fretwork panel of carved and gilded wood in a baroque design.

The interior of houses was cramped and airless, the heat trapped inside the small enclosed courtyards at the rear. The town's main pride was to be found in its canal streets, the finest of which was the Tiger's Canal, where the wealthiest Batavians chose to live. Flanked by the simple, regular lines of houses and shaded by trees—originally coconut palms but, by the end of the seventeenth century, the larger tamarind, *kanari* and *tanjong* trees—these streets evoked admiration from early visitors. Jan de Marre, the Poet Laureate of old Batavia, sang its praises in fulsome and leaden-footed verse;[12] other more disinterested travellers also left accolades. Visiting Batavia in the 1680s, the German Christopher Fryke thought it an even finer town than Amsterdam.[13] In 1718, the Portuguese Innigo de Biervillas wrote favourably of Batavia's beauty, abundant food and healthy climate[14]—the last a remarkable detail considering the town's later lamentable reputation. In the 1720s, Francois Valentijn waxed enthusiastic over the town's 'sixteen very fine canals', where the tamarind and flowering trees made it pleasant throughout the day.[15]

Although there were few buildings in Batavia which could compare with the best in the Netherlands, one which would not have shamed a Dutch city and which still stands today is the

Town Hall, completed in 1710. This impressive two-storey edifice, surmounted by a cupola-tower, could be seen as the civilian arm of government, as against the Company housed in the fort, which it directly faced at the end of a short street. In the Town Hall could be found most of the attributes of Dutch municipal administration: the Board of Aldermen, trustees of the orphanage, civil court and jail, the Board of Marriage Registration.[16] The dualism was, however, largely illusory, since the town was completely dominated by the Company: it appointed most of the Board of Aldermen, just as it appointed the ministers of the Reformed Church (for many years the only Church permitted in Batavia). Decisions of the Board had to be approved by the Governor-General, who also controlled the town's finances. An average journey of seven months away from the Netherlands, in Batavia people were at the mercy of the Company and its justice, embodied in a wing of prisons attached to the Town Hall and the dungeons underneath. The population had no civil rights. For Company servants, return to Europe depended on the Governor-General's whim; it was even difficult to marry against his wishes. Old Batavia, like most of the world in the seventeenth and eighteenth centuries, was a place of frequent and harsh punishment. In the cobbled square before the Town Hall it was commonplace to see people in the stocks. On one day in 1676 a visiting European witnessed four people beheaded, six broken on the wheel, one hanged and eight whipped and branded.[17]

A Mixed Society

Despite its great power, the Company was unable to imprint a strong European image on the town. Considering the very small number of Europeans present, it is surprising that the town appeared as European as it did. Contemporary accounts list a large number of different ethnic groups, none of which predominated. A population count within the walls in 1673 showed the following:[18]

Netherlanders	2,024
Eurasians	726
Chinese	2,747
Mardijkers	5,362
Moors and Javanese	1,339

Malayans	611
Balinese	981
Slaves	13,278
Total population	27,068

Many of the 'Netherlanders' would have been soldiers and sailors of the Company, who hardly set a high European tone. Ill paid, they drank heavily and fought in the streets. One observer in the late eighteenth century commented:

The military in Batavia and in general in all the Dutch East Indian possessions pine away their lives in a pitiful state. The common soldier there is surely the most miserable of all creatures.... They are given neither socks nor shoes and are obliged to go barefoot. Furthermore they are extremely harshly or rather brutally treated and beaten incessantly.[19]

As time went on, the vast majority of so-called Europeans in Batavia were really Eurasians. Unlike the British in Asia and following more closely the Portuguese model, the Dutch in the Indies often gave legal recognition of their offspring by Asian women and had little hesitation about marrying Eurasians or even Asians. In their view they had little choice in the matter. After their unhappy experience with the migration of Dutch women, the Company discouraged its servants from bringing out European wives, so in order to enjoy female companionship Dutchmen were obliged to marry local women or set up house with 'housekeepers' (*nyai* in Batavian Malay) who were really concubines.[20] Even if they desired to, it was not always possible for Europeans to marry Indonesian women, since up until the nineteenth century a law forbade the marriage of Christian and non-Christian, and very few Indonesians were converted to Christianity, despite the cash payment and regular rice ration offered as incentives. But the keeping of *nyai* was openly accepted and offspring were frequently recognized as Europeans—a simple matter merely requiring the father to register them with the local notary.

This is not to say that Eurasians were accorded as high a status in society as full-blood Europeans. In the Company preference was almost always given to Dutchmen from the Netherlands. Up until the nineteenth century the Dutch even took care to record officially the degree of European blood of citizens, using the

Portuguese terms *Mixtiezen* and *Castiezen*. Nor were they always fully trusted. The response to the real or concocted threat by a Eurasian 'traitor', Pieter Erbervelt, was a sign of Dutch insecurity.[21] Walking down what used to be Jacatra Way and what is now Jalan Pangeran Jayakarta, just south-east of the old walled town, passers-by can see by the side of the road an incongruous sight in that bustling commercial thoroughfare: atop a stone wall is placed a skull pierced by a spearshaft, and below it an inscription warns of the never to be forgotten treachery of Erbervelt. In the torture chamber in 1722 this landowning part-Asian son of a rich German shoemaker confessed to plotting the conquest of Batavia with various Javanese leaders, whereupon he was torn to pieces by horses driven in four directions. Dutch mythology converted Erbervelt into a bogeyman, yet the only research done into this obscure tale seems to indicate that the then Governor-General trumped up the charge to get rid of Erbervelt when the latter refused to accede to his designs on the Eurasian's estate. Guilty or not, the grisly way in which Erbervelt was done to death was intended to impress on all the motley Batavian population that the Company was indeed master and its will would prevail.

Slaves stood out as the single largest population group in Batavia until the last half of the eighteenth century.[22] Since they came from very diverse origins, however, it was only their status which gave them any unity. Company law forbade the taking of slaves from amongst the Javanese out of fear that they would conspire together against the Europeans. For menial labour the VOC preferred to import large numbers of slaves from outside, which had the added security advantage that slaves from distant and diverse origins were unlikely to join forces. At first slaves were brought mainly from South Asia, where the VOC had trading connections. However, as the Dutch trading empire there declined in the eighteenth century and its Indonesian contacts grew, it was more convenient for the VOC to exploit the existing local slave trade conducted on many islands of the archipelago. After all, the journey of slavers from Sulawesi took at most a few weeks, whereas that from India took months with much consequent wastage: a ship laden with 250 slaves from the Arakan coast was able to bring only 114 of them to market in Batavia.[23] Thus in the eighteenth century slaves came mainly from Sulawesi, Bali and lesser Sunda Islands of eastern Indonesia.

The vast majority of slaves were owned by Europeans, who used them as retinues to flaunt their wealth. The most well-to-do owned a hundred or more. Advertisements for slaves showed that they filled extraordinarily specialized domestic positions: cook, lamplighter, houseboy, housemaid, seamstress, pageboy, ironing maid, *sambal* (spicy side-dish) maker, breadbaker, tea maker, and coachman. Some ladies' maids only made tea, others were purely responsible for arranging her hair in the Indonesian style of the *conde* or large bun worn on the nape of the neck; gentlemen liked slave masseuses to soothe them expertly to sleep after the heavy European midday meal. Slave musicians were the height of fashion. Although Europeans owned most slaves, a slave register of 1816 showed that there were, in fact, slightly more Chinese owners.[24] Building up a fortune through business, the Chinese were less inclined than Europeans to use slaves merely for ostentation: many were employed in sugar mills and *arak* distilleries. The VOC also employed slaves in its workshops. The absence of free labour was reflected in the custom of some owners of making their living by hiring out their slaves. By the end of the eighteenth century it seems that there were almost as many Arab, Indian and Indonesian slave-owners as Europeans and Chinese—a reflection of their growing wealth in the town.

Treatment of slaves was probably not much worse than that of soldiers and sailors, which is to say that punishment could be severe. In large European households they were not overworked: observers even claimed they had so little to do that they resorted to gambling, which in itself was evidence of the control of money by slaves. Europeans (the only observers to comment on slaves) generally argued that other ethnic groups treated their slaves far worse, yet there is also plenty of evidence of ill-treatment by European owners, particularly in the seventeenth century: with the spread of Enlightenment ideas in the eighteenth century conditions seem to have improved. It was commonplace to use the services of the law to have one's slave whipped or imprisoned. For a long time, little was done to check inhumane treatment of slaves by their owners. For instance, in 1742 a Dutchman who shot dead one slave and injured three others was merely 'banned from the Company's jurisdiction for life'.

In cases of ill-treatment male slaves often took one of two courses: they fled or ran amok. Owners kept a weapon close at hand to deal with amoks, when the slave would suddenly go berserk and attempt to kill anyone in his path. As an exposé of injustice, Dirk van Hogendorp wrote a play in 1800 called *Kraspoekol*, featuring a European woman who so ill-treated her slaves that eventually one ran amok and killed her. While Batavia was still surrounded by jungle, it was easy enough for slaves to escape outside the town. For a long time the environs were unsafe due to marauding gangs of slaves, especially in the seventeenth century. One such slave, a Balinese called Surapati, attacked a VOC force near Batavia in 1684 and then was joined by a party from the Javanese court of Kartasura in a massacre of a Dutch embassy to that court in 1686. Surapati established an independent domain in East Java which he and his descendants ruled until the late eighteenth century.[25] Stern measures and gradual settlement eased the threat of escaped slaves during the eighteenth century. By then, the Company had begun to think that it was not so much the slaves they had to fear as the Chinese.

Batavia's Chinese

The Chinese had traded at Jayakarta long before the VOC appeared, and some had even settled in the area long enough to grow sugar and distil the *arak* famous among visiting sailors. When it struck roots in the area, the Company began on excellent terms with the Chinese.[26] Coen was anxious to encourage their trade and industry, and became close friends with their leader, So Bing Kong, whom he called Captain Bencon. Accompanied by his usual escort of umbrella-carrier, a dozen halberdiers and two dozen musketeers, Coen used to go on foot in the evenings to drink with Bencon. Frustrated in his desire to see a European society emerge in Batavia, he placed his hopes on the Chinese: '... there is no people who serve us better than the Chinese, and so easy to get as the Chinese'.[27] So keen was he to build up their numbers quickly in Batavia that in 1622 he sent ships to China to kidnap people on the coast. Once the port became established under the Company, however, it was unnecessary to resort to such measures: Chinese traders came of their own accord, bringing poor coolies from the south of China. The Europeans were heavily dependent on Chinese labour and on merchandise from East Asia brought in by Chinese junks. In 1625, the Chinese fleet trading in Batavia had a total tonnage at least as large as that of the whole VOC return fleet. Unlike the

Europeans, who were theoretically forbidden to trade privately, the Chinese were permitted and even encouraged to trade, since the goods which they brought to Batavia were useful to the local population and to the Company's trade with Europe. They took back to China, in addition to Dutch silver money, goods oriented to the home market—pepper, sandalwood, and delicacies like edible birds' nests and trepangs (sea cucumbers).

Just as important economically for Batavia was the skilled labour which the Chinese contributed. As Valentijn wrote (effusively as always) in the 1720s:

They are an uncommonly clever, courteous, industrious and obliging people, who provide great services to this town. Not only do they conduct wholesale trade in the town in tea, porcelain, silk cloth and lacquerwork, but they also engage very industriously in many crafts, being very good smiths, carpenters, very fine chair-makers, both drawing-room and unusually ornamental sedan-chairs. They make all the sunshades used here. They do very fine varnishing and gilt-work. They are also the foremost arak-distillers, rent-farmers, brick-makers and managers of sugar in the mills outside Batavia and purchasers of it within the town. Many keep eating-houses for sailors and soldiers, and tea-houses also for them, and a great many of them earn a living by carrying water, fishing or conveying people everywhere in Chinese *praus* (which is very convenient), on which vessels they always row standing up with two crossed oars. Many also ply sampans and big boats to take goods off ships. The whole agriculture of Batavia depends on them too, in which they are uncommonly ingenious and industrious, not only in ensuring that everything is available all year round, but they also travel around with everything imaginable, the whole day they carry around all sorts of vegetables, cloth, porcelain, lacquer-work, and tea and bring them to houses too for only a small profit . There is nothing that you can imagine that they do not undertake and practise. . . .

From all of which he concluded solemnly, 'If there were no Chinese here, Batavia would be very dead and deprived of many necessities.'[28] So dominant was the role of the Chinese, in fact, that a recent historian has argued that from 1619 to 1740 Batavia was, economically speaking 'basically a Chinese colonial town under Dutch protection'.[29]

There being no distinct Chinatown in Batavia before 1740, the Chinese were to be found throughout the city: according to Valentijn 'they live everywhere in the best places'. They adopted some European institutions, including their own orphanage, hospital and home for the aged. Their houses were an amalgam of European architecture and the shop-houses of southern China, distinguished by such features as upward curling roof ridges. They were not averse to converting European buildings to their own uses: when the Chinese cemetery was extended in 1760 they took over a Dutch house owned by a Councillor of the Indies and made it into a Buddhist temple, the Klenteng Gunung Sari or Klenteng Sentiong near Pasar Baru, which still has a Buddhist monk, the only one now left in Jakarta.

The VOC attempted to co-opt the Chinese by conferring titles of Captain and Lieutenant on leaders whom they appointed. To judge from the Chinese chronicles of these officers, however, it is highly likely that the Chinese saw the relationship as an equal one.[30] They celebrated the installation of their officers with as much pomp as if they had been mandarins appointed by the Emperor: one such ceremony was recorded as involving a procession of 156 Chinese honour pennants and lanterns borne by 312 slaves, and 190 Papangers (militiamen—the name deriving from their origins in the Pampangans of the Philippines) bringing up the rear with pikes and krises to the accompaniment of a musical band.[31] The town was studded with Chinese temples too, including the oldest extant temple in Batavia, what is now called the Wihara Dharma Bhakti, a Buddhist temple hidden among the back streets of Glodok. This large and much frequented temple complex, with an open impluvium shedding light into the main shrine, and a Chinese herbal clinic and massive paper-burner outside, was described by Valentijn as housing eighteen priests; now it has none.

The rapid influx of Chinese contributed to the opening up of the country around Batavia, and it was this development which caused anxiety to the Company, since outside the walls it was much harder to keep the Chinese under surveillance.[32] On the one hand the Government had to be grateful to the Chinese for farming the hinterland: it was they who spread the sugar estates which provided Batavia with its only original export in the seventeenth century in the raw form and as *arak*. But the opening up of new land brought a rush of Chinese coolies at the end of the seventeenth century, just as the capricious Chinese regime resumed trade with South-East Asia after a period of isolation. So entrenched had the position of Chinese officer become amongst the established élite of the Chinese in Batavia, that these leaders had little or no control over the newcomers, especially as they spread out so far into the hinterland. From 2,747 Chinese within the town in 1674 the registers show a jump to 4,389 in 1739; in the environs (a nebulous term denoting the hinterland as far south as the mountains) 7,550 Chinese were counted in 1719 and 10,574 in 1739 (likely to be an understatement).

Alarmed, the Dutch responded with harsher and harsher regulations. First they tried to put a quota on the number of Chinese who could be brought in by junk, but this was evaded by landing labourers outside the harbour of Batavia, thus smuggling them in. Then a crisis was precipitated when the Company, responding to a glut in the world sugar trade, dropped the prices and production quotas allotted to sugar mills around Batavia, throwing hundreds of Chinese coolies out of work. When these men began forming bands of thieves, the Government's reply in 1740 was to plan the forced transfer of unregistered migrants to another Dutch outpost in Ceylon, which, rumour had it amongst the distressed Chinese, was just a ruse for dumping them at sea.

In 1740, Batavia's environs witnessed a Chinese peasant revolt. Carrying home-made weapons and flying banners inscribed 'To assist the poor, the destitute and the oppressed' and 'Follow the righteous of olden times', the Chinese coolies marched on the city, where hundreds of their compatriots lived behind the walls. Although the latter had little or no contact with the Chinese outside, rumours spread that they were planning to assist the rebels. When the ill-armed Chinese force attacked the town on 8 October, the fact that they were easily repulsed did not save the Chinese inside. Europeans and Indonesians spontaneously attacked, plundered and burned six to seven thousand Chinese homes and massacred many of their inhabitants, probably more than a thousand of them. Although the Government did not order the action, it did little or nothing to stop it. Five hundred Chinese who were shut up in the jails of the Town Hall were brought out one by one and killed. For a week the town blazed with fire and the canals ran red with blood. Gradually the Government took control again, and by the end of the following month order was restored in and around the town, although the Chinese war was waged until 1743 elsewhere in Java.

The massacre of 1740 set the pattern for later incidents in Jakarta's history. Jealousy of Chinese commercial success simmered among many other citizens, who took advantage of a breakdown in law and order to attack the Chinese and loot their property. Little protection of the Chinese has been offered by Jakarta's governments, who have often seemed prepared to allow the Chinese to be treated as scapegoats for the inadequacy of their own administration.

Relations between the Chinese and the Europeans never returned to the easy friendliness of the days of Coen. The Chinese were the target of continual restrictive measures by the Dutch Government, despite the mutual dependence of the two groups. For some time after the massacre that dependence was only too obvious to the Europeans in Batavia, for the surviving Chinese fled the town, leaving it without services or food. Even then, the Government decided to apply to the Chinese the same policy as they had attempted towards the hostile Javanese: they were no longer permitted to live within the walls. Just to the south of the walled town a special suburb was created for them, which has ever since been the heart of Jakarta's Chinatown, around the area known as Glodok. Gradually Chinese immigration resumed, but not until the nineteenth century did it again reach high levels. The Chinese officer system which had worked well to control the population within the walls was ineffective when the Chinese population outside grew rapidly; suspicion had replaced the co-operative relationship between the Chinese and the Dutch.

However, the two groups still worked together on matters of mutual profit, such as the financial deals that went on between wealthy Chinese and Dutch officials. A substantial part of government revenue came from tax farming to the Chinese: selling off licences to operate markets, gambling dens, opium sales and other lucrative businesses. Being an officer was also a money-making position for the Chinese. So it is not surprising that the Chinese offered what we would see as bribes but what the Dutch preferred to regard as friendly gifts for being granted tax licences and officer positions. Generally this occurred at a discreet level, but there were occasional scandals, such as in 1793 when the incumbent Governor-General was revealed as having received unusually large monthly and annual payments from a Chinese Captain.[33] As with providing scapegoats, this kind of financial relationship with government was to prove a recurring theme in the history of Jakarta's Chinese. Apart from material advantage, the Chinese could be seen as attempting to buy security, which they have always felt to be dependent on the favour of those in power.

Mardijkers and Others

Apart from the two major groupings of slaves and Chinese, the rest of the non-European population of Batavia was a very mixed group.[34] Along with the Chinese, the Malays and the 'Moors' made up the Asian trading society. The latter were Indian Muslims, mainly from the thriving port of Surat in Gujerat, where the Dutch also had an outpost.

One unusual group whose name vanished with the VOC era in Batavia were the Mardijkers, later sometimes referred to as 'black Portuguese' because their origins lay with Portuguese settlements in Asia in the early sixteenth century. The first Mardijkers in Batavia in the early seventeenth century came from Portuguese territories conquered by the VOC in Malacca and India. Many had been slaves freed by the Portuguese on baptism into Christianity: hence the name Mardijker, which is connected with the Malay word *merdeka*, or 'free'. Their special characteristics were that they spoke Portuguese (albeit in a corrupted form) and as Christians were permitted by VOC law to dress as Europeans: in particular, they were privileged to wear hats. So great was their influence in early Batavia that they were able to keep Portuguese alive as a language for decades; they also left a mark on Batavian music in the form of *kroncong*, serenades played on mainly European instruments, especially a small guitar. Mardijkers and *kroncong* were also to be found in the other hybrid Portuguese–Dutch–Indonesian town of the VOC period: Ambon, in the Moluccas.

In Batavia Mardijkers worked in many capacities—as soldiers and guardsmen for the Company, as shopkeepers, and, as land was opened up outside the town, they became known as purveyors of poultry and vegetables. Towards the end of the eighteenth century most of them subsided into poverty, but one Mardijker family, the Michiels, stood out as big landowners. Augustijn Michiels, sometimes called 'the last of the Mardijkers', lived until 1833 and was renowned as a most generous host on his estates, where entertainment was provided by hundreds of slaves, some of them musicians accomplished in European, Chinese and Javanese modes.

As mentioned before, there were at first few Sundanese or Javanese in Batavia, despite the fact that they were the Indonesians closest to the town. Before the peace with Banten in 1686 the VOC actively tried to discourage them from settling there. Even when relations with the local rulers improved, there was no pressure on local Sundanese to move to Batavia since the surrounding region was relatively underpopulated until the nineteenth century. The established practice of slavery probably also discouraged the development of a market in free labour. The Company and Chinese employers had to take special measures to organize the recruitment of Sundanese and Javanese to be brought in gangs as seasonal labour to work on the sugar plantations and on public works in and around Batavia.

Far more numerous than the Javanese, especially in the eighteenth century, were the Balinese in Batavia, many of them mercenaries in the Company's army, which always consisted mainly of Indonesian soldiers.[35] In the eighteenth century there were also listed separately numerous other free Indonesian groups, including Ambonese, Buginese and Macassarese, who also fought as soldiers, and Bandanese, the descendants of the miserable survivors of the Company's attempts to exterminate the population of Banda as part of the imposition of a monopoly on clove production there. One of these Bandanese gave his name to a new settlement south of Batavia: Meester Cornelis, now Jatinegara and a district of Jakarta. Cornelis Senen, a Christian catechism teacher (Meester) from Lontor island, was granted the land next to the Ciliwung in 1661.[36]

The streets of Batavia contained the main public life of the city, accessible to all these heterogeneous groups. There, since most men assumed the distinctive garb of their ethnic group, it was quite easy to pick out the Chinese, who before the Manchu conquest of 1644 wore their hair coiled in a knot and afterwards in a long pigtail; the Mardijker men, proud of their Christian status which permitted them, by the Company's ubiquitous regulations, to wear a hat and shoes; Ambonese men with their hair long on their shoulders; Javanese with their neatly-folded head-kerchiefs; and Macassarese wearing their hair bound up in a turban.[37] Besides the normal street life of itinerant hawkers (often a Chinese merchant followed by a slave with the wares on a shoulder-pole), the varied transport of carriages, sedan-chairs, carts, boats on the canals, and the entertainers (including female *ronggeng* dancers), everyone mingled in the markets of Batavia, which were always described with great relish by European travellers. After long sea voyages and the more limited diet of home, they were delighted at the cheap and varied food available—the innumerable local fish and tropical fruits, the poultry, pigs and game, the European vegetables from market gardens—as well as the flower-market and the Chinese wares of silks and porcelain.[38]

And then there were the public festivals, enjoyed by all spectators, such as the Governor-General's birthday, celebrated as though he was an oriental potentate, which was altogether appropriate considering his power. Thus in the 1680s the German Fryke described the event:

All the Burghers and Freemen were in Arms, and drew up before the General's lodgings in the Castle (the fort), where after the Discharge of all the Cannon about the Castle and the City, they saluted his Excellency with several Vollies of Shot. Each Nation then came in a distinct Body with Presents to the General: at first the Chineses, Siamers, Japonneses, Macassars, Amboineses, Bandaneses etc., and even the Javians, who are not permitted to set foot in the Castle on any other time, were then let in; but all these come but after the Company of Burghers and Freemen, which is composed of Dutch, English, Danes, French, Portuguese and other Christians, born in the Indies, who altogether make one Body. These Presents are Magnificent, and one may judge they must needs be very considerable, when the very Soldiers who stood to their Arms under the Castle-Gate had some Hundreds of Guilders given them. Besides this, all the Streets were full of Lights, Bonfires, and Fireworks; wherein the Chinese employed their utmost Art and Skill; and for three or four days there was nothing but Feasting and Treating one another.[39]

In mentioning different 'Bodies', Fryke was referring to the town militia companies into which the VOC organized different ethnic groups. Clearly the Company considered that the mixed nature of the Batavian population afforded them some security, since the plethora of customs, religions and languages made it less likely that a combined conspiracy would be launched against their regime. They tried to freeze that diversity by such means as the militia, and even by designating separate living areas—*kampung* (literally villages) as they are called in Jakarta—

headed by 'officers' of their own ethnic group.[40] This accounts for some of the districts in Jakarta today with names like Kampung Bali and Kampung Bandan. The Buginese were given their own sections when the Boni leader Arung Pattojo was granted in 1663 the estate named after him, Petojo, and later in 1687 Kampung Bugis was given to that staunch ally of the Dutch, Arung Palakka. From early times the Moors lived in the area known as Pekojan after Koja, the current term for west Indian Muslims. One of the areas inhabited by Mardijkers was the swampy land opened up by the south-east gate of the city, across the river, where they built their second church, for long known as the Portuguese Church (now Gereja Sion) since services were given in that language for their benefit. (See Map 1.4.) An airy, whitewashed building in the simple Dutch Protestant style, erected in 1693, it still stands in good condition with its ornate organ, pulpit and heavy old church furnishings—brass chandeliers and individual carved wooden chairs.

Life in Eighteenth-century Batavia

This ethnic diversity persisted because the Batavian population continued to be supplemented by new immigrants from the various groups. Some individuals maintained strong ties with their homeland: Indians and Chinese frequently journeyed to and from Batavia on trading missions, which renewed ethnic traditions; soldiers, sailors and many other Company servants were often merely transients. A high mortality rate necessitated a constant flow of immigration merely to keep up the numbers in some groups. This applied especially to slaves, who were often kept in very cramped conditions in tiny out-houses; the Company had to encourage frequent shipments of slaves to make up the losses. But the artificial separation of ethnic groups by government regulation (on militias, residential areas, dress and so on) could not and did not last long. The smallness of the groups and the lack of females amongst many of them resulted in a high level of mingling.

In this way there developed a common language in Batavia.[41] In order to trade or to make settled domestic arrangements with other people, a lingua franca was required. In the very beginning, when relations with the Portuguese possessions conquered by the Dutch were still strong and the early Portuguese presence set the

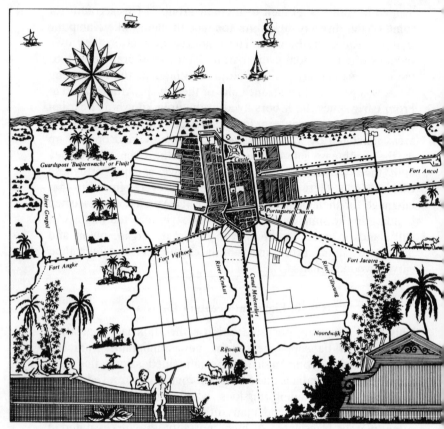

1.4 Batavia and Surroundings, 1740 (Reproduced from Adolf Heuken, *Historical Sites of Jakarta*, Jakarta, Cipta Loka Caraka, 1982)

standard for behaviour by and towards Europeans in the archipelago, it seemed that Portuguese would be the common language in the town. Such was the cultural unassertiveness of the Dutch that Portuguese was spoken widely: schools and church services for non-Dutch people were conducted in both Malay and Portuguese. When the Portuguese element in Batavia was not renewed by immigration, however, but rather was swamped by slaves and others from all over the archipelago, the traditional trading lingua franca of the islands, Malay, got the upper hand. By the eighteenth century, it had established itself as the language of Batavia, in a Sundanese and Javanese speaking region. With ethnic variations it was the only means of communication between different immigrant groups and between Batavian women and their immigrant menfolk; embedded in Batavian society and without formal education, few women ever learned their husbands' own language. And for the men, living with a local woman had the added advantage of allowing them to learn more quickly the essential local means of communication.

Although the development of cultural hybrids advanced further after the VOC period, even in the eighteenth century, however, ethnic groups seemed to be identified by their male component; the women floated about between groups and ranks.[42] Thus a 'European' woman might be the rare person who was actually born in Europe or, like many of the wives of high-status Batavians, an Asian-reared woman born into a part-Asian European family in Batavia, or a legally recognized child of a European man and his concubine, or the Asian wife of a European. In the same way, because almost no Chinese women migrated to Batavia, women bearing Chinese names were actually of Indonesian origin.

To speak of women 'floating' between groups does not, however, do justice to the very solid foundation that women often provided in Batavian families. Amongst the well-to-do, women were the means of creating powerful alliances between families. Often a newly-arrived Dutchman was bound into the élite through marriage with the daughter of an established Batavian family. Discrimination against Batavian-born sons within the Company obliged European parents to use their daughters as the main way of forming important connections. The wealth bestowed by their parents on such daughters brought a fortune to many a promising newcomer. And those women felt their own significance, and paraded their wealth for all to see. Observing them going to church in their silks and satins, damask and gold edging, laden with jewels and accompanied by their slave retinues, the visitor could not help feeling that 'the least of them seems like a princess'.[43]

In the Chinese community too, a Chinese visitor at the end of the eighteenth century remarked of relations with local women: 'Wives are called Niai or mistress, and men are very much afraid of them; the affairs of the family are all under their control and female slaves must obey their orders. They keep everything shut up very close and their jealousy is insupportable....'[44]

No doubt he would have been scandalized to hear that a Balinese concubine of a Chinese Captain was appointed to his position when he died in 1648.[45] According to Confucian custom, the important and even public role which women might play in the Chinese community in Batavia was unheard of, but was possible because these women were generally not of Chinese extraction, or because their mothers and slaves who brought them up were Indonesians with very different ideas about the role of women in society. Although in many ways these women were absorbed into the Chinese community, they were never completely subordinated to Chinese custom because the shortage of women in Batavian society gave them some leverage, and they derived strength from their constant contact with non-Chinese tradition.

At least in part as a result of the cross-cultural influence of women, the life of the different ethnic groups was changing in Batavia. Although visitors to Batavia under the Company always remarked upon the mixture of peoples in the town and tended to assume that people unfamiliar to them were behaving in ways characteristic of their ethnic origin, they were quick to notice how their own folk in Batavia had departed from the norms of the homeland, had to some extent 'gone native'. The Chinese observer mentioned above noted:

When the Chinese remain abroad for several generations, without returning to their native land, they frequently cut themselves off from the instruction of the sages; in language, food and dress they imitate the natives, and studying foreign books, they do not scruple to become Javanese, when they call themselves Islam.[46]

In religion Asians were certainly influenced by their neighbours in Batavia. At Ancol on the coast, next door to the present-day

Binaria 'funland' of Jakarta, stands a temple where Indonesians and Chinese have worshipped together since the second half of the seventeenth century. Although Muslims usually shun the idolatry of Chinese temples, this one contains a Muslim tomb which is considered sacred by Taoists and Muslims alike: they come from afar to consult the oracle there and even, in traditional Indonesian fashion, pass the night under the influence of the tomb. Another example of ethnic groups crossing religious boundaries is to be found in the little jewel of a mosque previously known as Mesjid Angke and now called Mesjid Jami Alanwar, hidden in the winding paths of Kampung Angke in north-west Jakarta, one of the districts originally inhabited by Balinese. Hindus in their home island, the Balinese seemed to convert rapidly to the prevailing Islam of Batavia, as this mosque bears witness. Built in 1761 for the local Balinese Muslim community, it is strongly influenced by both Chinese and Dutch architecture, seen in the upward-curving roof style and the ornamental stone door surround which is remarkably similar to that of the Dutch residence mentioned in Kali Besar. The architect was in fact Chinese, and in the graveyard behind the mosque one can see the tomb of a Chinese woman, evidence that some Chinese were also converted to Islam following the 1740 massacre.[47]

Europeans found themselves very ambivalent about the standards of urban life in Batavia. Immigrant males made earnest attempts to reproduce the main features of European civilization: so the town gained a hospital, schools, an orphanage, churches and, at the end of the eighteenth century, the first scientific learned society in the Far East—but not for many years a bookshop or theatre.[48] Yet so long as Europeans lived in a basically Asian society they had to compromise in many ways. It appeared that what was uppermost in the minds of most Europeans in Batavia was the desire to preserve the dominant status of their group in the eyes of society, and paradoxically this meant sacrificing much of what was characteristically European, for they were obliged to conform to ideas of status held by the Asian majority. Under the Company, this amounted to an obsession with the minutiae of rank, reaching its nadir in Governor-General Mossel's 'Sumptuary Code' of 1754, intended, unbelievably, to 'curb pomp and circumstance'. It made quite clear what could and could not be owned by Europeans of all ranks; for instance, only the

Governor-General's coach was allowed to have as many as six horses; none below the rank of junior merchant could wear golden shoe buckles; the code set out explicitly who could wear diamonds and pearls, carry gold betel boxes and wear velvet or silk.[49] Throughout Dutch rule, a basic status matter on which wrangles recurred was the right of people with pretensions to high standing to have an umbrella carried over them in public—a purely Asian symbol.

The richest Europeans aspired to houses that imitated the finest back at home. A few decades after the founding of Batavia, as the town filled up with people, they preferred to build country houses just out of town in healthier, less crowded areas, the most fashionable spot for many years being the Jacatra Way, the road to the south-east of Batavia leading to the outlying fort of Jacatra. (See Map 1.4.) A well-known artist of the period, Johannes Rach, has left pictures of these grand mansions, some of them very much in the baroque style with elaborate facades, gateways and gardens complete with fountains, statues and topiary.[50] Built on canals or the river, they were easily reached by boat, the most pleasant form of travel.

One of these mansions, in a more reserved style than the fantastic palace of Governor-General van der Parra, can be seen in all its glory by the canal that led directly south out of town, on what is now Jalan Gajah Mada. Although boats no longer glide on the canal which divides this major thoroughfare, people still bathe in its murky depths. But it is tempting fate to try to cross the road to look at the water, since there is scant respect for the pedestrian in Jakarta. Just as in colonial times when 'Might is right' was the motto of carriage owners, the flood of motorized traffic disregards every timid indication of pedestrian crossings. Both sides of the road are packed with Chinese shop-houses, modern shopping blocks and multi-storey hotels: it is difficult to imagine that in the eighteenth century this was a handsome and fashionable avenue lined with gentlemen's residences. The only remnant is impressive enough, a sudden haven of peace entered by heavy wrought-iron gates through an ornamental European garden. What is now the National Archives was once, in the mid-eighteenth century, the house of Reinier de Klerk, first a member of the Council of the Indies and later Governor-General. Recently restored, it presents a seductive image of the life of high-ranking Company servants of those days. The facade is still the plain, two-storeyed white one, pierced by the same severe regular windows as the older style Dutch house in the walled town, but lavish use is made of gilded carving above the doorways, and the rooms inside are large and cool, edged with imported Dutch tiles. Above all, there is space around the house; a garden in front and capacious wings of out-houses behind, which served for cooking, storage and accommodation for the scores of slaves. The closely hemmed-in streets of the walled city are another world.

Life for the European rich was indeed grand, but scarcely relaxed, despite the accepted custom that:

As soon as you enter a house, where you intend to stop for an hour or more, you are desired by the master to make yourself comfortable, by taking off some of your clothes, etc. This is done by laying aside the sword, putting off the coat and wig, for most men wear wigs here, and substituting for the latter a little white night-cap, which is generally carried in the pocket for the purpose.[51]

The fashion of European society struck outsiders as alien. For one thing, it was essential for the most highly placed to keep large numbers of slaves. These hordes of attendants often caused problems at dinners and in church, since there was insufficient room to accommodate the number which status-conscious people felt due to their rank. Social occasions amongst Europeans in Batavia puzzled European travellers by their extreme formality, again an expression of concern for rank:

Every individual is as stiff and formal, and is as feelingly alive to every infraction of his privileges in respect to precedency, especially in public companies, as if his happiness or misery depended wholly on their due observance. Nothing is more particularly attended to at entertainments, by the master of the house, than the seating of every guest, and drinking their healths, in the exact order of precedency.[52]

There was no social relaxation, no mingling of the sexes, no pleasantry.

If this pomp did not appeal to European visitors, it nevertheless had the desired effect of impressing at least some of the Asian population. The Chinese Ong-Tae-Hae, although firmly ethnocentric in outlook, could not avoid some sneaking admiration in his remarks about the Europeans in Batavia in the 1780s:

... when you get out into the campongs you meet with the gardens and parks of Hollanders, adjoining one another, for miles together. There you have high galleries, and summer pavilions, bridges and terraces, so

elegant and beautiful as almost to exceed the compass of human art. . . .
Every seven days there is a ceremony, when, from nine to eleven in the
morning, they go to a place of worship, to recite prayers and mumble
charms; the hearers hanging down their heads and weeping as if there
was something very affecting in it all, but after an hour's jabber they are
allowed to disperse, and away they go to feast in their garden-houses and
spend the whole day in delight. . . .[53]

This was hardly the intention of a Dutch Reformed Sabbath, but
it makes a nice counterbalance to similarly ethnocentric comments by Europeans on Chinese religious ceremonies in Batavia.
The German Schweitzer, for instance, recorded his fascinated
horror at seeing the Chinese make offerings before a wooden idol
in their home: 'I . . . continually expected to see the Devil eat the
victuals that were set before him.'[54]

The Decline of Old Batavia

By the end of the eighteenth century the Dutch East India
Company was bankrupt. Although not entirely dependent on the
Company, old Batavia's fortunes had mirrored its decline. The
city's golden age occurred around 1730, when the population
within the walled town numbered about 20,000 people and 15.000
in the suburbs.[55] The Chinese with their sugar industry around
Batavia contributed not a little to the town's prosperity. But in
the second half of the century that industry declined, disrupted
by the Chinese massacre and war and struck by a combination of
unfavourable government pricing policies and problems of finding
enough wood to fuel the sugar mills: as the jungle was cleared for
agriculture, wood had to be brought in over longer distances. A
European farmer (an unusual phenomenon, since few Europeans
there took farming seriously) wrote in 1792 that 'sugar planting
has led to the clearing of land up to seven hours' travel from
town; paddy cultivation and cattle-raising has also spread so that
up to the mountains no forest is left to provide fuel for sugar
mills'.[56] The number of sugar mills, which had grown to 131 in
the Batavian environs in 1710, had dropped to 55 in 1780.[57] The
decline in sugar production inevitably hit hard the distilling of
arak, which was one of Batavia's most profitable industries, not
to speak of other allied activities such as brickworks and potteries,
lime-burning and carpentry.

As far as most Europeans were concerned, Batavia had just

become unliveable.[58] The canal system had never managed to solve the city's drainage problems completely: high tides brought in sand and hindered the outlet of river water, and a growing quantity of silt was brought downriver as the uplands were cleared for farming, the combination causing frequent flooding. As early as 1634 a coralstone canal had to be built out to sea to prevent a sandbank from blocking the entrance to the river. The growing population within the town contributed to the clogging of the canals as they deposited their rubbish and sewage into the water, in defiance of government regulations. At some expense, the Government resorted to dredging operations by convicts or gangs of Javanese drafted from the coastal regions, without success. From the mid-eighteenth century some canals were even filled in. Visitors ceased to admire them:

The stagnant canals, in the dry season, exhale an intolerable stench, and the trees planted along them impede the course of the air, by which in some degree the putrid effluvia would be dissipated. In the wet season the inconvenience is equal; for then these reservoirs of corrupted water overflow their banks in the lower part of town, and fill the lower stories of the houses, where they leave behind them an inconceivable quantity of slime and filth: yet these canals are sometimes cleaned; but the cleaning of them is so managed as to become as great a nuisance as the foulness of the water; for the black mud taken from the bottom is suffered to lie upon the banks, in the middle of the street, till it has acquired a sufficient degree of hardness to be made the lading of a boat, and carried away. As this mud consists chiefly of human ordure, which is regularly thrown into the canals every morning, there scarcely being a necessary in the whole town, it poisons the air while it is drying, to a considerable extent. Even the running streams become nuisances in their turn, by the negligence of the people; for every now and then a dead hog, or a dead horse, is stranded upon the shallow parts, and it being the business of no particular person to remove the nuisance, it is negligently left to time and accident.[59]

This was the Batavia which had won a name as 'Queen City of the East'.

The water-table was so close to the surface in the old town that much well water was undrinkable: most people took their water from the river. At the 'waterplace' just south of the town watermen collected bucketsful and rowed them along the canals, offering water for sale. Despite the efforts of people to filter water, its impurity became a cause of many common and frequently fatal illnesses such as dysentery and typhoid. But the main killer, long the bane of Jakarta and also related to the water, was malaria, for anopheles mosquitoes bred in the stagnant water around the town, including the ponds widely used for farming fish along the marshy coast.

Batavians in the eighteenth century were quite unaware of the cause or even the nature of their illnesses. Most Europeans were inclined to attribute it to foul-smelling breezes, which made them close the windows and draw the curtains in their stifling houses. But the fevers which racked the population and carried them off in droves were unmistakable. Visitors to Batavia in the second half of the eighteenth century were astounded at the way in which the inhabitants had hardened themselves to the death of their acquaintances:

The frequency of deaths renders familiar the mention of them, and little signs are shown of emotion or surprise, on hearing that the companion of yesterday is today no more. When an acquaintance is said to be dead, the common reply is, 'Well, he owed me nothing'; or 'I must get my money from his executors'.[60]

Ships which had welcomed a stop in Batavia for its good provisions and water, now shunned the place. Forced to anchor there to repair his ship in 1770, Captain Cook noted in his diary that, whereas his crew had been healthy on arrival in October, by December most were sick and seven were dead. 'The unwholesome air of Batavia is the death of more Europeans than any other place upon the Globe....'[61]

Whatever their views on the causes of illness, Batavians could easily see that the old walled town was extremely unhealthy. Even in the late seventeenth century, following the peace with Banten and Mataram, settlement had begun to spread beyond the walls.[62] By 1730 there were an estimated ten to fifteen thousand people living in the suburbs.[63] Much less care was taken to regulate building outside, and some areas were even unhealthier than within. As an example, Javanese fisherfolk and sailors lived on the north-west bank of the river, just outside the walls and 'beyond the boom' (Luar Batang)—the customs boom across the river—in an area of poorly drained land and winding lanes; a kampung, nevertheless, with its own community life, centring on the eighteenth century mosque and holy grave of an Arab missionary, Said Husain Abu Bakar al-Aidrus, at which people still give offerings and make vows. Some land was leased out for agriculture by the Company-appointed Polder Board; some large estates were also sold to Europeans and Chinese. The markets on these estates, farmed out to Chinese tax-gatherers, served as focal points for growth: for instance, settlements grew up around markets granted at Tanah Abang and at Weltevreden in 1735. Industry also developed down the canal which the Chinese Captain Bingam had begun to dig south from the River Ciliwung in 1648 as a means of opening up the hinterland by providing transport for local goods. Along this waterway were built numerous waterwheels for ammunition powder works, cornmills and sawmills, giving rise to the name Molenvliet or Mill Race. (See Map 1.4.)

Gradually, rich Europeans took advantage of this development of the interior and the ease which canals such as the Molenvliet provided for their own transport, to move further and further out of the walled town in search of a more salubrious environment unpolluted by the stench of filthy canals and the rich smoke from the *arak* distilleries. In the mid-eighteenth century their mansions reached down the Molenvliet and the Jacatra Way as far as Weltevreden. Named after a local country estate (in English, Wellcontent), this area adjoined the vast open space known later as Koningsplein (King's Square) and, after Independence, as Lapangan Merdeka (Independence Square). Although the port was still the focus of Company business, making it necessary to attend their offices daily in town, those who could afford to build elsewhere and travel longer distances were abandoning old Batavia. In 1779, the population of the old town had dropped to 12,131, with 160,986 living in the environs, a large area extending south to the mountains.[64] Stavorinus, describing Batavia in the 1770s, commented on the depopulation of the city: 'The houses in which the greatest merchants dwelt, their counting-houses where they carried on business, and the warehouses which received their immense stocks of merchandise, are now either deserted or untenanted, or changed into stables or coach-houses.'[65] A great depreciation in the value of town houses resulted.

Decline of the Company

Some of the decay of the old town mentioned by Stavorinus was closely connected with the eclipse of its sponsor, the VOC. Batavian Europeans had contributed to this themselves by parti-

cipating in a widespread smuggling racket which undermined the
Company monopoly and thus its profits. Some of the funds for
those magnificent country houses derived from private enterprise
on the part of Company servants who illegally sent their own
goods by Company ships and in other ways manipulated their
positions for their own personal gain.[66]

The reasons for the decline of the VOC were, however, more
complex and far-reaching, with significance for Batavia's
changing role as a city. In trading competition, the Dutch East
India Company had lost out to the English; by the 1784 Treaty of
Paris which ended the Anglo-Dutch War, the Company was
obliged to abandon its monopoly and allow the English to trade
in the Indies, which meant English domination of some commodities. Long before this, the Company had experienced heavy
demands on its finances because it had really ceased to be a mere
trading concern and had become involved in extensive (and
expensive) territorial conquest and administration in the Indies.

In the Outer Islands the Company's control of land and population was still very small at the end of the eighteenth century.
Even its influence over inter-island trade was restricted to a
monopoly or pretensions to monopoly over certain commodities
only. The region where Batavia as a political and economic
centre had had its greatest impact was in Java, especially in the
years from 1677 to 1757, the time of most active VOC military
intervention. The Company had been drawn into local disputes in
order to ensure the security of its trade. The previously mighty
states of Banten and Mataram had disintegrated into civil wars in
which the VOC intervened, and the state of Cirebon had sought
VOC protection to escape from the suzerainty of Mataram. The
VOC could not, however, administer all of Java. Only on the
north coast and in the interior of West Java was it able to
exercise sovereignty in the eighteenth century. With the aid of its
allies the lords of Cirebon, the Company extended its coffee
cultivation in West Java throughout the Priangan highlands.
Elsewhere it attempted to cling to its prerogatives and to trade
profitably, two things made increasingly difficult as the VOC
slipped more deeply into that bankruptcy, nepotism, inefficiency,
corruption, maladministration and military decline of which
Batavia was cause, symptom and symbol.

Batavia was changing from an isolated coastal trading outpost
to the Company's centre of indirect government in west and

north coastal Java and a reception centre for goods from the hinterland. While sugar planting around the town was the work of the Chinese, the Company played an innovatory role by introducing the cultivation of another new crop, coffee.[67] Plants were first distributed amongst local district chiefs in 1707, but it was not until the second half of the century that coffee growing really took off in the mountain country south of the Batavian environs, the region called the Priangan, acquired by the VOC in 1677. 'Coffee sergeants' were appointed by the Dutch to assist the local rulers, or Regents, to ensure that the set amount required by the Company was grown by the peasants. In the course of the century, by means of these feudalistic 'forced deliveries', the Priangan was transformed from a sparsely populated, unsafe region into one of settled coffee plantations and rice-growing villages.

Batavia was now much more closely linked with the rest of West Java than at its inception. But one should not overestimate the land links, since road communications were still very poor, especially in the wet season.[68] At that time, only heavy, lumbering buffalo carts could provide transport from the mountains down to Batavia for travellers or for coffee; at times even buffaloes were not strong enough to haul a load through the mud and rivers, since bridges were non-existent. Ever since a country estate had been purchased there in 1745, Governors-General travelled regularly up to Buitenzorg (now Bogor), but the trip was considered so hazardous that in the eighteenth century thanksgiving services were held on a Governor-General's safe return to town. Water transport dominated as the easier form of communication, so Batavia's sea links were still most important, meshing it into a maritime hinterland around the Java Sea.

Batavia had turned away from the spice trade of East Indonesia into its own interior to find its most valuable commodity, coffee, in the course of the eighteenth century. But the wealth of coffee could not save the Company, whose expenses had been dragging it down for some decades. In the 1790s the Dutch Parliament took control of the VOC, whose charter was allowed to expire in 1799. It was a time of transition for the Company town within its fortified walls. The Company had failed, the walls had crumbled: everyone knew that the ramparts of the fort could not withstand a cannon being fired from it. Then the Netherlands fell to the French army in 1795, and the revolutionary Dutch Government

sent out a new broom, Governor-General Daendels, with orders
to prepare the colony for defence against the English enemy. At
a glance, he decided that the walled town was indefensible and
determined to move the seat of government further inland to the
suburb of Weltevreden. Daendels put the finishing touches to a
movement which had been occurring stealthily for decades: in
1810 he pulled down the town walls and began to demolish the
fort, symbolically using the stones for his buildings at Weltevreden.

Old Batavia had passed its zenith: although the businessmen
still sat at their desks there by day, many parts were depopulated
and neglected. Into its former mansions crept poor Indonesians,
Chinese and Mardijkers, all those who needed shelter near their
work and could not afford a healthier suburb. The Europeans
moved on, to create further south a new Batavia in their own
image—no longer merely a trading port but the capital of a
European colony.

1. Examples of Indonesian nationalist histories of Jakarta include R. M. Ali
and F. Bodmer, *Djakarta Through the Ages*, Djakarta, Government of the
Capital City of Djakarta, 1969 and Uka Tjandrasasmita, *Sejarah Jakarta*, Jakarta,
Pemerintah DKI Jakarta, 1977. Besides de Haan's work, Dutch histories include
H. A. Breuning, *Het Voormalige Batavia. Een Hollandsche Stedestichting in de
Tropen*, Amsterdam, Albert de Lange, 1954 and J. F. L. de Balbian Verster and
M. C. Kooy-Van Zeggelen, *Ons Mooi Indie: Batavia Oud en Nieuw*, Amsterdam,
Meulenhoff, 1921.

2. Evidence on early Jakarta is brought together in R. Z. Leirissa, 'Dari
Sunda Kelapa ke Jayakarta', in Abdurrachman Surjomihardjo (editor), *Beberapa
Segi Sejarah Masyarakat-Budaya Jakarta*, Jakarta, Pemerintah DKI Jakarta,
1977.

3. For the early history of the Portuguese and the Dutch East India Company
in Indonesia, see M. A. P. Meilink-Roelofsz, *Asian Trade and European Influence
in the Indonesian Archipelago between 1500 and 1630*, The Hague, Nijhoff, 1962.

4. For the origins of Dutch interest in Jayakarta and their first settlement
there and the siege of Jayakarta, see de Haan, op. cit., Vol. I, Chapter 1.

5. H. T. Colenbrander, *Jan Pietersz. Coen: Levensbeschrijving*, 's-Gravenhage,
Nijhoff, 1934, pp. 142–8.

6. Ibid., p. 156.

7. Descriptions of the Javanese sieges of Batavia are to be found in de Haan,
op. cit., Vol. I, Chapter 2.

8. For Coen's views on colonization, see ibid., Vol. I, p. 59. For discussion on
the subject, see Leonard Blusse, 'The Caryatids of Batavia: Reproduction,
Religion and Acculturation under the V.O.C.', *Itinerario*, Vol. VII, No. 1, 1983,
pp. 57–85.

9. Colenbrander, op. cit., p. 195.

10. For a description of the fort and of the development of the town, see de Haan, op. cit., Vol. 1, Chapters 4-7.

11. The quotation is from Francois Valentijn, *Oud en Nieuw Oost Indien*, Amsterdam, S. Keizer, 1862, first edition 1724-6, Vol. III, p. 536.

12. J. de Marre, *Batavia, Begrepen in Zes Boeken*, Amsterdam, A. Wor en de Erve G. onder de Linden, 1740.

13. Christopher Fryke and Christopher Schweitzer, *Voyages to the East Indies*, London, Cassell, 1929, first edition 1700, p. 26.

14. *Voyage d'Innigo de Biervillas, Portugais, à la cote de Malabar, Goa, Batavia et autres lieux des Indes Orientales*, Paris, Dupuis, 1736, pp. 2-9.

15. Valentijn, op. cit., Vol. III, p. 514.

16. For a discussion of Batavia's municipal administration, see de Haan, Vol. II, Chapter 21.

17. Fryke and Schweitzer, op. cit., p. 188.

18. *Dagh-Register gehouden int Casteel Batavia*, 1674, J. A. van der Chijs (editor), 's-Gravenhage, Nijhoff, 1902, pp. 28-9.

19. Jacob Haafner (1755-1809), quoted in R. Nieuwenhuys (editor), *Wie Verre Reizen Doet*, Amsterdam, Querido, 1975, pp. 94-5.

20. The subject of *nyai* is discussed in several sources, including Jean Taylor, *The Social World of Batavia: European and Eurasian in Dutch Asia*, Madison, University of Wisconsin Press, 1983 and Susan Abeyasekere, 'Women as Cultural Intermediaries in Nineteenth Century Batavia', in L. Manderson (editor), *Women's Work and Women's Roles*, Canberra, Australian National University Press, 1983. See also Leonard Blusse, op. cit.

21. For research on Erbervelt, see F. de Haan, *De Priangan*, Batavia, Kolff, 1910, Vol. III, pp. 472-6.

22. On slaves, see de Haan, *Oud Batavia*, Vol. I, pp. 451-68; S. Kalff, *De Slavernij in Oost-Indie*, Baarn, Hollandia-drukkerij, 1920; and Susan Abeyasekere, 'Slaves in Batavia: Insights from a Slave Register', in A. Reid (editor), *Slavery, Bondage and Dependency in Southeast Asia*, St Lucia, University of Queensland Press, 1983.

23. Kalff, op. cit., p. 5.

24. For the 1816 register and discussion of treatment of slaves, see Abeyasekere, 'Slaves in Batavia', p. 296, pp. 305-6.

25. A. Kumar, *Surapati, Man and Legend*, Leiden, Brill, 1976.

26. On the Chinese in old Batavia, see de Haan, *Oud Batavia*; Claudine Salmon and Denys Lombard, *Les Chinois de Jakarta, Temples et Vie Collective*, Paris, Cahier d'Archipel, 1977; and L. Blusse, 'Chinese Trade to Batavia during the Days of the V.O.C.', *Archipel*, No. 18, 1979, and 'Batavia, 1619-1740: the Rise and Fall of a Chinese Colonial Town', *Journal of Southeast Asian Studies*, Vol. XII, No. 1, March 1981.

27. Quoted in de Haan, *Oud Batavia*, Vol. I, p. 76.

28. Valentijn, op. cit., Vol. III, pp. 533-4.

29. Leonard Blusse, 'Batavia, 1619-1740', p. 160.

30. The chronicles of the Chinese officers are translated as 'Chronologische Geschiedenis van Batavia, geschreven door een Chinees', *Tijdschrift voor Neerlands Indie*, Vol. II, 1840, pp. 1-114.

31. Description of installation of officers is from B. Hoetink, 'Chineesche

Officieren te Batavia onder de Compagnie', *Bijdragen tot de Taal-, Land- en Volkenkunde*, Vol. 78, 1922, pp. 72–6.

32. Blusse, 'Batavia, 1619–1740', pp. 169ff describes the Chinese contribution towards opening up the hinterland, the influx of Chinese and the revolt and massacre which ensued. The other main source is J. T. Vermeulen, *De Chineezen te Batavia en de Troebelen van 1740*, Leiden, E. Ijdo, 1938.

33. De Haan, *Oud Batavia*, Vol. I, p. 498.

34. For Malays, Mardijkers and Javanese in Batavia, see ibid., Vol. I, p. 255 and pp. 482–9, 512–32, 476–7. On Mardijkers in particular, see Paramita R. Abdurachman, '"Portuguese" Presence in Jakarta', *Masyarakat Indonesia*, Vol. II, No. 1, 1975, pp. 89–101.

35. On the Balinese in Batavia, see C. Lekkerkerker, 'De Baliers van Batavia', *De Indische Gids*, Vol. 40, No. 1, 1918, pp. 409–31.

36. On the Bandanese and Meester Cornelis, see de Haan, *Oud Batavia*, Vol. I, pp. 124–5, 479–84.

37. The appearance of some different ethnic groups is described in *Batavia, de Hoofdstad van Neerlands O. Indien, in derzelver Gelegenheid* ..., Amsterdam, Petrus Conradi, 1782, pp. 33–6.

38. On markets, see Valentijn, op. cit., Vol. III, pp. 539–40; de Biervillas, op. cit., p. 6; and de Haan, *Oud Batavia*, Vol. I, pp. 360–8.

39. Fryke and Schweitzer, op. cit., pp. 153–4.

40. On 'apartheid' in Batavia, see de Haan, *Oud Batavia*, Vol. I, pp. 469ff.

41. On language in Batavia, see ibid., Vol. I, pp. 523–7.

42. On women in Batavia, see Taylor, op. cit.

43. Nicolaus de Graaff, *Oost-Indise Spiegel*, Hoorn, Warnsinck, 1703, p. 18.

44. Ong-Tae-Hae, *The Chinaman Abroad; or a Desultory Account of the Malay Archipelago, particularly of Java*, Shanghae, no publisher, 1849, p. 9.

45. 'Chronologische Geschiedenis', pp. 20–2.

46. Ong-Tae-Hae, op. cit., p. 33.

47. The mosques here are described in Salmon and Lombard, op. cit., pp. 86–97; Heuken, op. cit., pp. 126–32 and D. Lombard, 'A Travers le vieux Djakarta. 1. La Mosquée des Balinais', *Archipel*, No. 3, 1972, pp. 97–101.

48. On European attempts at Enlightenment in Batavia, see Taylor, op. cit., Chapter 5.

49. For Mossel's code, see J. A. van der Chijs, *Nederlandsch-Indisch Plakaatboek, 1602–1811*, Batavia, Nijhoff, 1889, Vol. VI, pp. 773–95.

50. Reproductions of the paintings of Rach can be found in the Platenalbum of de Haan's *Oud Batavia*.

51. Stavorinus, quoted by J. J. Stockdale, *Sketches, Civil and Military of the Island of Java and its Immediate Dependencies* ..., London, Stockdale, 1812, p. 109.

52. Ibid., pp. 97–8.

53. Ong-Tae-Hae, op. cit., p. 6.

54. Fryke and Schweitzer, op. cit., p. 191.

55. For a discussion of population statistics in old Batavia, see de Haan, *Oud Batavia*, Vol. II, pp. 346–50.

56. Andries Teisseire, 'Beschrijving van een Gedeelte der Omme- en Boven-landen dezer Hoofdstad', *Verhandelingen van het Bataviaasch Genootschap*, Vol. VI, 1792, p. 3.

57. Jan Hooyman, 'Verhandelingen over den Tegenwoordigen Staat van den Land-bouw in de Ommelanden van Batavia', *Verhandelingen van het Bataviaasch Genootschap*, Vol. 1, 1781, pp. 238–9.

58. On deteriorating conditions, see de Haan, *Oud Batavia*, Vol. I, pp. 237, 251, 265.

59. Stockdale, op. cit., quoting Stavorinus, p. 132.

60. Ibid., pp. 133–4.

61. *Captain Cook's Journal, 1768–71*, Adelaide, Libraries Board of South Australia, 1968, p. 364.

62. On the spread of settlement, see de Haan, *Oud Batavia*, Vol. I, Chapters 8 and 9.

63. Milone, op. cit., p. 143.

64. Ibid., p. 144.

65. Stavorinus is quoted in Stockdale, op. cit., p. 134.

66. On smuggling, see de Haan, *Oud Batavia*, Vol. II, pp. 13–17.

67. For the spread of coffee cultivation, see de Haan, *De Priangan*, Vol. I, Chapter 7.

68. On the state of the roads, see ibid., Vol. I, p. 169.

2

The Colonial City: Batavia in the Nineteenth Century

THE nineteenth century European view of Batavia focused on Weltevreden, the new seat of administration and European residence. It was to this area that they now transferred the title 'Queen of the East'. The old queen—Batavia proper, the old town, the 'lower town' (*benedenstad*) as they now called it—was dead. In every account of the capital of the Indies the same picture emerges, identical descriptions of what was noteworthy to the overseas visitor, a trend reinforced by the publication of official guide books from the later part of the century.[1] Let us take this tour of Batavia, seeing it as the Europeans did, if only to understand the image of the city which the colonial rulers presented to the world, before examining what this image distorted and concealed.

Harbour and Old Town

New international arrivals at Batavia in the nineteenth century naturally came by sea, and their first impressions were the unfavourable ones of a low-lying port area with only a distant view of mountains in the background. Before the 1880s ships still anchored in the roads of Batavia, the bay at the mouth of the Ciliwung River sheltered by the Thousand Islands behind. From the deck the visitor observed the bustle of activity into which the ship's arrival had thrown workers at the port. With curiosity he noted the crowds of *prau*, or native boats, the crocodiles at the river mouth and the lighters which came to unload the ships.

The delay in actually landing at the wharf was a prime cause for the ultimate removal of the main harbour from the roads to Tanjung Priok in the 1880s.[2] With the silting up of the river mouth, large ships had to anchor ever further from land, and keeping open the entrance to the river involved a continual fight against sandbanks by a combination of dredges and the building of canal walls out into the sea. Unloading and loading ships required a fleet of lighters, a task which was ordinarily time-consuming and, during the west monsoon when seas were heavy, either dangerous or impossible; at such times the Look-out Post (still to be seen at Pasar Ikan today) would fly a blue flag to indicate that no boats could leave or enter the river-canal. For steamships which operated all year round, speed of operation was essential to justify their expense; the only thing which excused Batavia's weaknesses was that no other north Javanese port had any better facilities. The opening of the Suez Canal in 1869 made changes unavoidable. The greatly increased volume of steamships which would obviously follow the shortening of the route to Europe made it urgent that Batavia, along with other Javanese ports, upgrade its harbour. Rivalry with Singapore, founded in 1819, also spurred on the search for improvements.

It was not easy for the administration to reach the conclusion that Tanjung Priok, some 9 kilometres to the east of the Batavia roads, was the best place. Dispute reigned for years, and to the end the Batavia Chamber of Commerce opposed the decision since they knew it would result in the rapid decline of the profitable lighter business and they feared a complete bypassing of the old town when cargo handling was diverted to the new port. Work on Tanjung Priok harbour began in 1877 and finished in 1886, providing Java with its first deep safe harbour where ships could tie up at the wharf, load coal and be repaired at a dry dock. The connection with Batavia proper was made through parallel road, canal and railway links. Doubtless to the relief of the Batavia employers, a rival commercial centre did not spring up at Tanjung Priok, whose malaria-ridden environment was so suspect that relatively few chose to live or work there. Henceforth, overseas visitors to Batavia would land at Tanjung Priok and travel by train into town, which served to remove all that was irregular and exotic about the earlier landfall.

Up until 1869, the new arrival would have to choose his means of transport from among the carriage drivers competing for his patronage. The most common vehicle for passenger conveyance was the *sado* (corruption of *dos-à-dos*, referring to the fact that passengers sat back to back). Batavia could offer *deleman, mylord, bendy* and palanquins also. It was common for European

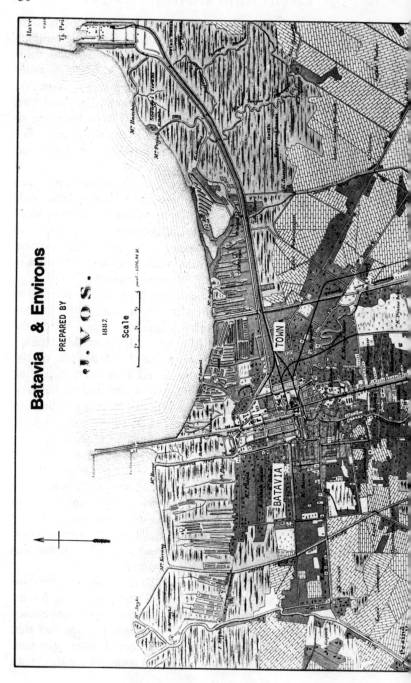

Batavia & Environs

PREPARED BY

J. VOS.

1887.

Scale

TOWN

BATAVIA

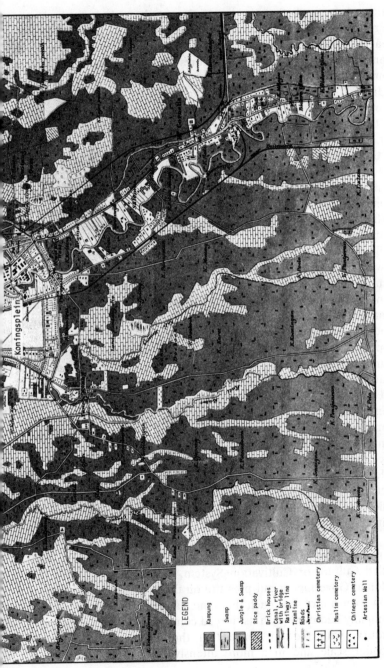

LEGEND

	Kampung
	Swamp
	Jungle & Swamp
	Rice paddy
	Brick houses
	Canal, river with bridge
	Railway line
	Tramline
	Roads
	Christian cemetery
	Muslim cemetery
	Chinese cemetery
	Artesian Well

2.1 Batavia and Environs, c.1885 (J. Vos, Batavia, 1887)

writers to remark that the horses were 'miserable beasts': they were small Sumbawan animals which did not thrive in the damp heat of Batavia. When in 1869 Batavia got its first horse-drawn trams, the toll on horses was enormous: in one year the tram company lost 545 horses.[3]

In fact, Batavia was very early in acquiring horse trams: few European cities had one in 1869. It was soon to become apparent to the visitor why some form of public transport was a necessity for Batavia: simply because it was such a sprawling town. Although not large in population terms (in 1850 there were less than 70,000 inhabitants and in 1900 about 115,000) the town was strung out over 10 to 12 kilometres in an awkward dog-leg shape from north to south. (See Map 2.1.) The situation was particularly difficult for Europeans because of the distance between place of work and residence.

So the new arrival was wafted into the old town, the lower town of Batavia. This was always a confusing experience, particularly if he or she arrived in the evening. Impressions were generally unfavourable. Everywhere one noticed signs of degeneration: of dilapidated canals and broken-down buildings. Those who had read of Batavia's former glory were especially disappointed. Visitors who arrived in the evening would find no Europeans in the town and could travel through it quite unaware that they had seen Batavia proper.

For those who passed through in office hours, the lower town presented a more lively appearance. Certainly the decline of some parts was evident, but the economic hub continued to be centred in the town. Batavia was still a great port, funnelling goods in and out, and being the capital of a large and growing colony it was increasingly the location of many overseas firms. Activity hummed around the warehouses and among the many offices. If some part of the town's economy was damaged by the shift of port facilities to Tanjung Priok, this was compensated for by the rapid growth in overseas private investment with the introduction of the Liberal System in the 1870s. Under the so-called Culture or Cultivation System, inaugurated in 1830, the colonial Government put pressure on the Javanese population to grow export crops in much the same way as the Dutch East India Company had done with its 'forced contingents' in the eighteenth century, with the difference that the system operated on a broader scale and in a more intensive manner. Export crops

(principally coffee in the Batavia region) continued to be conveyed to warehouses in Batavia, the monopoly now being
conducted by the Government rather than the Company (to
many Indonesians the distinction was never clear, and the Dutch
were always 'the Kompenie'). So successful was the system that
Dutch entrepreneurs finally prevailed on their Government to
hand the cornucopia over to private enterprise—the start of the
Liberal System. As a result, in Batavia the offices of European
firms multiplied. To make up for the demise of eighteenth-
century trading houses, Western insurance companies and banks
erected imposing new buildings in the old town.

During the day, Europeans, Chinese, Indonesians, Indians and
Arabs went about their business, presenting a varied picture to
the traveller. In the 1830s Roorda van Eysinga noted the hundreds
of carriages of European officials and shop-people raising clouds
of dust on the streets, while the 'Chinese, with their recognisable
and unpleasant features, with their long pigtails and silk caps, are
everywhere busy hammering, sawing, painting, sewing, building
and so on'. Rich Arabs and Chinese rode through the streets,
half-clad Javanese carried heavy loads, shabby Eurasian clerks
walked beneath their sunshades to their offices, old women sold
cakes, an Indian sat calmly eating his rice on a banana leaf, and
vegetable, milk and fruit sellers, butchers and hill-dwellers
offering monkeys and birds all mingled together in the crowd.[4]

In general the visitor did not stop to observe closely. His
destination was the hotels further south. Although many might
have had to work in Batavia proper by day, Europeans lived in
the more salubrious higher reaches of the city. The Dutch saw
Batavia in the shape of a barbell, the connecting bar between
lower and upper towns being the Molenvliet. After 1869 this
route could be travelled by horse tram, but Europeans found
such conveyance lowered their dignity, since it made no distinction
between races and classes. More popular was the steam tram
service which superseded the horse trams in 1881. The poor—
which meant Indonesians—travelled in a separate carriage. So
well patronized was this tram that in 1889 the regular ten-minute
service had to be changed to seven and a half minutes. Alternatively, after 1871 one could avoid the dust (or mud) of
Molenvliet entirely by taking the train, for the first section of the
Batavia–Buitenzorg railway opened in that year.

One can almost hear the sigh of relief of the nineteenth-century traveller as his carriage bowled down the Molenvliet road. Here at last was civilization. Important people's houses lined the road: first of all the mansions of Chinese officers, built as single-storey houses in large compounds rather than the cramped terrace style of the old 'Chinese camp'. Then a succession of European houses and finally, as the end of Molenvliet neared, the first of the large hotels that proliferated in the nineteenth century as travel became easier and more common. One of the best known lay at the south-west corner of Molenvliet—the Hotel des Indes, shaded by an enormous banyan tree.

Weltevreden

After relaxing in the hotel, the visitor could sally forth once more to view the noteworthy sights of the capital. It was now that he or she became aware of the 'new Batavia', the stretch of suburbs surrounding Koningsplein. This area, which came to be ringed by the Van den Bosch defence line in 1835, was generally known as Weltevreden, a term which might, however, also refer to a smaller part of it, the section next to Waterlooplein (now Lapangan Banteng). It was here that the bulk of the European population lived in the nineteenth century (see Figure 2.1). The formerly popular stretch around Jacatraweg had fallen out of fashion due to its poor health reputation; the Europeans were pushing southwards in search of better living. The main impressions gained of Weltevreden were those of distance and greenery half concealing spacious white residences. In the nineteenth century the Europeans built in a very different manner from that of the lower town, adopting the colonial empire style: uniformly white-painted, simple single-storey buildings with colonnaded galleries. Here the Europeans lived in a relaxed fashion in airy rooms overlooking potted plants, palms, sweet-smelling frangipani and massive tamarind, *kenari* and other tropical trees.

The visitor would first drive (no one of any status walked) through Noordwijk and Rijswijk, the suburbs immediately north of the Koningsplein. Here was to be found the oldest and most famous of the clubs around which European social life revolved—the Harmonie (recently demolished for road-widening), facing the end of Molenvliet. Completed in 1814, it was the most prestigious of clubs; sometimes the Governor-General held receptions there: for instance, when celebrating the birthdays of royalty, occasions close to the hearts of the monarchist Dutch. When fewer people were involved, he would meet with them at his nearby palace which was extended in 1861 to constitute the present Istana Merdeka, one of the impressive porticoed mansions facing Koningsplein. In fact, the Governor-General was rarely there in the nineteenth century: ever since the beginning of the century viceroys had moved their residence to the cooler mountain resort of Buitenzorg. Nevertheless, his regular appearances in the capital were marked with all the pomp and ceremony of old, and his authority was scarcely diminished despite the closer communications with Holland brought about, after the 1850s, by the era of steamships, the Suez Canal, and the telegraph.

The dominance of the colonial administration in Batavia would become clear to the visitor as he or she travelled east to the section surrounding the smaller city square, Waterlooplein. Here Governor-General Daendels, who was responsible for moving the army and the administration out of the old town, used the stones of the old fort to build an enormous palace facing the square where the soldiers drilled. So large that it was not completed until 1829, this broad, severe, two-storeyed building still stands today (it is now the Finance Department). In the nineteenth century the square in front featured a large white pillar topped by a poodle-like lion, in memory of the victory at Waterloo. Several other buildings of governmental and cultural importance clustered around this area. There one found the by now repetitive pseudo-Greek facades of the Departments of Justice and of the Army Commander's Office (now the Mahkamah Agung and Gedung Pancasila respectively). Rows of officers' houses, the barracks and the big Military Hospital (still there) clearly signalled the military might of the colonial rulers, who during the nineteenth century succeeded in conquering most of the archipelago. Celebrations of victories were frequent, although Batavians quickly learned to ignore triumphal news from Aceh, where guerrilla resistance dragged on until the early twentieth century.

On a lighter note, the military added to the culture of the city through their club, the Concordia, on the south side of Waterlooplein (now appropriately enough the site of another foreign hostelry, the Hotel Borobudur), and their frequent performances of band music. The visitor might even chance to see one of these concerts in the open air: at this early example of drive-in theatre, Europeans in their best dress would draw up their carriages in a circle around the band. Another artistic contribution by the army was to be found just north of the square: the Schouwburg (which now, as the Gedung Kesenian, serves as a cinema) was first built for amateur theatricals by officers but later housed professional performances, including immensely popular French operas. Several of Weltevreden's other public buildings were also designed by army surveyors.

Some exceptions to the rectangular neo-classical style of architecture could be observed by the visitor as he or she approached the gigantic Koningsplein. Two churches took pride of place, symbolizing the dominance of the Christian minority in Batavia. Europeans were proud of the unusual, circular style of the Protestant Willemskerk (opened in 1839 and still standing) and, at the end of the century, of the dark neo-Gothic hulk of the Roman Catholic Cathedral, its great spire pointing above the trees. But even the Cathedral was dwarfed by the Koningsplein. Most visitors were (and are) puzzled by this vast square. The existence of such a large piece of open public land in the middle of a busy city is even more of a miracle today. This trapezium measured 1 by 0.85 kilometres, and the Dutch were fond of saying that the town of Utrecht could be fitted inside it. In the 1880s one writer remarked that it was 'just an extensive grass field' which was unsightly in the long dry hot east monsoon.[5] Nevertheless, it still serves a useful function as breathing space for the city, and the tree-lined paths around its perimeter have always been popular for morning and evening walks. Its presence is due to the forceful Governor-General Daendels, whose short rule was so decisive for Batavia: he wanted it as another exercise ground for his troops, and indeed military exercises did occur there from time to time; a more peaceful use was made of the racecourse (a heritage of the English interregnum) which found a niche in the north-west corner in the nineteenth century.

By this time, the size of new Batavia had defeated many a nineteenth-century tourist. Merely noting the neo-classical museum (built 1868) and the stately homes of notable citizens scattered around the square, most visitors returned to their hotels and saw very little else of Batavia. Some hardy souls pressed onwards to see the later extension of European settlement to the south-east. During the century the built-up area crept towards the military and market settlement of Meester Cornelis, stimulated by the building of the tram and railway lines in that direction.

The fashionable newer areas of Batavia in the late nineteenth century were Kramat, Salemba, Kebon Sirih, Parapatan and Pegangsaan where more rows of white houses, with larger or smaller gardens, flanked the main roads. The traveller would undoubtedly have his attention drawn to the Botanical and Zoological Gardens (now the Taman Ismail Marzuki) at Cikini and would admire the enormous avenues of trees which marked this area, giving it, as with most of new Batavia, an idyllic countrified air. Although the darkness of Weltevreden's evenings was relieved by gas lamps after the 1860s, the stillness was profound. One visitor detected only the sounds of crickets, a distant cart, and a flute.[6]

Most visitors were now ready to pronounce Batavia, or rather Weltevreden in the wider sense, a beautiful city. One enthusiast wrote in 1873 that no one 'will dispute her the crown as Queen of the East'.[7] 'Everything in Batavia', wrote another, 'is spacious, airy and elegant.'[8]

European Society

Less laudatory were observers' comments on the life of Europeans in Batavia. True, the men had their daily work routines not very different from those in Europe, but it was immediately obvious to visitors in the nineteenth century, as before, that the so-called European women could barely lay claim to that title. Although the numbers of women who actually came from Europe increased during the nineteenth century, by 1900 there were still only 1,363 of them in Batavia (ten times as many as fifty years earlier).[9] Most women classified as European were Eurasian, and made only a few concessions to European life.

During the British interregnum (1811–16), Lieutenant-Governor Raffles' wife strove conscientiously to convert them away from the sarong and *kebaya* (favoured even by the wives of Councillors of State) to European fashions, and to inject her idea of elegance into the tiny circle of Batavian high society.[10] In 1815 the English Major Thorn was able to comment approvingly: 'After the arrival of the English, the younger ladies, and those who mix much in society with them, adopted the fashionable habiliments of our fair countrywomen, and in their manner as well as dress they are improving wonderfully.'[11] But Mrs Raffles made little lasting impression. Photographs of Europeans in Batavia in the nineteenth century show that at home women continued to dress in 'Indies' fashion and only when they went shopping or visiting did they 'dress up'.

There was little for wealthy European women to do aside from morning and evening visits. Slavery continued to provide labour in the home for the first twenty or so years of the nineteenth century, although Raffles sounded its death knell by abolishing the slave trade in 1812.[12] Despite Dutch reluctance to end slavery itself—it was not officially outlawed until 1859—it gradually went out of fashion. By the 1850s, the first independent newspapers remarked with approval that increasing numbers of slaves were being emancipated by their owners. The number of slave auctions declined, and slaves were often permitted to buy their own freedom. Apparently, Raffles had succeeded in his aim of demonstrating that free labour was more efficient; alternatively, it seems likely that Europeans found it cheaper to employ servants whom they effectively enslaved by keeping them perpetually in debt. In any case, visitors found European houses full of these barefoot Indonesians, each with his or her specialized tasks, which left European women idle.

Once the novelty wore off, this was a dull experience for women who actually came from Europe. Batavia managed to cater for their material needs very well: it had its own French quarter in Rijswijk where French fashions, pastries and other items, could be bought at a time when things French were much in vogue; pianos were imported, and life was transformed by the local manufacture of ice. One popular pastime which had been pioneered by the British was dancing; newspapers carried advertisements for *thés-dansants* at the clubs, and many descriptions of balls were written. Some women also wrote novels for this female clientele.[13]

Most Europeans who spent considerable time in Batavia complained of the boredom. A number of critics satirized Batavian life, the best-known being Bas Veth, whose *Het Leven in Nederlandsch-Indie* was written following a stay in the colony lasting from 1879 to 1891. The opening sentence launches the attack: 'Netherlands India is for me the incarnation of misery.'

What he detested most in cities like Batavia was the philistinism of European life. The men consisted of fortune-hunters, careerists and parvenus. Everyone was obsessed with rank and completely uninterested in ideas. This impression is reinforced by a reading of the novels of the period, notably those of the great Dutch author P. A. Daum. Several of Daum's satirical novels are set in Batavia, where he worked for some years as a newspaper editor. One of his works, *Hoe Hij Raad van Indie Werd* (How He Became a Councillor of the Indies), published in 1888, chronicles the way in which a mediocre civil servant works his way up the colonial bureaucratic ladder largely through the influence and intrigue of his wives. Another Batavian newspaper editor, the Dutch intellectual Conrad Busken Huet, wrote disdainfully to a close friend in 1868, 'Batavia, you must know, unites the pretensions of a world city with the attributes of Delft or Amersfoort'.[14]

The flatness of European public life was marked in the political arena. The deference to rank, the manoeuvring of officials mocked by Daum and Veth was in part due to the powerlessness of European society. The state was supreme. Until the introduction of the Liberal System in the 1870s, there were very few 'private' Europeans in Batavia: most were employed by some arm of government, either civilian or military, and were naturally very sensitive to its authority. Nothing approaching municipal representation existed. The city was governed by an Assistant-Resident as part of the wider Residency of Batavia. Above it all stood the Governor-General, whose word was law. Even the influence of the great Batavian families waned in the nineteenth century, as evidenced by the fact that only two viceroys were born in the Indies, and high-ranking officials had to have been educated in Holland.[15]

The first independent newspapers did not appear until 1850, and their timidity reflected the strict controls over freedom of speech; some newspaper editors including Daum were imprisoned for moderate criticism of government policy.[16] Freedom of association was virtually non-existent, as was made most obvious by the strange case of the 'May 1848 Movement' in Batavia.[17] On this occasion, the preacher W. H. van Hoevell sought permission to hold a small meeting of those dissatisfied with policies discriminating against Indies-born Europeans and with the lack of local educational opportunities. This tiny spark of dissent had been fanned by news of constitutional reform in Holland as a side-effect of revolutions elsewhere in Europe. Reluctantly, the Resident agreed to van Hoevell holding his gathering in the Harmonie Club. It was conducted with decorum, passing a respectful request to the Government to promote the interests of Indies-born Europeans. Van Hoevell left after, as he thought, closing the meeting, but some outspoken Europeans continued to discuss the matter in what was reported to be a rowdy fashion, although true to Indies traditions of early retirement, everything was over by nine o'clock. The administration held van Hoevell responsible for this intolerable insubordination and he found, to his astonishment, that high-ranking people snubbed him. When it became known that the Governor-General, previously quite affable with him, no longer spoke to him at receptions, van Hoevell's position became untenable and he was obliged to return to Holland, where he entered Parliament and became famous as a liberal critic of colonial policy. It was not merely the heat in Batavia that was stifling.

Eurasians, Chinese, Arabs

It is striking but hardly surprising how little the Europeans had to say about the other inhabitants of Batavia. Rattling along in their carriages down the main roads of Weltevreden, tourists were only vaguely aware of the fruit trees of *kampung* glimpsed between the European residences. The only way to enter *kampung* was on foot, and European visitors rarely walked. Nor did they have a language in common with the many other ethnic groups that made up the city. Their only contact was with servants. At the most, tourists dropped in at a market, to be entertained or repelled by the dances of *ronggeng*, the sight of opium dens, and the smell of durian fruit.

The Europeans who wrote about Batavia, even those who spent years there, were transients—*trekkers* as the Dutch called them. They found it hard to immerse themselves in the wider life of the town and indeed their books rarely feature anyone other than full-blood Europeans. Their view of Europeans was that of a minority within a minority, since most so-called Europeans in Batavia were not the officials who vied for high rank nor the ladies who patronized the French shops, but the less well-to-do Eurasians who filled in the lower office and army posts. This partly accounts for the treatment of van Hoevell: he was seen to be allying himself with the lower Eurasians. By holding services in Malay in the Willemskerk, van Hoevell was indeed seeking to identify with them. They bitterly resented the dominance of the *trekkers* with whom they could not compete because they could not speak good Dutch and had no chance of a good education until the first government secondary school, the Gymnasium Willem III, opened in Salemba in 1860. Even then, they faced discriminatory legislation which prevented anyone who had not been educated in the Netherlands from attaining higher positions in the civil service.

Life for the poorer Eurasian majority was very different from that of the inhabitants of the stately colonial mansions.[18] Many of them lived a precarious existence in the suburb of Kemayoran, just north of Weltevreden, struggling to keep up some of the expensive customs of the Europeans, like eating bread and wearing European clothes. European writers tended to speak disparagingly of these Eurasians: their sloppy way of speaking Dutch and the riotous *sinyo* or young toughs who always welcomed a fight, especially with European sailors. By the late nineteenth century, however, the poverty of many Eurasians was beginning to register among Europeans concerned to defend the prestige of their group and to display Christian charity. For instance, a ladies' organization called Dorcas took to conducting home visits among these unfortunates, to give alms and to warn against sin.[19]

Yet the Europeans as legally defined to include the Eurasians, amounted to less than 5 per cent of Batavia's population in the nineteenth century. The remainder of the city's population comprised Asian peoples, of whom only a few could be said to have been native to the Batavia region itself.

The Chinese made up almost a quarter of the total. Over the century their numbers grew steadily (see Figure 2.2), almost doubling to about 24,000. Immigration contributed to this growth, and since the influx was fairly gradual and the immigrants continued to be mainly Hokkien, they were absorbed into the existing *Peranakan* (Indies-born) Chinese community. Europeans noted with envy how the new arrivals were aided by their compatriots in establishing themselves in the economy. As in the previous century, many settled not in the city but in the rural environs as farmers, particularly in Tangerang, to the west of the town. The role of the Chinese in the Residency continued to excite anxiety and considerable jealousy amongst the Europeans. A particular cause of concern was the way that well-to-do Chinese bought up land. In their scramble for revenue in the late eighteenth and early nineteenth centuries, governments in Batavia had sold vast stretches of the Batavia Residency, which came to have the highest proportion of such private estates in Java. Although the original buyers were usually Europeans, during the nineteenth century most of this property fell into the hands of Chinese.[20]

Although many Chinese remained coolies or poorly paid tradesmen and street-vendors, there were undeniably an impressive number of successful Chinese businessmen in Batavia. One example was a prominent Batavian Chinese family by the name of Khouw. The first Khouw arrived in the city in the eighteenth century and began trading in a small way. In the nineteenth century, Khouw Tian Seck built up the family fortunes by purchasing rice plantations around Batavia and land in the business quarter. In the 1880s, three Khouw brothers lived in a grand house on the Molenvliet, where they owned valuable property; they also possessed rice fields in Tangerang and Bekasi, and three rice mills.[21]

It seems that Europeans had little real cause to fear the Chinese. Apart from an anti-tax campaign in 1832 (the Chinese contributed most of the revenue of the Residency), the Chinese were remarkably law-abiding settlers, perhaps because they had so many examples of rapid success before them and so much mutual support. Such peacefulness owed little to the power of the Chinese Council, consisting of the Dutch-appointed heads of the community, although wealthy Chinese continued to vie for the status involved in the position of officer.

It was these officers who sponsored the festivals which so enriched the public life of Batavia. Chinese theatre continued to be performed when ships arrived safely from China, thus providing the old town with frequent entertainment. Three annual festivals were also celebrated with especial pomp: the Chinese New Year, Pecun and Rebutan or Pu-du. On this last occasion, lavish offerings of food were made on a platform to the ghosts of the dead, after which the assembled poor were permitted to climb up and seize the food, resulting in a disorderly rush (hence the name Rebutan or Free-for-all).[22] The Pecun festival, celebrated in the middle of the year, was of obscure origin but it always involved a boat race. Even though the canals in the old town were low during the east monsoon, the Chinese continued to stage these races until the end of the century. A Malay-language newspaper in 1891 described the gathering of four Pecun boats, accompanied by others full of musicians and dancers, in the canals of the Chinese camp before the race along the River Angke.[23] The biggest festival was undoubtedly the Chinese New Year, which lasted for twelve days in January–February and culminated in the feast of Capgomeh. This involved enormous processions through the streets, like an evening one described by a European newspaper in 1884 as wending its way from Kramat through to the lower town: accompanied by torches and music, it featured various mythical creatures such as:

... a giant snake with protruding tongue on the end of which was seated a prettily clad child; also a colossal flower with a long stamen bearing a nymph; and a quaintly pointed crag on which sat one of the Chinese water-gods, and finally imitations of tigers and other animals ridden by neatly clad Chinese girls and boys.[24]

Indispensable at every Capgomeh was the *barongsai*, a dragon-like creature supported by a number of boys which visited house-holds through the Chinese camp to the accompaniment of a barrage of fire-crackers intended to drive away devils.

There were never more than a few hundred Arabs in Batavia, but they made their presence felt.[25] In some ways they replaced the 'Moors' or Indians of previous centuries. Because Indian trade had fallen off with the British conquest of India, their numbers diminished, although Indians continued to work as silk sellers in Pasar Baru, one of the main commercial centres near Weltevreden. Traders from the Hadhramaut began arriving at the start of the nineteenth century, it seems, and took over the Pekojan, the Moors' quarter of the old town. Because of their origins in Muhammad's homeland and the presence among them of a number of *sheikh* and *said*, they were highly respected as religious leaders by Indonesians in Batavia. Some of them were, like the Chinese, extremely successful businessmen who invested their wealth in property. The family of Alatas was one of the élite of Batavia. The first of the line to arrive in the early nineteenth century was Said Abdullah bin Alohsin Alatas, who established himself as a merchant; his best-known descendant was his grandson, Said Abdullah bin Aloie bin Abdullah Alatas, who bought up considerable property in Batavia and marked the move of wealthy Arabs from Pekojan to Tanah Abang in the south-west of the city by building a fine European style house which has now become the Museum Tekstil.[26]

Indonesians

Among the ethnic groups in Batavia in the nineteenth century, the Indonesians underwent the most interesting transformation. At the beginning of the century it was still possible to divide them up into a dozen fragments: Malays, Buginese, Balinese, Sumbawanese, Ambonese and others, and the catch-all category of slaves, who also came from all over the archipelago except Java.[27] It was true that during the century remnants of these groups could be traced in the newspapers: for instance, in 1869 a 'Makassarese house' in Kampung Bugis was sold by one man with a Makassarese name to another, and ten years later an auction was held 'on behalf of the Balinese woman Kalsoem'.[28] Yet immigration into Batavia in the nineteenth century ceased to be as diverse as before. When immigration of Mardijkers fell off, they died out as a separate group in the nineteenth century, leaving only a small pocket of 'black Portuguese' in the village of Tugu near Tanjung Priok, isolated by their Christian faith as much as by distance. The Tugu community is still distinctive, and its *kroncong* groups continue to perform the music which the Mardijkers appear to have originated. With the men wearing batik trousers and plain smocks and the women in long *kebaya* over their sarongs, their style of singing, in Malay larded with Dutch and Portuguese words, is rough and earthy, a far cry from the crooning style of *kroncong* which became popular in the city proper.

The end of the slave trade in 1812 meant that the gradual absorption of slaves into the wider Batavian society was not hindered by new arrivals from Bali, Makassar and elsewhere. Now that Batavia was the capital of a completely conquered Java, there was no bar to the influx of Sundanese and Javanese, who made up the main labour force. But it seems that the influx was sufficiently gradual to allow permanent immigrants to be absorbed into the developing culture of Batavia. The Indonesian population of the town more than doubled over the century (from about 33,000 in 1815, including all Indonesian ethnic groups and slaves, to almost 78,000 in 1900).[29] By the 1820s, however, intermixing had gone so far that observers could no longer divide the Indonesian community into distinct ethnic groups.[30] In the nineteenth century Indonesians born in Batavia generally came to be called Orang Betawi, a recognition that the Indonesians of the city formed a distinct ethnic group.

The Orang Betawi had several things in common.[31] First, they were Muslims; in fact, they had a reputation for being fanatically Islamic. Their strong religious feeling may have been fuelled by an Islamic revival brought about by the arrival of the Arabs. Alternatively, it may have been a reaction against the Chinese and Europeans, who held the dominant economic, social and political positions in the city. Orang Betawi clung to their faith as their only solace in a world over which they had very little control: if, for instance, Arabs or Europeans wished to acquire his land, it was most unlikely that the Indonesian could produce a title to defend his claim. Their religious adherence was blamed by others for their refusal to seek Western education—Muslim schools were the only ones to which they would send their children—but considering the scarcity and expense of such education in the nineteenth century, religion need not have been the main explanation for their illiteracy. However, they do seem to have avoided employment such as domestic service which would have brought them into contact with Europeans. Secondly, Orang Betawi spoke their own language, a distinctive dialect of Malay, remarkable in a region dominated by quite a different language, Sundanese. They also had their own customs, such as a wedding ceremony. Their houses combined elements of Buginese, Makassarese, Chinese and Dutch architecture, and they had their own dress, music, dances and oral tradition. For instance, *ondel-ondel*, a form of street theatre featuring giant dolls, was very popular, as was *rebana* music (singing to the accompaniment of a tambourine), particularly on religious occasions.

Although the Orang Betawi generally occupied the lowest rung on the social ladder in Batavia, there were other Indonesians in town as well. A sprinkling of aristocrats from outside the city lived quite apart from the Orang Betawi, who of course had no nobility of their own. (One consequence of this was that the Residency was unique in Java in having no Regent or Javanese ruler as part of the Dutch system of dual government.) In the nineteenth century, the best-known Javanese nobleman in Batavia was Raden Saleh, an extraordinary figure for his time.[32] A Westernized painter who had established himself on the artistic scene in Europe, he lived for a time in Batavia in the 1850s. He left his mark in the form of a Gothic mansion, designed by himself, on the land of his European wife in Cikini, where it now makes up part of a hospital; he also donated some of this estate for the Zoological and Botanical Gardens. At the other end of the social scale amongst the immigrant Sundanese there were large numbers of itinerant labourers, who could not really be called city-dwellers but who helped to build Batavia: it was, for instance, they who were mainly responsible for constructing the new harbour at Tanjung Priok.

The Orang Betawi themselves were divided by being spread out in *kampung* all over the city and in the surrounding district up to the mountains. Even in the *kampung* close to the centre, their way of living was surprisingly rural. Here is a description of a Betawi *kampung* in Weltevreden in the 1850s:

If you cross Parapatan bridge from Koningsplein in the early morning, you see the big kampung Kwitang on the river. Most of its inhabitants are bathing in the River Ciliwung. Praus bearing grass and vegetables float on the river, horses bathe in it alongside humans, linen is washed there. In the kampung one can see a woman stamping rice, another sewing on a *bale-bale* [string-bed] before her hut, another making red peppers into *sambal ulek*; men are climbing coconut palms to get the fruit and are preparing to take the fruit to market. Children dart around amongst hens, ducks, geese and dogs.[33]

The semi-rural character of the *kampung* is borne out by frequent newspaper reports of accidents caused by people falling out of coconut palms and the occasional mention of a *kampung*-dweller, while peacefully defecating into a river, being attacked by a lurking crocodile.

The Orang Betawi made their living from cash crops, a little handicraft production and performance of services such as cart- and *sado*-driving and laundering. Many grew *sirih* vines, selling the leaf to be used in betel-chewing. Men took fruit, firewood, grass (for the burgeoning horse population) and vegetables for sale to the city. Cottage industries were common: in some areas people engaged in hat- and mat-weaving, and many women earned money at home through batik work. The introduction of the *cap* or stamp technique in the nineteenth century reduced employment for women: whereas hand batik work was done by women, the heavy *cap* pressing was considered a man's job, and since it was best performed in factories it came to be dominated by people with capital—the Chinese.[34]

By nature the Orang Betawi seemed to prefer to be independent. What made this very difficult was the fact that most of the Residency, including about one-fifth of the urban land, was held as private estates by absentee landlords. So it is likely that most Orang Betawi were tenants, subject to the whim of the headman appointed by the landlords. By law tenants were obliged to give up to fifty-two days' labour a year to their landlords, plus a share of the harvest. Observers agreed that the treatment of tenants on the estates was harsh and arbitrary. In 1875, an editorial in a European newspaper claimed that people living in the Batavia Residency were lucky to have two-thirds of their crop left for themselves after they had paid their debts to the money-lender and their dues to the landlord (often the same person).[35] No legal form of redress existed for tenants, whereas the landlords could call in the police to prevent tenants from escaping their obligations. In these circumstances, it is not surprising that the Orang Betawi cherished so many stories of *jago*, folk heroes (usually reputed to have supernatural powers) who fought the landowners. At Marunda, near Tanjung Priok, stands a big timber Malay-style house on stilts, said to have belonged to Si Pitung, a famous *jago* of the nineteenth century who defended the local tenants against private estate owners. *Pencak*, a kind of martial art, was popular as part of this tradition. The private estates in and around Batavia were notorious for lawlessness and theft, and for gangs of thieves who the authorities often suspected were protected by the headmen in return for a share in the spoils.

The occasional riot in the environs did not pose any real threat to the Dutch. In town, six district officers (Kommandants) and *kampung* headmen (popularly known as Beks) were appointed by the Government to control the Indonesians. A Javanese aristocrat visiting the town in 1865 was greatly impressed by all the security measures in urban areas, such as the obligation of Indonesians to possess identity cards, to carry torches at night and to do duty as night-watchmen (hence the famous *tong-tong* or drums hanging from trees, to be struck in case of fire, theft, and other emergencies).[36]

Divisive Forces

While Indonesian groups living in Batavia merged to form the Orang Betawi, there were still a number of forces keeping the main ethnic groups apart in nineteenth-century Batavia. For one thing, they were divided by their roles in the economy. It was obvious to all that the Europeans held the dominant position. It was, after all, a European state which controlled the colony's main exports under the Cultivation System and then, after the introduction of the Liberal System in about 1870, it was the Europeans who owned and ran the big trading houses in the city. Only Europeans could enter the civil service, a highly significant fact in a bureaucratically controlled state. Second in line were the Chinese by virtue of their usefulness to the Dutch as middle-level traders and providers of more skilled urban services, and also by virtue of their relative wealth. Indonesians in Batavia provided the labour at wharves and warehouses and on public works, and fulfilled each others' needs as pedlars, *warung*-holders and so on.

The status division between Indonesians and Chinese was a powerful barrier to these two subject peoples forming a close liaison. However, one does occasionally glimpse some convergence in their attitudes towards the Dutch. A long Malay poem by a *Peranakan* Chinese celebrating the visit of the King of Thailand to Batavia in 1871 expresses some of the resentment of Chinese and Indonesians who were frustrated in their attempts to approach the distinguished Asian guest. When the King attended a ball at the Harmonie Club, non-European onlookers were held back firmly by hussars; the poet comments that the little people, both Muslim and Chinese, were pushed around and regarded with contempt.[37]

Religion also divided people. Despite the efforts of Christian missionaries in the nineteenth century, the faith of the Europeans made almost no headway amongst the Chinese and Indonesians (although the learned Englishman Medhurst had a small following in the Chinese camp in the 1830s).[38] The Chinese continued to bear witness to the strength of their own beliefs (and of their clan and guild associations) by building more and more temples,[39] and, as noted above, the Orang Betawi were fiercely Muslim, which hindered them in mixing with the infidels. Incidentally, it is very striking how little mention is made of Islam in Batavia by nineteenth-century writers or newspapers. Being poor, the

N

km
0 1 2 3 4 5

1 Old Batavia (now Kota)
2 Pasar Baroe
3 Koningsplein (now Medan Merdeka)
4 Weltevreden
5 Pasar Senen

Areas with relatively high
percentage of Europeans

Areas with relatively high
percentage of Chinese

Indonesian kampung

2.1 Ethnic Distribution of the Population of Batavia, c.1885

Source: 'Batavia en Omstreken', Samengesteld door J. Vos, Batavia, Albrecht & Co., 1887.

Indonesians could not build impressive mosques or celebrate their festivals in style. Hence the religion of the majority was almost invisible.

Ethnic divisions were reinforced by law and administrative practice. Up until 1848 marriage between Christians and non-Christians was illegal. The authorities continued to practise 'divide and rule' policies by a system of 'like over like', allocating each community its own official head who was responsible to them for law and order in that group and also acted as its spokesman to the Government. The different ethnic groups were subject to different legal systems. Special restrictions on their place of residence and their movements were imposed on the Chinese, and these were justified by the Government as intended to prevent them from oppressing the Indonesians. Many Europeans defended the restrictions as the only means of stopping the Chinese from growing too strong as rivals to themselves.

In the nineteenth century particular areas of town were associated with different ethnic groups (see Figure 2.1). The Europeans tended to move southwards in search of more salubrious land. The Chinese were at first to be found almost exclusively in the so-called 'Chinese camp', now Glodok, just south of the old walled city. In the nineteenth century they spread over virtually all of the old town and founded new settlements in the commercial areas of Pasar Baru and Pasar Senen. Most of them continued to live in the lower-lying areas of town, where their quarters were crowded and subject to flooding, and where they had poor access to safe drinking water. Of the old Chinese camp an observer wrote in 1844 that the 1,069 closely packed houses there mostly had only dirt floors, and when floods occurred the water sometimes stood 3 to 4 feet deep inside.[40]

Indonesian *kampung* sprang up all over town, and in every ward except the Chinese camp they predominated: Indonesians did, after all, comprise more than two-thirds of the total urban population. Their houses were almost always of wood, woven bamboo and thatch, surrounded by gardens which provided them with some food in the form of hand-raised poultry, fruit and vegetables. Even in these picturesque surroundings, the lack of sanitary provisions was striking and the location was often swampy land, the parts of town spurned by the more well-to-do. In the crowded inner areas, housing for Indonesians in the nineteenth century was already notorious, particularly the *pondok* or boarding-houses, where the coolies lived packed together. The numerous fires in these areas occasionally raised the veil on conditions there: for instance, in 1854 an estimated 1,500 Bantenese coolies were reported to have been living in *pondok* in Blandongan (still a squalid area) which were destroyed by fire.[41] It was always very difficult to halt a fire in these wards where lanes were too narrow and twisting for fire engines to approach. Another disaster which often struck the *kampung* was flooding, which happened so frequently that only when there were particularly bad floods, as in the 1870s, did the authorities feel obliged to undertake large drainage works. In general, Chinese and Indonesians in the lower town suffered from water-related problems—either too much of it or too little, polluted or in the wrong place. All manner of waste was thrown into the canals, yet ordinary people were obliged to resort to canals for much of their water, with predictable consequences. During droughts they had great difficulty finding drinking water, and lacking safe or reliable wells they were often forced to spend part of their meagre wages on buying it from water-carriers.

Health

The different areas in which ethnic groups lived were clearly related to what patchy evidence exists about their health in the nineteenth century.[42] On the one hand, Batavia lost its reputation as being a graveyard for Europeans. Various researchers estimated a steep decline in mortality among Europeans over the century—from a stunning 228 per 1,000 in 1819 to 29 in 1903–11 (still well above the average in Holland).[43] Since European medicine showed little advance in practice in the Indies during the century, except for smallpox innoculation and the increasing use of quinine for malaria, the main reason for better European health must be put down to their movement away from the malaria-ridden lower town to an area less subject to flooding and with access to better water supplies. Wells in the upper town reached safer water than elsewhere, and in the late nineteenth century the administration sank deeper artesian wells, mainly in the 'European' areas of town.

Better housed they might be, but because of their lack of understanding of the nature of disease and the absence of any reliable remedies, the Europeans were not immune from the scourge of all big cities in the nineteenth century—cholera. This disease, new to most countries, including the Indies, was one of the negative results of greatly improved transportation. It caused panic among Europeans: not surprising when one considers that in the 1864 epidemic, for instance, 240 Europeans died.[44] One of Daum's novels (*Hoe Hij Raad van Indie Werd*) portrays the demoralizing effect on Batavia's Europeans of an epidemic in the 1880s; even the dashing young Connie who dominates the book is terrified: she drinks champagne heavily as a preventive and has a medicine chest full of patent remedies. Some individuals worked heroically against fearful odds. Roorda van Eysinga wrote of the 1821 epidemic:

There were days when in Batavia 160 people were carried off by [cholera]; seized by strong cramps, they gave up the ghost in a few moments ... I had the good fortune not to be infected, and to see many of my patients recover; but I was so weary that I could hardly keep going. It was very difficult, in an intensely hot climate, to treat patients who, if they belonged to the lower class, mostly lived in little brick rooms. These rooms had to be kept closed to prevent any draught. Then the patients had to be bathed with warm water, and the terrible condition of the victims, whom I instructed to be rubbed with arak (which I did myself when help was lacking) made the treatment one of those unbearable employments which should rightly be described as *hellish*. . . .[45]

Cholera was so new and so dramatically fast-acting that it called forth unusual responses from the Indonesian and Chinese communities as well. Individually Indonesians placed great reliance on the powers of 'holy water' (water from sacred spots or blessed by Muslim leaders). There were also community rituals to fend off illness. In a Malay language paper of 1888 we read of *kampung* notables forming processions to chant prayers through Indonesian living areas. Amongst the Chinese it was apparently customary to call in the *barongsai*, the dragon-players, to roam through the Chinatown at the approach of an epidemic, since they believed the cholera demon feared the *barongsai*.[46]

Not only cholera but also outbreaks of malaria plagued the Chinese and Indonesians in nineteenth-century Batavia to a far greater extent than for Europeans, simply because these groups inhabited the malaria-prone, low-lying parts of town. A glance at a graph (Figure 2.2) of the growth of the different ethnic groups shows, where data are available, quite big fluctuations in popu-

2.2 Population of Batavia by Ethnic Group, 1820–1900

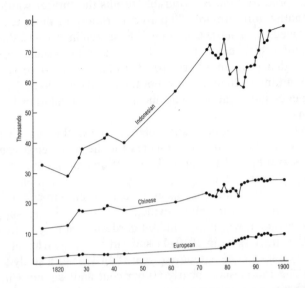

Note: Before 1860, when they were emancipated, slaves are included amongst the Indonesian group.

Sources: Raffles, 1817, Vol. 1, Table No. 1 and Vol. 2, p. 246; Van Hogendorp, 1824, p. 31; Bleeker, 1846, pp. 449–51, 456; *Statistische Gegevens*, 1862; *Koloniaal Verslag* 1875–90, 1892–97, 1902 (Bijlage A).

lation size, which coincide with epidemics. What is less obvious is that the underlying health level of the Chinese and Indonesians was generally very low, largely due to poor living conditions. Since reliable mortality statistics are just not available for the nineteenth century, it is difficult to speak definitively. Better surveys in the early twentieth century, when conditions were unlikely to have been much different, reveal death rates for Chinese considerably higher than those of Europeans but lower than those for Indonesians; it has sometimes been suggested that the Chinese habit of drinking boiled water in tea offered them better protection against some of the mainly water-related diseases that struck the Indonesians. In the more elevated area of town the Indonesians enjoyed better health than in the lower part. Even in the 'upper town', however, the death rate among Indonesians reported for 1903–8 (not significant cholera years) was 48 per 1,000 (almost double that of the Europeans); in the 'lower town' it was as high as 98.[47] A survey in the same period for enlargement of the spleen (a good and simple indication of malaria) produced more favourable results the further south one went. In one northern area 90 per cent or more of those examined displayed the malaria symptom.[48] Research in 1911–12 showed a shockingly high death rate of Indonesians in certain parts of town. In that year, in a very crowded older area where *pondok* were found, more than one-third of the population died.[49] Only a high rate of immigration could maintain the population in such locations.

Despite the dramatic nature of epidemics, the big killer in Batavia was infant mortality. Figures for the nineteenth century are non-existent, but it seems likely that among the Indonesians and to a lesser extent the Chinese, the main causes of the problem were the same then as in the early twentieth century, for which we have documentary evidence. Polluted water supplies meant diarrhoea, which hit children hardest. A survey of Muslim cemeteries in Batavia in 1910–11 showed that a quarter of those buried died under the age of one year.[50] In 1935–7 a study found that among Indonesians nearly 60 per cent and, among Chinese 50 per cent, of total mortality was due to deaths of children below the age of five.[51]

Little was done by the authorities to alleviate the appalling health situation of the Indonesians and Chinese. Apart from a good campaign of smallpox innoculation, the administration contributed little in the way of doctors and hospitals, although it did take the first step of setting up a small training programme for Indonesian paramedics in 1851. Most medical care in this age of territorial conquest was devoted to the army: hence the large Military Hospital at Weltevreden. Since European medicine at this stage could not claim to have much better results than other varieties, it did not matter greatly that the medical scene for most Batavians was dominated by Chinese and Indonesian healers, whose methods were likewise unable to deal with the hazards of urban life: polluted drinking water and poor housing, sanitation and drainage.

Some public works measures, involving forced labour, were undertaken by the Government to try to improve drainage: canals in the lower town were filled in and new ones dug further upstream to divert water from the river during the wet season. Continual reports of flooding bear witness to their lack of success. Efforts to provide better drinking water through artesian wells were also limited due to the Government's reluctance to spend money on non-Europeans. The fact that Batavia was the capital of the Indies and contained the largest concentration of Europeans in the colony justified some expense, but belief in government non-interference died hard. As a result, health in Batavia depended on the environment and income that one enjoyed, which in turn were determined by one's position in the racial hierarchy created by the colonial rulers. Batavia might be an increasingly attractive and healthy place for the Europeans, but the conditions of life for Chinese and Indonesians still cast a shadow over its general health record. Studies in the early twentieth century comparing it with other areas showed Batavia as firstly, more unhealthy than West Java as a whole; secondly, worse than other Javanese cities including Surabaya; and, finally, as having a higher mortality than other large Asian cities— including Calcutta.[52]

Culture and Women

Ethnic groups in Batavia differed from one another in socio-economic status, employment, areas of residence and health records. What brought them together was women.[53] Already in the eighteenth century the fact that there were so many more foreign men than women meant that immigrant men sought sexual relations with local and slave women. In 1844, men made up about 56 per cent of the population.[54] In the nineteenth century, the absolute numbers within each ethnic group had increased to the extent where it was only necessary for a minority of males to look for a partner outside their ethnic group, but the fact remained that relatively few women moved into Batavia: they were the stable force within the city, helping the men to adapt and exerting a constant influence on the children. So it was the women who shaped Batavian cultural traditions.

As a result of their influence, the life of the Europeans and Chinese became more Indonesian. During the nineteenth century this process reached its apogee. Amongst the wealthier Dutch, even the *trekkers* adapted their life-style to eating *rijsttafel*, wearing sarongs at home, taking siestas, and so on. Poor Eurasians spoke Malay rather than Dutch, or a kind of Dutch that was ridiculed by *trekkers* because its grammatical structure was Malay. It was the Eurasians who popularized two cultural forms which had a wide following in Batavia: *kroncong*, the type of music which derived from the Mardijkers, and *stambul*, eclectic theatre where dramas borrowed from European, Middle Eastern, Indonesian and Chinese sources (amongst others) were performed in Malay with frequent songs set to current Western dance tunes.

A rather similar picture holds true for the Chinese community. The day-to-day life of *Peranakan* (Indies-born) Chinese, who made up the vast bulk of the Chinese population in Batavia, was intermingled with belief in Indonesian spirits, consultation of *dukun* (Indonesian healers) and so on. The Chinese language was no longer current among *Peranakan*, who used Batavian Chinese Malay, a Malay influenced by Javanese, Dutch and Hokkien, in which some Chinese were publishing newspaper articles, verse and novels by the late nineteenth century. Certain cultural forms, such as the *gambang kromong* orchestra and *cokek* (a dance performed by girls in semi-Chinese dress accompanied by *gambang kromong*) were shared by both Indonesians and Chinese in Batavia.

Most so-called European women were Eurasians, who continued to raise their children in an Indonesian atmosphere; those who could afford it allowed them to be brought up in the care of Indonesian slaves and servants. European boys might be given some Western education in the few schools to be found in Batavia, but such education was not thought important for girls.

Presumably it was the strangeness, the Indonesianness, of Eurasians which produced the torrent of abuse poured out against them by Dutch writers in the nineteenth century. Eurasian women in particular were described by writers like Couperus as promiscuous, selfish, cunning, lazy, superstitious—and sexually attractive. Indies women were seen as failing to live up to the European standard as wives, and as intruding an alien element into European marriage.[55]

Since the Chinese who emigrated to the Indies were not from the scholar class, their culture derived from the folk tradition which was adept at absorbing many and often contradictory influences. In Batavia, where there were very few and poorly run classical Chinese schools, there was little to prevent children of Chinese–Indonesian unions and their descendants from absorbing the Indonesianized *Peranakan* culture from their mothers, slaves and nurses. The traditional Chinese subordination of women failed to take hold in *Peranakan* Chinese households; for instance, the custom of foot-binding never caught on, daughters as well as sons inherited property, and some *Peranakan* women were held in public esteem in Batavian society.

In the nineteenth century, most European and Chinese men did not marry the Indonesian women with whom they had relationships: casual sexual encounters and concubinage seem to have been much more prevalent. Prostitution existed in an officially countenanced though controlled fashion. The keeping of *nyai* or housekeepers was accepted in both European and Chinese communities. Although the liaison was unmentionable in polite Batavian society, unofficially it was recognized that since many young European males (especially those in the army) could not afford to marry a European woman, it was preferable for a man to lead a healthier, more settled life with a *nyai* than for him to indulge in heavy drinking parties with his bachelor friends, often followed by visits to brothels.[56] Moreover, in this way he could learn Malay, which was essential for commercial and official intercourse in Batavia. Such Indonesian women in established relationships could be very influential in introducing their masters to Indonesian practices. At the same time, they acted as cultural brokers within the Indonesian society. *Nyai* acquired wealth and status through their association with Europeans and Chinese; for these and other reasons they were often influential in Indonesian society, so that even if they were unable to marry their foreign masters, or were obliged to leave the service when the latter went home, married elsewhere, or dismissed them for bearing unwanted children, they could usually set up in business on their own and/or find husbands among other groups in which they could introduce the new tastes they had acquired.[57] This may account for some of the Chinese and European cultural influences in the Indonesian group; for instance, *gambang kromong, tanjidor* and *stambul* were popular among Indonesians as well as Chinese and Eurasians. An aristocratic Javanese visitor to Batavia in 1869 considered that Indonesians there had been infected by foreign customs such as using table and chairs.[58]

One of Batavia's best-known folk tales concerns a *nyai*—the tale of Nyai Dasima. Based on fact, it tells of an Indonesian woman who lived as a *nyai* with an Englishman in Batavia in the early nineteenth century. Although treated well by him (or, according to some versions, precisely because her remuneration

made her so tempting to outsiders), she was persuaded by some
Orang Betawi to leave him and return to Muslim society. The
story ends in tragedy when her new Betawi family has her
murdered for her money. The pull of religion on the woman is an
interesting sidelight on the Betawi culture, and her wealth
supports the view that *nyai* could acquire considerable prestige.

Apart from sexual relations, well-to-do Chinese and European
households had to seek servants and slaves outside their own
population groups. These people were in a position to exert
considerable social influence, especially strategically placed
women servants like nursemaids, cooks and seamstresses. They
were able to influence the upbringing of children, the kind of
food eaten and the clothes worn by the family. In wealthy
European families it was considered essential to have a cook who
could prepare both European and Indonesian dishes; it was in the
nineteenth century that *rijsttafel* became a regular daily meal.
Many European novels and memoirs pay tribute to the close
relations between European children in Batavia and their female
Indonesian nurses and servants, who spoke to them in Malay,
taught them Indonesian folk tales and songs and generally
brought them up in the only way they knew how. Relations
between European adults and their servants also seem to have
resulted in cultural exchange, to take a positive view of an
exploitative situation. Some travellers describe the popularity of
Indonesian massage, administered by skilled female servants or
slaves in European households. It was common for European
masters to have sexual relations with female domestics, often
resulting in Eurasian children. Sometimes these children were
legally recognized by their fathers, carrying further Indonesian
influence into the European community; more often it seems they
were raised in the *kampung*, clinging to their vestige of European
prestige-by-descent.

The integrating role of women can best be seen by comparing
the lives of women across ethnic groups: there were striking
similarities. Most notably, almost all Batavian women spoke
Malay as their first language. Then again, almost all of them wore
sarong and *kebaya*. True, there were distinctive variations on this
Indonesian dress form: European women and *nyai* tended to
wear lace-trimmed, white *kebaya*; those of the *Peranakan* women
had long points, and the batik of their sarongs was differently

patterned and coloured; Betawi women wore longer, coloured *kebaya*. There is plenty of evidence, too, that most women had habits which were regarded by foreigners as Indonesian: frequent bathing, chewing *sirih*, gambling at Chinese cards, consulting *dukun*, using *jamu* (medicinal herbs), and believing in *guna-guna* (black magic). During the English interregnum, a correspondent with the *Java Government Gazette* criticized the prevalence of gambling amongst European ladies, one of whom asked in a spirited reply what else they should do when the men spent all night at all-male card parties. 'Is it just that their wives and daughters should have no amusement whatever, but sit quietly at home in the society of their slaves?'[59]

Since women made up almost half the Batavian society, clearly cultural integration had gone a long way in the town; at the least, Indonesian influences pervaded domestic life across the ethnic spectrum. In European and Chinese communities, the foreign men often appeared to be of marginal significance domestically; certainly Breton de Nijs, in his colourful memoirs of a Batavian Eurasian family, gives the impression that full-blood European husbands, although much sought after, never really belonged in households dominated by Eurasian women close to the Indonesian world. Some of these Eurasian women were respected personalities in their domestic sphere: they wrote household handbooks published in the late nineteenth century on Indies-style cooking and medicine.[60]

Even outside the domestic scene, social and cultural mixing occurred frequently in nineteenth-century Batavia. Indonesians and Europeans participated in Chinese religious festivals and in gambling intended by the authorities only for the Chinese. For instance, at Capgomeh, Indonesians joined in the festivities, which included a range of entertainments: in 1884, besides the usual Chinese processions, there was a Eurasian *dangsu* (old Portuguese-style dance) performer, twenty or thirty Malay *dendang* (singing) groups, Arab *gambus* (six-string lute) and *kroncong* played by Eurasians.[61] A European traveller reported in 1851 that Eurasians were very fond of Chinese *wayang*; they wandered around all night eating Indonesian snacks of *kemelo*, sugar-cane, *kacang-goreng* (fried peanuts) and *kwee-kwee* (cakes).[62]

Close relations between Chinese and European élites were

fostered by the introduction in 1809 of the so-called opium farm, a method of tax-farming which worked to the mutual benefit of Chinese entrepreneurs, the colonial finances, and high-living colonial civil servants who were dependent on indirect Chinese bribes, usually offered in the form of gifts on festive occasions.[63] As a sign of this collaboration, wealthy Chinese and Europeans liked to offer entertainment of all types to their mixed visitors. Europeans commonly invited *ronggeng* (Indonesian female dancers) to their parties, and in 1894 the Chinese Captain Khouw Kim Po was recorded as throwing a party for European friends, at which Chinese and European entertainment was offered, dinner was brought from the Cavadino restaurant, and the wine and champagne flowed freely.[64]

It seems likely that women, as the most mobile group in this society, carried cultural forms into different ethnic groups. Certainly they were prominent as public performers. Unlike in China where female roles were usually taken by eunuchs, in Batavia Chinese *wayang* was performed entirely by girls, and *ronggeng* and *cokek* were public dances for women. Women also featured in *topeng* (mask) dances and in *stambul*, and joined in improvising verses in *kroncong* competitions. All these hybrid types of home-grown entertainment flourished at a time when there was little competition from imported varieties.

Reading the newspapers, novels and reports of nineteenth-century Batavia, one is struck by the relative lack of communal friction. To be sure, there were complaints by Europeans about the wealth of the Chinese, occasional disturbances of the peace when off-duty soldiers amused themselves by roughing up Asian shopkeepers, and more serious rumblings in the private estates from Chinese defying Europeans or Orang Betawi resisting their landlords. But even taking into account the likely effects of censorship and administrative repression, Batavia at this period stands out as unusually harmonious.

Compared with earlier times, Batavia in the nineteenth century seemed in the process of consolidating itself socially. Immigration was sufficiently slow to allow this relatively small urban society to pursue its own cultural forms in peace, undisturbed by economic or political upheavals. In such a society women were able to play a vital role as cultural intermediaries, helping to shape a distinctive Batavian culture with ethnic variants.

Batavia: Growth and Role

Such a social idyll stands in stark relief against the rapid developments of the twentieth century. What were the reasons for this relatively peaceful interlude in Batavia's history? What was happening (or failing to happen) in Batavia can be better appreciated if the town is compared with its nearest rival, Surabaya.

In the nineteenth century Batavia was not the largest city in Indonesia. Whereas Raffles reported Surabaya in 1815 as having a population of about 24,500 compared with 47,000 for Batavia,[65] by 1900 Surabaya with 147,000 people outstripped Batavia's 116,000.[66] There are a number of possible reasons for Batavia's slower growth. One is the apparently greater unhealthiness of Batavia. Apart from van Gorkom's figures for the early twentieth century which make this claim, it is significant that from 1873 to 1894, the death rate in the Residency of Batavia (mortality was recorded only at the Residency level, not at the smaller urban level) was consistently reported as higher than that of Surabaya; indeed the records frequently show the death rate there exceeding the birth rate.[67]

Another possible reason for Batavia's slower growth is its less crowded hinterland, which probably created less pressure for migration to town. This merely raises the further question as to why the region around Batavia was so sparsely populated. West Java had always had fewer people than the other provinces of the island, and (or because?) it was much slower to adopt irrigated cultivation which could support a larger population.[68] In the nineteenth century the province saw rapid growth with the spread of irrigation, but because it started off from a much lower base than the other provinces, increased numbers could easily be absorbed on the land, except in Banten, where irrigated cultivation was reaching its limits and from where large numbers of coolies were supplied to Batavia. West Java was also affected by the so-called Preanger System: until 1870 the Government cut the highlands area (the Preanger or Priangan) off from the world, refusing people permission to migrate and outside influences (principally the Chinese) to penetrate the area, with the aims of 'protecting' the people and of forcing them to grow crops for export.

Migration to the cities depended on good transport. Only in

the late nineteenth century did road and rail systems allow easy movement in West Java. Even then, some of the problems in obtaining labour experienced at the Tanjung Priok construction works (1877–85) give insight into the relative scarcity of population in Batavia's region. Reports of progress on the harbour continually reveal the shortage of labour, which went so far that at times convicts and women workers had to be employed. Admittedly the work was onerous (coolies refused to dig the undersea foundations for the breakwater) and dangerous (accidents abounded and the region was notoriously malaria-prone), but even north Banten could not provide the requisite work-force for much of the time.[69]

In the nineteenth century, the sugar industry was much more important for Surabaya than for Batavia. Under the Cultivation System, and even more so under the Liberal System after 1870, sugar exports poured out of Surabaya's port. East and Central Java were the heartland of sugar, following the decline of West Javanese production, and Surabaya grew to be its main exit point.[70] In the late nineteenth century, ship movements, not only international but coastal too, in Surabaya were the largest of any Indies harbour. Part of this activity resulted from the fact that in 1811 Surabaya had been designated as the naval centre for the Indies. Surabaya came to outstrip Batavia as a port within the Indies, just as Singapore did at the wider regional level: during the nineteenth century, it displaced Batavia as the main South-East Asian entrepôt.

Then again, sugar production, unlike coffee in West Java, gave rise to industry. Especially after 1870, sophisticated machinery involving steam engines was used to mill sugar, and Surabaya developed its own facilities to service and even manufacture this equipment. What with the machine workshops and the large shipbuilding and repair works which were associated with the naval centre, it is not surprising that in the nineteenth century Surabaya developed into the foremost industrial city in the colony. A survey in 1898 showed Surabaya with large engineering factories employing hundreds of workers each; by comparison, Batavia had relatively fewer and smaller industrial establishments.[71]

In the nineteenth century Batavia also lost some of its government departments to Buitenzorg and Bandung as the European élite discovered the more temperate climate of these hill resorts and could reach them more easily with the improvement of main roads at the start of the century and with the extension of the railway system in the 1880s. The Governor-General and his co-ordinating secretariat were located in Buitenzorg, as were the Departments of Agriculture, Arts and Education. In 1894, the Railways Department set up its head office in Bandung, which became West Java's second biggest city. Still, the bulk of the departments were left in Batavia. As the Dutch expanded their colonial control in the nineteenth century to cover virtually the whole archipelago, Batavia's political influence grew. Under the Cultivation System the colonial administration grew in size and rigour, spreading its tentacles right down to the village level. Hence the frantic political machinations that observers found so obsessive amongst the European population in Batavia.

In the nineteenth century, Batavia had to share many of its functions with other colonial cities in the region, as the Dutch consolidated their hold. This helped to explain its quieter history in the nineteenth century. Even then, the last quarter of the century was beginning to see faster change as a result of rapid economic development in the Indies and increased immigration, both connected with communications improvements. Socially, the ethnic groups were drawing further apart as their ties with their homelands strengthened. By the twentieth century, the colonial urban society built up in the nineteenth century was under threat. For Europeans it meant the beginning of the end of what they later saw nostalgically as *tempo doeloe* (the old times), their era of unquestioned privilege and superiority. For others, perhaps the dissolution of an autonomous urban culture was a small price to pay if the other side of the coin of change was greater political power and urban improvements which would destroy Batavia's dubious claim to be one of the unhealthiest cities on earth.

1. Travellers' accounts of Batavia in the nineteenth century include: Ph. P. Roorda van Eysinga, *Verschillende Reizen en Lotgevallen*, Amsterdam, Johannes van der Hey, 1830–2; M. D. Teenstra, *De Vruchten Mijner Werkzaamheden gedurende mijner Reize over de Kaap de Goede Hoop naar Java en terug ...*, Groningen, H. Eeckhof, 1828–9; J. B. J. van Doren, *Reis naar Nederlands Oost Indie*, 's-Gravenhage, J. and H. van Langenhuysen, 1851; Johannes Olivier, *Land- en Zeetogten in Nederlands Indie*, Amsterdam, Sulpke, 1827–30; A. W. P. Weitzel, *Batavia in 1858*, Gorinchem, J. Noordvijn, 1860; Eduard Selberg, *Reis*

naar Java en Bezoek op het Eiland Madura, trans. W. L. de Sturler, Amsterdam, Oldenburg, 1846; W. A. van Rees, *Neerlands Indie. Batavia*, Leiden, A. W. Sijthoff, 1881; Greiner, 'Over Land en Zee: van Rio Janeiro naar Java', *Tijdschrift voor Nederlandsch Indie*, nieuwe serie, Vol. 2, No. 2, 1873, pp. 341–83; Jules Leclerq, *Un Sejour dans l'Ile de Java*, second edition, Paris, Plon, 1898. For photographs taken of Batavia by Europeans from about the 1860s, see E. Breton de Nijs (R. Nieuwenhuys), *Batavia: Koningin van het Oosten*, 's-Gravenhage, Thomas en Eras, 1976, and his *Tempo Doeloe*, Amsterdam, Querido, 1961. Good illustrations of existing buildings are also to be found in A. Heuken, *Historical Sites of Jakarta*. For descriptions of locations, the author has also used H. A. Breuning, *Het Voormalige Batavia*.

2. On Tanjung Priok, see entry 'Havenwerken' in *Encyclopaedie van Nederlandsch Oost-Indie*, 's-Gravenhage, Nijhoff, 1918, Vol. II, and *Rapport der Kommissie ingesteld bij Gouvernementsbesluit van den 9e Jan. 1873 no. 28, met het doel om de kwestie omtrent de geschikste plaats waar Eene Zeehaven voor Batavia kan worden daargesteld, te beoordelen*, Batavia, Landsdrukkerij, 1874.

3. For information on trams in Batavia, see H. J. A. Duparc, *De Elektrische Stadstrams op Java*, Rotterdam, Wyt, 1972.

4. Van Eysinga, op. cit., pp. 247–8.

5. J. H. W. Cordes, 'Flora en Pomona te Batavia', *De Indische Gids*, Vol. 11, No. 1, 1889, p. 672.

6. Van Rees, op. cit., p. 27.

7. Greiner, op. cit., p. 368.

8. Van Rees, op. cit., p. 22.

9. *Koloniaal Verslag 1856* and *1902*, Bijlage A.

10. On Mrs Raffles, see V. I. van der Wall, *The Influence of Olivia Mariamne Raffles on European Society in Java (1812–1814)*, no place, publisher or date given (c.1930).

11. William Thorn, *Memoir of the Conquest of Java*, London, T. Egerton, 1815, p. 248.

12. On slavery in nineteenth-century Batavia, see Abeyasekere, 'Slaves in Batavia'.

13. On women novelists of the late nineteenth century, see Taylor, *The Social World of Batavia*, and Rob Nieuwenhuys, *Oost-Indische Spiegel*, Amsterdam, Querido, 1973.

14. Quoted in Nieuwenhuys, *Oost-Indische Spiegel*, p. 181.

15. Taylor, op. cit.

16. For the history of European newspapers in Batavia, see *50 Jaren 1885–1935 Bataviaasch Nieuwsblad*, Batavia, Kolff, 1935 and H. F. Joel, *Honderd Jaar Java-Bode*, Djakarta, Koninklijke Drukkerij de Unie, 1952.

17. On the May 1948 Movement, see Nieuwenhuys, *Oost-Indische Spiegel* and J. Th. Canter Visscher, 'De Waarheid over 22 Mei 1848', *Tijdschrift voor Nederlandsch-Indie*, Vol. 10, No. 2, 1881, pp. 401–34.

18. On the Eurasians, see Victor Ido, *De Paupers*, 's-Gravenhage, J. C. Opmeer, 1912, reissued 's-Gravenhage, Thomas en Eras, 1978; J. Th. Koks, *De Indo*, Amsterdam, H. J. Paris, 1931; and Hanneke Ming, 'Barracks-Concubinage in the Indies, 1887–1920', *Indonesia*, No. 35, April 1983, pp. 74–9.

19. On Dorcas, see *Verslag van de Vereeniging 'Dorcas' te Batavia over 1908–1909*, Batavia, 1909.

20. On the Chinese, see G. W. Skinner, 'Java's Chinese Minority: Continuity and Change', *Journal of Asian Studies*, Vol. 20, No. 3, May 1961, pp. 353–62. See also J. F. W. van Nes, 'De Chinezen op Java', *Tijdschrift voor Nederlandsch-Indie*, Vol. 13, No. 1, 1851, pp. 239–53, 292–313 as well as articles in *Java-Bode* (e.g. 24/4/1858; 29/5/1861).

21. Information on the Khouws from A. Wright and O. T. Breakspear (editors), *Twentieth Century Impressions of Netherlands India*, London, Lloyds Greater Britain Publishing Company, 1909, pp. 481–2.

22. Examples of descriptions of Rebutan can be found in *Pembrita Betawi*, 14/9/1893 and *Bintang Barat*, 14/8/1875.

23. *Pembrita Betawi*, 12/6/1891.

24. *Java-Bode*, 12/2/1884.

25. On the Arabs in Batavia, see Milone, 'Queen City of the East', pp. 212–13.

26. Wright and Breakspear, op. cit., p. 483.

27. On Batavia's population in 1815, see T. S. Raffles, *The History of Java*, first edition, London, 1817, reissued Kuala Lumpur, Oxford University Press, 1965, and Singapore, Oxford University Press, 1988, Vol. II, p. 246.

28. *Java-Bode*, 13/11/1869; 27/12/1879.

29. Raffles, op. cit., and *Koloniaal Verslag 1902*, Bijlage A.

30. Discussion of Batavia's population in 1824 is found in C. S. W. van Hogendorp, 'Algemeen Jaarlijksch Verslag van de Staat der Residentie Batavia over 1824', Collectie van Hogendorp nr. 83, Algemeen Rijksarchief, Den Haag.

31. On the Orang Betawi, see Budiaman, *Folklor Betawi*, Jakarta, Pustaka Jaya, 1979 and Milone, op. cit., pp. 250–63.

32. On Raden Saleh, see Harsja Bachtiar, 'Raden Saleh, Aristocrat, Painter and Scientist' in *Papers of the Dutch-Indonesian Historical Conference*, Leiden/Jakarta, Bureau of Indonesian Studies, 1978.

33. Weitzel, op. cit., pp. 23–4.

34. On occupations of Indonesians in Batavia, see van Hogendorp, op. cit. On small-scale manufacturing (including batik) in Batavia, see *Koloniaal Verslag 1892*, Bijlage A.

35. *Java-Bode*, 31/11/1875. For discussion of the private estates, see Emile van Delden, *De Particuliere Landerijen op Java*, Leiden, S. C. van Doesburgh, 1911 and H. van Kol, *Uit Onze Kolonien*, Leiden, A. W. Sijthoff, 1903, pp. 813–22.

36. R. A. Sastradarma, cited in S. Z. Hadisutjipto, *Sekitar 200 Tahun Sejarah Jakarta (1750–1945)*, pp. 54–5.

37. The poem is given in Claudine Salmon and Denys Lombard, 'Le Poème en Maleis d'un Peranakan sur la Visite du Roi Chulalongkorn à Batavia en 1871', *Archipel*, No. 22, 1981, pp. 133–66.

38. On Medhurst's efforts, see Roorda van Eysinga, op. cit., pp. 261–2.

39. On Chinese temples, see Salmon and Lombard, *Les Chinois de Jakarta*.

40. P. Bleeker, 'Bijdragen tot de Geneeskundige Topographie van Batavia. IV Bevolking', *Tijdschrift voor Nederlandsch-Indie*, Vol. 8, No. 2, 1846, pp. 495–6. For numbers of ethnic groups in different districts of the town, see this article and his later contribution, 'Nieuwe Bijdragen tot de kennis der Bevolkingstatistiek van Java', *Bijdragen tot de Taal-, Land- en Volkenkunde van Nederlandsch-Indie*, Vol. 3, No. 4, 1869, pp. 464–5.

41. *Java-Bode*, 20/9/1854.

42. Data in the following section on health is taken from Susan Abeyasekere,

'Death and Disease in Nineteenth Century Batavia', in Norman Owen (editor), *Death and Disease in Southeast Asian History*, Singapore, Oxford University Press, 1987.

43. P. Bleeker, 'Bijdragen', 472 and C. D. Ouwehand, 'Mortaliteit te Batavia', *Geneeskundige Tijdschrift voor Nederlandsch-Indie*, Vol. 52, 1912, p. 298.

44. *Java-Bode*, 21/9/1864.

45. Roorda van Eysinga, op. cit., Vol. III, pp. 146–7.

46. Chinese and Indonesian reactions to cholera are based on reports in *Sinar Terang*, 21/8/1888 and *Pembrita Betawi*, 12/7/1901.

47. Ouwenhand, op. cit., p. 298.

48. W. J. van Gorkom, *Ongezond Batavia, Vroeger en Nu*, Batavia, Javasche Boekhandel, 1913.

49. Ibid.

50. Ouwehand, op. cit.

51. J. H. de Haas, 'Sterfte naar leeftijdsgroepen in Batavia, in bijzonder op den kinderleeftijd', *Geneeskundige Tijdschrift voor Nederlandsch-Indie*, Vol. 79, 1939, p. 713.

52. See *Koloniaal Verslag, 1873–1894*, Bijlage A. for comparative mortality figures by Residency, and also van Gorkom, op. cit., p. 61 and Ouwenhand, op. cit., p. 298.

53. Most of the data in the section about women is taken from Abeyasekere, 'Women as Cultural Intermediaries'.

54. Bleeker, 'Nieuwe Bijdragen', p. 456.

55. L. Couperus, *The Hidden Force*, trans. A. Teixeira de Mattos, London, Cape, 1921. The portrayal of women in colonial literature is discussed in Taylor, op. cit.

56. On women and the army, see Ming, op. cit., pp. 65–94.

57. As evidence of the wealth of *nyai*, a study of the register of slaves in Batavia in 1816 shows that ninety-eight *nyai* owned slaves, Abeyasekere, 'Slaves in Batavia', p. 304.

58. R. A. Sastradarma, summarized in S. Z. Hadisutjipto, op. cit., pp. 55–6.

59. *Java Government Gazette*, 20/2/1813 and 27/2/1813.

60. Examples of handbooks are Njonja E. van Gent-Detelle, *Boekoe Obat-obat voor Orang Toea and Anak-anak*, Djocdja, fourth edition, 1880; Njonja Johanna, *Boekoe Masakan Baroe*, Batavia, 1897 and Nonna Cornelia, *Kokki Bitja*, Batavia, ninth edition, 1881.

61. *Bintang Barat*, 9/2/1884.

62. J. B. J. van Doren, op. cit., p. 97.

63. On opium farms, see J. R. Rush, 'Opium Farms in Nineteenth Century Java', Ph.D. dissertation, Yale University, 1977, Chapter 5.

64. *Bataviaasch Nieuwsblad*, 20/2/1894.

65. Raffles, op. cit., Vol. II, p. 277.

66. *Koloniaal Verslag 1902*, Bijlage A.

67. Ibid., *1873–1894*, Bijlage A.

68. The discussion of West Java's population relies on Graeme J. Hugo, 'Population Mobility in West Java, Indonesia', Ph.D. dissertation, Australian National University, 1975, Chapter 3.

69. Reports on building Tanjung Priok: *Maandverslagen omtrent de werkzaamheden aan den bouw der Havenwerken van Batavia, 1877–1885*, Batavia, Landsdrukkerij, n.d.

70. On Surabaya, see 'Soerabaja' in *Encyclopaedie van Nederlandsch Oost Indie*, Vol. IV.

71. *Koloniaal Verslag 1899*, Bijlage JJJ.

3
Batavia, 1900–1942:
The Colonial City under Challenge

AFTER the relative tranquillity of Batavia in the nineteenth century, in the twentieth the tempo increased so dramatically and Batavia became so entangled in momentous national events that it is hard to concentrate on the city itself. The temptation is to be so engrossed by Batavia/Jakarta as the political centre of Indonesia that the history of the city becomes a catalogue of all the national political struggles which have occupied the attention of so many of its prominent inhabitants and visitors. Of course, these events do reflect something of the role of the city in Indonesia and in the world: the character which those events took on was in some part moulded by the nature of the place, and those events in turn have helped to shape the city. But for most of its residents, most of the time, other preoccupations were more important.

In order to highlight the changes and continuities which were most obvious for ordinary citizens, we will compare Batavia in 1940 and in 1900. Starting from this general view, we can then seek the roots of political change in the city—the awakening political consciousness of the different ethnic groups and the resulting conflicts within and between them.

Batavia in 1940

One of the biggest contrasts between Batavia in 1900 and in 1940 is sheer size. By 1930, the population of the city of Batavia (including Weltevreden) had grown to 435,000, trebling the 1900 level.[1] Immigration caused it to expand, so that in 1935 the southern appendage of Meester Cornelis had to be absorbed into the municipal boundaries, bringing the total population to well over half a million. (See Map 3.1.) By this time, Batavia was

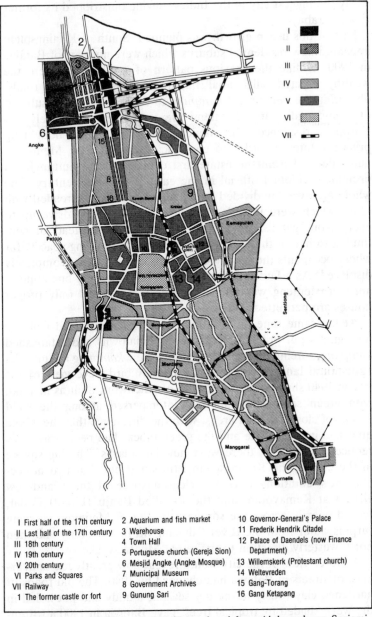

I First half of the 17th century	2 Aquarium and fish market
II Last half of the 17th century	3 Warehouse
III 18th century	4 Town Hall
IV 19th century	5 Portuguese church (Gereja Sion)
V 20th century	6 Mesjid Angke (Angke Mosque)
VI Parks and Squares	7 Municipal Museum
VII Railway	8 Government Archives
1 The former castle or fort	9 Gunung Sari

10 Governor-General's Palace
11 Frederik Hendrik Citadel
12 Palace of Daendels (now Finance Department)
13 Willemskerk (Protestant church)
14 Weltevreden
15 Gang-Torang
16 Gang Ketapang

3.1 The Growth of Batavia to 1938 (Reproduced from Abdurrachman Surjomihardjo, *Pemekaran Kota* (The Growth of Jakarta), Jakarta, Djambatan, 1977)

easily the biggest city in the Indies, having outstripped its former rival, Surabaya.

Part of this urban growth was planned. South of Koningsplein appeared new residential suburbs which were not part of Batavia in 1900. Unlike the previous pattern of settlement, where the wealthy erected substantial buildings along the main roads, obscuring the network of *kampung* to the rear, the new suburbs of Gondangdia and Menteng were planned exclusively for European residence. The municipal government had bought up private estates in order to construct these suburbs: Menteng's name derived from the estate first owned by van Muntinghe, a prominent colonial official in the early nineteenth century. The whole area was subdivided into smallish plots and threaded with roads which were intended to allow motor cars to drive up to every front gate. Former *kampung* residents, instead of continuing to live in the interstices of European building spaces, for whose occupants they provided various services, were completely displaced. As a Dutch architect put it, the unusually fine appearance of Menteng was 'due to the care taken that only proper houses are permitted there'.[2]

At the same time, large numbers of Indonesian and Chinese immigrants put pressure on the old Chinatowns and established *kampung*, forcing up the price of land. New *kampung* ate into the agricultural land surrounding the city. A bird's eye view of the city in 1940 showed the same kind of patchwork quilt as in 1900, with green semi-rural *kampung* interspersed among the solid blocks of closely settled areas, with the difference that the whole quilt had grown in size and the green blocks had been drastically reduced. Moreover, there were new landmarks. The big square in the centre, the Koningsplein, still stood out, but two noticeable new additions were the cleared space of the brand-new airport at Kemayoran, and the so-called Banjir (Flood) Canal, scored heavily across the southern border of Menteng, carrying surplus water from the River Ciliwung off in a westerly and then north-westerly direction to the sea at Muara Angke.

A closer view of the city would reveal how greatly the appearance of streets in Batavia had changed by 1940. The old roads of hardened clay (dusty in the dry season, muddy and pot-holed in the wet), shaded by tropical trees, gave Batavia in 1900 a softened countrified look. In 1940, most of the road network had been asphalted and many trees cut down to make way for electricity and telephone wires and poles. The effect was to make it much harder on the eye.[3] Along these thoroughfares drove a greatly increased volume of traffic, as the population growth would lead one to expect, and that traffic included at least three types of vehicles not seen in 1900: hundreds of motor cars, thousands of bicycles (one for every eight residents according to a 1937 count),[4] and the first *becak* or pedicabs. This last conveyance deserves a special fanfare, since it has played such a colourful part in the life of twentieth-century Jakarta. In the 1950s, the great anecdotist of Jakartan street life, Tjalie Robinson, looked back on the origins of the *becak*, which he claims first appeared in Batavia in about 1936, a contraption of a modified tricycle propelling a passenger-box:

In the first year these construction attempts clearly bore the character of experiments. Rather similar to aeroplanes and sometimes just as fatal. But the Jakartan had great fun in the process. Taking a ride on a *becak* became a sort of sport. Despite the scornful commentary of *sado*-drivers, *becak* men had fares enough to really test out their vehicles. In the first place it had to be investigated what was the ideal application of aero-dynamic and other laws for a perfect distribution of energy and balance. The first *becak* overturned rather easily on bends, lost their braking at critical moments. . . . Moreover, *becak* like radium had the mysterious quality of spontaneous disintegration. It was a difficult evolution and much blood of passenger-martyrs was necessary to raise sufficient *becak*-seed, for every other wheeled road-user hated the *becak*, and if there was any acceptable excuse, the *becak* was joyfully smashed to bits. But the Jakartan seemed to have set his heart on the *becak*, and after a year a couple of hundred rode around the capital, while elsewhere in Indonesia the *becak* was still quite unknown.[5]

So it seems at least one contribution to transport technology has come out of pre-war Jakarta.

As for the buildings which lined these newly surfaced streets, the architecture of the 1920s and 1930s has left many mementoes. The most imposing were usually commercial offices and banks in central and northern Batavia. As most visitors to Jakarta have observed, there are very few impressive public buildings from the colonial period; true to their home architecture, the Dutch style of building was more modest than the imperial heritage of the British. However, many modern public buildings indicated new aspects of urban life. By 1940 Batavia had numerous schools, hospitals, clinics and entertainment centres like cinemas and swimming pools. On the surface it seemed that Westernization was far advanced now that so many people could receive a Western education, consult doctors and watch the latest European and American films.[6]

This impression would be strengthened if one picked up at the bookshops in 1940 some of the recent publications from Batavia. For instance, in 1900 there was not a single Indonesian novel. In 1940 not only could one have a choice of many, but the two most notable recent works of fiction featured a completely new type of Indonesian. Takdir Alisjahbana's *Layar Terkembang* (With Sails Unfurled) of 1937 opens in the City Aquarium, a brand-new public building in lower Batavia, where two young Indonesian women in Western dress have just arrived by bicycle. During the rest of the novel these women, sometimes accompanied by a Western-dressed Indonesian man, proceed to cycle around the city, study or teach in educational establishments, address political meetings and discuss the latest nationalist play. The other controversial novel of the time, Armijn Pane's *Belenggu* (Shackled), published in 1940, features an Indonesian doctor whose professional life revolves around his telephone and motor car, whose wife determinedly pursues her own independent life, and who falls in love with a singer whose gramophone records he plays constantly. It appears almost incidental that this story is set in Batavia rather than in any other big city in the world.

With all these changes, what was still recognizable in the Batavia of 1940 as compared with that of 1900? For most people the Westernization was largely superficial. When one went beyond the bitumen roads into the twisted lanes of the *kampung*, community life showed continuity.[7] This is not to say that *kampung* everywhere were the same: ethnic groups often congregated in distinct *kampung*; inner-city ones differed from those on the outskirts in being more congested, and accommodation varied from *pondok* housing the poorest coolie labour to the substantial homes owned by the lower middle classes, who lived in the *kampung* only because land values had risen so high that they could not afford a house on the road. Certain *kampung* had their own peculiarities, for instance as the haunts of *banci* (transvestites), whose origin in Batavia seems to go back to the late nineteenth century.[8] But *kampung* had a certain closed life of their own which came from being differentiated from people in the real suburbs, from sharing facilities like water, and from providing their own largely self-sufficient services to each other, like tailoring or making *tahu* (soybean curd) in backyard workshops or front rooms. *Kampung* had their separate organizations like mutual aid societies, where people contributed small sums weekly to insure against sickness and funeral expenses. In the twentieth century, they also had sporting clubs. *Kampung* were enlivened by a constant stream of humanity through their lanes: children ran off to bathe in canals and rivers, or kicked footballs in empty plots; street vendors with their distinctive cries and noises paraded their wares and set up their *warung* for noodles and *saté* at appropriate times of the day; street performers wandered from house to house. On Fridays, men gathered at the mosque; more frequently tiny *langgar* (prayer-houses) served as social as well as religious meeting places.

Beyond the *kampung* there was also the life of the streets in which all could join, and frequent occasions for festivals which differed little from the past. The big religious festivals drew large crowds. Muslim celebrations like Lebaran, Mi'raj and Maulud saw thousands at the big mosques, especially when a favourite preacher officiated: for instance, people from Batavia and beyond swarmed to the Pekojan mosque to hear the Mi'raj sermons of Said 'Ali bin 'Abd-al-Rahman al-Habashi.[9] Devoutly Islamic though Batavia's Indonesians mainly were, they still enjoyed other people's festivals too: just as the Chinese often paid respects to their Indonesian friends at Lebaran, Indonesians enjoyed the big processions of the Chinese holidays: Capgomeh was still a great event in the Batavian calendar.

Secular festivals seem merely to have grown in number and size, and many acted as magnets for well established kinds of entertainment. Early in the twentieth century the Dutch introduced Pasar Gambir, an annual exhibition-cum-fair held on Koningsplein around the time of the Queen's birthday. Here Batavians could enjoy nearly two weeks of *kroncong*-singing competitions, exhibitions of turtle-doves (*kampung*-dwellers often kept dovecots), football matches and performances of *stambul*. In 1936, more than 300,000 visitors attended the Pasar Gambir.[10]

There is no need to romanticize daily life in Batavia in the last decades of Dutch rule. Colourful it might have been in many ways, but it had its harsh and seamy side. Prostitutes were part of street life, as were pimps and pickpockets. In the Depression the homeless who drifted in from the villages to seek work sometimes ended up sleeping on the streets.[11] A study of municipally employed coolies in Batavia in 1937 found that most earned 30–35 cents a day, of which more than half was consumed by the family in food; the best housing they could afford was generally a *pondok* with an earthen floor, a privy shared by ten to thirty families, and drainage through open sewers.[12] A *kampung* study of Batavia in the same period found that most Indonesians were living in impermanent dwellings of the *petak* (one-roomed apartments giving onto a shared verandah) or *pondok* types.[13] By 1940, epidemics had been brought under control in Batavia by means of cholera innoculations, isolation measures and mosquito-eradication campaigns. However, infant mortality among Indonesians and Chinese was still alarmingly high: in 1935–6, 30 per cent of Indonesian and 15 per cent of Chinese infants were estimated to have died (compared with less than 6 per cent for Europeans), which gave Batavia a worse record than any other Asian city except Hong Kong.[14] So disease, filth and misery were also elements in the continuity of daily life for most people in Batavia. If this were to be described in terms of Westernization, the only comparison could be with Western cities one hundred years before.

This picture of Batavia in 1940 does not tell the whole story of changes since 1900; for instance, 1940 saw the city recovering from the Great Depression but plunged into a political malaise. It merely serves as a reminder of the more humdrum considerations of ordinary life which for most people were more real than the unfolding political and international changes.

The Impact of Education

Fundamental to the changes which began in Indonesia in the early years of the twentieth century was the new colonial policy presented by the Dutch Government in 1901: the so-called Ethical Policy. Although the motivations for the policy were a mixture of humanitarian concern for the 'diminishing welfare' of the Javanese and a desire by Dutch exporters of manufactured goods to raise the buying power of this large potential market, the practical thrust of the policy everywhere was the same: increased government intervention to improve health, education and productivity, and to open up the political scene for more local initiative. More schools, more health centres, more political freedom and respresentative assemblies were among the most obvious signs of the Ethical Policy in Indonesian towns like Batavia.

Education was one of the driving forces of the age, and more particularly in Batavia which, with the most secondary and higher institutions in the colony, was its greatest educational centre. Tremendous faith was invested in the powers of modern schools by the leaders of every ethnic group. Without modern education it is impossible to envisage the development of nationalism. The dynamism of Batavia was largely due to the endeavours of educated élites.

The expectations of education were extremely diverse. Dutch willingness to support an expensive school system in Batavia had several causes. The government and foreign businesses required an educated workforce. The increasing numbers of Europeans arriving in the city wanted an education system of Dutch standard so that their children would not be disadvantaged by a stay in the colony. Eurasians were anxious to equip themselves to compete with these newcomers. And the Ethici, the Europeans ideologically committed to the Ethical Policy, hoped that education would benefit Indonesians and create bonds between colonial subjects and their rulers. In the early years of the twentieth century, this last feeling was remarkably strong, and was referred to as the 'Association Idea': the belief that once Indonesians, even the most devoutly Islamic amongst them, were inducted into Western culture through modern schools, they would recognize its greatness and learn to appreciate the sincere desire of the colonial rulers to uplift them. This would result finally in co-operation between rulers and ruled in a great common cause of bringing the benefits of Western culture—individualism, material advancement, scientific thought—to the Indonesian people at large.

Several young Indonesians in Batavia were involved in this great Association experiment. Hand-picked from élite families in the archipelago, they were brought to European schools in Batavia where they were entrusted to the care of sympathetic Europeans. One of those who wrote his memoirs of this experience is P.A. Achmad Jayadiningrat. Son of the Regent of Serang, the young Jayadiningrat at the turn of the century became the protégé of the famous Dutch Islamicist and Adviser for Native Affairs.

Christiaan Snouck Hurgronje, who placed him with a respectable Dutch family for schooling in Batavia and invited him to lunch on Sundays to review his progress. Despite a brief periòd when, according to his memoirs, he was led astray by a Eurasian ne'er-do-well, Jayadiningrat was obviously considered a credit to his patron; he became one of the most enlightened of the new breed of Javanese Regents and in 1924 was even appointed as the first Regent of Batavia when, as part of administrative reforms, Batavia was finally fitted into the Regency system.[15]

Did the policy of making Western education available to Indonesians fulfil the expectations of Europeans? Certainly the schools and colleges in Batavia succeeded in turning out sufficient qualified workers for European purposes; in fact, by the 1930s, there was even a surplus of educated Indonesians in some fields. Considering the very small size of the Indonesian-educated class, this was a reflection both on the relevance of the education system (which produced too few practically-oriented graduates) and on the colonial economy: the demand for such people was limited because the Dutch commitment to transforming Indonesia's agrarian base was very limited. What Batavia did above all was to produce a modern-educated élite; what the Dutch failed to do was to educate the bulk of the Indonesian population. This is especially striking in Batavia: although a large number of educational institutions were concentrated in the town, the 1930 census found that 88 per cent of its Indonesian population was illiterate in any language; amongst women the level was as high as 96 per cent. One of the handful of well-educated Orang Betawi, Mohammad Husni Thamrin, is famous precisely because he was in many ways different from his people. The son of a *wedana* (the highest-ranking of Betawi officials), he attended a Christian primary school and government secondary school, and, until he was able to set up independently in the property business, he worked for a Dutch company: all activities which for most Betawi were both undesirable and beyond their financial means. In only one respect was he true to Betawi tradition: he decided against a career in the bureaucracy. In other ways he was very Western-ized: his fluency in Dutch and confident familiarity with European customs enabled him to move easily in European circles, where he had many friends.[16]

Thus, it was amongst only a tiny minority in Batavia that

education could have the cultural effects which the Ethical Policy hoped for. European schools certainly attempted to instil loyalty to the Dutch Empire. School children of all ethnic groups learnt Dutch history and geography and celebrated all the Dutch festivals: the Queen's birthday in particular was a great occasion on which children turned out to sing Dutch songs in their best white clothes with orange sashes (for the Royal House of Orange). More important, however, was the exposure to Western ideas, which changed the lives of Indonesians who received a modern education. It was the possibilities both for employment and for intellectual revival which created such an appetite for Western education among Indonesians that many private schools had to be opened up to compensate for the scarcity in the government system. Indonesians were forced to question traditions accepted by their own people, and many preferred to adopt the new learning. Several Indonesians educated in Batavia in the early twentieth century wrote books about the struggle they experienced between the new and old values, which flared especially in relation to family matters such as arranged marriages.

Many of these Indonesians carried the new ideas out to the rest of their society, often with very disruptive effects. Takdir Alisjahbana, transported hundreds of miles from his Sumatran home to attend school in Batavia, later wrote movingly about the shock caused to his family by his display of learning. They had sacrificed much to support him through school in the hope that he would gain material advancement which would benefit all his kindred, but his father found to his horror that Takdir had imbibed sacrilegious ideas like Darwin's theory of evolution.[17]

After the first rapturous response to new ideas, however, Indonesians educated in Batavia began to think more independently about their own culture and about colonial rule. They read widely in European political history and theory, and began to apply European views of liberty and the right of national self-determination to their own situation. They wondered where their main loyalties should lie. Part of the impact of education in Batavia derived just from the mingling of students from all over the country: young Javanese were for the first time meeting not only Europeans but also Sumatrans, Ambonese and Sundanese. The effect was both confusing and electric. Although at first their new appreciation of regional differences led them to form organizations like Jong Java and Jong Ambon, the need to mix with others produced in many a recognition of cultural similarities and a common questioning of colonial power.

So it is not surprising to find a political revival occurring in the early twentieth century amongst Indonesian students in Batavia. The beginning of modern Indonesian nationalism is conventionally dated as 1908 with the formation of Budi Utomo, an organization founded by students at STOVIA, the training school for native doctors in Weltevreden which is now preserved as a national monument. At this time, it was the only institute for higher learning in Batavia; it was followed in 1926 by the Law School and in 1940 by the School of Arts. (Bandung acquired a Technical College in 1920.) Budi Utomo was not in fact overtly nationalist; it was basically Javanese and concentrated on the importance of social and economic advancement for society, but it was the first modern-style organization founded by Indonesians.

Jayadiningrat, who was in many ways the fulfilment of Ethical Policy hopes and who was awarded the highest honours by the Dutch Crown, was one of these early nationalists who maintained good relations with Europeans. Several prominent Dutchmen in Batavia fostered the early development of pride in Indonesian culture and the struggle for political rights. For instance, M. H. Thamrin learned politics from the Dutch socialist Daan van der Zee, who encouraged him to join an Association-based electoral organization of Europeans, Chinese and Indonesians which got Thamrin into the Municipal Council in 1919. The stages of Thamrin's career reflect the development of the nationalist movement, for from Association politics he went on to join the Kaum Betawi, an organization founded in 1923 to promote the interests of the Orang Betawi.[18] It was this group which he represented in the Municipal Council and later in the People's Council (Volksraad) to which he was elected in 1931. But he was soon attracted to the broader nationalist movement; he became treasurer of the Federation of Indonesian Political Parties founded by his friend Sukarno in 1928 and in 1935 he joined the nationalist party, Parindra. He also donated a hall in Gang Kenari (in Salemba) as a meeting place for the nationalist movement.

Students in Batavia went down in Indonesian nationalist history by proclaiming the Youth Oath in 1928 at a house at Jalan Kramat 106. This building (still standing) was rented in 1925 by

Javanese students, mainly from STOVIA, for use as a hostel. It became a centre for many nationalist student activities: the board outside called it 'Indonesische Clubgebouw' (Indonesian Club building). One of the sessions of the Second Youth Congress was held there in 1928. The assembled youth organizations voted in favour of an oath stating that they belonged to one fatherland and nation, Indonesia, and would uphold the language of unity, Bahasa Indonesia. They also declared the national flag to be the Red and White, and adopted a national song, 'Indonesia Raya', composed by W. R. Supratman, which was sung for the first time.[19] Because all these resolutions are now an accepted part of the Indonesian Republic, it is hard to realize how revolutionary and idealistic they were in those days, when the concept of Indonesia as a nation was quite new (for most people there was no term other than Dutch East Indies for the archipelago) and the decision to adopt one national language was also more of an ideal than a reality. Although Malay, on which Bahasa Indonesia is based, had long been a trading lingua franca, it was still only a minority language in the colony. These were notions that the nationalists had to promote, not just to their colonial rulers but, even more importantly in the long run, among their fellow Indonesians.

The Potential for Indonesian Nationalism in Batavia

What was the response of Indonesians in Batavia to the views of such intellectuals? What was the particular nature of nationalism in the capital city? Answers to these questions depend on explaining a little about the changes in the Indonesian population of the city.

That population grew rapidly in the last decades of colonial rule. The number of Indonesians in the municipality in 1930 was almost four times what it had been in 1900, rising from 77,700 to almost 326,000. About half of these came from outside, overwhelmingly from West Java.[20] Most of them came because in the countryside a rapidly growing population had outstripped the supply of land, and it was now possible for them to travel easily and cheaply to the city by train and bus. As a result of immigration, the character of Batavia's Indonesian population changed considerably. By 1930, fewer than 45 per cent of Indonesians in the city had been born there; 36 per cent were Sundanese and 13 per cent Javanese. This meant that the Orang Betawi, the distinctively Batavian Indonesians, were being swamped by newcomers, who arrived in numbers too great to be readily assimilated to the Indonesian urban culture which had been developing in the nineteenth century. Because of divisions within the Indonesian community in Batavia, there were likely to be several responses to nationalism.

The picture is further complicated by the economic circumstances of the Indonesian inhabitants of the city. The 1930 census shows the main jobs for Indonesians were as coolies, domestic servants and in all the most menial aspects of transport, industry, trade and government service.[21] Very few new occupations seem to have been added to the Indonesian repertoire in the twentieth century. For the small number with a Western education, professional positions were opening up, but for the vast mass of the unskilled, only a handful of new industries emerged, such as the cigarette industry, which began in Batavia in the early twentieth century. Even that industry was, like the batik industry, at a very low technical level: Indonesian cigarettes were hand-rolled by women.[22] Unlike some other towns which began to develop a sizeable modern labour force armed with new skills and working together in large numbers (one thinks of railway workshops in Bandung and Semarang and machine shops in Surabaya), Batavia's workers were scattered in innumerable tiny work-places with no chance of acquiring better qualifications. This applied particularly, of course, to women, whose main paid tasks were the isolating ones of domestic service and home crafts like batik.[23]

This work-force was fragmented not only by location, but also ethnically. Observers frequently noted that different regional groups in Batavia tended to take up different occupations. The Orang Betawi had their own preferred ways of making a living and appeared to avoid those that involved close contact with non-Indonesians. The 1930 census observed that coolies at Tanjung Priok were usually seasonal workers from Banten and Tangerang, Batavia's closest hinterland. People from Central Java and Buitenzorg tended to work as servants, market gardeners, wharf labourers, vegetable sellers and laundry workers. Even more specifically, a study of a ward near Pasar Senen in 1936 found that hawkers of particular goods came from different areas: so sellers of lemonade and ice cream came mainly from Sundanese districts and Central Java, while almost all *gado-gado* hawkers were from Cirebon and Kuningan.[24] It seems likely that such preferences and expertise were the result of newcomers gravitating towards kinsfolk who might help them in a competitive environment.

The nationalists faced an uphill task in winning over this Indonesian population to the new ideology. Indonesians generally lacked any education which might give them some understanding of the new ideas; very few could read, for instance. Their work divided rather than united them; many were seasonal immigrants who were quite unaccustomed to urban life and whose only concern was to find shelter and income. Since most of them rarely had contact with Europeans, they could not take in the idea of colonial rule.

There is no need to assume that newcomers to Batavia were discontented, that they found life in the urban *kampung* much worse than at home. Driven as most of them were by dire poverty from the rural areas and attracted by the knowledge conveyed to them by friends and relatives that the prospects of earning money in town were better than at home, they were unlikely to form a potential pool of urban unrest.

The nationalist movement in some other cities of Indonesia was closely allied with labour organization. For instance, Semarang and Surabaya feature prominently in the history of labour agitation from 1910 to the 1920s. By comparison, Batavia's contribution was remarkably small.[25] In contrast to those other towns, very little large-scale industry developed in Batavia, which remained in the twentieth century what it had been in the nineteenth, primarily an administrative and commercial centre, with the addition of some educational institutions. Admittedly, there were a few scattered strikes in Batavia, mainly involving more skilled workers and mainly occurring during the rapid inflation following the First World War: for instance, strikes by pawnshop administrative employees in 1922.[26] There was very little labour organization amongst the unskilled, the worst exploited of the work-force. It is extraordinary indeed to hear of any such strikes succeeding, so special mention should be made of a strike by women employees in a rubber factory, who won a small rise in their pay in 1925.[27] It is more usual to learn that strikes failed miserably as employers organized their superior force to crush agitation: for instance, the pawnshop employees' strike in 1922 soon faltered when the Government immediately filled the places of strikers and ruled that they could never again be employed by any public authority. When shipping companies at Tanjung Priok experienced labour unrest among their seamen in 1913, they simply joined together to decide that no seaman who left work as part of an industrial dispute would be employed by any other company; in the same year a similar tactic was used by major printing companies in the town.

Indonesian workers in Batavia were generally in a very weak position. Their dispersed work-places made it difficult to organize them, they had few if any skills to bargain with, and the rising tide of immigrants meant that employers always had a ready-made reserve work-force prepared to accept even lower wages and worse conditions. Being directly under the eye of the central government must also have had an intimidatory effect.

The plight of labour was most starkly seen in the Depression of the 1930s. Many work-places retrenched employees and those who remained had to sustain a drastic cut in wages. In 1936 the Labour Inspectorate reported that daily wages in most industries were 25 to 45 per cent of their 1929 level.[28] Although this could be justified in part by a fall in food prices during these years along with the prices of most goods, the suffering of ordinary people was indicated by a number of signs such as a marked decline in income tax revenue.[29] Throughout these years the Government took the view that the workless should be cared for by private initiative; the only official support available was for Europeans. Indonesians and Chinese, the authorities proclaimed, had plenty of compatriots to assist them and it was well known that city-dwelling Indonesians could easily return to their villages in times of need. The Resident of Batavia reported complacently in 1934: 'Thanks to the adaptability of the Native population in particular (generally the unemployed worker returning to the village is received hospitably) and to the support committees set up by private initiative, there is no need to appeal to the Government for assistance in what are difficult times for the Government also.' Unfortunately this argument was contradicted by an earlier statement from the same report commenting on agriculture in the Residency: 'Now that so many industries lie idle and many people have left town to return to the countryside, the supply of labour is great. Sometimes at harvest time the village administration even has to be called in to restore order amongst all the harvesters competing for work.'[30]

Since there are no statistics available, it is impossible to tell how many Indonesians were unemployed (remembering anyway that only a minority were ever in regular, paid employment) and how many actually left town. But people did note an increase in the number of street-vendors and prostitutes.[31] Various philanthropic organizations were formed to raise and distribute funds and food for the workless: for instance, an Unemployment Night Fair was held in Batavia in 1933 where the performers provided their services for charity.[32] Perhaps, as some officials claimed, Batavia suffered less than some other cities in Java during the Depression: certainly it was not as dependent on the sugar industry which was so badly hit in East and Central Java, and imports into the city declined less during these years than in the rest of Java.[33] As far as the reaction of Indonesian workers was concerned, there were almost no signs of organized protest in Batavia. Whereas inflation in the aftermath of the First World War had provoked a wave of discontent, Batavians suffered the Depression silently.

If nationalists were unable to attach themselves to a labour movement in Batavia, they had rather more success when they appealed to other local preoccupations. The most prominent of these seemed unrelated to urban life: they were the old ones of religion and the private estates. Batavians did respond when nationalists pulled these strings, and the parties which did so most assiduously were the Sarekat Islam and the PKI, the Indonesian Communist Party.

Sarekat Islam, the Communist Party and the Aftermath

The years from 1910 to the 1920s were years of unrest. The colonial government, still imbued with the warm glow of the Ethical Policy, extended unprecedented political freedom to groups to contend among themselves and seek representation in the newly formed local councils and, from 1918 onwards, in the national representative body, the Volksraad or People's Council. Several Indonesian parties emerged to take advantage of these opportunities.

Sarekat Islam, the first great nationalist party in Indonesia and always the largest in the colonial period, was founded on the issues of Islam and trade.[34] Indonesian traders happened to be more devoutly Muslim than most, and their Islamic identity was strengthened by competition from Chinese traders. The party actually had its origins in Batavia with a Javanese journalist called Tirtoadisuryo, who in 1909 founded the Sarekat Dagang Islamiyah, or Muslim Traders' League, which was intended to help Indonesians against Chinese traders. In 1912, Sarekat Islam was formed, an offshoot of the earlier organization and without specific emphasis on trade. The Chinese were a target for attack by the Sarekat Islam in the Batavia region for two reasons: firstly their role in trade, where what were regarded as traditionally Indonesian fields like batik were being taken over by the better organized Chinese; and secondly, their role as the main owners of private estates, which dominated the Residency and where conditions were backward and oppressive. Support for Islamic and nationalistic slogans was not difficult to find amongst people who regarded themselves as the victims of foreigners and heathens, although the enemy was seen by most ordinary Batavians as more obviously the Chinese than the Dutch.

Around Batavia Sarekat Islam became embroiled in a number of local issues, which encompassed inter- and intra-village quarrels, outright economic grievances against (Chinese) landlords, resentment at local officials, and religious revivalism. Although the Dutch authorities accused the Sarekat Islam leaders of fomenting disputes and encouraging violence, it is likely that Sarekat Islam was equally used by local people for their own purposes, as a means of organizing people against common enemies. A couple of examples from the district of Meester Cornelis may illustrate this. In May 1913, the Assistant-Resident of Meester Cornelis reported the establishment of a local branch of Sarekat Islam, led by a well-to-do local Indonesian butcher, a teacher, two clerks and a trader. One result was a considerable increase in mosque attendance: at one mosque more than ten times the normal number of people were reported. About 4,600 members were rapidly enrolled, half of them in the town. Certain people were not permitted to join: those considered to be engaged in sinful activities which included, significantly, not only those carrying pigs but also a man whose daughter was a *nyai* with a European. In November that year, the Sarekat Islam was involved in a dispute on the private estate of Cakung, where people protested against the landlord's requirement to cut grass for him and against the low wages paid by Chinese farmers for planting rice.[35]

None of these small disputes ever amounted to anything more

than a few localized clashes which were quickly suppressed by the authorities. The Government took care that the Sarekat Islam in the region was unable to organize effectively on a large scale; for one thing, the central leaders of Sarekat Islam were unable to exert any control over the branches because the League was not permitted to exist legally except as separate local groups.

That political parties were merely part of a continuing wave of discontent on the private estates around Batavia is proved by the number of similar incidents which did not involve political organizations, all in direct line with a history of disturbances since the foundation of the city. An example from Tangerang in 1924 may give something of the flavour of popular unrest.[36] This was an area just to the east of the city dominated by Chinese private estates and where the protest of peasants was influenced by religion. One of the leaders of the movement, a *dalang* or shadow-puppeteer called Kaiin, worshipped at the shrine of two saints in Manggadua in lower Batavia, where, he claimed, it was revealed to him that he was the rightful owner of the private lands of Tangerang. He formed an alliance with an Orang Betawi who was a well-known *dukun* or healer and teacher of the mystical science of invulnerability (*ilmu keslametan*). Linking together a number of *dukun* and mystical teachers (several of them female), an organization grew up which drew its support from both Tangerang and Batavia. In February 1924, Kaiin led a band of followers to attack the houses and offices of landlords in Tangerang; they then proclaimed their intention of marching on Batavia in order to destroy it. When the procession reached Tanah Tinggi it was ended by gunfire from the local police.

This pathetic tale is just one of the many which could be told. It proves both the potential for unrest and how far removed local belief systems and unofficial networks of authority could be from the thinking of Batavia's nationalist intellectuals.

In the city itself, Sarekat Islam leaders rallied large crowds when they spoke about issues close to the hearts of urban Indonesians. One of the leading figures of Sarekat Islam in Batavia was Abdul Muis, who, like Jayadiningrat, had been a protégé of a high-ranking Dutch official during the early years of the Ethical Policy.[37] Born in central Sumatra and educated at STOVIA, Muis had been encouraged by J. H. Abendanon, the Director of Education, to work in his department. Muis later made his mark as a nationalist leader, journalist and novelist. In

1916 he became the vice-president of the Central Sarekat Islam and was elected first to the Municipal Council and then as a member for Batavia to the People's Council. During 1918, in the prelude to the opening of the People's Council, he and other Sarekat Islam leaders spoke at public meetings where conditions in Batavia were vigorously criticized. Muis attacked the policy of the Municipal Council of forcing Indonesians off land in Batavia in order to open up new residential areas for Europeans. For instance, he claimed that the former inhabitants of Menteng had been forced out with only paltry compensation. At several Sarekat Islam meetings in Batavia in 1918, speakers were applauded when they attacked conditions on private estates within the municipal boundaries. The issue of high prices was also taken up in meetings during these years of rapid inflation. In July 1918, about two thousand people crowded into the cinema at Decapark on the Koningsplein to hear one Sarekat Islam speaker call for fixed rice prices, and another deplore the dreadful situation of inhabitants of the estate Kwitang Oost (whose owner was a rich Arab, Bassalama): it was claimed that the landlord had driven up rents and did nothing to help tenants during severe floods. A similar situation was said to prevail on the estate of Kemayoran owned by a Chinese, Tjeng Boen Tok.[38]

The popularity of Sarekat Islam was short-lived. The leadership was unable to sustain the momentum of the movement or to direct it, and members who had joined in the revivalist atmosphere from 1910 onwards drifted away in disappointment in the 1920s when Sarekat Islam failed to make any headway with its increasingly radical political demands against a Government which granted few or no reforms.

Much of the radical fervour aroused by Sarekat Islam was soon transferred to the PKI, which was formed in 1920.[39] PKI leaders at first tried to hitch their wagon onto industrial labour unrest, which gained strength in Semarang, Surabaya and Bandung. Following harsh Government repression in those industrial centres, the PKI turned its attention to other areas, including West Java. In 1925, the party endeavoured to enrol more members. An atmosphere of millenarianism was created, even stronger than in the Sarekat Islam days, so that people were led to believe that the communist revolution, here pictured in Islamic terms, was imminent. The leaders in Batavia felt pressured by their followers to launch the revolution, and by 1926 considered that they had no alternative but to do so. Hence the ill-fated revolt of November 1926, one of three squibs lit by the PKI in Banten, Batavia and Minangkabau, which spluttered and were ignominiously extinguished by the colonial authorities.

The revolt lasted one night. A number of armed bands sprang up in the lower town, at Tangerang and at Meester Cornelis, with the apparent aim of cutting off communications, breaking into the prisons and attacking police and officials. The most that was achieved was the momentary seizure of the telephone exchange. The operation was so poorly organized that the authorities had no trouble in restoring order by morning. Three hundred people were arrested at once; some later found themselves in the detention camp in Boven Digul, deep in the wilds of Dutch New Guinea. It seems likely that it was only because of a slip-up in co-ordination by the authorities that the revolt in Batavia was not nipped in the bud earlier, as rebellion had already been prevented in the much more revolutionary environments of Semarang and Surabaya.

Achmad Jayadiningrat, who was Regent of Batavia at the time of the revolt, was puzzled by the origins of the movement. He did not believe that it had broad mass support (which was perhaps proved in the event), but in at least one area he thought there was a local economic base for discontent. The unrest in Tangerang might have been linked to the generally poor and infertile land of the area, owned by Chinese landlords. The share of the harvest received by the tenants was, he considered, not sufficient to live on; many people supplemented their livelihood by small trading and coolie work, both of which occupations took them often into town, where they came in contact with 'people called communists'. Insurgents within the city also came from areas with high concentrations of coolies, illustrating the connections between Old Batavia and the surrounding private estates which had also existed in the 1924 uprising.[40]

The 1926 revolt marks the turning of the tide of nationalist radicalism and agitation in Batavia. This incident brought down such a storm of European wrath upon the nationalist movement that it was never again able to establish a base amongst the Indonesian masses of the city. Although followers of Sukarno did try quietly to set up educational courses in the *kampung*, there is little evidence of any impact by intellectuals on ordinary Batavians. Nationalist activity in the city returned to its earlier paths, in which its strength lay: developing and disseminating ideas and serving as a centre for negotiations with other groups. With its large concentration of Indonesian intellectuals, Batavia was the main publishing centre of works in Bahasa Indonesia: daily newspapers, journals and books. For instance, writers for the magazine *Pujangga Baru* in the 1930s devoted their energies to refining and developing the language in preparation for its official use in an independent Indonesia.[41]

Considerable thought was given to a question which naturally preoccupied educated Indonesians in the city: was it necessary to distinguish between Westernization and modernization in order to adopt the latter while avoiding the former? Intellectuals in Batavia were the most Western-influenced in the Indies, precisely because they were uprooted from their birthplaces and families and subjected to life in a city which the Dutch had striven to make as European as possible. Their view of a modern Indonesia was more urban and Western-oriented than that of other nationalists.[42]

The women's movement was especially concerned with trying to find an appropriate role for modern Indonesian women. Some women's organizations operated as adjuncts to the main nationalist parties; others devoted themselves to social work. The Western image of femininity filtered into Indonesian life; in Indonesian newspapers in Batavia in the 1920s, for instance, the women's page emerged with its emphasis on cooking, etiquette and household duties. Educated urban Indonesian women were under considerable social stress, which was depicted in the novels of the period, like *Layar Terkembang* and *Belenggu*.

As a centre of government, Batavia served as a focus for the nationalist movement's attempts to influence the colonial authorities and to persuade other groups in the colony of the justice of their cause. In the People's Council and in the Municipal Council, nationalist politics in the 1930s took on the appearance of negotiation rather than confrontation. Since radical political activity was banned, nationalists had no choice but to retreat into non-political areas like education or to join the so-called 'co-operating' parties which sought reforms by constitutional means. One such party was Parindra, in which Thamrin was a prominent leader. As their name suggests, co-operating nationalists were aware that reform required the support of non-Indonesian groups.

Arabs and Chinese

The rest of Batavian society was also changing as the Indonesian feeling of identity and assertiveness was growing, and in ways that ran parallel to Indonesian development, ensuring that reconciliation was as impossible as parallel lines meeting. In the first decades of the twentieth century, every foreign minority in Batavia was deeply stirred by the influx of migrants bearing new ideas sanctified by their origin in the home country.

One of the smallest foreign groups in Batavia, the Arabs, represented a microcosm of the transformation of these communities in the early twentieth century.[43] They are of particular interest because of their influence on their co-religionists, the Indonesians. Increasing numbers of Arabs migrated to Batavia (their population in 1930 exceeded six thousand), bringing with them modernist notions of Islam from the Middle East, which was grappling with the challenge of Western ideas and attempting to reform Islam accordingly. In 1905, a group of Arabs in Batavia founded an organization called Jam'iyyat Khair (Association for the Good) and proceeded to set up an elementary school based on modernist Islam, which preached that Muslims should combine the scientific advances of Western learning with a purified Islam. The egalitarian ramifications of reform divided the Arab community. Whereas Arabs bearing the hereditary title of Said had always been considered superior beings in Batavia, their authority was now defied by democratically-minded Arabs, leading to a bitter split. A rival Arab organization, Al-Irshad, was formed. Through their close association with Arabs in Batavia, some Indonesians seem to have imbibed the modernist doctrine, which was not widely accepted within their Muslim circles either; the main Indonesian modernist Muslim organization, Muhammadiyah, did not find strong support in Batavia.

Developments within the Chinese community were similar but more complicated.[44] Changes began along the same lines: immigrants arriving in Batavia in the late nineteenth century brought news that in China a reassessment of Chinese thinking was gaining ground. In particular, a new form of Confucianism was being put forward by K'ang Yu Wei and other statesmen as the Chinese answer to the West. The Peranakan Chinese in Batavia were also under pressure from Dutch colonialism; they felt that the spirit of the Ethical Policy was directed against them and in favour of Indonesians. Evidence of this was the dismantling of the whole tax-farming system which had contracted out various tasks to the Chinese. This system, and especially the opium farm (whereby Chinese bought the licence to sell opium), had formed the economic and political base of the authority of the recognized leaders of the Chinese in Batavia, the Chinese officers. Now the Government had taken direct control of such fields as opium manufacture and distribution, pawnshops and credit, turning them into bureaucracies employing Europeans and Indonesians. In 1897, restrictions on Chinese travel and residence in Java were tightened, with the intention of limiting their contact with Indonesians: the Dutch viewed the Chinese as exploitative and a prime source of the 'diminishing welfare' of the Javanese. One effect in Batavia was that Chinese required a travel pass even for the short distance between Batavia and Meester Cornelis. It is not surprising then that the Chinese in Batavia could feel great sympathy with the Government in China in its sufferings at the hands of Western Powers. Some responded with the same demands that Chinese should recover their national pride and strengthen themselves by returning to their spiritual roots, which to the leaders meant neo-Confucianism, although Confucianism had never taken hold in Batavia.

As with the Arabs, the first move of the Chinese was to establish in 1900 a modern-style organization called Tiong Hoa Hwee Koan (THHK), which tried to 'spread Confucian doctrines and erase many superstitions'. The THHK frowned on worship in temples, which did not prevent fourteen new religious establishments being founded in the first four decades of the twentieth century in Batavia.[45] There was little sympathy for attempts to alter the very un-Confucian culture of the *Peranakan* Chinese in Batavia (for instance, they resented THHK opposition to gambling), but there was a better response to what came to be THHK's main activity: running Chinese schools. Among the Chinese, as amongst other groups in Batavia, education was seized upon as the solution to the challenges of the twentieth century. Although there were already a few schools teaching Chinese language and classics in Batavia, they were of such low calibre that the THHK had little difficulty, when it opened its first school in 1901, in demonstrating that teaching Chinese along modern lines was far more efficient. So successful was THHK in this enterprise that it soon served as a model for branches formed elsewhere in Java. The organization imported Chinese teachers and textbooks, thus serving as another conduit for modern Chinese ideas. They also financed a visit to Batavia in 1903 by K'ang Yu Wei himself. At about this time, the Chinese Government began to take an interest in its compatriots overseas, and in 1906 the first of a number of officials began arriving in Batavia to exercise paternal supervision over Chinese activities there: a steady stream of school inspectors, commercial representatives and others attempted to advise and guide the Batavian Chinese. For instance, an official representative persuaded them to form a Chinese Chamber of Commerce (Siang Hwee) similar to those found in other parts of South-East Asia.

This intervention in itself proved a source of trouble, because China was rent by bitter controversies in the twentieth century. Some of the well-to-do *Peranakan* Chinese who supported the THHK were dismayed when the Imperial Government was overthrown by republicans in 1911; they felt the waves of that revolution rocking their position in Batavia. The Chinese officer system came under challenge from their more egalitarian-minded and more China-oriented compatriots, especially now that the patronage exercised by the officers was destroyed by Ethical Policy reforms. Such hostility was levelled against the Chinese Council in 1912 that its members felt compelled to submit their resignations. Although the Government refused to allow this, it was obviously embarrassed by the declining authority of the Council; it tinkered with the appointment of officers and the size of the Council during the remainder of the colonial period without managing to shore up the prestige of the institution.[46]

Large numbers of Chinese immigrants into Batavia further disrupted the Chinese community. In the municipality, the numbers of Chinese increased by almost half between 1900 and 1920, and almost doubled in the next ten years to reach 72,000 in 1930.[47] These immigrants differed in important ways from those of the nineteenth century; for one thing, they included far more women, which diminished the need to adjust to the local society, and most of them were not Hokkiens like the former immigrants but rather Hakkas and Cantonese. For these reasons, plus the sheer rapidity of the influx, adjustment to *Peranakan* culture was both less probable and less necessary. Yet in one field—language—*Peranakan* society still exerted great influence.

According to the 1920 census, almost 80 per cent of the Chinese in the Residency of Batavia spoke Malay rather than Chinese as their daily language. This was the highest level of Malay usage amongst the Chinese in any Residency in the Indies.

In the first decade of this century, the Chinese in Batavia showed considerable unity in their opposition to the trend of colonial reforms. They lobbied the Government for more schools for their children, for the abolition of discriminatory laws and for further political rights. In this campaign they met with success. The Government set up Dutch–Chinese schools in 1908, where Dutch was the medium of instruction, and many Chinese were also permitted to join ordinary European schools. The Chinese were given generous representation in both the Batavia Municipal Council founded in 1905 and in the national People's Council of 1918. From being subject to Indonesian law, the Chinese were brought under the jurisdiction of Dutch civil law, and travel and residential restrictions were abandoned.

Then came the parting of the ways in the Chinese camp. Many *Peranakan* were content with the concessions they had gained, and became reconciled to the colonial regime. They were repelled by the Indonesian nationalist movement, since they regarded the Indonesians as inferior and felt their own position in society would deteriorate under an Indonesian Government. Probably the best-known example of this kind of Dutch-oriented *Peranakan* Chinese in Batavia was H. H. Kan (1881–1951). A wealthy landlord, he attended Dutch schools in Batavia and became founder-president of the Chung Hwa Hwee, a Chinese party which supported the Dutch in representative councils: Kan himself was a prominent member of the People's Council.[48]

Against the Chinese whose first loyalty was to the Indies were those who felt more drawn to China. These could include both *singkeh* (new arrivals) and *Peranakan*. In Batavia this stream of thinking was strongly represented by the newspaper *Sin Po*, founded there in 1910. One of the biggest Chinese daily newspapers, it was printed in both Malay and Chinese and generally took a pan-Chinese and anti-colonial stand. This at least gave it something in common with the Indonesian nationalists. The paper's editor, Kwee Kek Beng, later pointed out that W. R. Supratman, composer of 'Indonesia Raya', was a journalist with *Sin Po*, for which he regularly reported Indonesian nationalist meetings.[49] Sympathetic though these Chinese might be to anticolonialism in the Indies, however, they did not identify with Indonesian nationalism because they regarded China as their motherland.

In Batavia the division within the Chinese community between Indies-oriented and China-oriented Chinese was obvious in many ways. In the education system there were both Chinese and Dutch language schools. Only the most nationalist Chinese sent their children to the former, since vocationally they offered little chance of advancement within the colony. Amongst the *Peranakan*, Chinese Malay literature had a marvellous flowering.[50] Hundreds of novels which focused on life in the capital appeared. Many were sensationalist and crudely written, but the best give a lively feel of the mixed society of the town. For instance, *Aannemer Tan Ong Koan* by Lim Khoen Giok, published in Chinese Malay in 1920, portrays the obsession of a Chinese contractor for a European woman; the prevailing mores made this a hopeless case, but the author describes sympathetically a variety of Indonesian, Dutch and Chinese characters. As European education spread, these novels often took as their theme the impact of that education on Chinese children, especially girls. In *Nona Lan-im* (1919) by Tan Boen Kim, two sisters, one Westernized and the other in the traditional Chinese mode, are compared in favour of the latter. The romances of the 1930s, no doubt popular with Chinese girls, sometimes raised the dilemmas facing Western-educated Chinese women. For instance, *Pelita Penghidoepan* by Yang Lioe in 1937 shows a Chinese typist working for a big firm in Batavia who is subjected to various temptations beyond the range of the secluded girls of the past. Chinese national pride also appears here: in *Kesopanan Timur* (1932) a Dutch employer falls in love with his *Peranakan* Chinese typist, but she rejects him in favour of her Chinese sweetheart. And on the other hand, opposed to this literature firmly rooted in Batavian society, the yearning for the homeland was satisfied by a flood of imported Chinese works.

It was hard for Batavia's Chinese to escape the call of China. When Western cinema entered the scene early in the century, it was quickly followed by Chinese films. The latest films from Hong Kong and China could be seen in Chinatown cinemas. But the Chinese also pioneered the film industry in the colony, adapting popular old themes for cinema audiences: in 1929, the most successful Chinese team, the Tan brothers, made a film of the Batavian favourite story, *Nyai Dasima*. One of the most popular film stars in the country in the pre-war period was Tan Tjeng Bok, born in Jembatan Lima in lower Batavia of a Chinese father and an Indonesian mother. After attending a THHK school, he joined a *stambul* theatrical troupe and then worked his way into film.[51]

So the Chinese contribution to Batavian life diversified in the early twentieth century. Some of them preferred to withdraw from the old mixed urban society and reaffirm their Chineseness; others extended their commitment to the Indies into new cultural and political fields. For most Chinese, it was as if the Indonesian nationalist movement did not exist: they were not preparing themselves for an independent Indonesia.

Europeans

The Ethical Policy had seemed to bode well for relations between the Europeans and Indonesians, since it laid a moral responsibility on the former to improve the welfare of the latter. The Association Idea did, in fact, bring together many educated people on both sides for a time. Even without the changing conditions of the age, however, this kind of relationship could not have lasted long, founded as it was on condescension on the part of the Europeans, a conviction that it was they in the position of superiority who had an obligation to uplift the Javanese. Some Indonesian nationalists were soon to find the Ethici impossibly naïve and sentimental.

Probably the Ethical Policy was never very popular among Europeans in Batavia anyway. Many felt it to be an unnecessarily expensive and intrusive policy formulated by bureaucrats who did not understand the real needs of the country. In any case, reaction was not long coming when the Europeans saw the fruits of the policy. Reaction was all the stronger because at the same time as modern education and political freedoms were giving rise to Indonesian nationalism, Europeans were drawing apart from the rest of Batavian society.

In the 1920s and 1930s, life for many Europeans in Batavia closely resembled that in their home country. For one thing, the numbers of European migrants had grown so much that they could live in an almost closed community. The influx was particularly great in the first twenty years of the century when their numbers almost trebled to 24,500. At that stage, Europeans made up almost 10 per cent of the municipality; over the next ten years their ranks swelled by another 6,500 but as a percentage they dropped to 7 per cent. By 1930, the numbers of women migrating had increased so greatly that there were more than nine women to every ten males.[52]

Outgrowing their residential area of Weltevreden, the Europeans opened up new housing estates further south and south-east. The new suburbs of Nieuw Gondangdia and Menteng were built along contemporary Dutch lines: smallish plots of land containing neat houses with garden plots at the front and back, all looking onto bitumen roads, and all supplied with electricity and water. Instead of the dark, spacious interiors of the past, the smaller new houses were decorated by their fashion-conscious owners with European-style furniture and hangings.

Filling middle-level administrative and commercial ranks, the new migrants were solidly bourgeois and lived accordingly. Certainly there were more servants than in Holland, but fewer than in the old days and they no longer lived around the house as in the times of larger residences. Contact with Indonesians declined in another way too: *nyai* were not even faintly acceptable amongst Europeans. Even in the army, where officers had commonly taken *nyai*, the custom changed in 1914 when the authorities discouraged it and raised salaries to allow men to take European wives. It was now felt that there was no excuse for a European to demean himself by going outside his own community to find a partner.[53]

The entertainments of many Europeans excluded all but the most wealthy Indonesians, Chinese and Arabs. There were still the clubs of course, but the range of possibilities was greatly extended. Sports were all the rage: European soccer clubs, tennis clubs, yachting, and swimming-pools proliferated, some of them, like the Cikini swimming-pool, out of bounds for Indonesians. The coming of cars opened up wider horizons too, and Batavia Residency had the greatest number of private cars and motor cycles of any in the Indies.[54] A weekend trip to the mountains became popular; the wealthier had a holiday house at the Puncak Pass. Europeans tended to patronize the well-appointed cinemas where the latest American and European films were showing, and which few Indonesians could afford.

This life was held up as the norm for European society, but it was still difficult to attain for most Eurasians. Although they continued to enjoy the more easy-going Indonesian-influenced home life and to participate in non-European entertainments like *stambul* theatre and *kroncong*, Eurasians felt under pressure from the Dutch immigrants. Many struggled to conform: as a class, Eurasians improved their Dutch education significantly through the expanded school system (the 1930 census showed fewer than 5 per cent of Europeans in Batavia were illiterate), and tried to adapt their appearance and homes to fall into line with the image they saw projected by the films, the newspapers and their wealthier neighbours. Some advertisements played upon the search by Eurasian girls for 'real European' husbands: 'Whitex makes your skin white. No tropical sun will rob you of the fresh, young colour which men so admire.... See how much whiter your face, hands and arms become at once.'[55]

But within the European society, as within the Chinese, those born in the Indies also resisted pressure from the *totoks* (full-bloods). An early sign in Batavia was the editorship of *Bataviaasch Nieuwsblad* by F. H. K. Zaalberg. A Eurasian himself and an aggressive journalist, Zaalberg used the paper to support the moral and social uplifting of this group. He was associated also with the founding in 1919 of the Indo-Europeesch Verbond (Eurasian League). The leader of this party, Dirk den Hoog, championed the cause of the poorer Europeans (in other words, Eurasians) who, unlike the transient migrants, were said to be the backbone of colonial rule. In the social, educational and economic field, the IEV did much philanthropic work for poor Eurasians, which was particularly important during the Depression years. Politically, the party was something of a maverick. It became increasingly critical of the colonial Government's alignment with the *totoks* and with big business; this dissatisfaction went so far that in 1936 in the People's Council the IEV supported the Sutarjo petition calling on the Dutch Parliament to discuss autonomy for the Indies. On the other hand, because the IEV was determined to defend and extend the privileges of the European group against Indonesians and Chinese, it had no sympathy at all for the idea of Indonesian independence.

As time went on, opinion among Europeans hardened against the Indonesian nationalist movement. The Communist revolts encouraged Europeans to reject the political ideas of the Ethical Policy. Signs of reaction were the formation of the Vaderlandsche

(Patriots) Club, an intensely conservative European party, and some support for the Nationaal-Socialistische Beweging, or NSB (the Dutch fascist party), as shown by great interest in the visits to the colony by NSB leaders.[56] European newspapers in Batavia in the 1930s conveyed the feeling of the times: news from Europe predominated and almost nothing about Indonesians was reported except in the form of ridicule. In 1932, the editorship of one of the two biggest European papers in Batavia, the *Java-Bode*, was taken over by the redoubtable H. C. Zentgraaff, the leader of the Vaderlandsche Club and one of the most virulently racist men in the colony.

It was at this period of Dutch rule that a French connoisseur of colonialism, G. H. Bousquet, visited the Indies and cast a censorious eye over Batavia. In the tradition of Conrad Busken Huet and Bas Veth, he wrote:

The atmosphere of this 'city' lacks even the slightest suggestion of intellectuality or culture. The young Indonesian is sincerely to be pitied, for to him this agglomeration represents Europe. Batavia is neither Europe nor the Orient; it is a plot of ground on which for some centuries the Dutch have pitched their tents, as other Europeans have done in the Klondike or at Witwatersrand.[57]

Of course, there were Europeans in Batavia who went against the tide, such as Zentgraaff's greatest opponent, the writer Edgar du Perron. Born and bred in Meester Cornelis and Batavia, du Perron returned to the Indies in the 1930s after some time in Europe. A liberal intellectual, he was horrified by the reactionary and philistine nature of European society in Batavia, and sought instead to befriend Indonesians. Although he managed to establish a remarkable rapport with leading Indonesian intellectuals, many of whom remembered him with affection and gratitude, he found he could not bear the tension within the society, which seemed to allow a well-meaning European no further role, so far had the communities drifted apart. Finally, he returned to Europe in 1939.[58]

A Forum for Urban Debate: the Municipal Council

With all the various ethnic groups bristling with new-found national consciousness and divided loyalties, it is not surprising that there was conflict in Batavia over the stresses inflicted by rapid population growth in the last decades of Dutch rule. And for the first time, political dissent had some legal outlet because in 1905 the Batavia Municipal Council was formed, one of the first fruits of the hesitant decentralization of power which was one of the aims of the Ethical Policy. The history of the Council offers some insight into colonial life in Batavia.[59]

In fact, the much-vaunted 'decentralization of power' amounted to very little. The origins of the municipal councils lay mainly in a desire by the colonial Government to slough off its urban responsibilities at a time when it was finding Java's cities a growing financial and administrative burden.[60] Initially the powers and finances of the Batavia Council were severely circumscribed, and only in 1908 were limited elections introduced for some European Council members. In 1917, all twenty-seven seats were opened up for election but the conditions for election were still such as to protect European dominance, since fifteen seats were reserved for Europeans, leaving four for 'Foreign Orientals' (almost always Chinese) and eight for Indonesians. Voting was limited to males over twenty-three; Europeans who paid a yearly income tax of fl.900 could vote, as could others who paid income tax of fl.600 and could speak and read Dutch. Although the voting age and financial requirements were lowered in 1925, and literacy in a local language was accepted as an alternative to Dutch, the electorate remained small and male (women were finally permitted to vote in 1941, too late for the last elections before the war). At its greatest in 1938, the electorate for the Council consisted of 8,563 Europeans, 3,468 Indonesians and 718 Foreign Orientals. The proportion of European Council members was reduced so that by 1938 they made up only half the total,[61] and at the same time the scope of the Council's activities and its financial resources increased: its annual budget grew by eight times during the years 1905 to 1930.[62]

Judging from participation in elections, interest in the Council's activities was never great, even among its limited electorate. Generally, less than half of those eligible bothered to vote. Moreover, voter turn-out could not be interpreted merely as an indication of interest in Council affairs, since Council elections were also one step towards the indirect system of elections for the national People's Council which opened in 1918. The importance of local councils was boosted by their connection with national politics in this way.

In many respects politics in the Batavia Council could be seen as a smaller version of that in the People's Council. The political groups and parties were the same, created with national rather than local issues in mind. Apparently the Municipal Council had not had time to establish itself in its own right before the People's Council took the limelight; it was also typical of the way in which Batavia, as the colony's capital, tended to dominate and to be dominated by national affairs. Several prominent Municipal Council personalities, notably M. H. Thamrin, were concurrently or later active in the People's Council.[63] The fortunes of political parties in the Municipal Council followed the national trend: after 1910, Association parties thrived and radical parties attracted support from Europeans and Indonesians alike; by the 1920s the Indonesians and Chinese had their own nationalist parties and amongst the Europeans the Indo-Europeesch Verbond (IEV) emerged as an important force; in the 1930s, the Indonesians were united in a nationalist alliance, while the IEV and the Vaderlandsche Club dominated the European ranks. As in the People's Council, voting increasingly followed clear divisions between Indonesian and European members, with the Chinese almost invariably siding with the Europeans.

Discussion of financial matters brought to the fore the main differences of opinion about priorities for Batavia. As is usual, what was accepted without comment was as telling as what aroused most controversy. Significantly, most of the items of budget expenditure were never queried, and every budget was weighted in favour of European interests in the city. Most of the biggest items, such as road-building and maintenance, street-lighting, drinking-water provision, and payment of municipal personnel were items of expenditure largely on behalf of Europeans, since they were the ones who lived along and used roads most; street-lighting and drinking-water were largely restricted to their areas; and expenses on Europeans' salaries, overseas leave and pension provisions were a heavy burden on the budget. Rarely did this pattern of European-oriented expenditure come into question, apart from occasional sniping during the heavy retrenchment of the early 1920s and the Depression of the 1930s.

Rather than the Europeans having to justify this established system, controversy centred around the introduction and extension of items of expenditure in the interests of the Indonesian majority. The reason for this was not merely that European members dominated Council meetings (vocally as well as in voting), but that it was the European community which contributed most to the Council's income. After all, the vast majority of Indonesians were too poor to pay much if anything in the way of taxes. Local taxes and surcharges on central government taxes made up the bulk of Council income, to which in 1923 Europeans contributed about fl.40 per head, Arabs fl.76, Chinese fl.15 and Indonesians a mere 66 cents.[64] Because of their political and financial weakness in the Council, the Indonesian members were on the defensive on issues involving increased expenditure on their section of the community, despite the fact that they constituted three-quarters of the population. Any additional expenditure was hindered by the reluctance of all population groups to pay any further taxes. Although studies showed that Europeans in Batavia paid less in municipal taxes than in other major Indies towns and much less than in Holland, many Europeans protested fiercely at the introduction or raising of any tax.[65] Indonesian members were just as vociferous in rejecting taxes which affected their section, although there were many like themselves who could well afford to pay extra. For instance, Thamrin and Sapi-ie who were prominent speakers on behalf of the oppressed Indonesian community were both wealthy men, the former the owner of considerable property and the latter a successful businessman—two quite exceptional Orang Betawi.[66]

Kampung Improvement

The extreme political and economic imbalance in Batavia made the issue of *kampung* improvement a thorny subject. The enormity of the task of tackling the neglected areas of the city where most Batavians lived daunted the financially conservative Council members. Yet, as the Indonesian members continually stressed, although the *kampung* were overwhelmingly Indonesian in complexion, most of the Chinese and Arabs and the poorer sections of the Eurasian community also lived there. Moreover, *kampung* settlements tended to be scattered around the city in close proximity to European places of work and residence. Thus, health conditions in the *kampung* necessarily concerned Europeans too. The frequent fires in closely settled *kampung* also aroused fear amongst Europeans on their own behalf.

Although from the start the Council had accepted in theory some responsibility towards the *kampung*, their improvement was at first blocked by the existence of private estates in Batavia. The Council was not permitted to interfere with *kampung* on these private lands, despite complaints from tenants. However, the owners of these estates, mainly Chinese with a sprinkling of Arabs and Europeans and an occasional Indonesian, had no political power: the colonial Government and the Municipal Council, with their civil servant outlook, condemned the anachronistic and notoriously bad conditions on the estates. The Municipal Council therefore received Government political and financial support in its policy of buying out and dispossessing the private estates in order to bring them under Council control. As early as 1908, the large estate of Menteng was purchased, and by 1927 the Council had acquired eleven estates covering 10 square kilometres.[67] Although there was disagreement within the Council about the method of acquiring these properties (purchase versus expropriation) and their cost, everyone approved of this way of improving conditions and of providing new housing areas while preventing land speculation. The Council created a large property industry to develop its acquisitions. Indonesian members rightly complained that the estates were developed to provide housing mainly for Europeans; even when the Council decided to build special low-income housing for Indonesians, they met with little success. The new 'model *kampung*' were beyond the financial reach of the poor Indonesians for whom they were intended, so that the Council was obliged to allow wealthier people to move into them.[68]

Similar problems and criticisms dogged the Council in its attempts to improve established *kampung*. Despite good intentions, for a long time it was accepted that effective *kampung* improvement was beyond the financial scope of the Council. Under concerted pressure from Indonesian nationalists in the Municipal Council and in the People's Council, the situation began to change in the 1920s. Increasing budget allocations were voted for *kampung* improvement; a big step forward was made in 1927 when the colonial Government agreed to pay half of the total cost of improving various city *kampung*. In 1928, an overall plan of *kampung* improvement was drawn up for Javanese cities. But the Depression brought an end to government subsidies, making a mockery of planning. In 1932 an Indonesian member pointed out that the item for *kampung* improvement took up only 1.25 per cent of the budget and that at this rate it would take thirty-five years to improve all *kampung*; but when he moved to increase the allocation, the Indonesian bloc was defeated by a combined European and Chinese vote.[69]

The *kampung* improvement programme consisted basically of building paved roads and paths with accompanying lined gutters. In terms of impact on *kampung*-dwellers' lives, other projects were probably of equal benefit, in particular the flood relief works of Ir van Breen completed in 1918, vaccination campaigns and the extension of the artesian well system. Not only the level of expenditure but also the method of *kampung* improvement was criticized by Council members. In 1935, Sapi-ie summarized the essence of some complaints when he commented that the dominance of European interests in the municipality meant that the central areas were made as European as possible, and *kampung* people were more and more driven to the periphery. For example, when good roads were built through *kampung* land, rent and land prices rose, inducing the poor to move to areas further from their place of work. Similarly, strict municipal building regulations led to *kampung*-dwellers being forced out when their houses were demolished as below standard. Less favourably placed *kampung* in the northern area were neglected although they were more and more overcrowded. When other members asked why very few public privies or wash-places were built in *kampung* or if built became unusable through lack of maintenance, the municipal administration replied that the facilities could not be extended when *kampung* people were unwilling to provide land for them and did not care for them themselves.[70]

It was useless for Indonesians to complain that *kampung*-dwellers often had to pay high prices for scarce drinking water from hydrants because they could not afford the installation costs for the ultimately cheaper (and better quality) piped water, useless to comment on the utter inadequacy of the drainage, sewerage and rubbish removal in the northern *kampung*. The system was geared to those who could afford to pay. In 1936 Thamrin referred savagely to the great expense incurred by the

Council in controlling the purity of the city's supplies of milk: a commodity consumed only by Europeans. This, he said, was typical of the colonial arrogance of the European in the tropics.[71]

There is no doubt that the work of the Municipal Council improved Batavia. A publication written for the Municipality in 1937 could point to a doubling of the road surface in the city over the period 1913–33; the improvement of 308 hectares of *kampung* over the period 1921–36; vaccination on a large scale against smallpox, typhoid, cholera and dysentery; a modern cattle abbatoir; council-run schools; municipal clinics; a piped water system deriving from mountain springs; and other benefits. The death rate for Europeans was only 10 per 1,000 in 1936, and although for Indonesians and Chinese it was still much higher at 29 and 21 respectively, this represented a marked improvement on the 1926 figures of 40 and 39.[72] Most of the new services introduced by the Council, however, benefited Europeans disproportionately; for example, in 1929, European areas received almost four times as much of the water provided by the municipality as did *kampung*. Moreover, it seems that the Council was unable to keep up with the growth of population in Batavia. A careful study of *kampung* life conducted from 1937 to 1941 concluded that for *kampung*-dwellers 'the housing problem is just as acute as it was twenty years ago'.[73]

The key to the problem was that, in Dutch eyes, Batavia was still essentially a Western enclave where the Indonesians were largely ignored. A crude English version of a book on Batavia published for the Municipality claimed that when the newly-arrived European

... walks in the beautiful environment of this Eastern town, which has been created by Western hands from what was no more than a marsh at the mouth of the Tjiliwoeng, he inwardly feels the mastery of the white race as if he himself has taken a part in the sublime work of his fathers.

The description of the town which follows does not mention the *kampung,*

... and this with a purpose, for the kampungs of Batavia have never been cooperating factors in Batavia's beauty, in spite of a long-lasting Western rule. Modern Batavia, which not so long ago was called by a famous architect one of the most beautiful cities in the world, is not an Eastern but a Western Batavia, built by the Dutch, and it is this Westernized town which today boasts the title of 'Queen of the East'.[74]

It is interesting that the Dutch version, written by an Ethically-inspired European, hints that when the East rouses itself to participate in its own way in the world, Batavia will perhaps no longer be primarily a Western city 'but an Eastern town, the centre of an energized millions-strong population, a town in which the Western spirit exists as something from the past'. Apparently, the English reader could not be expected to tolerate such a prospect.

Increasingly, Indonesian members of the Municipal Council pointed out the contradictions and injustices which resulted from such a blinkered view of the city. Looking back on the debates today, one is struck by the fact that the same issues were expressed in much the same terms in later decades. As early as 1918, at the time of Municipal Council elections, Abdul Muis had exhorted Indonesians to remember the way in which they were neglected and oppressed by the city authorities: 'Remember the "transformation of *kampung* into Dutch suburbs (Gondangdia)", and the way traders are driven away from the sides of main roads, because in those places live many Dutch people who don't like to see those dirty street-sellers!'[75]

Within the Council nationalists defended such hawkers; they championed the cause of Indonesian *kampung*-dwellers and squatters forcibly evicted for 'urban development'; and when *becak* appeared on the streets in the late 1930s they joined in a debate about regulation of *becak* which revealed all the later doubts about these vehicles: on the one hand they seemed a humiliating man-powered vehicle which appeared to be a backward step in urban transport, but on the other hand they were an efficient, cheap means of conveyance over short distances and provided much-needed employment.[76]

To a contemporary Dutch analyst of urban affairs, this appeared to be a typically colonial dilemma: the views of a European minority in opposition to those of the mass of the urban population.[77] Certainly the nationalists presented it in this light: Thamrin's remarks about milk were an example of this way of thinking. In retrospect it does not appear a strictly colonial matter, since the same conflicts persist today. Rather it is a question of differing views about and interests in the city: the image of Batavia as a modern capital which could be proudly exhibited to the world, set against the reality of a poor and burgeoning urban population desperately trying to make a living.

During the colonial period, the Indonesian nationalists, effectively excluded from positions of responsibility, could whole-
heartedly champion the cause of the downtrodden masses. Later
it would be a different matter.

The Coming of War

Not until the Nazis invaded the Netherlands in May 1940 did
Batavia begin to take on the appearance of a wartime city. Until
the last possible moment, the Dutch had been convinced that
they could keep out of the war by remaining neutral. For a brief
space after the German invasion, attempts were made to seek co-
operation from all groups in the Indies population, to support the
exiled Dutch Government in Britain. In Batavia rallies were held
at which Dutch, Indonesian and Chinese speakers all called on
the crowds to back the war effort. Superficial attempts were
made to prepare the city for war: air-raid practices were held,
and a black-out was enforced at night.[78]

Few believed that war would touch the Indies. Japan was not
at war with Europe and was believed to be so fully occupied with
the conflict in China that it would not take on targets further
afield. If it did, it would get no further than Britain's impregnable
fortress of Singapore and would never risk provoking the United
States, which had the greatest fleet in the Pacific, by an attack in
South-East Asia.

Dutch complacency was a great blow to the Indonesian nationalists, who had hoped that their expressed sympathy for
occupied Holland would lead a frightened Government to seek
their help. When it was clear that this would not happen, most
nationalists ceased to pretend to support the Dutch war effort.
They took a malicious delight in watching Dutch dismay at
pressures being exerted on the Indies by Japan to make generous
economic concessions, but hardly dared to hope that Japanese
veiled threats would amount to anything.

War with Japan had been in the wind for years: nationalist
leaders like Sukarno and Thamrin had hinted at this possibility as
a way out of their impasse with the Dutch. Colonial intelligence
sources occasionally reported contact between Japanese spies and
Indonesian nationalists, but never had evidence of more than
vague conversations. In February 1941, Batavia was rocked by
scandal and tragedy when the already seriously ill Thamrin was

arrested under suspicion of treacherous dealings with the Japanese and died before he could defend himself. The whole affair remained shrouded in secrecy, and no proof of the charge against him was ever provided. The feelings of Batavians for their most famous son, the only Orang Betawi in the ranks of na-tionalist leaders, were revealed when an enormous crowd turned out for his funeral. Even Europeans wrote respectful obituaries for a man who had proved himself a consummate parliamentarian in both the national and local councils of Batavia.

Thamrin's death marked the passing of the politics of the colonial era. With the Japanese attack on Pearl Harbor at the end of the same year, Batavia stood on the brink of an era of uncertainty and upheaval. The Indies were now genuinely at war. The Japanese swept through South-East Asia, conquering Singapore and attacking the Indies in a matter of weeks. As the air-raid sirens sounded in the city, many people evacuated into the countryside, and those who remained began to hoard food.[79] The colonial Government also left town: indeed, many of its top officials left the colony, flying into exile in Australia. The airport at Kemayoran and the harbour at Tanjung Priok were bombed, but Batavia was spared any real warfare by being declared an open city; the colonial army withdrew into the interior.

At the beginning of March 1942, this open city was left rudder-less, awaiting the Japanese arrival. Most of the Europeans and the Chinese were terrified of the future, knowing the fate of their compatriots elsewhere at the hands of the Japanese. The In-donesian leaders, after years of stultifying inertia, welcomed any prospect of change, especially when so many of them expected that the Japanese as fellow-Asians could only represent an im-provement upon the Dutch.

1. *Volkstelling 1930*, Batavia, Landsdrukkerij, 1933, Vol. I, pp. 122–3.

2. G. E. Jobst, 'Stedebouwkundige Ontwikkeling van Batavia', *Indisch Bouwkundig Tijdschrift*, No. 6, 1926, p. 91.

3. The contrast between the late nineteenth century and the 1930s is clearly seen in a book which compares photographs of Indies towns across time: *Het Indische Stadsbeeld voorheen en thans*, Bandoeng, Stichting Technisch Tijdschrift, 1939.

4. *Batavia als Handels-, Industrie- en Woonstad/Batavia as a Commercial, In-dustrial and Residential Centre*, Batavia, Amsterdam, Kolff, 1937, p. 180.

5. Tjalie Robinson (Jan Boon), *Piekerans van een Straatslijper*, Den Haag, Tong Tong, 1976, first edition, 1953, pp. 99–100.

6. Western facilities are comprehensively listed and illustrated in *Batavia als Handels-*. . . .

7. Descriptions of *kampung* conditions in this period include J. W. Tesch, *The Hygiene Study Ward Centre at Batavia: Planning and Preliminary Results 1937–1941*, Leiden, University of Leiden, 1948; 'Living Conditions of Municipally Employed Coolies in Batavia in 1937' in *The Indonesian Town: Studies in Urban Sociology*, The Hague, Van Hoeve, 1958 and H. C. H. Gunning, 'Het Woningvraagstuk', *Koloniale Studien*, Vol. 2, No. 1, 1908, pp. 109–26. More cheerful aspects of *kampung* life have been gleaned mainly from the newspapers of the period.

8. *Sinar Terang*, 2/3/1889 refers to *banci* in Kampung Tanah Sareal, and *Pembrita Betawi* of 13/5/1901 says they were to be found in Kampung Petojo and Kampung Kebon Djahe.

9. For a description of the Mi'raj ceremony, see G. F. Pijper, 'Mi'Radj' in his *Fragmenta Islamica*, Leiden, Brill, 1934.

10. *Batavia als Handels-* . . . , p. 191.

11. *Java-Bode*, 4/4/1934.

12. Tesch, 'Living Conditions of Municipally Employed Coolies', p. 13.

13. Ibid.

14. J. H. de Haas, 'Zuigelingensterfte in Batavia', *Geneeskundige Tijdschrift voor Nederlandsch Indie*, Vol. 78, 1938, pp. 1467–1512. See Widjojo Nitisastro, *Population Trends in Indonesia*, Ithaca, Cornell University Press, 1970, Chapter 6 for comments on the problems involved in deducing urban infant mortality in this period.

15. P. A. A. Djajadiningrat's memoirs are *Herinneringen*, Amsterdam, Batavia, Kolff, 1936, Chapter 3.

16. Biographies of Thamrin include Matu Mona, *Riwajat Penghidupan dan Perdjuangan M. Husni Thamrin*, Medan, Tagore, third edition, 1952 and Soekanto S. A., *Matahari Jakarta: Lukisan Kehidupan M. Husni Thamrin*, Jakarta, Pustaka Jaya, 1973.

17. S. Takdir Alisjahbana describes his education in *Indonesia in the Modern World*, New Delhi, Congress for Cultural Freedom, 1961, Chapter 4.

18. It seems that some time after its founding (the first meeting is reported in *Neratja*, 11/2/1923), the Kaum Betawi became inactive; it needed to be reformed in 1937, when it issued a journal, *Berita Kaoem Betawi*.

19. For a short history of the building and of the Youth Oath, see Mardanas Safwan, *Peranan Gedung Kramat Raya 106 dalam Melahirkan Sumpah Pemuda*, Jakarta, Pemerintah Kota Jakarta, 1979.

20. *Koloniaal Verslag 1902*, Bijlage A. and *Volkstelling 1930*, Vol. I.

21. *Volkstelling 1930*, Vol. I, p. 87.

22. For a report on the cigarette industry in Batavia, see B. van der Reiden, *Rapport betreffende eene gehouden enquete naar de arbeidstoestanden in de Industrie van Strootjes en Inheemsche Sigaretten op Java*, Deel I. West Java, Bandoeng, Landsdrukkerij, 1934.

23. P. de Kat Angelino, *Batikrapport*, Weltevreden, Landsdrukkerij, 1930.

24. Tesch, 'The Hygiene Study Ward Centre', p. 67.

25. On the early Indonesian labour movement, see John Ingleson, *In Search of*

Justice: Workers and Unions in Colonial Java, 1908–1926, Singapore, Oxford University Press, 1986.

26. *Java-Bode*, 2/2/1922 and 3/2/1922 give details of pawnshop strikes.

27. *Api*, 11/5/1925.

28. *Zestiende Verslag van de Arbeidsinspectie*, Batavia, Landsdrukkerij, 1937, p. 31.

29. L. G. C. A. van der Hoek, 'Memorie van overgave van Batavia 1931–1934', *Mailrapport* 1320/1934, Ministry of Colonies Archives, Den Haag.

30. Ibid.

31. Ibid., and *Pemandangan*, 24/11/1933.

32. *Pemandangan*, 24/11/1933, 30/11/1933, 5/12/1933, 8/1/1934.

33. Van der Hoek, op. cit., was one official who claimed Batavia suffered less than other Javanese cities during the Depression.

34. On the origins of the Sarekat Islam, see Robert van Niel, *The Emergence of the Modern Indonesian Elite*, The Hague and Bandung, Van Hoeve, 1960, pp. 89–90.

35. *Sarekat Islam Lokal*, Jakarta, Arsip Nasional R.I., 1975, pp. 15–18, 29–40.

36. For the story of the 1924 Tangerang uprising, see Sartono Kartodirdjo, *Protest Movements in Rural Java*, Singapore, Oxford University Press, 1973, pp. 45–57.

37. For the activities of Muis, see Deliar Noer, *The Modernist Muslim Movement in Indonesia, 1900–1942*, Kuala Lumpur, Oxford University Press, 1973, pp. 108–16.

38. *Java-Bode*, 25/11/1918 and 22/7/1918.

39. This account of the PKI is based on Ruth T. McVey, *The Rise of Indonesian Communism*, Ithaca, Cornell University Press, 1965.

40. Djajadiningrat, *Herinneringen*, pp. 299–341.

41. On Pujangga Baru, see Heather Sutherland, 'Pudjangga Baru: Aspects of Indonesian Intellectual Life in the 1930s', *Indonesia*, No. 6, October 1968, pp. 106–27.

42. A view of Indonesian students in Batavia as Western-oriented is presented in Abu Hanifah, *Tales of a Revolution*, Sydney, Angus and Robertson, 1972, Chapter 1. See Achdiat K. Mihardja, *Polemik Kebudayaan*, Jakarta, Pustaka Jaya, third edition, 1977, for the debate in the 1930s about modern culture.

43. On the Arabs in Batavia, see Noer, op. cit., pp. 56–69.

44. This discussion on developments in the Chinese community is based on Lea E. Williams, *Overseas Chinese Nationalism: The Genesis of the Pan-Chinese Movement in Indonesia 1900–1916*, Glencoe, Free Press, 1960; G. William Skinner, 'Java's Chinese Minority: Continuity and Change', *Journal of Asian Studies*, Vol. 20, No. 3, May 1961, pp. 353–62; and Leo Suryadinata, *Peranakan Chinese Politics in Java, 1917–1942*, Singapore, Institute of Southeast Asian Studies, 1976.

45. On Chinese religious establishments in Batavia, see Salmon and Lombard, *Les Chinois de Jakarta*, pp. xxii–xxiv.

46. Reports on the fate of the Chinese Council in Batavia in the twentieth century are found in Williams, op. cit., pp. 124–33, van der Hoek, op. cit., and *Java-Bode*, 30/1/1929.

47. *Volkstelling 1930*, Vol. VII, p. 183.

48. Suryadinata, op. cit.

49. Kwee Kek Beng, *Doea Poeloe Lima Tahun Sebagai Wartawan*, Batavia, Kuo, 1948, pp. 35–6.

50. On Chinese Malay literature, see John B. Kwee, 'Chinese Malay Literature of the Peranakan Chinese in Indonesia 1880–1942', Ph.D. dissertation, University of Auckland, 1978.

51. On the cinema in Indonesia in this period, see 'Dossier Cinema', *Archipel*, No. 5, 1973.

52. *Volkstelling 1930*.

53. On the end of official support for *nyai*, see Ming, 'Barracks-Concubinage in the Indies', pp. 65–94.

54. *Indisch Verslag 1939*, Vol. II, p. 404.

55. *Java-Bode*, 12/4/1941. See also Paul van der Veur, 'Race and Color in Colonial Society', *Indonesia*, No. 8, 1969, pp. 69–79. On the Eurasians generally, see ibid.; 'The Eurasians of Indonesia: A Problem and Challenge in Colonial History', *Journal of Southeast Asian History*, Vol. 9, No. 2, September 1968, pp. 191–207; J. Th. Petrus Blumberger, *De Indo-Europeesche Beweging in Nederlandsch-Indie*, Haarlem, Tjeenk Willink, 1939.

56. On European parties, see J.Th. Petrus Blumberger, *Politieke Partijen en Stroomingen in Nederlandsch-Indie*, Leiden, Leidsche Uitgeversmaatschappij, 1934 and S.L. van der Wal, 'De Nationaal-Socialistische Beweging in Nederlands-Indie', *Bijdragen en Mededeelingen van het Historisch Genootschap*, Vol. 82, 1968, pp. 35–56.

57. G.H. Bousquet, *A French View of the Netherlands Indies*, London, Oxford University Press, 1940, p. 96.

58. On du Perron in Batavia, see his *Indies Memorandum*, Amsterdam, Bezige Bij, 1946 and Soewarni Pringgodigdo, 'Over du Perron en zijn invloed op de Indonesische intellectuelen (1936–1939)', *Cultureel Nieuws*, Vol. 2, No. 16, January 1952, pp. 135–49.

59. The two sections of this chapter on the Municipal Council are largely based on Susan Abeyasekere, 'Colonial Urban Politics: The Municipal Council of Batavia', *Kabar Seberang*, Vol. 13–14, 1984, pp. 17–24.

60. For documents on the debate leading up to the creation of the municipal councils, see S.L. van der Wal, *De Volksraad en de Staatkundige Ontwikkeling van Nederlands-Indie*, Groningen, J.B. Wolters, 1964, Vol. I, section 1.

61. Information on the Council electorate is from *Verslag van de Commissie tot Bestudeering van Staatsrechtelijke Hervormingen* (Visman Commissie), Batavia, Landsdrukkerij, 1941, p. 144.

62. E.J. Eggink, *Na 25 Jaar. Beknopt Gedenkschrift ter Gelegenheid van het 25-jarige bestaan der Gemeente Batavia*, Batavia, Indonesische Drukkerij, 1930, p. 37.

63. Thamrin was a Municipal Council member from 1919 to 1941 and in the People's Council from 1927 to 1941. Other examples were W.M.G. Schumann, Khouw Kim An, F.H. de Hoog and Landj. gelar St. Tumenggung.

64. *Gemeenteblad 1924*, No. 442, pp. 611–12.

65. Studies on European tax-paying from Ibid., *1937*, No. 412 and *1924*, No. 442.

66. Moh. Sjah Sapi-ie was a member of Kaum Betawi and a well-to-do businessman with a big shoe store in Pasar Baru.

67. Information on the Council's estates from *Gemeenteblad 1927*, pp. 243, 290. A problem associated with buying up of private estates was the apparent desire of some landlords to drive tenants off the estates before making a deal with the municipality. Cases were reported where landlords threatened tenants of Kampung Kebon Klapa and Sawa Tanah Tinggi and even burnt their houses in order to force them to leave, *Neratja*, 2/7/1918 and *Sin Po*, 12/6/1929.

68. An example of an experiment with housing for the poor is the 'model *kampung*' of Taman Sarie, built on land acquired from the Chinese Council. See *Verslag van de Toestand der Gemeente Batavia over 1917*, Weltevreden, Landsdrukkerij, 1919, pp. 116–19.

69. *Notulen der Vergadering van de Gemeenteraad van Batavia*, 21 March 1932.

70. Ibid., 20 May 1935.

71. Ibid., 9 December 1936.

72. Information on health and water supplies from *Batavia als Handels-*. . . .

73. Tesch, 'The Hygiene Study Ward Centre', p. 107.

74. D. van der Zee, *Batavia. De Koningin van het Oost/The Queen of the East*, Rotterdam, Dr. Gustav Schueler, 1926, p. 47.

75. *Neratja*, 31/7/1918.

76. On its first appearance the *becak* was referred to as *roda tiga* (trishaw). See the debate on regulations for *roda tiga* in *Notulen* . . . , 11 March 1940. By the following year the vehicle was being called *becak* in the Council.

77. 'Town Development in the Indies', in *The Indonesian Town*, translation of Explanatory Memorandum on Town Planning Ordinance for Municipalities on Java, Batavia, 1938.

78. For discussion of the early war period, see Susan Abeyasekere, *One Hand Clapping: Indonesian Nationalists and the Dutch, 1939–1942*, Clayton, Monash University, 1976.

79. The last weeks before the Japanese arrival are described in Satyawati Suleiman, 'The Last Days of Batavia', *Indonesia*, No. 28, October 1979, pp. 55–64 and Hanifah, op. cit., pp. 118–19.

PART II
Interregnum

4

Japanese Occupation and the Struggle for Independence, 1942–1949

THE history of Jakarta in the period 1942–9 is confused. The city had a number of different masters, not only in succession but at one stage as many as three concurrently. In 1942, when the Japanese occupied the archipelago and divided it into regions, Jakarta (the new name for Batavia) was treated as the capital of one such region, Java. While the outcome of the Pacific War was in doubt, so was the country's and thus the city's future. As the tide of war turned, Japan promised independence to Indonesia but did not actually have time to grant it. Immediately after Japan surrendered, Indonesian nationalists in Jakarta seized the opportunity to declare that Indonesia was an independent Re- public and Jakarta its capital. Before the Republic could con- solidate its position, however, British forces arrived in Jakarta to supervise the surrender and disarming of the Japanese. Returning to Indonesia on the heels of the British, the Dutch attempted to reclaim their colony and for more than a year the British acted as referee between the Republic and the Dutch: in Jakarta this involved a tripartite form of urban government. After helping to engineer a shaky agreement between the two sides in November 1946, the British were only too happy to withdraw. Not long afterwards, the Dutch used their superior military strength to crush the Republican presence in Jakarta. For the Republic the centre of the struggle for independence was Yogyakarta in Central Java, and for the Dutch Jakarta was again Batavia, the capital of their East Indies. It took a further two years of guerrilla resistance, international intervention and another sweeping military advance by the Dutch before the conflict was finally resolved in favour of the Republic. At the transfer of sovereignty in December 1949, Jakarta assumed its role as the capital of an independent Indonesian nation-state.

Through all these vicissitudes, it is not surprising that little attention or resources could be devoted to improving the lives of Jakarta's inhabitants. Japan was primarily intent on winning the Pacific War, while the Netherlands and the Republic were locked in competition for control of the country as a whole. For most of this period, Jakartans found themselves powerless to exert their influence against the vastly superior military might of occupying foreign forces. Some individuals gloried in the turbulence of the times: it proved a fruitful period for the young and military-minded and even for artists. In an atmosphere of often agonizing uncertainty, however, most people were absorbed in the struggle for sheer survival.

Japanese Reorganization of Batavia

At 3 a.m. on 7 March 1942, the Dutch mayor of Batavia was summoned from bed by Japanese soldiers and taken in his night-clothes with the Resident of Batavia to the police headquarters for questioning. When they refused to sign a statement pledging loyalty and obedience to the Japanese army they were marched through the streets of the city to the main jail at Glodok. This deposition and humiliation of former colonial rulers was typical of the Japanese regime in the city.[1]

The Japanese set out to obliterate as far as possible all signs of Dutch influence. Almost immediately, the statue of Batavia's founder, Jan Pieterszoon Coen, was removed from its place of honour on Waterlooplein. This move foreshadowed a decree later in 1942 changing the capital's name to Jakarta, a version of the pre-colonial Jayakarta. European street names were replaced by Indonesian or Japanese ones; so, for instance, Van Heutsz Boulevard appropriately became Jalan Imamura—one conquering general's name succeeding another—and Oude Tamarindelaan became Jalan Nusantara. By October 1942 all signs and advertising in Dutch had to be replaced by Japanese and Indonesian. Speaking or writing in Dutch was forbidden: in Jakarta, Indonesian or Japanese alone were acceptable. As soon as was practicable, full-blood Europeans in the city were interned.

Most of this was to be expected. What was not clear was who or what was to replace Dutch rule. Initial signs encouraged Indonesians to hope that they would be granted independence. When the Japanese entered Batavia, they flew the Indonesian red and white flag on their trucks together with the Rising Sun. Delighted crowds applauded their arrival and proffered gifts of food and drink to Japanese soldiers.[2] A few days later, however, the Japanese forbade the flying of the Indonesian flag or the singing of 'Indonesia Raya'. It now appeared that the new rulers, exalted by their early triumphs, were interested only in their own ultimate victory and the incorporation of Indonesia into a Greater East Asia Co-Prosperity Sphere led by Japan. One early sign of this intention was the way in which the archipelago was split into three different regions under different military commands, completely disregarding Indonesian concerns for national unity. For the duration of the war, Jakarta was cut off from the rest of the islands beyond Java and Madura.

The Japanese wanted to put their own stamp on Jakarta in much the same way as the Dutch had tried to make it a European city. Re-training courses were organized for Indonesian administrators and teachers to introduce them to Japanese culture and customs. Pressure was placed on government servants to learn Japanese. In schools, Dutch and English language teaching were replaced by Japanese, and at the start of every school day children had to sing the Japanese national anthem and stand to attention while the Japanese flag was raised. It took some time to reform higher education: when the Medical College finally re-opened as the Ika Daigaku in March 1943, it taught along Japanese lines, much to the dislike of many students. The front page of every issue of the only daily newspaper permitted in Jakarta, *Asia Raya*, was covered in news and photographs of Japanese military victories. Calendars and even clocks were most inconveniently altered to give Japanese time. Instead of Queen Wilhelmina's birthday and St Nicolaas, Jakarta now had to celebrate the Emperor's birthday and the eighth of every month, but more particularly 8 December, commemorating the start of the Pacific War. Official occasions had to begin with a deep bow towards the Emperor in Tokyo (determining the direction could cause problems) and meditation in honour of Japanese war dead. In their initial enthusiasm, the Japanese launched the Three A's movement, which took its name from the slogan that Japan was the leader of Asia, the protector of Asia and the light of Asia. In Jakarta, the headquarters of this campaign as of all political organizations in Java in these years, frequent mass meetings on this theme were organized by its leader, Samsuddin.

The Japanese effort to transform the city was restricted by the very fact which made it so urgent: the war. Because priority always had to be given to winning battles far outside Java, Japan simply could not devote many resources to Jakarta. There were few Japanese in the town, and even fewer who understood the local situation, which meant that the new rulers had, reluctantly, to rely heavily on Indonesian personnel. In urban government, for instance, although a handful of Japanese held the top positions, it was Indonesians who took most of the responsibility. After some months during which an Indonesian, H. Baginda Dahlan Abdullah, was head of the municipal administration, a Japanese filled the position of mayor, a position entailing much greater powers than during the Dutch era. At the broader level of the Jakarta *syu* (pre-war Batavia Residency), however, the leading position was taken by Sutarjo Kartohadikusumo, the nationalist civil servant who had initiated the Sutarjo Petition in the People's Council in 1936.

Indonesian feelings about working with the Japanese varied. Most regarded it in the same light as their previous employment under the Dutch: in their eyes they had no choice about it and there was no reason why they should feel any personal antagonism to the Japanese merely because they had gone to war against the previous colonial master. Some Indonesians in Jakarta at this time have recorded their esteem for the Japanese with whom they worked; others were repelled by them.[3] Partly because of the war situation, Japanese rule was more brutal than that of the Dutch. Abu Hanifah, a doctor in the Jakarta General Hospital at the time, had to treat *romusha*, Indonesians who had been recruited to labour on Japanese public works projects: most of those he saw were dying of starvation.[4] And everyone was afraid of the military police, the Kempeitai, who set up their headquarters in the former Law College next to the Central Museum; the screams of agony issuing from the building bore witness to the torture of suspected dissidents.

Working for the Japanese often produced a transformation of attitudes in ways which the Japanese had certainly not intended. Although the Japanese hoped to impress Indonesians with their ineffable superiority—a strong part of their war ethic—the opposite generally happened, and the result was doubly liberating for the Indonesians' perceptions of themselves. Although they expected that the new masters would naturally be more capable than the ones they had defeated, most Indonesians found this was not true. Few Japanese understood the task as well as the local workers, and Japanese behaviour often seemed unnecessarily crude and cruel; their readiness to hit people over the head, for instance, deeply offended Indonesian custom. Many thinking Indonesians went on to reassess their subordination to the Dutch: why had it been necessary to wait to be freed by this Japanese *deus ex machina* whose feet were so obviously of clay? This reflection on the frailties of both their conquerors, plus the experience they were now gaining in positions of greater responsibility, increased the confidence of Indonesians that they could rule themselves.[5]

Realizing that it would take a long time to instil Japanese values, the new masters appealed to two local sources of ideology as a means of galvanizing the Indonesians to withstand the rigours of the war years: Islam and secular nationalism. As soon as they entered Jakarta, the Japanese attempted to woo the city's Muslim leaders to speak in their favour.[6] Japanese Muslims participated in mosque ceremonies. Unprecedented publicity was given to Islamic celebrations: political leaders attended mosques, and sermons were reported and broadcast at length. And Javanese Islam was centralized and supervised as never before: the main Islamic organizations were forced to amalgamate, with their new headquarters in the capital under the stern eye of the Japanese authorities. From all over Java, local Islamic leaders were brought to Jakarta to attend conferences and training sessions which were treated as great occasions by the new rulers.

But Islamic leaders did not serve Japanese purposes very satisfactorily. They resisted including political matters in their sermons and some refused to bow towards Tokyo as directed by the Japanese. Moreover, they did not reach that large section of the Javanese population which was not piously Muslim. As the war situation worsened, the Japanese turned increasingly to the Indonesian nationalist movement to help mobilize the population. In order to do so, they were obliged to tone down the emphasis on Japanese domination in favour of an Indonesia-oriented message. Thus after about a year the Three A's movement, with its Japanese and pan-Asian theme, was abandoned. Instead, well established nationalist leaders were brought to the fore: Sukarno and Hatta were harnessed to the propaganda effort in the organization known as PUTERA, founded in March 1943.

In his usual flamboyant style, Sukarno preached a message which combined support for Indonesia's 'liberator', Japan; hatred for the Western colonialists who were also Japan's war enemies; and above all, a fiery Indonesian nationalism. For Jakartans it was difficult to escape the barrage of propaganda. Apart from frequent mass meetings, Sukarno's voice rang out through the so-called 'singing towers', public address systems mounted on poles throughout the city. It was during this period that Sukarno came to be known by the affectionate title of Bung Karno, *bung* coming from the Jakartan Malay for brother, a form of address which he later popularized as being most appropriate to the egalitarian, fraternal spirit of the Revolution.

As the tide of war turned against the Japanese, they grew more willing to make real political concessions to the Indonesian nationalists in return for an assurance that Indonesians would co-operate in opposing an allied invasion. In October 1943, the Japanese took the very significant step of forming an Indonesian volunteer army with the stirring name of Pembela Tanah Air (Protectors of the Homeland), generally known as Peta. This was to become an important element in the army of independent Indonesia. Less than a year later, in September 1944, the Japanese Prime Minister promised independence at an unspecified date and permitted the flying of the Indonesian flag.

Life under the Japanese

Obviously the Japanese Occupation brought important political changes. But how did Japanese rule affect people's lives in other ways? Was the city a different place now that Dutch domination had ended and Indonesia had entered the Japanese Co-Prosperity Sphere?

The groups who felt the change most acutely were the Europeans and Chinese. The former were treated by the Japanese as war losers and the latter as untrustworthy; as wealthy communities, both were fair game for economic exploitation.

As soon as their services could be replaced by either Japanese or Indonesians, full-blood European men were put into prison camps, mostly outside Jakarta, although one prison existed in the old army barracks next to Waterlooplein. There was considerable movement between camps as men were transported to work on various Japanese war projects, the most notorious being the

Burma–Siam railway. The treatment of European prisoners by the Japanese in South-East Asia has been well documented; those in Jakarta experienced their share of harsh treatment, lack of medical care, and poor food.[7] Full-blood European women and children were interned in three main camps in Jakarta: in Petojo (the Cideng camp), in Salemba and at Manggarai (the Adek camp). Although at first conditions were not too bad (women were free to move around the city, and they retained servants and most of their possessions), as the war progressed more people were brought in from other areas, the size of the camps was reduced, freedom of movement ended, and the food situation grew very difficult.

Most European internees did not realize that austere conditions were shared by other inhabitants of the city. Imports of most consumer goods to Java ceased, and everything was thrown into supporting the war effort, to the detriment of the population behind the lines. Food, medicine and clothing were extremely hard to come by and very expensive. Some Europeans did recognize that they were being brought to the same level as the population at large. In the Adek camp (ironically a former transition camp for Javanese coolies being transported to Sumatra), Mevrouw van Mook, wife of the post-war Lieutenant Governor-General of the Indies, is reported to have remarked in 1944: 'We are now just like the Natives who are permanently underfed, and half of whom always have malaria or hookworm which makes them weak and inclined to hang around doing nothing or lie down rather than work hard.'[8] For most Europeans, however, the conditions they suffered did not bring them closer in sympathy to Indonesians but merely embittered them against the Japanese and all who collaborated with them.

Japanese treatment of the Chinese in Jakarta was similar to their handling of Europeans. The support of the Chinese in Indonesia for the anti-Japanese struggle in their homeland was well-known; so too was the close economic co-operation that had existed between many Chinese and the Dutch. On both counts the Chinese were suspect in Japanese eyes. Many Chinese political leaders in Jakarta were interned during the war, and others left the city to go into hiding. Chinese and Eurasians outside the camps were treated in much the same way. Political organizations were manufactured to control them and ensure their contribution to the war effort: P. F. Dahler and Oei Tiang Tjoe respectively led Eurasian and Chinese movements which claimed that their followers were loyal Indonesians with no links to other homelands. Both groups were also subject to special levies on behalf of the war: they were required to register themselves, which meant paying a head-tax, and were called upon to make 'donations' to Japanese coffers.[9]

Such financial pressure fell hard upon them at a time when whatever wealth most Chinese and Europeans had was undermined by the Japanese Occupation. Private estates were taken over by the occupying forces in 1942. Trade slumped, and most of what remained was also expropriated. Many firms never reopened their doors during the war. An observer in the lower town in December 1942 remarked that commerce was dead: many *toko* (Chinese shops) were closed or operating on little stock: others had to put up iron railings to protect their shops against looters.[10] (Some plundering of Chinese wares had occurred in the first days of the Occupation but had been brought to an abrupt halt by savage punishment.) Nevertheless, Chinese and Arab shopkeepers were continually suspected by the Japanese of hoarding goods and demanding excessive prices for them. In August 1942, fifty such traders were arrested in Jakarta for charging above the set prices for necessities.[11] The Japanese apparently intended to shift trade away from the untrustworthy Chinese into the hands of Indonesians. Basic goods, like rice, were controlled by the government and distributed through Indonesian *warung*.

It would be wrong to give the impression that Jakartans suffered intense hardship throughout the Occupation. During the first months of Japanese rule, life probably did not change very much for most Indonesians in the city. Prices did not rise greatly, basic necessities were still available, and the day-to-day services of the town went on much as usual.[12] The fact that, initially, many people fled into the countryside probably made things easier for those who stayed behind, people like the Orang Betawi who had no village to return to. But the drift back to town began when the situation settled down and it became clear that, far from being safer in the countryside, it was better to remain in town. It was country folk who were forced by the Japanese to produce more and to provide 'voluntary' labour as *romusha*. The greater security of the town seems to be indicated by high population figures at the end of the war: Van der Plas, the first

Dutch official to return to Jakarta in September 1945, reported that the official figure (really an estimate) for the city's population was 844,000, or a quarter of a million more than before the war.[13]

Such growth in numbers overstretched the declining resources available in Jakarta during the war. More and more people had to make their living on the street as the formal sector of the economy stagnated. *Becak*-driving, begun before the war, became increasingly common: according to one source, 3,900 of the vehicles were registered in Jakarta municipality in July 1943.[14] Given the decline in motorized traffic following petrol shortages and commandeering of cars and trucks by the Japanese, this was a logical development. The horses in the city were slaughtered for food. By December 1942 also, an observer commented on the growth in petty services offered on the pavement: bicycle repairers, people selling empty bottles and old clothes.[15] As time went on, inflation rose steeply, forcing more and more people on fixed incomes to try to earn a little extra. First of all, household and personal goods were sold, then people developed new skills to make ends meet, such as making and selling their own soap, candles and cigarettes. Many people earned a little by travelling out to the rice-surplus areas of Krawang and Bekasi just east of Jakarta by bicycle or on the appallingly overcrowded train, to bring back some rice to sell at a small profit.[16]

By the end of 1943, rice and every kind of food was hard to find. There were long queues at the *warung* and sometimes fighting occurred over what was available.[17] The Japanese encouraged people to grow their own food as far as possible; city-dwellers, who had never done so before, grew vegetables during the war. At the end of 1944, a Eurasian woman noted the misery in the *kampung* and beggars in gunny sacks lying by the side of the road, swollen with hunger oedema. In the lower town she saw bodies being loaded onto rubbish trucks. Her servant reported that the *kampung* was flooded with people from the country who were so weak they could hardly walk. 'Just listen to the mosque drum,' she said. 'It sounds for mourning almost every day and the worst is that there is no white cloth to wrap the bodies in. . . .'[18] Another younger Eurasian woman wrote maliciously in her diary at the beginning of 1945: 'Our Queen of the East, our glorious Batavia, can now properly be called Jakarta. It has become an Eastern town, disorderly, filthy, dusty, full of natives and stinking beggars, emaciated with hunger, half-naked due to lack of clothes, etc. The roads are full of holes.... You find *pasar*s [markets] everywhere on the street....'[19]

Although European commentators might be suspected of bias, Indonesian reports tell much the same story about life at the end of the Occupation. Some of the short stories of Idrus, for example, give humorous and often touching insights into daily life at this time. In a story entitled 'New Java', he reported widespread complaints about the cost of food and naked, starving beggars on the main roads and in front of restaurants. Idrus commented, 'Every day journalists are sent out to observe the situation around the town, but all they write about is co-prosperity.'[20]

Jakarta and the War Effort

It was precisely during this last period of the Occupation, however, that the Japanese put most pressure on Indonesians to sacrifice for the war effort. Even the lowest levels of society were expected to co-operate. Jakarta was divided administratively into units called *tonarigumi*, comprising twenty to thirty households, who were supposed to send one representative to regular meetings which organized defence against fire and air raids and spread information from the Government. *Tonarigumi* also worked to allow closer supervision of the population. *Kampung*-dwellers had never before been so closely drawn into the network of the administration.

For the Japanese, the more desperate the war situation the more necessary was Indonesian involvement. Women were not exempt: special women's organizations were formed to carry the message into families. Indonesians must have found the Japanese position on women rather puzzling. They were informed that Japanese women were modern outside the home but traditional within it, and that this combination provided the backbone of Japanese society.[21] The few Japanese women in Jakarta itself filled stereotyped roles as prostitutes, nurses and typists. At a meeting for educated Indonesian women in Jakarta in 1944, the Japanese official present was reported to have confessed that the position of Japanese women was probably lower than that in Indonesia.[22]

Unlike in Japan, where many men were absent because of the

Inter-island boats unloading at Sunda Kelapa, the oldest port area of Jakarta: A timeless scene.
Jan Pieterszoon Coen (1587–1629), founder of Batavia.

3 The oldest extant Buddhist temple in Jakarta, the Wihara Dharma Bhakti, founded in the mid-seventeenth century. Preparations are being made for New Year celebrations.

4 Town Hall of Batavia, built in 1710, now the Jakarta City Museum.

5 Mesjid Angke, a mosque built by a Chinese architect for Balinese Muslims in Batavia in 1761.

6 House of the former Governor-General Reinier de Klerk, built in 1760 and now the National Archives.

7 Tiger's Canal, sketched by Johannes Rach in the 1770s. The carriage belonged to Director-General van Riemsdijk, as did the pleasure-house perched over the canal. Note the cramped European-style buildings.

8 Old houses in Glodok, the 'Chinese camp' built after the massacre of 1740. In the foreground is a *becak*.

9 Auction of slaves in Batavia, early nineteenth century.

10 Waterloo Square in Weltevreden, about 1840. While the military band played by the Waterloo memorial, Europeans circled around it. The palace begun by Governor-General Daendels in 1809, and now the Department of Finance, is seen in the background.

11 A street-stall in Batavia in the
   mid-nineteenth century.
12 Coolies waiting for work at a
   Batavia warehouse, mid-
   nineteenth century.

3 Woman making batik, mid-
nineteenth century.

4 Chinese playing cards in
Batavia, mid-nineteenth
century.

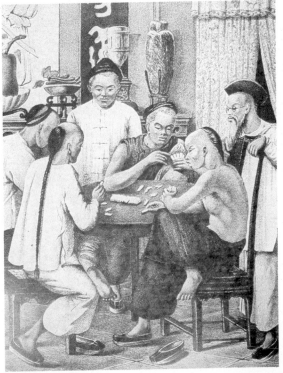

15 *Kampung* on outskirts of
Batavia in the nineteenth
century. The picture features a
mosque. Note the drum,
beaten for the call to prayer,
the bird-cage hoisted on a
pole, and women pounding
rice.

16 A *nyai*, photographed in about
the 1860s.

Toekang sepèn.
Deprès jongen.

Toekang lampo.
Lampen jongen.

Roemah blanda.
Woning van Europeanen.

Toekang mendjait.
Naaister.

Paroet kalapa.
Klappers raspen.

Boedjang stal.
Staljongen.

Toekang kebon.
Tuinjongen.

Baboe anak.
Kindermeid.

Kokki.

Ajam-ajam.
Kippen.

Dikbewerkten olèh

Anak boedjang.
Kinderen van bedienden.

Koesir.

7 The numerous Indonesian servants employed in a European house, around 1870.

8 Interior of a horse-drawn tram in late nineteenth-century Batavia, illustrating the city's ethnic diversity.

19 A *ronggeng* (Indonesian dancer) with orchestra performs at a European house in the late nineteenth century.
20 A Eurasian family in the late nineteenth century.

The Batavia 'roads', now known as Sunda Kelapa, in the late nineteenth century. Ships had to anchor in the bay, their passengers and cargo being brought in by lighter. Smaller craft could (and still do) moor in the canal.

Said Abdullah bin Aloie bin Abdullah Alatas, a successful Arab merchant, and his house in Tanah Abang (now Museum Tekstil) at the turn of this century.

23 Officers of the Chinese Council of Batavia at the beginning of the twentieth century.

24 *Ondel-ondel*, a form of street theatre associated with the Orang Betawi, in a *kampung* early this century.

Mohammad Husni Thamrin
(1894–1941), a nationalist
leader and the most famous
Orang Betawi.
Flooding in a *kampung* in
about the 1930s.

27 A street in the new European suburb of Menteng in about 1935.

28 Pasar Baru, the main shopping centre in Weltevreden for Europeans, in about 1935.

The rally of 19 August 1945 to celebrate the declaration of independence.

Independence slogans on the Dutch monument to General van Heutsz, conqueror of Aceh, greet Allied troops arriving in Jakarta at the end of 1943.

31 Jakartans enjoy a snack from a street vendor in the 1940s.

32 One of Jakarta's last trams, typically overcrowded, passes Chinese shops on Jalan Senen Raya in the 1950s.

3 President Sukarno (in dark glasses) and Mayor Sudiro (in safari suit) contemplate a pile of garbage in Jakarta in 1957.

4 President Sukarno and Governor Sumarno (both wearing black headgear) inspect a model of the cloverleaf bridge in the Blueprint Building in 1962.

35 The National Monument
   erected in the central
   Independence Square.
36 Inauguration of the Welcome
   Monument and Hotel
   Indonesia, ready for the Asian
   Games in 1962.

37 A suspected communist is
arrested in Jakarta at the end
of 1965.

38 Ali Sadikin, Governor of
Jakarta 1966–1977.

39 Market building at Glodok: New-style shopping centre of the 1970s.

40 Street vendor: Old-style shopping.

1 Squatter housing in Jakarta in the 1970s.
2 Lane in a relatively prosperous inner-city *kampung* in 1980, after the Kampung Improvement Programme had paved footpaths and drains. The sign indicates a Family Planning post.

43 A leafy street in spacious Kebayoran Baru. Note the *becak*.

44 New house in a recent wealthy residential suburb, 1980.

Scavengers recycling waste paper.

Bamboo rafts on the River Ciliwung in southern Jakarta: A timeless scene.

47 Jalan Thamrin, the main road of modern Jakarta at the end of the 1970s.

48 The inner-city *Kampung* of Kebun Kacang before demolition in 1980.

war, it was not immediately clear what women could do to assist the war effort. Yet every new propaganda body had its special women's wing. What were they doing? A report of a women's campaign in April 1943 referred to a meeting of more than two thousand 'ordinary women' at which the women's organization requested the audience to make socks for the army. The accompanying photograph shows women kneeling on the ground together knitting; as always in *Asia Raya* captions on the war effort, they are described as working 'enthusiastically' (*dengan gembira*).[23] In the previous month, meetings were organized in the *kampung* to inform mothers about their duty to contribute to the struggle.[24] One of Idrus' short stories ('Fujinkai') satirizes a women's organization meeting in a Jakarta *kampung* in 1944. After a tediously long speech praising Japan for promising independence, the chairwoman tells the assembled women that she has received directions that on 8 December they must visit sick Japanese soldiers with gifts of cakes, for which she requests a donation of one rupiah. The outraged women, some of whom have been trying to interject complaints about the food shortage, are silenced by the information that their remarks will be reported to higher authorities.

Reading between the lines, however, it seems that the women's stream within the nationalist movement was doing the same as Sukarno: using the war propaganda machine to take the nationalist message out to Jakarta's women. As often as they mentioned the war, they spoke of the need to forge a new society in Indonesia. Kartini Day, in honour of Indonesia's feminist and nationalist pioneer, was officially celebrated during the Occupation, and in the last months of the war *Asia Raya* featured prominently photographs of women doing various kinds of work. A picture of a woman dentist, for instance, was subtitled 'Indonesian women can also become dentists. It can truly be said that the advancement of our women into new fields in the movement to make a New Society will not be neglected'.[25]

Artists, too, were drawn into the war effort by the Japanese. An official Cultural Centre, with headquarters as usual in Jakarta, was created to cover all people in the cultural field. The Japanese were interested in fostering Indonesian culture at the expense of Western influence. Several large exhibitions of Indonesian painting were organized and a few journals published which judiciously combined Japanese and Indonesian contributions.[26] There were many opportunities for Indonesians to perform publicly. For instance, *pasar malam* (night fairs) were held, featuring the full gambit of Jakarta culture: *sandiwara* (plays), *gambus* and *kroncong* competitions, *topeng, ronggeng, pencak, gambang kromong* and Chinese music, in addition to art exhibitions and the usual sports contests.[27] Specially emphasized were performances which developed physical strength; the papers were full of photographs of men and women athletes.

Many Indonesians felt ambivalent about the exploitation of their culture by the Japanese. On the one hand, there is no doubt that official encouragement and the removal of the Dutch brought a great blossoming of the arts in Jakarta during the Occupation years. A number of famous artists, for instance the painters Affandi, Otto Jaya and Basuki Abdullah, spent these years in the Cultural Centre and seemed to benefit at least from the exchange of ideas that went on there. Yet many also resented Japanese censorship and direction and sought their own independent sphere. A cultural circle called Maya offered a refuge for those who chafed at official restrictions: it included the playwright (later film producer) Usmar Ismail; Abu Hanifah, a doctor turned playwright who was later to become a politician; Rosihan Anwar, the poet and journalist; the composers Cornel Simanjuntak and Ismael Marzuki; and Indonesia's greatest poet, Chairil Anwar.[28]

Chairil Anwar's name evokes the level of society perhaps most strongly influenced by the war years: the young, known in Indonesian as *pemuda*, a word with a special resonance in the early Revolution.[29] Unlike any previous leadership in Indonesia, the Japanese especially cultivated the young: it was the group which responded best to the dynamic, martial and theatrical style typical of their own *bushido* ethic. They taught the *pemuda* that in order to win, what was wanted above all was *semangat*: spirit or will power. In believing that material strength was less important than spiritual, Japanese and Javanese culture were similar; indeed, the training given by the Japanese in many ways resembled that of the *pesantren* or Muslim religious centres. In Jakarta the *pemuda* ethos also had links with the tradition of *jago*, the people's champions who relied on such arts as *pencak* and the mystical science of invulnerability in their struggle against landlords and other oppressors.

In the poetry of Chairil Anwar, who came to Jakarta from

Sumatra as a teenager in 1940, could be seen the release of energy by young people in the 1940s, an outpouring of intense emotion by individuals searching for freedom. Part of one of his poems, published in 1943 and called simply 'Me', expresses it all:

Here I am, a wild beast
Driven out of the herd
Bullets may pierce my skin
But I'll keep on,
Carrying forward my wounds and my pain
Attacking,
Attacking
Until suffering disappears
And I won't care anymore
I want to live another thousand years[30]

Valuable though such indomitable spirit might be in war, it is understandable that the Japanese had difficulty harnessing the *pemuda*. Training exclusively for the young occurred in *asrama* or hostels in Jakarta. Some of the courses were straightforward enough, featuring paramilitary drilling with bamboo spears and teaching techniques of mass mobilization. Not only boys received training: for instance the Barisan Srikandi (Srikandi Corps) consisted of girls aged from fifteen to twenty who were prepared as fighting troops and for behind-the-lines activities, being taught first aid, self-defence, use of arms and air raid defence.[31] What was extraordinary was the way some Japanese authorities tolerated anti-Japanese feeling in these *asrama*. This was most marked in the Asrama Indonesia Merdeka, established by the Japanese Admiral Maeda at Kebon Sirih 80 in October 1944. A legendary and controversial figure, Maeda was known to be particularly sympathetic to Indonesian independence. Under his protection, *pemuda* were lectured not only by prominent nationalist collaborators like Sukarno and Hatta, but also by Syahrir, who was known to have refused to co-operate with the Japanese. Courses at this hostel emphasized anti-imperialism and anti-capitalism: the anti-Japanese feeling which it engendered may have been tolerated because it was balanced by anti-Westernism.

The *pemuda* associated with the *asrama* included a variety of people, such as *kampung* children, *becak*-drivers, labourers and students, who were encouraged to carry what they learned out to the wider community. Japanese rule filled them with disgust.

They despised the older nationalist leaders who had compromised their principles by collaborating with the Japanese and disguising inhumane policies like the recruitment of *romusha*. From early signs of token resistance like the refusal of medical students to have their heads shaved in the Japanese fashion, some *pemuda* began to make trouble for the Japanese: it was *pemuda* in the volunteer army, Peta, who revolted against the Government in Blitar in East Java in February 1945.

Jakarta: Kota Proklamasi

Tension in Jakarta between the *pemuda* and the collaborating leadership flared into open conflict over the question of the declaration of independence.[32] At the beginning of August 1945, it was known unofficially that the end of the war was near. News filtering through about the bombing of Hiroshima on 6 August sent the *pemuda* in Jakarta into a frenzy of anxiety about the timing of Indonesian independence. To them it was imperative that the leadership announce independence of their own free will before the Japanese surrender; to do so under Japanese auspices would be to make independence seem to be Japan's last move to frustrate the returning colonial powers. They longed for it to be a declaration in keeping with the spirit of *merdeka*, of freedom: a defiance flung equally in the faces of the Japanese and the Allies.

Sukarno, Hatta and the older generation of nationalist leaders were more cautious. Although they, too, did not desire an independence which would be interpreted by the world, and more particularly by the Allies, as a gift of Japan to a puppet government, they saw no sense in antagonizing the Japanese, who were still the strongest military might in Java at the time, whether or not they had lost the war. Apart from a few armed units, the nationalists had no troops with which to take on the Japanese militarily.

As it happened, the *pemuda* forced a compromise. On 15 August, several members of the Menteng 31 Asrama approached Sukarno and Hatta, urging them to declare independence immediately because news of the Japanese surrender had been secretly received and was expected to be officially announced at any moment. When the leaders refused, the *pemuda* group kidnapped them that night and took them to Rengasdengklok, outside Jakarta. Among historians there is some debate about the intention behind this move; some consider there was a possibility at this point that the older leadership could have been deposed and the nationalist movement revolutionized by putting radical *pemuda* at the helm. The *pemuda*, however, seem to have felt that they were unable to take charge, that it was the older leadership which still had legitimacy in the eyes of the public, an assessment which seemed to be justified by events. That path not taken offers tantalizing glimpses of a very different subsequent history of Jakarta and Indonesia generally.

Sukarno and Hatta managed to convince the *pemuda* that it was possible to declare independence without the official approval of the Japanese but without openly defying them either. Here Admiral Maeda's help proved invaluable; he offered his house as a safe place for the working out of the final moves and guaranteed Japanese absence during the vital declaration. So, after a sleepless night at Maeda's house, the statement was read on the morning of 17 August outside Sukarno's house at Pegangsaan Timur 56. In the eyes of the *pemuda*, it was an anti-climax, for the wording of the announcement of independence was remarkably short and flat: 'We the people of Indonesia hereby declare the independence of Indonesia. Matters concerning the transfer of power and other matters will be carried out in an orderly manner and in the shortest possible time.' Unexciting though it might look on paper, this pronouncement came at a highly charged moment which gave Jakarta the honour of being Kota Proklamasi, the City of the Proclamation of Independence for the Republic of Indonesia.

The *pemuda* then moved rapidly to give substance to that title. While the older leaders hesitated, waiting to judge the mood of the Japanese, the Menteng 31 Asrama group set up an organization called Angkatan Pemuda Indonesia, with the evocative acronym of API (Fire), to co-ordinate *pemuda* groups in the city. At the instigation of API, workers at railway stations in Jakarta took over the railway system from the Japanese, a move quickly imitated by the tram workers and the central radio station personnel. They then planned a mammoth rally for 19 September in the central square to allow the population of Jakarta and environs to confirm the announcement of independence.

Again, they acted against the orders of both the Japanese and the nationalist leadership. General Nagano had forbidden the meeting but on the morning of 19 September an enormous crowd gathered in the square, waiting for their leaders to address them. They were surrounded by Japanese tanks and armed soldiers. The Republican Cabinet spent hours debating whether or not to address the meeting. The situation was felt to be fearfully precarious: the huge crowd, whipped up by the *pemuda* organizers, could easily provoke the Japanese into firing on them, resulting in stampede and massacre. After all, it was one thing for the Japanese leaders to pretend not to notice a declaration of independence made behind their backs and before an official statement in Jakarta about the end of the war; it was another matter for them to appear to condone an enormous public confirmation of that declaration more than a month after the surrender, according to the terms of which they had promised to retain the political status quo as of 15 August. Yet on the other hand, if Sukarno did not address the crowd they might in their impatience do something reckless and he would lose credibility as their leader.

At last, at 4 p.m. Sukarno decided to attend the rally. Although the Japanese soldiers surrounding the square at first challenged his arrival, finally they let him through to speak to the sea of 200,000 people who had come from throughout the city and beyond. His appearance was greeted by tumultuous shouts of 'Merdeka! Merdeka!' and 'Long live Bung Karno!' Red and white flags waved everywhere. Sukarno's speech was uncharacteristically short and low-key, reassuring them that Indonesia was now indeed an independent Republic, and requesting them to disband quietly and go home. Miraculously they obeyed, and the Japanese soldiers stood aside to let them pass.[33]

Indonesians everywhere thrilled to the news of independence spreading out from Jakarta to the rest of the archipelago: the capital had reasserted its authority over a nation divided by occupation. It was Jakarta which set the pace.

Jakarta in Dispute

The tide quickly turned in October 1945 when British troops landed in Jakarta, charged with receiving the surrender of the Japanese on behalf of the Allies. The British had undertaken simply to maintain law and order and supervise the evacuation of Allied prisoners of war before handing over the reins of government to the sovereign power in the archipelago, the Netherlands.

The Dutch authorities themselves were champing at the bit to return but immediately after the war they lacked the transport or manpower to do so. Neither the British nor the Dutch had heard more than a rumour of what they assumed to be a Japanese-orchestrated independence movement in Jakarta.

The responses of the Republic's leaders and the *pemuda* in Jakarta to the Allies' arrival were once again at variance.[34] *Pemuda* groups, proud of their *Merdeka*, were prepared to fight anyone to defend it. Hundreds of small, largely unco-ordinated groups of both sexes called Badan Perjuangan (Struggle Organizations) sprang up throughout the Jakarta region, clustering around accepted local leaders. The weeks before the British landing they had spent stealing Japanese arms; they would fight even with bamboo spears if necessary, protected as they felt themselves to be by their impenetrable righteousness and *semangat*. Sukarno, Hatta and the older generation, on the other hand, were anxious to impress on the British that they were an established Government, accepted by the society and able to keep peace and order in their own right. It was hoped that the Allies might then regard the Republic as a *fait accompli* and persuade the Dutch that all that could be done was to negotiate a transfer of sovereignty.

The *pemuda* might be tolerated when they daubed slogans all over Jakarta; the trams in particular were adorned in English with 'Hands off Indonesia' and 'We want freedom' to greet the British troops, the majority of whom were, ironically, British Indians. But the Republican Government was seriously embarrassed when fighting broke out between British troops and the *pemuda*, since that challenged Sukarno's promise that the Allies would be permitted to fulfil their limited tasks in peace. What enraged the *pemuda* was the way in which Dutch soldiers were creeping back into Java under the cloak of the British. On this issue full-scale fighting broke out between British troops and the *pemuda* in Surabaya in late October and early November. In Jakarta conflict never approached the level of the 'Battle of Surabaya' but there were almost continuous clashes in the last part of 1945. The fact that the Republican Government had its seat in Jakarta no doubt did much to dampen the fighting there.

The Republican Government was not strong enough to hold sway in Jakarta in the face of British and Dutch troops. It had to accept that the British neither could nor would recognize it as the rightful Government of Indonesia, no matter how much they were prepared to work with it in the short term to maintain law and order; and the Dutch would not countenance the thought of an independent Indonesia formed, as they saw it, by collaborators with the Japanese, people whom they regarded as war criminals. Moreover, on their return to Jakarta (which of course they still referred to as Batavia), the Dutch were shocked to see the state of the city. High-ranking officials like van Mook and van der Plas, who had known Batavia before the war, felt that the place was almost unrecognizable in its dirt, poverty and untidiness.[35] Along with the insecurity created by the aggressiveness of the *pemuda*, this was sufficient justification in their view for the full restoration of Dutch rule. The Indies must be returned to normality, to peace, order and prosperity before there could be any discussion of the prospect of independence. This they regarded as a matter of high duty.

At the end of September 1945, Sukarno had appointed Suwiryo as the first mayor of the Republic's capital, Jakarta. However, a month later, the British commander announced that henceforth the city was under the government of the Allied Military Forces. The Republic instructed its officials to help the Allies while standing firm on the principle of independence. It also announced that Jakarta was not to be made into a combat zone. This was directed at the *pemuda*, who by the end of the year were engaged in continuous fighting with NICA (Netherlands Indies Civil Administration) troops in and around the town. The city was unsafe for Europeans or those suspected of being loyal to the Dutch and, on the other hand, zealous supporters of the Republic ran the risk of being roughed up or worse by NICA soldiers who included Ambonese and Dutchmen embittered by their experience in internment.

Outside the town, long-standing social tensions in Tangerang came to a head. A populist group led by Haji Akhmad Khaerun, a veteran of the 1926 communist uprising in Banten, set up a separate Government in the area and forced local officials to resign. A reign of terror was conducted against Chinese, Japanese and Europeans in the area; in the following year thousands of Chinese were forced by a local massacre to flee into Jakarta. Haji Khaerun's domain was not destroyed until March 1946. In the Krawang area to the east of the city there was another popular uprising in retaliation against the Japanese and local officials who had implemented the harsh policies of the Occupation years. Many people were killed.[36]

Elsewhere in Indonesia, too, old ruling groups were being overthrown in local revolutions. Jakarta city knew nothing of this. True, it did not have indigenous élites who opposed the Republic. The ruling power in Jakarta had been the Dutch and the next strongest economic power the Chinese: they were the groups most directly under attack. On the old private estates around Jakarta, landlords and their henchmen were being ousted, but within the town the aim of Republican leaders appeared to be a smooth transition of power, with the new élite stepping quietly into the shoes of the old, and no fundamental questions raised about the nature of the new social order.

In retaliation against rising violence in the city, the British introduced strong measures. Frequent searches of *kampung* were conducted to unearth arms, to capture suspects and generally to try to prevent these areas being used as refuges for urban guerrillas. The last two months of 1945 were known as the *bersiap* period from the cry 'Bersiap!' (Watch out!) which went up whenever an Allied patrol or Dutch troops entered a street or *kampung*. By the end of 1945, and with 743 people in detention, the city was under British control, although they permitted certain tasks of urban government to be carried out by the Republican administration. Most Badan Perjuangan were forced to retreat outside the city, where they blockaded food supplies into Jakarta and formed alliances with local leaders, often to the annoyance of the newly created Indonesian regular army.

Kidnappings, murders and robbery made the city unsafe for the Republican Government also. In early 1946 it decided to withdraw to the relative security of inland Yogyakarta where there was no Dutch presence, since the Republic controlled most of Java. Although the Town Hall was left under Suwiryo's care and a few ministers remained in Jakarta, from mid-1947 (following the first 'police action' mentioned below) until 1949 the Republican capital was Yogyakarta.

Jakarta: Kota Diplomasi

Throughout the period known as the Indonesian Revolution or the Struggle for Independence, from August 1945 to the transfer of sovereignty in December 1949, there was conflict in the

Republican camp between the proponents of *diplomasi* or diplomatic negotiations as the best way to secure independence and those who favoured *perjuangan* or armed struggle. In this division Jakarta represented *diplomasi*. This was not a matter of choice, since the city was occupied first by the British, then by the Dutch and British together during 1946 and finally by the Dutch alone until the end of 1949. It was all very well for critics in the Republican strongholds to advocate *perjuangan* but that was possible in Jakarta only to a very limited extent.[37]

In 1946, Jakarta formed a disputed enclave in a sea of Republican territory. The surrounding rice-lands were held by the nationalists, and the city itself was divided between British, Dutch and Republican control, with the balance shifting in favour of the former two. (Map 4.1 illustrates the centres of divided authority in the city.) The Republican Government's main interest in Jakarta was in keeping it open as a forum for negotiations with the outside world, as a *Kota Diplomasi*, or City of Diplomacy.

The Republican leaders were constrained by the usual preoccupation of rulers of Jakarta that the city's appearance should convince foreigners that Indonesia was a well-run state. In the eyes of the *pemuda*, their leaders had been trapped by Dutch logic into believing that the main attributes of good government were order and regularity. In fact, this was a result not just of Dutch influence but of the Republican leaders' reasoning about the means of attaining independence: they were relying on international recognition of the view that the Dutch had no right or need to return because the country already had a viable, responsible national Government. Most important was the need to convince Britain and the United States of this viewpoint, since the former briefly held the upper hand in Indonesia, both were powerful members of the new United Nations, and the USA had an economic stranglehold over the Netherlands through its postwar aid programme. Neither was likely to be favourably impressed by trigger-happy *pemuda*.

In some respects Jakarta in 1946 succeeded in conveying an appearance suited to a *Kota Diplomasi*. A British aide, comparing Yogyakarta and Jakarta at the time, wrote:

At Batavia the atmosphere was cooler, calmer, more matter of fact, there were no cheering crowds, the waving banners decreased in num-

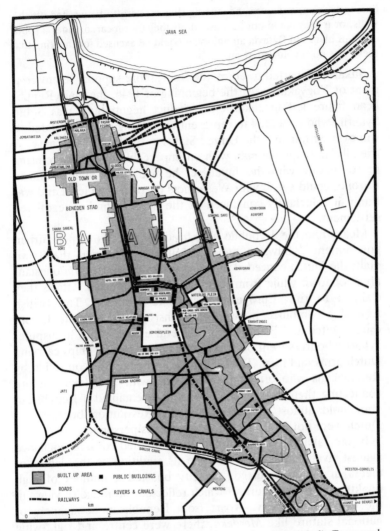

4.1 Batavia in 1946 (Based on a map from J. Fabricius, *Hoe ik Indie Terugvond*, Den Haag, Leopoldus, 1947)

bers every day, and even the stirring slogans were to be washed off the
walls, or if they could not be washed off they disappeared under a sober
cloak of black. In Batavia an onlooker could be excused for thinking that
there was no revolution at all....[38]

Sukarno departed to enjoy the freer, more supportive environment of Yogyakarta. At the beginning of 1946, the main Republican figure left in Jakarta to conduct negotiations was Sutan
Syahrir, who appeared to represent everything most calculated to
win over Britain and the United States to the Republic's cause. A
friendly and equable man with an impeccable history of refusing
to co-operate with the Japanese, he had spent many years in
Europe, could speak with Westerners on their own level and was
firmly if reluctantly convinced of the need to find a negotiated
settlement.

Meanwhile the Republic also tried to hold its own in urban
government.[39] Suwiryo and his followers occupied the Town
Hall; the Dutch conceded Suwiryo's right to control 'Indonesian'
areas of town while from their Office of Municipal Affairs they
claimed to run 'European' areas like Menteng. The British
formed a combined police force consisting of separate Indonesian, Dutch and British corps. Several utilities were in dispute.
Wharf labourers went on strike, refusing to unload ships carrying
Dutch arms and men. The telephone exchange was controlled by
Republicans who often greeted callers with 'Merdeka!' before
connecting them. The General Hospital remained a Republican
stronghold almost to the end of the Revolution because the
Dutch were not in a position to replace its personnel.

In the Jakarta press nationalists maintained constant vigilance
against rival newspapers. True to its tradition as the centre of
media in the archipelago, the city boasted a number of high
quality papers and journals which reflected the range of views in
the disputed territory. Apart from Republican newspapers of
national stature like *Merdeka*, there were centre and right-wing
Dutch dailies (*Nieuwsgier* and *Het Dagblad*), Chinese papers and
the English language *Independent* which was sympathetic to the
Republic. Despite newsprint shortages, the battle for the minds
of Indonesians and of the international community raged in a
lively fashion in the pages of the Jakarta press.

The urban economy was another arena of rivalry between the
Dutch and the Republic. On the one hand, the Republic, through
its control of the rice-bowl area of Krawang to the east of the

city, was able to organize the distribution of the main staple of the population. On the other hand, the Dutch, through their sea blockade were in charge of imported consumer goods. Although at first they were able to bring in only a trickle of such goods, as time went on they commanded an increasing supply of desperately needed requirements like textiles and medicines.

Ordinary people found themselves in the front line of the economic battle in Jakarta when they had to decide which currency to use. Both the Dutch and the Republic introduced their own currencies in 1946 to replace that of the Japanese which had been in use since 1942. The Republican rice distributors were instructed to accept only Republican money, while shops selling foreign imports would take only Dutch notes. To make matters more difficult, armed *pemuda* who still operated clandestinely from the *kampung* were likely to search passers-by and make examples of people found to be carrying Dutch money, which branded them as disloyal to the Republic. The fortunes of the Republic in Jakarta were mirrored in the fate of its currency: as the Dutch introduced a ready supply of consumer items and food, and when a blockade by the *pemuda* prevented the Republic bringing in rice, the exchange rate of Republican money fell dramatically. By the end of 1946, it was clear that the Republic had lost the currency battle in the city.[40]

Conditions in Jakarta continued to be tough for most people. Not enough rice came in to feed the population adequately. The Republican administration estimated that about forty destitute Indonesians died of starvation or disease every day in Jakarta. In April 1946, according to the Dutch, there were 20,000 beggars on the city streets. Republican officials found it impossible to live on their salaries (paid in Republican money): the cost of rice alone for a family exceeded any official's income, and Yogyakarta could not afford to make higher allowances for the extra expenses of Jakarta. Sometimes Republican employees received no pay at all. Not surprisingly, more and more of them reluctantly changed camps.

Despite the declining influence of the Republic in the city and the Republican Government's attempts to transform it into *Kota Diplomasi*, the *pemuda* did not give up their efforts to keep *perjuangan* alive there. True, most of them had retreated to the outskirts, taking up positions beyond the demarcation line which the British drew around the city. Some had even left the region completely to carry the message of independence to other parts of the archipelago. But there were still occasional attacks within the city and harrassment of those regarded as enemies of the Republic; the Chinese in particular suffered from extortion and intimidation. The *pemuda* were not, after all, a collection of entirely high-minded people: their ranks contained opportunists and even criminals who abused the nationalist cause to loot and to victimize others. It was a constant struggle for *pemuda* leaders to discipline their followers: admittedly some leaders were pure bandits anyway.

Be that as it may, the *pemuda* could point with pride to signs that they kept *Merdeka* in the minds of the people of Jakarta. A highlight of 1946 was the struggle of young Republican women to celebrate the anniversary of the Proclamation of Independence at Pegangsaan Timur 56. The British authorities forbade the ceremony and posted armed soldiers around the building, but the women broke through to hold their peaceful observance.

Yet the Dutch strengthened their hold on the city, returning to all their old haunts. Veenstra, a Dutchman sympathetic to the nationalist cause, described taking a pro-Republican Chinese Indonesian friend to a Jakarta restaurant in 1946. The friend pointed out that when the Dutch were in the camps, Indonesians regularly patronized all the big cafes and the Japanese organized weekly meetings with them in the luxurious Hotel des Indes. Now that the Dutch had returned, he said, they had again appropriated the big restaurants and hotels: for the Indonesians little *warung* were good enough. 'And no one even thinks that we have the feeling that the city has been taken from us again. We have to shoot to make you notice that we still exist.'[41]

With British permission the Dutch reoccupied many buildings which had been taken over by the Republic for official purposes. Their stronger economic position allowed the Dutch to stock their old shops with imported goods, to provide a network of buses as an alternative to the Republican-run trams and trains, to reopen schools and even to set up an emergency medical college as early as January 1946. Although Suwiryo's administration responded with their own schools and an emergency faculty of law and letters, they had insufficient funds to run most services efficiently. Local rates could not be collected properly and staff could not be paid adequately.

A turning-point was reached when the British army withdrew from Java at the end of November 1946, following the signing of the Linggajati agreement between the Dutch and the Republic. Each side acknowledged the territory held by the other and undertook to work towards a federal United States of Indonesia, but there was little good faith on either side. The Dutch found the situation intolerable; in Jakarta itself they felt it was impossible to continue in a city cut off from its hinterland. So on 20 July 1947 as Dutch forces in Java, Madura and Sumatra pushed out into Republican-held territory, in Jakarta they occupied the Town Hall and most other Republican buildings. The first 'police action' had begun.

Batavia Again

Suwiryo, Mayor of Republican Jakarta, was arrested at the time of the first 'police action' and packed off to Yogyakarta. The only Republican presence permitted in the city was a delegation which kept up contact between the Dutch and the remaining Republican territory in Central and East Java and parts of Sumatra. In Batavia, Republican schools were closed down and political censorship of Republican meetings and newspapers introduced. The Dutch Office of Municipal Affairs moved into the Town Hall. Batavia was now theirs and the Dutch did their best to restore it to its former role as the capital of their Indies possessions.

As a result of their advance, the Dutch were masters of most of West Java, although guerrilla resistance continued there. In the areas under their control the Dutch set about fostering regional movements and creating federal states despite the Republic's expressed desire for a strong unitary system.

Within the city the Dutch were so confident that they began planning for the future growth of Batavia. Fighting in the region had forced many people, especially Chinese, to seek safety in Batavia. The Dutch estimated that there were 1,050,000 people in the city in 1948, almost double the figure for 1930. This had put further strain on the city's housing capacity, particularly since housing stock had deteriorated badly during the Japanese Occupation. In 1948, there was an estimated shortfall of 80,000 houses. Within the municipal limits of the time there was insufficient suitable land to accommodate that kind of growth. A desperate scarcity of building materials in the post-war years added to the problem.[42]

In August 1948, the Indies Government took the historic step of approving plans for a satellite city just south-west of Batavia's boundary in the district known as Kebayoran. This was an area sparsely populated by poor Orang Betawi, some 10,000 in all, who made a living as fruit-growers, handicraft workers and coolies. At first, the Dutch persisted in maintaining that, despite an atmosphere of guerrilla warfare, they could conduct fair compensation negotiations with the inhabitants of Kebayoran. The local people demanded what the authorities considered exorbitantly high prices, which 'obstinacy' was attributed to the machinations of Republicans. At the end of 1948, the Government therefore abandoned negotiations and set its own levels of compensation. The displacement of Orang Betawi, begun in the early twentieth century, continued apace.

In the event, Kebayoran Baru (New Kebayoran), the so-called 'satellite town', proved to be another Menteng. This was hardly surprising. The Dutch stated that it was planned as a residential complex of 100,000 for lower income groups, but as a purely residential area only 4.5 kilometres from the city, it was unable to generate much work locally and therefore appealed only to those who could afford to travel to town. Moreover, in a time of acute housing scarcity, it was those with more money who monopolized new homes, especially the moderately expensive kind built in Kebayoran Baru. But these were still early days in the suburb's history, for by the end of 1949 only a few dozen houses were ready for occupancy.

Some official policies tried to restore the pre-war situation. The Government extended trading privileges to Dutch commercial houses and European banks re-established themselves. Chinese businesses were assisted; for instance, Batavia's Chinese batik producers were given ready access to scarce imported cloth.[43] The Municipal Council was resuscitated, although the population was still not trusted to participate in elections.

The city's population did not believe that the clock could be turned back, however much some of them might long for it. Even among the Europeans, opinions were divided: a small so-called Progressive Group led by Mr B. van Tijn supported Indonesia's right to self-determination. The Chinese community was in ferment.[44] Some *Peranakan* Chinese tried to reassure their compatriots that they would be welcomed by the new Republic and they could point to the Republic's generous citizenship law of 1946 which gave citizenship to all Chinese born in Indonesia unless they repudiated it within a given period. Such pro-Republican Chinese formed a group called Sin Ming Hui (New Light Association) in Jakarta in 1946, which gave birth in 1948 to an integrationist party called Persatuan Tionghoa (Chinese Union). Attacks on Chinese in Republican territory in 1945–6, however, inclined many to prefer the protection of Dutch rule. The attention of many Chinese at this time was diverted by events in their homeland so that the Indonesian conflict was for them secondary to the battle between the Communists and Kuomintang in China. Finally, there were the Chinese (perhaps the majority) whose response to living in a foreign country was attempted neutrality: they pleaded to be allowed to avoid choosing sides in favour of just conducting business as usual.

For many Indonesians it was impossible to behave as though the dramatic events of 1945–6 had not changed Jakarta for good. Women's organizations struggled to support the remnants of Republican institutions.[45] For instance, Wanita Negara Indonesia (Women of the Indonesian State), formed by Suwarni Pringgo-digdo in Jakarta in 1945, ran public kitchens and provided foodstuffs for families of fighters and needy citizens. To assist the families of officials who refused to work for the Dutch they organized food and credit co-operatives. They also ran clandestine Republican schools. Another change which left its mark on society as a result of the Revolution was the disruption of family life. Teenagers who had lived dangerously and supported their kindred by black marketeering found it difficult to accept again the role of a subordinate in a routine of school and regular jobs.[46]

After the first 'police action' a few armed groups still operated within the city, occasionally throwing grenades at Dutch soldiers. Outside the city irregular units continued to fight, although the Indonesian army increasingly co-opted and suppressed their independent activities. Fighting had died down considerably. Chairil Anwar, one of the *pemuda* who fought at Krawang, urged Indonesians to remain faithful to their spirit:

We who are lying, now, near Krawang–Bekasi,
We can no longer cry out 'Freedom', no longer lift our rifles

But who cannot still hear our moans?
Still see us marching forward, unafraid?[47]

Certainly the Revolution was kept alive at the cultural level in Jakarta. Dutch occupation did not deter artists from enjoying one of the most intensely productive periods of Indonesian history. Although Yogyakarta might house the Republican Government, a truly Indonesian culture was being forged in more cosmopolitan Jakarta. The vigorous paintings of Affandi and others gave visual images to the spirit of *Merdeka*. The poetry of Chairil Anwar, the archetypal wild-eyed and loose-living *pemuda*, relived the *perjuangan* period and already reflected the disillusionment of these anti-climactic years in Jakarta. He died, burnt out, in 1949 at the age of twenty-seven. Prose writers like Pramudya Ananta Tur and Idrus developed new styles to suit the harrowing events they described and to convey the questioning of man's behaviour which they felt as a result of the inhumanity they observed. Divided loyalties, trials of conscience, heroism, and hardship were all themes of the work of the so-called Angkatan 45 or Generation of 1945. Although Jakarta had experienced revolution for only a few brief months, it provided the raw material for artists for years to come.[48]

Transfer of Sovereignty

Meanwhile, the rest of Indonesia was in turmoil. After the first military action, the United Nations intervened in the dispute between the Dutch and the Republic, insisting on negotiations which resulted in the Renville agreement of January 1948. The terms of that agreement were most unfavourable to the Republic, but, as it turned out, the critical thing was that it had been made under UN auspices. When the Dutch later broke the terms, they called down the full wrath of the UN and more especially the USA, on their heads.

In February 1948, continuing in their efforts to create federal states in Indonesia, the Dutch formed the West Javanese state of Pasundan. However, although the Republican forces had been pushed back easily, the Dutch were disconcerted at the strength of the resistance against them within 'conquered' territory. In West Java, devout Muslim fighters rallied around a charismatic leader to fight against the Dutch on behalf of Darul Islam, an

Islamic State. Amongst the leaders of the states they had created, the Dutch found strong sympathy for the Republic. Tempted by their own military might and the weakness of the Republic following the abortive Communist coup at Madiun in September 1948, in December that year the Dutch launched their second 'police action', which swept over almost the whole of Java and Sumatra, swallowing up Republican towns including Yogyakarta, where the Republican Cabinet was captured.

Immediately, the United States suspended some of its aid funds to the Netherlands while guerrilla resistance was maintained in the wake of the Dutch advance. The opposition was too great for the Dutch. They accepted a United Nations call for a ceasefire at the end of 1948 and began negotiations with the Republican Government in the following year, with the result that in December 1949 the Netherlands transferred sovereignty over Indonesia (minus West New Guinea, which they retained) to a federal Indonesia, which within a year had been replaced by a unitary Republic.

Within Indonesia, the transfer of sovereignty occurred in Jakarta at the former Governor-General's palace, now Istana Merdeka (Freedom Palace) on 27 December.[49] An enormous crowd was present as the Dutch flag was lowered for the last time and the Red and White raised, to the singing of 'Indonesia Raya'. Jakarta was once more the capital of an independent nation.

Now, after years of uncertainty, Jakarta's inhabitants would see what it meant to live in a city free of colonial rule. Return to the relative tranquillity of the colonial era was out of the question. Jakarta's population had doubled in size and it was surrounded by countryside stirred into revolt by armed *pemuda* and Muslim extremists. A new order was imperative. During the preceding years, there had been no time or inclination to envisage what an independent Jakarta might be like, since all the attention of the authorities had been concentrated on winning acceptance from the outside world. Long-haired, unconventionally attired, the *pemuda* had indeed focused on something rather different: *merdeka* to them meant personal liberty—an intense, unfettered experience which challenged all constraining traditions. Their sheer anarchism gave no direction as to what a free city might be like, and by 1949 their strength had been defeated by the more conventional older leaders of both the State and the army.

1. Japanese treatment of Europeans is described in I. J. Brugmans *et al.* (editors), *Nederlandsch-Indie onder Japanse Bezetting: Gegevens en documenten over de jaren 1942–1945*, Franeker, Wever, second edition, 1960. For general coverage of the Occupation period, see Anthony Reid, 'Indonesia: from Briefcase to Samurai Sword' in Alfred W. McCoy (editor), *Southeast Asia under Japanese Occupation*, New Haven, Yale University Press, 1980.

2. The Indonesian welcome to the Japanese is described in G. Pakpahan, *1261 Hari di bawah Sinar Matahari Terbit*, Jakarta, no publisher, 1979, which is a useful memoir of Jakarta under the Japanese.

3. Examples of good relations between Indonesians and Japanese are described in the memoirs of Margono Djojohadikusumo, *Herinneringen uit 3 Tijdperken*, Jakarta, Indira, 1969 and M. Gani, *Surat Kabar Indonesia pada Tiga Zaman*, Jakarta, Departemen Penerangan, 1978.

4. Abu Hanifah described his experiences in *Tales of a Revolution*, p. 123.

5. The view about increased Indonesian confidence is strongly put by Soetan Sjahrir in *Out of Exile*, New York, Greenwood, 1949, pp. 248–9.

6. On Japanese policy towards Islam, see Harry J. Benda, *The Crescent and the Rising Sun: Indonesian Islam under the Japanese Occupation, 1942–1945*, The Hague and Bandung, Van Hoeve, 1958.

7. A Dutchman who was imprisoned in Jakarta has described his experiences: Rob Nieuwenhuys, *Een Beetje Oorlog*, Amsterdam, Querido, 1979. Descriptions of life in internment camps in Jakarta are to be found in Brugmans, op. cit. and Margaretha Ferguson, *Mammie ik ga dood. Aanteekeningen uit de Japanse tijd op Java 1942–1945*, Den Haag, Leopold, 1976.

8. Ferguson, op. cit., p. 235.

9. On Japanese policy towards Chinese and Eurasians, see Brugmans, op. cit. and Charles A. Coppel, 'Patterns of Chinese Political Activity in Indonesia', in J. A. C. Mackie (editor), *The Chinese in Indonesia*, Melbourne, Nelson, 1976.

10. Brugmans, op. cit., p. 146.

11. S. Z. Hadisutjipto, *Sekitar 200 Tahun Sejarah Jakarta*, p. 134.

12. The view of the early occupation years as relatively normal is held by Tan Malaka, who lived in Jakarta in the first year of the Occupation (*Dari Pendjara ke Pendjara*, Djogjakarta, Pustaka Purba, n.d., Vol. II, p. 138) and is confirmed by other sources.

13. S. L. van der Wal (editor), *Officiele Bescheiden betreffende de Nederlands-Indonesische Betrekkingen 1945–1950*, 's-Gravenhage, Nijhoff, 1971, Vol. I, p. 152.

14. Hadisutjipto, op. cit., p. 137.

15. Brugmans, op. cit., 286.

16. Information on how people made extra income is from Pakpahan, op. cit., pp. 40–1, and interviews with Paramita Abdurachman (13 April 1980) and Soebardi (30 August 1979).

17. Pakpahan, op. cit., p. 75 and Brugmans, op. cit., p. 489.

18. Brugmans, op. cit., p. 601.

19. Ibid., p. 602.

20. Idrus' Japanese stories are reprinted in *Dari Ave Maria ke Jalan Lain ke Roma*, Jakarta, Balai Pustaka, 1978.

21. An example of Japanese propaganda about women is in *Asia Raya*, 18/1/2603 (1943).

22. Brugmans, op. cit., pp. 564–5.

23. *Asia Raya*, 16/4/2603 (1943).

24. Ibid., 4/3/2603 (1943).

25. Ibid., 28/3/2605 (1945).

26. On Indonesian culture in Jakarta during the Occupation, see Claire Holt, *Art in Indonesia*, Ithaca, Cornell University Press, 1967 and A. Teeuw, *Modern Indonesian Literature*, The Hague, Nijhoff, 1967.

27. For a description of a *pasar malam*, see *Asia Raya*, 3/9/2602(1942).

28. On Maya, see Hanifah, op. cit., pp. 136–8.

29. On the Japanese and the *pemuda*, see Benedict R. O'G. Anderson, *Java in a Time of Revolution: Occupation and Resistance, 1944–1946*, Ithaca, Cornell University Press, 1972.

30. Translation of Chairil Anwar's poem by Burton Raffel, *The Complete Poetry and Prose of Chairil Anwar*, Albany, State University of New York Press, 1970, p. 21.

31. Brugmans, op. cit., p. 532.

32. On the declaration of independence, see Anderson, op. cit. and George McT. Kahin, *Nationalism and Revolution in Indonesia*, Ithaca, Cornell University Press, 1952, Chapter 5.

33. Descriptions of the rally are to be found in Anderson, op. cit. and H. Rosihan Anwar, *Kisah-Kisah Jakarta Setelah Proklamasi*, Jakarta, Pustaka Jaya, 1977.

34. On the actions of the Republican leadership and the *pemuda* at this time see Anwar, op. cit., Anderson, op. cit., Robert B. Cribb, 'Jakarta in the Indonesian Revolution, 1945–1949', Ph.D. dissertation, University of London, School of Oriental and African Studies, 1983, and *Republik Indonesia: Kotapradja Djakarta Raja*, Djakarta, Kementerian Penerangan, n.d. General descriptions of the Revolution years (1945–9) are found in Kahin, op. cit. and Anthony J.S. Reid, *Indonesian National Revolution 1945–1950*, Melbourne, Longmans, 1974.

35. Van der Wal, op. cit., Vol. I, pp. 121, 401.

36. On developments in the region surrounding Jakarta, see especially Cribb, 'Jakarta in the Indonesian Revolution'.

37. On the *diplomasi/perjuangan* dichotomy, see Reid, op. cit., Anderson, op. cit., and, for its applicability to Jakarta, see Robert Cribb, 'Kota Diplomasi? Jakarta in the Early Revolution', paper presented at the AAS Annual Meeting, Toronto, 14 March 1981.

38. David Wehl, *The Birth of Indonesia*, London, Allen and Unwin, 1948, p. 86.

39. On urban government, see Cribb, 'Jakarta in the Indonesian Revolution' and The Liang Gie, *Sedjarah Pemerintahan Kota Djakarta*, Djakarta, Kotapradja Djakarta Raja, 1958.

40. On the currency battle, see Robert Cribb, 'Political Dimensions of the Currency Question 1945–1947', *Indonesia*, Vol. 31, April 1981, pp. 113–36.

41. J. H. W. Teenstra, *Diogenes in de Tropen*, Amsterdam, Vrij Nederland, 1947, p. 109.

42. For population figures and information on Kebayoran Baru, see Jac. Zwier, 'De Opzet van het Bestuur van de Satellietstad Kebayoran nabij Djakarta (1948–1950)', *Indonesie*, No. 4, 1950–51, pp. 419–41.

43. Information on Dutch economic policies at this time from D. Sutter,

Indonesianisasi: Politics in a Changing Economy, 1940–1955, Ithaca, Cornell University Press, 1959, p. 438 and Chapter 16.

44. On the Chinese in this period, see Coppel, 'Patterns of Chinese Political Activity'.

45. On women's activities, see Kongres Wanita Indonesia, *Sejarah Setengah Abad Pergerakan Wanita Indonesia*, Jakarta, Balai Pustaka, 1978, pp. 70–5.

46. For a fictionalized account of the problem of children, see M. Balfas, 'A Child of the Revolution', *Indonesia*, No. 17, April 1974, pp. 43–50.

47. Raffel, op. cit., p. 127.

48. See Holt, op. cit. and Teeuw, op. cit. on art and literature in the Revolution.

49. For a description of the transfer of sovereignty, see *Republik Indonesia: Kotapradja Djakarta Raja*, pp. 49–51.

PART III
The New Masters

5

Sukarno's Jakarta: 1950–1965

Sukarno's Influence

JAKARTA is full of statues of people shouting, waving their arms and shaking their fists. It may seem surprising that a city which had played so small a part in the Revolution of 1945–9 is nonetheless studded with so many monuments to the heroism of those years. It is a further irony that this should be the work of President Sukarno, who during the Revolution had urged caution and opposed any fundamental change other than the overthrow of the Dutch. In the post-independence period Jakarta became a perfect vehicle for Sukarno, for like him it was strong on rhetoric and symbols and weak on revolutionary reality.

It is somewhat misleading to imply that Jakarta was dominated by President Sukarno during the whole period of fifteen years following independence. Only after the transition to Guided Democracy in 1957–9 did he cease to be a figure-head president and move to take control of the country in general and its capital in particular. Up until that time, there was not one leader but rather a form of constitutional democracy at both national and local levels.

But Sukarno more than anyone else shaped Jakarta during this period. He had a vision of the city which has in part been realized, if not in his time in office then afterwards, and he is responsible for most of Jakarta's familiar landmarks today. The National Monument, that soaring obelisk surmounted by a gilded flame in the centre of Jakarta; Hotel Indonesia, the country's first modern multi-storey hotel; Sarinah, its first department store; the Jakarta bypass and the Senayan clover-leaf bridge, the first modern highways in Indonesia: these and many more were his heritage. In the confusing years after independence, Sukarno appeared to be the only person giving any direction to the city's development. Like his vision for the country as a whole, it lacked any firm basis in economic reality but, in Jakarta more than in the rest of Indonesia, he was able to give his dream some concrete form.

Sukarno had graduated in 1926 as a civil engineer and practised as a private architect for a year before becoming a professional politician.[1] He was passionately devoted to the idea that architecture and town planning could serve to create the ideal society; in this he had much in common with the contemporary utopian architect Le Corbusier. He harnessed architecture to the cause of the Indonesian Revolution, which he proclaimed was the greatest in history since it would lead the world in the fight against imperialism. As time went on his rhetoric became increasingly strident, elevating Indonesia to leadership of what he called the New Emerging Forces, the progressive nations which were locked in combat with the old imperialists. His view of Jakarta as the 'lighthouse', the city which would personify the new spirit, was expressed in this speech of 1962:

Comrades from Jakarta, let us build Jakarta into the greatest city possible. Great, not just from a material point of view; great, not just because of its skyscrapers; great, not just because it has boulevards and beautiful streets; great not just because it has beautiful monuments; great in every aspect, even in the little houses of the workers of Jakarta there must be a sense of greatness....

... Give Jakarta an extraordinary place in the minds of the Indonesian people, because Jakarta belongs to the people of Jakarta. Jakarta belongs to the whole Indonesian people. More than that, Jakarta is becoming the beacon of the whole of humankind. Yes, the beacon of the New Emerging Forces.[2]

Sukarno took up residence in the old Governor-General's Palace, now renamed Istana Merdeka (Palace of Independence). He took a keen personal interest in the city, stressing the importance of art in urban life. At home in the presence of artists (the Istana became the country's main art gallery), he gathered around him a large group of architects and artists to discuss the progress of projects for buildings, statues, streets and gardens. To inspire and educate, Sukarno took architects with him on his overseas tours.[3]

An early example of the impact of Sukarno's ideas on Jakarta was the development of its central square. In 1950 the President expressed his desire that it be renamed Lapangan Merdeka (Independence Square), and that all temporary structures on it be razed to make way for the building of a tall monument 'like the Eiffel Tower in France'.[4] His wishes were fulfilled. The National Monument combines tradition and modernity in the way Sukarno liked best. Its form harks back to the *linggam-yoni* sculptures of Indonesia's Hindu days; its dimensions are based on the numerals of the date of the proclamation of independence, 17/8/45; and its base contains a museum of Indonesian history, depicting in dioramas scenes in Indonesia's long evolution towards independent nationhood. Placed in the centre of Jakarta's huge main square, it managed to dominate that expanse as no previous structure ever did, and its gilded flame, visible from afar across the city's flat, low profile, reminded Jakarta's citizens and visitors of the country's past and its aspirations for the future.

Just as the Dutch had twice created new Batavias, first at Kota and then at Gambir, so during this period Sukarno shifted the hub of the city. He was determined to give independent Jakarta a modern image which focused on the newly constructed Jalan Thamrin leading from Lapangan Merdeka south-west to Jalan Sudirman and Kebayoran Baru: an area free of colonial connotations, and one which would feature the bold work of Indonesian architects and builders.

As the seat of national government, Jakarta has always felt the central administration weigh heavily on its shoulders. One instrument of central control was the Mayor, from 1957 onwards the Governor, who as in colonial days was appointed by the central government. This official's powers were gradually increased in relation to the Municipal Council, and during Guided Democracy he was more or less the creature of the President. Clearest recognition of this fact was given by Henk Ngantung, Deputy Governor from 1960 to 1964 and Governor in 1964–5. A Christian from Menado, Ngantung was an artist with no previous experience in administration. He had advised on the decoration of cities and ceremonial places and had been appointed to parliament by Sukarno. According to Ngantung, one day in 1958 or 1959 Sukarno informed him that he intended at some time to appoint him to the Jakarta city government: 'I would like you to represent me. I want this city to become beautiful.' When he did take up office, Henk Ngantung was keenly aware that he was expected to bring an artist's contribution to the city and to perform the will of the President. He wrote later that his position as Governor was due to Sukarno and 'throughout my term of

office there was practically no development or important event
... that was not blessed or tackled directly or indirectly by Bung
Karno'.[5]

Sukarno's dreams for his city and his personal involvement in
its planning were seen in one place above all: the Gedung Pola,
or Blueprint Building. The original simple monument to the
Proclamation of Independence at Jalan Pegangsaan Timur was
pulled down as insufficiently impressive for his city. (It was
replaced as the symbol of Jakarta by the new National Monument.) On the same site he ordered built a sleek six-storey glass
building containing the blueprints of projects for Indonesia's
development. Although some of these, like the proposal for a
nuclear reactor, were flights of fancy, most of the plans for
Jakarta were brought to fruition. Here Sukarno was frequently
photographed showing guests scale models of such projects as the
Asian Games Complex at Senayan, the Planetarium at Taman
Ismail Marzuki, the National Monument, the plan for Jalan
Thamrin, the clover-leaf Overpass, the reconstructed Senen'
Market, Sarinah Department Store, the Istiqlal Mosque and the
Ancol Funfair. Each of them was the subject of consultation
betweeen the architect and Sukarno, who had often conceived
the original idea and made suggestions for alterations. Each of
them bore his signature of approval, without which no action
could be taken.

The hallmark of such plans was modernity and monumentality.
Sukarno liked grand symbols which would impress on the world
that Jakarta was the equal of any great modern city and had a
strong sense of its own worth and revolutionary tradition. He
favoured skyscrapers and bold statuary. Most of Jakarta's statues
of this period were elevated on huge pylons and gestured histri-
onically to the heavens. Examples are the Liberation of West
Irian monument in Lapangan Banteng and the so-called
Welcome Statue next to the Hotel Indonesia. Curiously, although
the work of Indonesian sculptors, neither seems at first glance to
evoke Indonesia past or present: they feature people in Western
dress. A more 'Indonesian-looking' statue of this period, portray-
ing a guerrilla fighter and a peasant woman to commemorate the
Revolution was, ironically, made by a Russian sculptor. Nonetheless, Jakarta's statues symbolized unforgettably the President's
rhetoric: as he said, he was in love with the romance of the

Revolution, whose goal in his eyes was to satisfy not only the material but also the spiritual needs of the Indonesian people.

But did Sukarno's Jakarta meet this goal for its inhabitants? Did they want his conception of modern urban life? And what, apart from the obvious construction boom which his dreams launched, was done for their material requirements?

Straining at the Seams

Sukarno's visions had little relevance to the dominant fact of Jakartan life in this period: the most rapid population expansion in the city's history. Official figures show the population doubling from 1948 (823,000) to 1952 (1,782,000), and, after a plateau in the mid-1950s, rising steeply again to 3,813,000 in 1965.[6] These figures exaggerate the early rate of growth, since the city boundaries were altered in 1950: the new Kotapraja Jakarta Raya (Municipality of Greater Jakarta) of that year was three times the area of the old municipality. (See Map 5.1.) The expansion in area was itself a response to population growth, a recognition that the urban population had spread beyond the old limits and that most of these new districts were relatively sparsely populated. The bulk of the population was still concentrated in the confines of the old municipality. All the official statistics understated the actual number of people in the city at any time, since they failed to count the large number of temporary migrants.

Apart from an altered definition of the city, population growth was due mainly to a massive influx of people. In 1953, a survey of selected districts within the inner city found that 75 per cent of people there were born outside Jakarta, and of that number, half had come to Jakarta since 1949.[7] In 1961, the first census since 1930 showed that only 51 per cent of the population of the city were actually born there; the overwhelming majority of the remainder had come from West and Central Java.

Why did they come? A great many arrived in the wake of the Republican Government's move back to Jakarta from Yogyakarta in 1949. After the transfer of sovereignty, the new Government rapidly increased the public service in line with ambitious plans to develop the country, and also as a matter of political expediency. The census of 1961 found that 16 per cent of Jakarta's work force was employed in the government service.

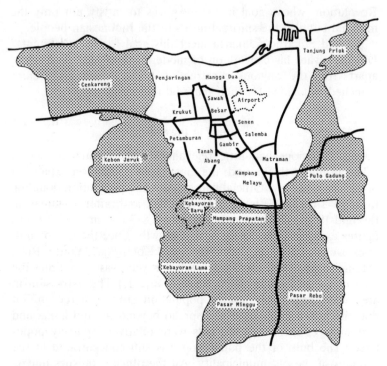

5.1 Jakarta in 1965, showing municipal boundaries and sub-districts. The shaded area was annexed to Jakarta in 1950. (Reproduced from Lance Castles, 'The Ethnic Profile of Djakarta', *Indonesia*, Vol. 3, 1967)

Some found refuge in Jakarta from the unrest that plagued the countryside even after war ended with the Netherlands. In some areas rebels resisted the authority of the Republican Government. In West Java, the biggest threat to law and order was the Darul Islam, an army of Muslim rebels fighting for an Islamic state in opposition to the secular Republic. Their revolt lasted for many years after the transfer of sovereignty. Travellers on the road from Jakarta to Bandung were frequently robbed and even killed by Darul Islam guerrillas. A smaller leftist group of rebels, called Bambu Runcing (Bamboo Spears), expressed its dissatisfaction with the terms of the transfer of sovereignty by fighting on in the outskirts of Jakarta.[8] Finally there were the remnants of the gangs which had sprung up during the Revolution as the direct descendants of the bandits who had operated in Jakarta's environs for centuries. In 1953, for instance, there was a news-paper report of the shooting by soldiers of Mat Item, the leader of a criminal gang which had raged through the district of Kali Angke on the north-west outskirts of Jakarta: his body was photographed with his weapons and *jimat* (amulets).[9] Such gangs were particularly likely to terrorize the Chinese, many of whom fled into the city.

The 1953 survey of immigrants found, however, that the vast majority came to Jakarta for economic reasons. At the end of the struggle for independence, Indonesia was at a very low economic ebb; production was down and there were few goods available. Jakarta, the home of the new nationalist Government which had promised that independence would bring prosperity, seemed to offer new hope to many country-dwellers. Many came from extremely densely populated areas of Java. Unknown thousands were seasonal migrants, spending only a few months in the city before returning to their villages for the busy times of the agricultural year and, of course, for Lebaran, the end of the Muslim fasting month. Lastly, there were commuters using rail and bus to work in Jakarta during the day: it was estimated in 1957 that 10,000 people used the train to come to Jakarta each day from Bogor.[10]

This tide of humanity put unbearable pressure on the facilities of a city which had been intended in the pre-war years for a population of less than half a million, most of whom, not being European, were not expected to enjoy those facilities anyway. Most critically felt was the housing shortage. Houses could not be built quickly enough even for those able to pay for them; for the rest, land was generally not available within their means. The results were overcrowding of existing housing stock and the explosion of illegal squatter settlements. And a sizeable minority sought shelter where they could, on the streets or under bridges.

The loudest complaints about the lack of accommodation came from civil servants. Aware of its obligations to them, the Government opened up new land and stepped up construction of Kebayoran Baru: from 1948 to 1956, 6,033 houses were completed there, largely for the bureaucracy.[11] Large apartment blocks were erected to house employees of particular ministries. Progress was unbearably slow for these middle-class people who had to spend years awaiting the allocation of a house or apartment. Many were accommodated meantime in hotels and even school buildings, exacerbating shortage of these facilities also.[12] Others crammed into already occupied houses, or if they were lucky acquired the Jakarta phenomenon which seems to date from these years: the pavilion, an outbuilding in the garden of the older and more spacious houses of former Dutch residential areas. Not surprisingly, one of the most popular Indonesian films of these years, called *Krisis* and released in 1953, took as its theme the daily social drama caused by overcrowded housing in Jakarta.

The majority of Jakarta's new immigrants shared existing housing, bought on the private market or built their own houses. Such was the competition for houses that government regulations about minimum rents or prices were bound to fail: the notorious practice of demanding 'key-money' was used to extort large sums from the unhappy victims of the shortage. The state of affairs is described by the poet Ayip Rosidi, who arrived in Jakarta as a boy in 1951. Coming from Jatiwangi in West Java, he was appalled at the place his uncle took him to live in. It was an alley in Galur sub-district, east of Senen Market. The area was only a few years old, very muddy and full of huts with grass-thatched roofs. Rosidi lived for several years in one of these huts backing onto a river lined with privies. Houses were built in an unbroken row; his row measured 33 feet by 23 feet, and contained 57 inhabitants. The boy shared a bed with two other men in a small room inhabited by five people. He wrote later:

It was entirely beyond anything I had imagined before actually coming to Djakarta, and I felt nauseated. I had never, never thought I could live in such squalor. Yet little by little ... I grew familiar with Djakarta housing, knowing that it was sometimes possible to live in a row of shacks, as we did, only after some stroke of good luck.[13]

From time to time, the authorities produced estimates of the extent of the housing problem. In 1952, municipal officials claimed there were 30,000 illegal dwellings in the city; in 1957, they thought there were 70,000. At least 275,000 people were estimated in 1957 to be living in unsanitary homes and a further 80,000 in grossly overcrowded conditions. The most densely populated parts of town were found in the inner city where in 1957 Sawah Besar had 300 people per hectare, and the areas of

Menteng, Salemba, Tanah Abang and Kota housed 250 residents per hectare. Considering that residences were no more than two storeys high, it can be imagined how congested conditions were.[14]

The housing shortage was exacerbated by frequent fires. Great stretches of *kampung* in the inner areas consisted of flimsy buildings built far too closely together, occupied very often by country people who had not yet adapted to the precautions required in such conditions when cooking over wood fires (as most people did). There were some spectacular conflagrations in these years. One in Kampung Krekot Bunder near Pasar Baru destroyed 600 houses in 1952, rendering 10,000 people homeless; another in Tanah Tinggi in the following year did similar damage. In 1962, it was officially reported that there were 183 fires causing the loss of 5,056 houses and leaving 45,197 people homeless and 12 dead.[15]

Houses could not be serviced properly as municipal departments were unable to meet the demand. Rubbish and sewage disposal was still at its pre-war level, or worse. In 1951, there were only 47 rubbish trucks and 600 hand carts available to remove rubbish, and at any one time about one-sixth of these were out of action because of their poor condition. Three years later, the situation had deteriorated further: some vehicles had given up entirely, and the breakdown rate for the rest had increased. For the whole of Jakarta there were only 60 men and 4 trucks employed to empty privies, and again the trucks, which were more than thirty years old, were never all in use. Most *kampung* houses did not have their own privy, so it is particularly shocking to learn that this city of almost two million people possessed only 84 public privies in 1954, none of which had water laid on.[16] One of the great luxuries of the new suburb of Kebayoran Baru was that the area was actually sewered.

Similarly, not all houses could be connected to the electricity grid, even if their occupants could afford it, as most could not. There was simply not enough power generated. In 1951, the city experienced black-outs on average once every three days. As for telephones, the subject aroused pained comments from all visitors. In 1951, the city had fewer than 400 connections more than in 1940, a grand sum of 8,204.[17] And the switching system was so antiquated and inefficient that several observers joked that it was quicker to deliver one's message across town on foot.

Such a journey would surely then provoke comment on the inadequacy of Jakarta's roads and transport system. Pre-war trams and buses, in a decrepit condition, could not cope with the demand. The buses were driven recklessly, racing one another in their competition for passengers. Although the number of buses was increased in 1956 by a gift of a hundred modern diesel vehicles from Australia, lack of proper maintenance and spare parts removed more than half of them from the road in three years.[18] Although slow, the trams were extremely cheap and popular, so much so that they were extraordinarily crowded. Jakarta's anecdotist, Tjalie Robinson, referred to the envy which passengers felt for the freedom of sardines in a tin and pondered the tale of the woman who, on descending from a tram, was seen to shake out her sarong to release from its pleats the flattened bodies of her children.[19] In such a throng it is not surprising that many travellers failed to pay their fares, which contributed to the downfall of the tram service. Its uneconomic performance, compounded by lack of maintenance, led to trams being phased out in the early 1960s. This step was urged upon the municipal administration by Sukarno, who felt that trams were not suited to a modern city, thus following a misguided trend in the Western world and ignoring the wishes of Jakartans.[20]

Public transport requirements were increasingly met by motor buses called *oplet*, which carried six or more people and operated on fixed routes, and by *becak*. These last were a common form of employment for new arrivals from country areas, hence their frequent brushes with urban traffic laws. In 1951, there were estimated to be 25,000 *becak*, each employing up to three drivers per day on a shift system. Colourfully painted and decorated, *becak* and their jaunty, daredevil drivers clogged the roads for motor vehicles. From 1952 to 1956, the number of motorized vehicles per head of population more than doubled in Jakarta. In 1962, Jakarta had one-third of the nation's cars—a total of more than 43,000.[21] And then there was the most common type of private transport: the bicycle. In fact, the only vehicle to decrease in numbers during these years was the horse-drawn carriage: it was possible to find *sado* and *deleman* only on the city outskirts.

While leaders like Sukarno might have had ambitions to make Jakarta into the city beautiful, the hard reality was that the main task of urban government was to come to terms with massive population increase and its attendant squalor.

Modest Achievements

While Sukarno took the limelight in Jakarta, the business of trying to keep the city afloat was left to the Jakarta Municipal Council. As if the problems it had to tackle were not great enough, it was hampered by internal divisions and tangled lines of responsibility.[22]

In 1950, Indonesia had a political system based on constitutional parliamentary democracy in the Western style. At every level representative bodies were created, although national elections were not actually held until 1955 and provincial council elections only in 1957–8. In Jakarta before 1955 the Provisional Municipal Council comprised members elected in a curious way by and from a large number of parties and organizations. The parties continually bickered about their numbers in the Council. After the national election the membership was adjusted according to the voting in Jakarta. In 1957, Jakarta had its first and last free municipal election with universal adult suffrage, giving it a Council made up of representatives who reflected the preferences of the city's population. This state of affairs did not last long, at either national or local level. In response to regional military take-overs in Sumatra and Sulawesi, a State of Emergency was declared by the President in 1957, after which all political structures were altered to conform with Sukarno's ideas of Guided Democracy. He disliked the divisiveness of the party system and preferred a corporate state in which an authoritarian leader consulted widely with representatives of many different types of organizations. For the Jakarta Municipal Council this meant the removal of some party representatives and the inclusion of non-elected members appointed by the Minister of the Interior.

Even before 1957, however, the power of the Municipal Council was constrained by its relationship with the central government. The Mayor (later Governor) was appointed by and responsible to the Minister for the Interior. Together with the Executive Body of the Council he formed the Municipal Government. Although the Executive Body was initially elected by the Council, from 1957 onwards it, too, was appointed by and answerable to the Minister. Cabinets changed frequently during the period of constitutional democracy, so there could be little continuity of central government policies for Jakarta at that time.

A Mayor appointed by a Minister of one political party might soon find himself being instructed by one of a different political allegiance. And when, in mid-1965, the Governor was elevated to the status of a Minister, relations with the Cabinet must have been even more confusing. Responsibility for urban decision-making in Jakarta was divided between the representative Council, the Mayor/Governor and the Minister for the Interior. On occasion each would find itself overridden by a higher authority: during Guided Democracy this was most frequently the President himself.

As far as the Council was concerned, this lack of autonomy was the main disadvantage of its close relationship with the central government. The main benefits were financial. Jakarta's municipal budget depended heavily on central subsidies, which was felt to be only fair considering that many of the large projects undertaken in Jakarta, particularly those initiated by Sukarno, were intended for national or international purposes, for building an impressive national capital. Much of that money came from foreign loans: for instance, Hotel Indonesia was built with Japanese funds, the Asian Games Complex at Senayan with Russian loans, and the Jakarta Bypass with the help of the USA. On average, half the total Jakarta budget came from the central government.[23]

Perhaps this access to national funds merely allowed the Jakarta administration to avoid more difficult means of seeking local sources. Certainly the latter were few, being limited by law to local taxes like road, advertising and property taxes, but most were also not collected properly. It could be argued that it was more difficult for an Indonesian administration to collect taxes than for a colonial one: people expected to be taxed less after independence, and ensuring the implementation of unpopular measures was hard for a Council whose members wanted to increase their voter support. Nevertheless, it does seem extraordinary that in a time of very high land values and property speculation, property taxes contributed little to municipal revenue: the most lucrative taxes were the more easily collected ones like cinema and restaurant taxes.

Even with central government subsidies, Jakarta was always desperately short of funds to provide for its burgeoning population. But it would be quite unfair to give the impression that no advances were made in these years: in fact there was much to be proud of as administrations seized the initiative to compensate for neglect during the colonial period. Especially in the early 1950s, in the years directly following independence, many people revelled in the excitement of constructing a new order in Indonesian society.

One such field of endeavour was education. A massive effort was made to teach everyone to read and write. In 1957, the authorities could report that whereas before the war Jakarta had had only 140 elementary schools, by that year the number had increased threefold. Of course, the population had grown even more than that, but school buildings were used for teaching two shifts per day to make up for the shortage of classrooms—and this was still not sufficient. Even more impressive was the campaign to combat illiteracy: informal short courses were conducted by local groups in the *kampung* in *langgar* (prayer-houses) and any other available space. At the end of each course, tests were conducted and the *kampung* proudly recorded the number of their newly literate. The campaign came to an end in 1962 when the Governor stated that it had brought literacy to 268,000 men and 364,000 women. It seems unfortunate that the courses were not made a permanent institution, for despite a great improvement Jakarta was far from eliminating illiteracy. The 1961 census revealed that 64 per cent of the city's population over the age of ten was literate compared with 12 per cent in 1930. The almost total illiteracy of women in the earlier census had changed markedly for the better: by 1961, half of Jakarta's women could read and write, although they still trailed the 77 per cent literacy rate of the men. As could be expected, the young had higher educational levels than the old: most children in 1961 had been or were at school, while amongst those over twenty schooling was much less common.[24]

Since the turn of the century, Jakarta had always been a centre of higher education, but it increased its educational standing in the post-independence years. Government and private secondary and tertiary institutions proliferated, the latter accounting for more than 10,000 students in 1957. Although there were universities in other cities too, the University of Indonesia at Salemba was the country's best known. Jakarta contained the greatest number of highly educated people in the nation, concentrated in just a few suburbs where the well-to-do lived, principally Gambir and Kebayoran Baru. By contrast, the outer districts of the city were inhabited by people whose education was well below the national average: Tanjung Priok with its large number of temporary migrants working on the wharves, and Cengkareng, Kebon Jeruk, Pulo Gadung and Pasar Minggu, the areas with the greatest concentration of Orang Betawi still living by agriculture and handicrafts.

Another area where significant improvements were made in Jakarta was in health services. Several new hospitals and clinics were quickly opened, including a mobile clinic to service the more scattered population on the outskirts of the city. Mass innoculations were conducted against smallpox, tetanus and typhus. As in the nineteenth century, the most common illness was malaria, which was fought partly by spraying houses with DDT.[25] Harder to tackle were the more basic causes of ill health: malnutrition, poor hygiene and inadequate water supply. Although rubbish and sewage disposal defeated the authorities, considerable headway was made in providing good drinking water. With the opening in 1957 of the water purification plant at Pejompongan, one of the largest and most modern in the world, the flow of water through city pipes became relatively dependable for the first time since the war. But most of the population could not afford to pay for the connection to the piped water supply, and wells continued to be the main source of *kampung* water.[26]

One of Jakarta's governors during this period was a former army doctor who naturally took a particular interest in urban hygiene. Brigadier-General Dr Sumarno (Governor 1960–4) encouraged cleanliness campaigns. *Kampung* organizations were urged to compete with each other in cleanliness, and the competition was carried through to the national level, so that every year on Independence Day a prize was awarded to what was judiciously called 'Kota Besar Paling Tidak Kotor' (The Least Dirty City). Not surprisingly, Jakarta never won the prize, although Sumarno considered it had benefited from the campaign. He conducted another pet project in 1960 when, at about eight o'clock every morning, the 'cleanliness siren' was sounded in Jakarta. All traffic stopped and passengers had to alight and clean up the area around their vehicle. Peak-hour traffic was held up for ten minutes or more. Looking back on this exercise, Sumarno conceded that, although it was at first successful, when it went on for week after week the complaints mounted and the economy was disrupted. He was obliged to call it off.[27]

What impact did Government measures actually have on people's health? In 1955, the death rate in Jakarta was officially reported to be 14.1 per thousand, more than one-third of those deaths being among children below the age of one and about two-thirds among children below the age of five. This was a distinct improvement over the estimated death rate of between 20.1 and 15.6 per thousand in 1935–7, although the proportion of infant deaths had apparently risen.[28]

Some interesting comparisons with the pre-war period can be gleaned from a public health survey made of Tanah Tinggi ward in 1955–6,[29] because a similar study was made of roughly the same area in 1937–8.[30] The character of the ward seems to have changed little over time. Just east of Pasar Senen, it was a well established area with a relatively high concentration of Chinese, who were of above average wealth. Densely populated (about 11,000 people per square kilometre at the times of both surveys), its intake of migrants in 1956 was about the same as that of the city as a whole: 43 per cent of households had settled there since 1942. In general, it seems that conditions in the ward had improved appreciably since 1937–8: more houses were permanent structures (20 per cent in 1956 as compared with 10 per cent in 1937–8); fewer had earthern floors (44 per cent as against 74 per cent); more were connected to piped water (54 per cent compared with 20 per cent). The improved environment, coupled with better health services, seems to have contributed to lowered mortality: in 1955–6 the death rate was 16.2 per thousand compared with about 21 in 1936–40.

Education and health were the areas where the authorities (both at municipal and central level) made the biggest strides in improving conditions in Jakarta. There were other successes too, like the Pluit flood control scheme, which drained excess water off to a new reservoir on the north-west side of the city, surrounded by reclaimed land used for industry and housing. Considering the political conflicts and lack of trained staff with which the Jakarta administration had to contend, these were remarkable achievements.

The Urban Economy

No matter how poorly endowed Jakarta might appear, it was the most privileged place in the country. The wealthiest people lived there and it received investment on a bigger scale than anywhere else. Of the total of government loans in 1956, for instance, almost two-thirds went to Jakarta.[31] This kind of favouritism made Jakarta the envy of the rest of the country (thus attracting more immigrants) and a source of great resentment. At the time of the Sumatran regional resistance to Jakarta in 1957, the Minangkabau intellectual Takdir Alisjahbana put the case against Jakarta and for the neglected regions:

Not only has most of the revenue of the new State accumulated in Djakarta, but most of it has also been spent there. Djakarta has become the center where the money collected from the rest of the country is divided up.... Djakarta, with its population of top officials and business leaders who are all tied to each other by a whole range of political and financial connections, is like a fat leech sucking on the head of a fish, the fish being Indonesia....[32]

To some extent this is an argument against a Javanese capital of an Indonesian nation. Jakarta happened to be the locus of Governments which were biased in favour of Java, perhaps understandably so, since almost two-thirds of Indonesians lived there. Their policies, which sought to redistribute the wealth of the export-producing but under-populated Outer Islands in favour of the majority of the population on the island of Java, were bound to draw the wrath of Outer Islanders. But more than this, Takdir's speech implies that Jakartans were corrupt and lazy, doing nothing to earn their keep. So strong was the feeling against Jakarta on the part of politicians in other regions that from 1955 onwards a campaign was waged in the national parliament to move the capital elsewhere, except that no one could agree on where. It was only in 1960 that Sukarno put an end to speculation by confirming that Jakarta would remain the capital.[33]

What was done to try to create a more dynamic economy in Jakarta, to allow that city to do more to support its own large population, independent of national funds? Heavy central government subsidies to the municipal government could not be a long-term solution; ultimately the city had to find sufficiently remunerative employment for Jakartans to finance their own needs.

Indonesia's first Governments aimed to foster indigenous private enterprise as the basis for economic growth.[34] Legislation favoured indigenous Indonesians (*asli*) at the expense of aliens. This had important consequences for Jakarta's economy, where it was hoped that *asli* businessmen would displace Chinese and Dutch entrepreneurs. The urban economy inherited at independence was virtually the colonial one, much the worse for wear: Chinese and European businessmen still controlled the higher reaches of the economy, such as manufacturing, banking, export and import firms and the main urban utilities. As Europeans moved out after the transfer of sovereignty, it was the Chinese rather than the Indonesians who stepped into their shoes. According to the terms of the Round Table Conference on which the transfer of sovereignty was based, the Indonesian Government had undertaken to respect the position of foreigners in the economy. Moreover, the first Governments of the 1950s were only too uncomfortably aware of the lack of expertise and capital on the Indonesian side, which made it impractical to expropriate foreign firms overnight.

Since it was difficult to establish Indonesians quickly in other sectors, the most well-known and ultimately notorious policy of 'Indonesianization' was undertaken in the importing sector. Only indigenous Indonesians were granted licences necessary for importing goods. Intended to create a niche in the economy for enterprising Indonesian businessmen, this policy merely gave rise to an enormous racket. Instead of running the firms themselves, many Indonesians with a licence acted as a sleeping partner for Chinese businessmen. It was an easy way of making money, exploited by many politicians who won licences from their cronies in government. The policy was finally abandoned in 1957, after doing untold harm to the party system and little to promote Indonesian enterprise. Since the spoils (the licences) were to be obtained in Jakarta, it also contributed to the rise of that wealthy, corrupt élite which typified the city in the eyes of people in other parts of the country.

Some new Indonesian businesses did start up in Jakarta in the early 1950s. The Indonesian film industry flourished there with the help of government protection, and some Indonesian manufacturing concerns started in the fields of enamelware, tanning, and ink and varnish-making. With the help of *Peranakan* Chinese capital two ex-politicians, Dul Arnowo and Mohamad Tabrani, became successful businessmen, the latter in the bottling industry. But these were exceptions: a glance at the list of industrial enterprises in Jakarta in 1956 shows most still in European and Chinese hands.[35]

Discouraged by their lack of success in promoting Indonesian entrepreneurs, Indonesian governments began to rely more on nationalization as a means of displacing foreigners in the economy. In Jakarta this resulted in a large part of the economy falling into the hands of the State. Anxious to get rid of the 'feudal' institution of private estates, governments (both central and municipal) proceeded to buy out the owners, who were mainly Chinese. Already by 1952, the Jakarta administration owned 1,765 hectares and the central government 29,750 hectares of Jakarta's land—more than half its total area of 56,000 hectares (much of this had been acquired during colonial days). Finally, in 1958, all freehold estates were abolished by law. Some of the former estates were sold to their Indonesian residents but much was retained for planning purposes or public housing, so that the Government collected rent as a landlord.[36] Gradually, the various utilities—tram and bus lines, electricity and gas supplies—which had previously been in private European hands, were also nationalized. And the State moved into areas of manufacturing and banking: Indonesian national banks were established, and in Jakarta the Government bought out the Dutch-owned Scheepwerf Antjol in 1952 and the American General Motors plant in 1955, converting them into State-run shipping and motor vehicle manufacturing establishments. In 1957, a wave of nationalization occurred when, following a breakdown in negotiations with the Dutch over the future of West New Guinea (now Irian Jaya), all Dutch businesses were summarily expropriated.

While the government role in the economy expanded in Jakarta, there was not much growth in manufacturing industry, the area most likely to provide modern, reasonably paid employment for new immigrants. Larger-scale manufacturing was still dominated by the Chinese, who can have felt little incentive to expand in the prevailing xenophobic climate. Industries relying on imported goods or spare parts were badly hit by government cuts in imports and the confusion caused by the licensing system.

The work-force in Jakarta at the time of the 1961 census had changed little from colonial days: the vast bulk of people were employed in various services such as in transport and storage, in commerce and in government. Altogether, about a quarter of the work-force were occupied in manufacturing and construction. As far as women are concerned, this record of work is most misleading. The census reported only 19 per cent of women as 'working' and 60 per cent as 'looking after the home', which in census terms are, of course, mutually exclusive categories. Countless numbers of women in irregular occupations were no doubt overlooked: it is highly unlikely, for instance, that the census took into account the large number of prostitutes in Jakarta, estimated to be 20,000 in 1952.[37]

Work was mainly labour-intensive. In 1957, most industrial establishments in Jakarta were based on manual labour, and the number of workers employed in plants using power machinery was about 80,000, of whom only 25,000 to 30,000 were in factories with more than a hundred workers.[38] The service sector contained a very large number of women working as servants. Observers often commented that the bureaucracy, a major part of the service sector, was grossly overstaffed, to the extent that most were underemployed. Since cutting the civil service was politically unacceptable, the choice was made in favour of employing too many people at too low wages, so low that most had to find second jobs to make ends meet, especially when inflation bit into fixed wages from 1954 onwards. The price paid was inefficiency: red tape proliferated, and paperwork moved extraordinarily slowly from desk to desk. Since almost no transaction could avoid administrative documentation, every sector of the economy was slowed down unless bribery was used, an important extra source of income for public servants.

Did Jakarta's population benefit economically in these post-independence years? The answer depends on what is being compared. Since about half the city's people came from outside, they would have compared their lot with conditions in other areas. The 1953 survey of Jakarta immigrants indicates that most had improved their position by coming to the city. After all, the great attraction of Jakarta was the well-founded promise it held that immigrants could earn more there. Even though the city did not have large numbers of ready-made jobs to offer, it was possible for almost all to find a niche: the 1953 survey showed that male immigrants found work mainly in industry and transport, and the rest in street vending and government service; women were employed primarily as labourers and domestic servants.

Two roughly comparable surveys of lower-income family budgets in 1937 and 1953–4 give some idea of change in the living conditions of Jakarta's workers. The 1953–4 survey shows that a remarkably high 74 per cent of the families' expenditure was on food, compared with about 57 per cent in 1937. Since the proportion of family expenditure on food generally falls with increasing wealth, this does not offer support for the view that workers were generally better off in Jakarta after independence. The only redeeming feature of the comparison is that in 1953–4 families surveyed were eating a much more varied diet than in 1937, with less emphasis on rice and more on meat, fish and vegetables.[39] Later surveys seemed to show that the situation was deteriorating: for instance, a Ministry of Health survey in 1957 of Jakarta workers' families found that only 30 per cent ate three times a day, the average worker's calorie intake was only 70 per cent of calculated minimum requirements, and vitamin deficiency was widespread. A Health Ministry report in 1959 considered that the situation was becoming worse.[40]

One of the causes of decline in real income was inflation, the dominant economic feature of most of these years.[41] The cost of rice rose by more than half in Jakarta over the two-year period 1953–5 and continued to climb with the rampant inflation of the 1960s. From January 1958 to July 1965, the cost-of-living index increased tenfold. Those on fixed incomes like government employees were hit particularly hard; people selling goods and services were better able to adjust by raising their prices. A study of Kampung Kebun Kacang, the *kampung* just west of Jalan Thamrin, whose residents lived mainly by petty trade, has found that they remembered the Sukarno years as a time of relative comfort and freedom: inflation did not bother them.[42]

The Government tried to soften the blow of rising prices, while failing to attack the causes of inflation, which included flagging production, a skewed exchange rate and hoarding in the face of increasing political uncertainty. Besides their wages, civil servants received rice rations, which came to exceed the money wage in real value. In order to bypass private sellers, who were blamed for raising prices unfairly, the Government under Guided Democracy established so-called *sandang-pandang* (basic necessities) shops and *kampung* co-operatives where shoppers required a ration card to buy fixed-price goods. Like other aspects of *Socialism à la Indonesia* (Sukarno's term), this effort did not succeed: the shops and co-operatives lacked capital and experienced staff and were often unable to buy goods because of a faulty delivery system.[43]

The increasing poverty of most ordinary Jakartans was noted by visitors, many of whom in the late Sukarno years found it a depressing city. Immediately after independence that poverty had seemed a challenge to those intent on creating a just Indonesian society, but in the late 1950s and early 1960s it was the obvious inequality of suffering which disturbed people. A small minority of well-placed politicians, civil servants, military officers and businessmen were prospering, very often through corruption. The numbers of luxury cars and other such imports rose, and the city buzzed with stories of ill-gotten gains. One such scandal which broke in 1959 centred around Tanjung Priok, a favourite place for illegal business. The army had taken charge of the supervision of import and export trade there: just one example of the growing economic role of the military in these years. Some officers were charged with using their position to go into business for themselves. The army investigated the matter; although the men were found guilty, they were very lightly punished because they argued that they had used their profits on behalf of the army.[44]

'The Foreigners'

In the 1950s, Indonesian governments were trying to displace foreigners from positions of dominance. It was a time of reckoning for the most important alien groups in Jakartan society, the Europeans and the Chinese.

The problem of the position of Europeans was solved fairly rapidly if not painlessly. According to the Round Table Conference of 1949, Europeans (which of course meant mainly Eurasians) were given two years to decide whether to take Indonesian nationality.[45] The vast majority opted for Dutch citizenship and subsequently left the country with assistance from the Netherlands. Fear of loss of status and income in an Indonesian republic, coupled with financial incentives from Holland, seems to have determined the outcome for these people. By 1956, there were less than 17,000 Dutch people in Jakarta.[46] After a sustained anti-Dutch drive by the Indonesian Government, incensed by the Netherlands' refusal to cede West New Guinea, by 1961 there were only 530 Hollanders left.[47] The decision to leave Indonesia was a difficult one for many Eurasians, whose hearts were really in the land of their birth. In Holland they kept alive the old memories in journals like *Tong Tong* (later *Moesson*). It is hard to imagine such a confirmed Jakartan as Tjalie Robinson in a Dutch city, and indeed he continued for some years to muse wistfully on the contrasts between the two: Dutch streets all neat and careful; Jakarta relaxed, with growth and decay flourishing together, and nothing hidden.

Those Eurasians who chose Indonesian citizenship appear to have been gradually absorbed into the rest of Jakartan society. After all, they spoke Indonesian and they shared Christianity with Indonesian ethnic groups like the Menadonese. For a while Eurasians gathered together in the Gabungan Indo untuk Kesatuan Indonesia (Indo Association for Indonesian Unity). This organization, the descendant of the old Indo-Europeesch Vereeniging, continued to operate schools in Jakarta until all foreign language schools were prohibited to Indonesian citizens in 1958.

The question of the Chinese was not so easily settled.[48] In Jakarta their numbers after independence were greater than before the war, not through immigration from overseas, which had ceased, but because of the influx from insecure rural areas. In the following years, while many Chinese citizens left for mainland China, Indonesian government measures forced more of them to leave rural areas and settle in towns. In 1961, there were perhaps 294,000 Chinese in Jakarta.[49] Their citizenship was a vexed question; Indonesian governments kept changing the law to make it increasingly hard for the Chinese (even those born in Indonesia) to take Indonesian citizenship. It is likely that in 1961, when the citizenship issue finally seemed to have settled down, almost two-thirds of Jakarta's Chinese were Indonesian citizens and the rest were mainly citizens of the People's Republic of China.

Their position was extremely difficult. Unwilling to lose their separate identity, the vast majority of Chinese at first sent their children to their own private schools, many of which used the Chinese language. In 1954, the Jakarta Municipal Council passed a motion directly aimed at the Chinese to prohibit Indonesian citizens from attending foreign schools, a practice which it regarded as highly undesirable from the point of view of national unity. When this policy was adopted by the central government, the result was that Chinese pupils became divided educationally into foreign citizens attending Chinese language schools and Indonesian Chinese at their own private Indonesian-language schools. Many Chinese parents argued that it was hard to get their children into State schools, where the shortage of places was used as an excuse to discriminate against Chinese in selection. For similar reasons they also established their own university. Under the State of Emergency the army forced all Chinese language newspapers to cease publication in 1958; only a few resumed publication when the ban was later lifted. Government policy apparently aimed to separate the Chinese community into aliens and Indonesian citizens, and seems to have achieved this result.

Choosing Indonesian citizenship still left open the question whether Indonesian Chinese would retain their separate ethnic identity or merge with the rest of the country's Indonesians. The Chinese were divided on this issue, which became a highly political one. The leftist organization Baperki maintained that the Chinese had a right to a separate culture, like any other *suku* (ethnic group) in Indonesia; other organizations favoured trying to assimilate by taking Indonesian-sounding names and even converting to Christianity or Islam. There were prominent examples in Jakarta of different choices: Sung Chung-ch'uan, a Chinese citizen, was president of the Ch'iao Tsung, an organiz-ation which encouraged the city's Chinese to identify with the People's Republic of China; Siauw Giok Tjhan, as president of Baperki, championed the cause of Indonesian Chinese loyal to their homeland but keeping their own culture; and Tan In Hok, a wealthy businessman from colonial days, won official approval by becoming a staunch supporter of an Islamic party.[50]

Whatever the Chinese did, they still suffered discrimination from governments and individuals who regarded them as an excessively privileged and exclusive race. Government practice was contradictory: it abolished old methods of separate treatment for the Chinese, like the Chinese officer system, only to invent new ones. Even those with Indonesian citizenship were the target of discriminatory practices, and most feared outbreaks of violence against them. Although there were in fact no serious anti-Chinese riots in Jakarta such as occurred in other places in these years, there were some ugly incidents. In 1956, there were two interconnected cases of anti-Chinese demonstrations involving rich Indonesian-Chinese businessmen, Han Swie Tik and Lie Hok Thay. What was disturbing about the treatment of these two was that the State permitted and the press condoned a campaign of accusation and intimidation against them before they were finally brought to trial. Anti-Chinese feelings were allowed full play, short of actual violence against persons.[51]

So what remained of the Chinese contribution to Jakarta culture? They had their own newspapers, but, as time went on censorship reduced their individuality. Long-standing Jakarta Chinese papers like *Sin Po* and *Keng Po* had to adopt Indonesian names during Guided Democracy and take on indigenous Indonesian staff. As a result, they ceased to present the views of *Peranakan* Chinese.[52] A similar fate befell the Chinese Malay literature which had been so prolific before the war. The authorities considered that the language and style of these works were not in keeping with their view of Indonesian culture; pressure was applied to publishers so that Indonesian Chinese writers stopped writing differently from other Indonesians.[53] There were distinguished exceptions, however, to the decline of the Chinese role in the great amalgam of Jakarta culture. The artist Lee Man Fong contributed his own delicate version of Chinese tradition to Indonesian painting, which was received with favour by the President. (Unlike many of his fellow politicians, Sukarno fostered good relations with China and the Chinese.) And *gambang kromong*, that Chinese-influenced Betawi music from the previous century, was popular on Jakarta radio, especially when performed by Pak Kodok, a Jakartan of Chinese descent whose real name was Tjian Hok San.[54]

Chinese culture did not disappear in Jakarta: it was just harder to keep it alive publicly under the weight of government disapproval. Chinese temples continued to be built and the old ones restored in the 1950s.[55] Certain areas of town, notably Glodok and Senen, where their commercial ventures were concentrated, still had a distinctly Chinese appearance with shop-houses, cinemas, restaurants and specialty stores, yet *Peranakan* Chinese seemed to prefer to live more dispersed among the rest of the urban population. Capgomeh celebrations for the Chinese New Year still involved large street processions around Senen, Sawah Besar, Glodok and Jatinegara in the 1950s, but the scale of

The ethnic mixture was as varied as that of eighteenth-century Batavia, but the proportion of non-Indonesians had declined greatly and most Indonesians came from Java, not the Outer Islands.

What of the old Orang Betawi, who were already seen to be a minority in 1930? It now becomes harder and harder to trace them. In the central districts of the city they seem to have been outnumbered; their strongholds were the more isolated outer regions of the city, generally on the former private estates. Here communications were still poor and people still made a living in the old ways by fruit-growing and handicrafts. Betawi folk theatre, including *lenong* and *bangsawan* (a dramatic form like *stambul*) was still performed frequently in places like Pasar Minggu, although the number of such theatrical troupes in the city generally seems to have fallen.[57] In the post-1949 period, however, Betawi culture reasserted itself in a new and more sophisticated form. The first generation of Betawi intellectuals gathered regularly at Senen in the 1950s and produced many works in Betawi dialect. Prominent among the 'Senen Artists' group were S. M. Ardan, who wrote short stories, and Syuman Jaya, a writer and cinematographer, many of whose films, notably *Si Doel Anak Betawi*, featured Orang Betawi.[58]

As for the vast mass of immigrants to the city, it was remarkable how quickly they became Jakartans. Of course, it was still possible to distinguish what certain ethnic groups had to offer: there was a disproportionately high number of immigrants from the Outer Islands, who were generally much better educated, among the intellectual élite of the city; dances from East Sumatra became popular in Jakarta; Christian Bataks built churches and trained their famous choirs; and a Sundanese repertory group called Miss Tjitjih's long formed the mainstay of Jakartan theatre, with a style strongly influenced by *stambul*. Yet it was even more striking to see how people adapted themselves to the city. For example, new arrivals seem to have readily learnt the Indonesian spoken in the capital. Again, ethnic groups were dispersed through the city instead of forming ghettoes: the 1953 survey noted that there were no strong concentrations of immigrant groups in particular *kampung*. It observed also that the children of immigrants to Jakarta already regarded themselves as native Jakartans rather than identifying with their parents' ethnic group.

One reason why Indonesians fitted in so easily can be found in the help they got in settling into Jakarta life. Most immigrants to Jakarta seem to have been received by friends and relatives, who advised them before they made the decision to migrate.[59] So it is likely that in the post-independence period new arrivals knew that they would have to learn a new language and fit into a cosmopolitan society, and that their contacts helped them to do this and to find employment. Many ethnic groups had their own associations in Jakarta which assisted new arrivals to adapt, even teaching them the local etiquette: loud-voiced Bataks were advised how to tone down their behaviour to make themselves acceptable.[60] Because Jakarta has a reputation as a go-ahead place, the young in particular are only too anxious to conform to a new, modern image.

A study of a Jakarta railway workshop *kampung* reveals another way in which people settled in the city and learned to live with people of different ethnic groups.[61] In this case, the neighbourhood was based on housing provided for the workers by the National Railway Authority. The *kampung* consisted of new arrivals from West and Central Java living in dormitory buildings and sharing the same work place. Working together helped to create a bond across ethnic groups. People who arrived later deferred to those who had come when the *kampung* was first formed soon after independence. Probably much the same thing occurred in other residential areas where accommodation was built by government departments or industries.

No one ethnic group dominates in Jakarta, so all have learned to give and take a little in the interests of living together. Tjalie Robinson referred to it as Jakarta's *gado-gado* culture: a dish which could be prepared with all kinds of vegetables, mixed with a spicy sauce. He revelled in the variety and liveliness of Jakarta, typified by its inhabitants' approach to eating out. The Jakartan, he wrote, is an adventurous eater, able to nose out the best *saté*-seller, the tastiest *lotek*, the finest *bakso* and the most generous *nasi-rames* tent in town. He is willing to try all foods and develop his own variation of them.[62] For some new arrivals the apparently rootless cultural permissiveness of Jakarta could produce indigestion, yet for most people the tolerance seems to have grown out of confidence in the city's ability to cope with diversity. This surely is a cultural trait fundamental to life in a metropolis.

The leaders of Jakartan society did not, however, take such a relaxed view of its development. At the same time as the new nation was trying to find a specifically Indonesian national identity, Jakarta's leading lights were contemplating whether a modern Jakartan culture could blaze a trail for the Indonesia of the future. Some intellectuals despaired of such a thing emerging. Pramudya Ananta Tur described Jakarta scornfully as 'just a large collection of villages'; in his view no real urban culture existed: everything had been brought in from outside, from the provinces or abroad.[63]

Some of the more well-to-do clearly felt that Western influences had most to teach about shaping a modern urban society. They watched Western films frequently and tried to keep in touch with trends abroad. This troubled many nationalists, who feared that Jakartans were absorbing all the worst aspects of Western culture. In 1952, Vice-President Hatta noted that Indonesia's large cities were much influenced by Westerners: 'In these places, most of our people just become imitators. As usual, the easiest thing to imitate is the shallow, the superficial. . . .' He put this down to the fact that 'most of our cities did not arise from our own society but rather as appendages of a foreign economy. These cities are not the centres of the creative activity of our own people but primarily distribution centres for foreign goods'.[64]

In the Jakarta of the 1950s, Hatta's remarks seemed to be supported by the appearance of so-called 'cross-boys'. These were gangs of youths who modelled themselves on the juvenile delinquents portrayed in Western films and who were usually associated with jeans and motor bikes. Some viewed them suspiciously as a sign of imported social decadence, but they also had much in common with the *pemuda* of the Revolution days. When martial law was introduced in 1957, the military authorities in Jakarta banned 'cross-boy organizations', of which there seemed to be a large number: thirty-six were listed by name, including Cross-Boys Club, Deddy [*sic*] Boys Club, and James Dean Club. And for good measure, the wearing of jeans in public by anyone over the age of ten was forbidden. This was no hollow threat: arrests were subsequently made at cinemas.[65]

Suppression of undesirable foreign influences was one side of life in Jakarta under Guided Democracy. Sukarno strongly opposed rock-and-roll and other American cultural imports, which he regarded as incompatible with Indonesian national culture. Such views became the subject of intense intellectual debate. While many well-to-do people simply ignored the President and continued to jive at private parties, different artistic, political and religious groups felt strongly about it. Jakarta was, after all, the main literary and publishing centre of Indonesia, the place where most films were made and most cultural criticism was produced and printed. Increasingly the cultural arena divided into entrenched camps: those who stressed nationalism and social responsibility as against those who favoured a more cosmopolitan and individualistic approach. The former position was held by LEKRA, the communist-sponsored cultural organization. In the final years of Guided Democracy they supported noisy campaigns to boycott Western films considered to purvey imperialist values.

Regardless of which camp they belonged to, many writers and artists of these years were studying urban life. Some of them, recent immigrants like most Jakartans, had difficulty in coming to terms with it. Ayip Rosidi, the poet who migrated to Jakarta in his boyhood, felt torn between the city and his Sundanese place of origin. His ambivalence dated from his arrival, when he found that Jakarta was not the glorious and beautiful place he had expected. Later in life he felt called to return to his rural origins for a while:

... I felt that I'd been placed in a sickening cage, that I'd lost my roots, that I stood right in the middle of an international city's whirling confusion, a city that opened itself to every current and never flinched away, a bustling activity without direction or purpose, a city of lies and tricks.[66]

Yet he could not settle down in his home village and had to return again to Jakarta, for as he wrote:

I love you Jakarta
Because you are the city of my second birth.[67]

For him, Jakarta was both a liberating and a bewildering experience.

Curiously enough, what seemed to Indonesians an excitingly cosmopolitan city appeared to many Western visitors to Jakarta at the time as a dreary backwater.[68] They complained about Jakarta's lack of international-class hotels and night-clubs, about its film censorship, about its undistinguished and pot-holed streets and cracked footpaths, and its beggars. Each was a very subjective picture, prejudiced by the very different backgrounds of the observers.

Probably the best-known writer on Jakarta in this period was the journalist and novelist Mochtar Lubis, whose novel *Twilight in Djakarta* was written in Indonesian in 1957. It constitutes a scathing attack on the corruption of the time, which seeped down through all levels of society. He continually contrasts glimpses of the pitiful life of Jakarta's common folk—its *becak*-drivers and rubbish collectors—with the temptations to bribery facing civil servants battling the housing crisis and inflation, the endless vapid debates among Jakarta's intellectuals about national culture, and corrupt dealings between politicians, businessmen and newspaper editors. Lubis was only one of several writers about Jakarta who took corruption as a theme, regarding it as the city's great sickness.

It was not only intellectuals who were concerned about the failure of Jakarta to conform to their notions of a modern urban society. It also preoccupied the Jakarta authorities. Many of the city's residents were originally country-dwellers; in fact, some were only temporary migrants who felt no commitment to urban life. Like the colonial rulers of old, Jakarta's leaders sighed at the impossibility of preventing these peasants from bathing and defecating in the canals and throwing their rubbish into the waterways, thus blocking the drainage system. But they persisted in their attempts to mould a modern city.

Urban Regulation and Planning

Naturally enough, the urban administration felt it had to have a hand in mixing the *gado-gado* of Jakartan society: in such an overcrowded environment a cook was desperately needed. For much of the time the authorities were running hard just to stay in the same place. But beyond merely maintaining basic urban facilities they wanted to give direction to the city's development.

Jakarta's mayors and governors and the President himself were disturbed by the lack of order and beauty in what was, after all, the capital of a great nation. When they tried to create those qualities they came into conflict with many of the city's inhabitants and their representatives in the Municipal Council. There were three main sources of conflict: illegal occupation of land, homeless people and street traders and buskers.

The immigrants to Jakarta had to find shelter somewhere. Many were forced to build their own huts or even quite substantial houses on land which they did not own, simply because insufficient residential land was made available or it was beyond their price range. This problem was a constant headache for the municipality.[69] As early as 1950, the municipal government tried to regulate the situation by giving some rights to squatters on unpartitioned land, but land which was required for city planning purposes had to be vacated as soon as possible, and shacks were to be cleared from areas which threatened safety or hygiene, such as along railway lines and waterways. For some time, however, little was done about squatters: the problem was considered too sensitive, money was not yet available to develop the public land occupied by squatters, and the municipal administration was distracted by reconstruction tasks. Most Jakartans must have found this a period of great freedom.

When, in the mid-1950s, the municipality began to push through major development projects, clashes with illegal settlers became inevitable. The administration recognized the complexity of the issue: it knew that registration of land had for so long been in a confused and neglected state that many people had been unable to straighten out their claims to land; moreover, during the struggle for independence, the Republican leaders had encouraged people to squat on land in Jakarta in defiance of the Dutch. The municipal government felt some obligation to arrange new land for squatters to settle on and to compensate them for removal. It became quite an expensive and time-consuming task to clear squatters from land required for new urban projects. This was the reason given by the administration for the very slow construction of Jalan Thamrin, which opened up a new six-lane thoroughfare from Medan Merdeka to Jalan Sudirman, the highway to Kebayoran Baru. Planned by the Dutch in 1946, the road was still not finished in 1953, when the authorities explained that in order to complete the last few hundred metres the municipality had to provide compensation for about 500 houses on the site which had to be pulled down and moved to resettlement areas in Kebon Sayur and Dukuh Atas.[70]

In 1956, the Municipal Council became concerned that nothing was being done about illegal occupation of land. It authorized the administration to shift buildings erected illegally between 1950 and 1955, giving assistance to the owners and providing suitable alternative land, but it also wanted harsher action against those who had erected buildings illegally after January 1955: following a warning, these buildings were to be demolished. From this time onwards it seems that the problem was tackled much more vigorously, especially after martial law and Guided Democracy introduced an era of authoritarianism. The public works associated with the Asian Games of 1962 were completed with considerable dispatch: within two years, about 47,000 people were moved to make way for these projects. Governor Sumarno commented later that 'freeing land' for the Pluit flood control scheme and the Ancol recreation area 'was easy because of the martial law situation'. In other words, the authorities did not have to worry about opposition.[71]

What happened to the so-called *gelandangan* or homeless people in Jakarta was rather similar. The authorities found them an embarrassment, a blot on their vision of the city. In a revealing passage in the official municipal history of the mayorship of Syamsurijal (1951–3), it is stated: 'In an effort to beautify Jakarta, [he] took steps to clean it of homeless people.... Unlike now, they were sleeping in shop verandahs, under bridges, in little huts alongside railway lines, so that foreign people stared at them and they lowered the status of the nation....'[72]

Some measures taken to deal with this problem were more humane than others. Orphanages were established for homeless children. Another method was to move *gelandangan* onto newly opened land in South Sumatra. When the problem became particularly pressing, that is when important foreign visitors were expected, raids were made on areas where beggars and other homeless people congregated and, as Governor Henk Ngantung later explained, these homeless people were rounded up, put on trucks and taken to temporary camps where they were fed; usually, after one or two days, they escaped and returned to the same spot. Ngantung understood that the problem of homeless immigrants was not one which could be solved at the local level: it was a consequence of failures of national policies to provide work outside Jakarta.

On a bigger scale was the question of uncontrolled street

vendors and entertainers. Such activities were the main source of income for a very large proportion of Jakarta's population. The authorities objected that they cluttered up streets and footpaths and lowered the tone of the city. Again, measures against these 'nuisances' were slow to appear, so for some years Jakartans had considerable freedom to trade and offer services where they liked. Losing patience with the mess, in 1956 the Municipal Council authorized the executive to enforce cleanliness regulations on street vendors and, after a warning, to find other suitable places for their operations. One of the bottlenecks was lack of market space: until this was made available, the Council did not wish illegal hawkers to be punished.[73]

On occasion, however, the municipal government did move rather peremptorily. A case in point, and one with unpleasantly anti-Chinese overtones, is that of the *tanjidor* performers.[74] *Tanjidor* groups consisted of Indonesians playing semi-European music influenced by old Dutch military bands. They were out in strength during Capgomeh celebrations. In 1954, the then Mayor of Jakarta, Sudiro, took a dislike to the behaviour of *tanjidor* troupes at Capgomeh: he thought it unseemly that they entered Chinese houses and requested money. One suspects that he was ashamed of Indonesians being seen begging from Chinese, although it had always been customary at Capgomeh for all sorts of performers, Chinese as well as Indonesians, to seek payment for their entertainment. Pressure was applied to *tanjidor* players with the result that in the 1955 Capgomeh there was no *tanjidor*. Itinerant musicians objected to the move against *tanjidor* and some formed an organization rather provocatively called Persatuan Musik Rendah (Union of Low Music), which formed a delegation to explain to the Mayor that he was preventing them from making a living. The outcome was unsatisfactory. It was decided to form a committee to help the musicians improve their music and find suitable employment for them. The Persatuan Musik Rendah was persuaded to change its name to the more respectable Persatuan Seni Musik Pantjaroba or Union of Musicians in Transition. Sudiro met with restaurant owners to encourage them to hire musicians. Government sponsorship of musicians had begun, starting the process of removing music from the street to the more artificial haunts of restaurants (few of which responded to Sudiro's plea), public park entertainments and ultimately to the Cultural Centre at Taman Ismail Marzuki, where Jakarta culture became ossified and transformed into a museum piece for middle-class people.

It may be significant that all the people in authority who had to deal with Jakarta's folk culture were born and bred outside Jakarta, so that *tanjidor* and its ilk had no place in their affections. This is not the whole story, however, for class differences also clouded perceptions of street entertainment.

The authorities' most ambitious move was to commission a Master Plan for Jakarta.[75] The history of this exercise reveals the many obstacles facing urban planners at that time. In 1956 Kenneth Watts from the United Nations was appointed to form a town planning team within the Jakarta administration. Because of the lack of qualified personnel, several Indonesians were sent overseas (mainly to the USA) for training. Meanwhile, planning surveys were conducted throughout the city to gather necessary information about traffic, population, housing, and so on. In 1957, the preliminary or Outline Plan for Greater Jakarta was finished. It began by pointing to what it considered the main problem areas: employment, traffic congestion, housing, social facilities. In each of these areas it made recommendations: expansion of industrialization on the basis of a regional plan which would also provide employment in Jakarta's catchment areas; investment in a housing programme; a system of ring roads for Jakarta; schemes for extension of the water supply, drainage and electricity systems and for rubbish collection; and a proposal to create a Green Belt around the planned built-up area of the city.

In 1958, the Outline Plan was approved by the municipality and work began on the more detailed preparation of the Master Plan. A British architect-planner, George Franklin, joined the Master Plan Section. He was struck by the many practical difficulties facing the team. One of the biggest was the severe shortage of staff, even after the crash training programme. In 1957, there were only eight trained planners in Indonesia. Tremendous pressure was placed on them because the Jakarta Master Plan was intended to serve as a pilot for other cities.

But worst of all in Franklin's view was the politics, which ultimately rendered the whole scheme null and void. His assignment, lasting from 1957 to 1960, coincided with the introduction of Guided Democracy and the ascendancy of Sukarno in Jakartan as in national affairs. Staff changes occurred on the whim of the

President; Sukarno imposed his own priorities on the planning team. The biggest such distraction was the Asian Games, due to be held in Jakarta in 1962. Since the President was determined to make this the biggest and most successful Games ever, large projects were begun to prepare the city for international eyes. Jalan Thamrin and Jalan Sudirman had to be completed, the Senayan Games Complex, Hotel Indonesia and the Jakarta Bypass built. Although the funds for these projects and planning help came from the Japanese, Americans and Russians, implementation depended on trained personnel in Jakarta. Several members of the Master Plan team were seconded, including the only qualified traffic engineer in Indonesia.

By 1960, the Master Plan was essentially finished but it was impossible to get it discussed and approved. Many qualified staff were otherwise engaged and most government officials did not want to make any decision for fear it would meet with Sukarno's disapproval. The Master Plan was simply allowed to slip into oblivion, very like the concurrent Five Year Plan for Indonesia's economic development which was never implemented.

In retrospect, it seems that Jakartans had reason to be grateful that at least some of the planning of these years was not carried through. Plans were concocted totally without consultation with those likely to be affected. Sudiro, Mayor during the period of the Outline Plan, acknowledged the great difficulties in planning for a city undergoing rapid transformation; in these circumstances, he stated, it was hard to know the wishes and needs of Jakarta's citizens, especially those newly arrived from the countryside.[76] A major problem area was the future of the *kampung*, where most Jakartans lived. Significantly, the Master Plan avoided this issue. It aimed to spend about 11 per cent of its budget on housing, which it admitted was quite inadequate: it would provide about 1,000 houses each year, when about 14,000 were required. And housing expenditure would include a 'slum clearance programme'—an ominous note, since this would involve the destruction of more houses. As for existing *kampung*, it is not clear what was to become of them apart from their possible demolition. The planners knew that money was just not available to rehouse *kampung*-dwellers in the type of houses they proposed to build.

The main planner of the Guided Democracy period, President Sukarno, had a fancy for multi-storey buildings, which Jakarta could scarcely afford. His insistence that all construction along Jalan Thamrin be at least five storeys high held up building there for a long time, since most government departments which owned the land could not comply with the demand.[77] He also favoured slum clearance and rehousing of people in high-rise buildings. Apparently he believed that this was the 'modern' thing to do, since it was happening in Western cities and some developing countries like Singapore. (During the Crush Malaysia campaign, Sukarno was particularly anxious that Jakarta should outstrip Singapore.) He waxed lyrical about the sense of pride which young Indonesian builders would feel when they were able to 'build more sky-scrapers, more parks, more hospitals, more schools and clear more slums ...'.[78] There can be no clearer expression of the 'architect's dream' approach to city planning, oblivious of the economic or social consequences. It was perhaps a blessing that Sukarno's vision of Jakarta was not fulfilled: as it was, *kampung*-dwellers in the 1950s and early 1960s escaped the experiments which other large cities were doing in slum clearance and high-rise apartment building, experiments which proved very costly in financial and human terms and which many of them came to regret. Multi-storey office blocks and hotels began to be built in Jakarta, but the profile of the city's housing remained low: two- to four-storey apartment blocks for departmental accommodation were the main exceptions.

Contentious Years

The intrusion of politics into urban planning, which exasperated the technocrats, was unavoidable in Sukarno's Jakarta. The fifteen years after independence were intensely political, dominated as they were by party rivalry under parliamentary democracy and the President's own strenuous variety of politics during Guided Democracy. Sukarno always maintained that party politics were divisive, whereas his leadership united the people behind the national Revolution. What effect did politics have on Jakarta life during these years?

Before the introduction of Guided Democracy in 1958, there certainly was political party infighting within the Municipal Council, rivalry which grew stronger as the 1955 general elections approached. Resentment was felt by some parties against the Mayor, Sudiro, who quite openly belonged to the secular nationalist party, Partai Nasionalis Indonesia (PNI), in a city where, as the 1955 elections revealed, only about one-fifth of the population supported that party.[79] In that election and the municipal poll of 1957, Jakartans gave stronger support to the Islamic parties Masyumi (29 per cent of the vote in 1955) and Nahdatul Ulama (17 per cent in 1955).[80]

In the long lead up to the 1955 elections, the Jakarta population was given a thorough political wooing. Parties moved into the *kampung* for local meetings and decorated the city with their posters, banners and daubed slogans. The PKI was the most active at the *kampung* level, using social welfare work as well as direct electioneering as a means of winning mass support. Members helped to clean streets and drains, and constructed public privies and bathing-places. Communist election manifestos were carefully worded to cover local issues. The reward was reaped in the 1957 municipal election in Jakarta, when the PKI improved its vote at the expense of all other parties: with 19 per cent of the total it became the second largest party in the city after Masyumi.

Not just parties but also governments aimed to involve people in politics. For instance, the Government wanted to assemble crowds for rallies to support its campaign to win back West Irian: an enormous rally involving about one million people took place on this issue in 1957.[81] At the local government level, Mayor Sudiro launched a strong campaign to organize *kampung*-dwellers through the formation of Rukun Tetangga and Rukun Kampung (neighbourhood and *kampung* associations) which were to serve as the lowest rung of the municipal administration in an informal way: the leaders of these associations (*lurah* and *kepala kampung*) were locally elected although they were expected to assist the government authorities. In setting up this structure in 1954, Sudiro hoped to encourage the co-operative spirit in *kampung*; in particular, voluntary labour was wanted for local projects like road making.[82]

The trouble was, of course, that the authorities liked political mobilization which they controlled for their own purposes, but found it irksome when people organized against them. Then they spoke of political manipulation of the ignorant masses. What is particularly interesting about politics in Jakarta in the 1950s is that it was the only time in the city's history when ordinary Indonesians were free to express themselves: to join the party of their choice, to vote for it at elections; to publish their views without much censorship; to hold meetings and rallies; and to form deputations on various issues. Although the parties certainly attempted to turn these opportunities to their own advantage, they also had to respond to local wishes if they wanted support. So ordinary people used the parties as well as the reverse.

During the 1950s there were many examples of Jakartans getting organized and using political channels to present their views. Trade unions were one such method. Although unionism was not strong in Jakarta due to the continuing backwardness of the economy and oversupply of labour, trade unions were important to the life of some *kampung*. In the railway workers' *kampung* mentioned earlier, from 1955 onwards local factions became identified with particular unions which, like all unions, were associated with political parties. Most railway workers were members of the PKI-dominated union, probably because it represented their interests more vigorously than did others. Unions were just one of the large number of voluntary organizations which mushroomed in these years: women's groups also made great efforts to draw women more into public life and to win members by offering a range of services like literacy courses, women's banks and credit co-operatives.

The Municipal Council also served to channel political interests. It was by no means representative of the Jakartan population: in 1957, for instance, among forty-three members only six were women and few were born in Jakarta.[83] However, the points of view of identifiable *kampung* groups came through to Council level, to such an extent that Mayor Sudiro (1953–60) commented rather ruefully: 'The revolutionary spirit burned fiercely in Jakarta: there were always hot debates in the meetings of the provisional representative council of Jakarta. Everyone defended the rights of an independent people which had to be held in high esteem.'[84]

One example was the case of Krekot Bunder.[85] This area close to the busy commercial centre of Pasar Baru had, during the colonial period, been a private estate owned by the Chinese Council. In July 1952, a huge fire destroyed two *kampung* in Krekot Bunder. The Municipal Government, seeing a chance to renew a depressed area, bought up the land and announced a special plan involving a new street joining Pasar Baru with Jalan Lautze, a street which was to be lined with multi-storey buildings.

In the meantime, the former inhabitants were temporarily accommodated elsewhere, having been promised new housing in their old *kampung*. By 1955, still nothing had been done for these people, who feared they would be unable to return because they were unable to afford the kind of buildings specified in the new plan. The grievances of these *kampung*-dwellers were very eloquently voiced in the Municipal Council: members of several factions supported their case, pointing to the proud history of resistance which Krekot Bunder had had during the period 1945–9 when its *pemuda* had fought and died for the Republic in the hope that *Merdeka* would bring a better life. Now, said Council members, the redevelopment of Krekot Bunder had forced out the poor *kampung*-dwellers in favour of wealthy foreign traders (presumably Chinese and Indian) who could afford the 'luxurious' buildings on the new street. The Municipal Government agreed to look into the case of the displaced fire victims. This was one occasion where the Municipal Government, which favoured multi-storey accommodation for high-density areas, was resisted by the Council.

This kind of representation of local interests seems perfectly legitimate in municipal politics, however much of a nuisance it might appear to people in power. What was more questionable was the disturbance caused to Jakarta life by national politics. The city became the forum for playing out national rivalries, often subjecting Jakarta to great tension and uncertainty. There was, for instance, the so-called 'October 17 Affair' of 1952 when a large demonstration outside the President's Palace, backed by army tanks and guns, tried to pressure Sukarno into dissolving parliament. He refused, defying what was really an expression of military frustration at civilian politics. On this occasion a military leader made use of contacts among some *kampung* organizations to rally a large crowd. Although the affair fizzled out in a few days, it caused considerable tension in the city. At the end of 1956, there were large rallies and attacks on the British Embassy library in connection with the Suez dispute. In early 1957, Sukarno first aired his idea of Guided Democracy, which was met with mass demonstrations for and against; supporters daubed the city with slogans. In the same year the city was rocked by an attempted assassination of the President at Cikini.[86]

Having decided to dissolve parliament, Sukarno and his supporters amongst the army and the parties (the PNI, PKI and NU) orchestrated the introduction of Guided Democracy. For Jakarta it meant the decline of local politics in favour of heightened fervour for national issues. Masyumi, which had been the most popular party in Jakarta, was banned, largely because of its involvement in the Sumatran rebellion. The power and representativeness of the Municipal Council was reduced when Sukarno restructured both national and local institutions to diminish the role of parties and increase central control. In 1960, the power of the Jakarta Mayor, now renamed Governor, was increased, and he in turn was brought more firmly under the President's direction. Sukarno began to resemble the Governors-General of Dutch times. Like the viceroys of eighteenth-century Batavia his retinue was immense, and it was impossible for anyone to survive publicly without his personal approval. Sukarno appointed a new team for Jakarta which seemed to encapsulate the politics of Guided Democracy: the new Governor in 1960 was an army man, Sumarno, and his deputy was Henk Ngantung who was nominated by PKI members of the Council. This looked like a balance of the two main forces—the army and the communists—who supported the President and vied for the succession. Significantly, just as the President became increasingly radical in his speeches in later years, in 1964 Ngantung was promoted to the governorship.[87]

Having replaced parliamentary democracy with his own brand of authoritarian politics, did Sukarno manage to put into practice his ideals for Jakarta? He was successful in having some large projects constructed or at least begun, but once resources had been diverted to big monuments it was much harder to carry out more mundane tasks which were necessary to fulfil Jakartans' material and spiritual needs in the way he wished. Henk Ngantung, Sukarno's Jakarta man, was painfully aware of this. He recalled later that Sukarno believed that anything could be done simply by decreeing it. Although in fact nothing could be done in those days without the President's authority, that did not ensure execution. Ngantung recounted a dressing-down he had received from the President in mid-1965. Sukarno asked him why he had not carried out the President's order to requisition private trucks in Jakarta to dispose of rubbish when there was a shortage of municipal trucks due to breakdowns and lack of spare parts. Before Ngantung had a chance to answer, Sukarno added sharply, 'You mustn't consult with people too much!' Ngantung did not retort but reflected rather bitterly that if he had done the 'easy thing' by using all the authority of the 'President, Highest Commander, Great Leader of the Revolution and so forth' (using Sukarno's many titles), then it would have been quite counter-productive: private trucks would simply have vanished from Jakarta. He knew this from what had happened to rice in the city at the beginning of that year. Rice prices had risen steeply with inflation, and delegations and demonstrations demanded a re-duction in the price of daily needs. When the Government intervened to arrest traders selling above the fixed price, rice just disappeared from the market altogether. Ngantung preferred to confer with those concerned in order to avoid that kind of reaction.

Meanwhile, Sukarno's desire to mobilize the population on what he regarded as crucial national issues involved frequent large rallies and political campaigns in Jakarta.[88] The city became a theatre for huge meetings held to show solidarity for liberating West Irian and crushing Malaysia (opposed as a British neo-colonial conspiracy). Most grandiose of all was the staging of the Asian Games and the Games of the New Emerging Forces in 1962 and 1963 respectively, which gave Sukarno a new forum for speech-making: the huge stadium at Senayan where he could play on the emotions of 100,000 people. Popular frenzy was whipped up against first the Dutch, then the British and Malayan govern-ments, resulting in the burning of the British Embassy in Sep-tember 1963. Huge banners with slogans such as 'Hail Bung Karno—Father of the Revolution' and 'Crush Every Form of Imperialism' hung across the main streets. Women volunteers (*Sukarelawati*) marched and drilled in uniform in the streets as part of the heightened defence awareness: Indonesia was con-sidered a nation under threat from imperialist powers. All of this represented a considerable drain on urban resources. How, pondered Ngantung despairingly, was it possible to deal with a crisis in public transport when all available buses were com-mandeered to take people to a big Government rally?

In this atmosphere of 'living dangerously' as Sukarno put it in his speeches, an Australian visitor, Maslyn Williams, noted the reactions of some Jakartans. Peak hour traffic to work was brought to a halt, but this time not for Sumarno's clean-up. Williams heard rifle shots, mortar shells exploding and whistles being blown, and learned that this was an army exercise: quite a normal thing, to judge by the bored looks of passengers. The traffic stopped for half an hour while soldiers in camouflage used the vehicles as cover. On being told by a soldier that the objective of the exercise was to capture the telephone exchange, an Indonesian official in Williams' car said, 'They are crazy. This telephone exchange is a very inefficient installation. Whoever holds it will be handicapped and lose the battle.'[89]

It was possible for Jakartans to regard these exercises and big political demonstrations with indulgence or cynicism (although the President's speeches thrilled most listeners). What was harder to ignore was political feuding in the work-place, which reached worrying dimensions in these years of Guided Democracy.[90] From 1960 onwards, campaigns were waged to bring all civil servants into line with Sukarno's stated policy of MANIPOL-Usdek, one of the era's many acronyms, which summarized the President's ideology; amongst other things this ideology amalgamated Nationalism, Islam and Communism. Calls were made to 'retool' (remove from office) people and organizations suspected of diverging from this line. Indoctrination committees were set up in government departments and civil servants were required to undergo short indoctrination courses. The Municipal Government was bombarded with telegrams, letters and deputations demanding the 'retooling' of this or that local official. At the University of Indonesia academics lost their positions when staff were 'purged'. Newspapers were censored so heavily that they did little more than carry Government propaganda; the city became rife with rumours as an alternative news medium. Bitter political divisions reached some *kampung* too. The railway workers' *kampung* mentioned previously in this chapter was split into two main factions aligned with communist and anti-communist unions. The latter was aided by the army which gave it considerable resources for recruitment. Inflation meant that workers became increasingly dependent on material benefits which their unions could provide.

The whole system lurched towards a crisis in 1965. Inflation reached bizarre levels in that year, corruption mounted and the bureaucracy ground to a near halt. Sukarno's rhetoric became ever shriller, ever more revolutionary, painting Indonesia as a nation defying the wicked imperialists who were doing their best to isolate and destroy her. The army and the PKI eyed each other nervously, jockeying for position and wondering what would happen when Sukarno died, as no plans for succession had been made. Since Sukarno's health appeared to be deteriorating rapidly, this was a matter for urgent concern. By this time, the army and the communists were mortal enemies and whoever seized power would surely cripple if not eliminate the other.

The End of Sukarno's Rule

This was the background to the attempted coup of 30 September 1965.[91] The details of that event are still subject to heated debate, but its effects on Jakarta are clear enough. The main events of the first days occurred in the capital. Elements of the presidential palace guard, the army and the air force captured the radio station and kidnapped six of Indonesia's top generals in the city. The generals were murdered and their bodies buried at the air force base at Halim on Jakarta's outskirts. The radio announced that Colonel Untung had taken command, that the coup perpetrators were loyal to Sukarno and that they had acted to prevent a coup by a 'Council of Generals', a counter-revolutionary body disloyal to the President. That was as far as the coup went. General Suharto, a lesser-known army leader, took charge of the situation and recaptured installations taken by the rebels. The Untung coup was over in Jakarta in twenty-four hours but the Suharto coup had just begun.

From the start, Suharto charged the PKI with masterminding the coup. The party's Jakarta daily, *Harian Rakjat*, indeed issued an editorial supporting Untung and some Communist Party members and sympathizers who had been drilling at Halim at the time of the generals' death had been involved in their murder. This was sufficient for Suharto to lay responsibility at the party's door. The President was silent on the matter and left Jakarta for Bogor on the night of 1 October. Whether he was implicated in the coup is not known, but his presence at Halim during the day certainly condemned him in the eyes of Suharto and the army, whose leading generals had been killed there. Suharto staged a grand state funeral for the murdered generals on 5 October. After a lying in state at the army headquarters on Merdeka Square, the funeral procession paraded slowly through the city streets to the cemetery. Two days later military leaders gave permission for a campaign against the communists. The first moves were against communist property in Jakarta: army units stood by and allowed crowds to burn the PKI headquarters on 7 October and later to attack other buildings of communist-related mass organizations.

This was just the beginning of an avalanche of anti-communist actions throughout Indonesia involving up to a million arrests, of whom perhaps half a million people were massacred and 200,000 interned. However, Jakarta was fortunate in being spared many of the horrors that were perpetrated elsewhere. Killings occurred mainly in rural areas; in the capital the army moved swiftly to make arrests, forestalling unbridled revenge. By the middle of November 1965, it was stated that about 2,200 PKI members and activists in organizations connected with the party had been arrested. Most of the unofficial anti-communist activity in Jakarta was directed against property, not persons. The fact that there were foreigners in the capital probably helped to cool the violence there. Sukarno tried to protect his erstwhile communist allies from the wrath of the army and other anti-PKI forces.

Although Sukarno was not formally relieved of his office until March 1967, it was clear that General Suharto held real power. The Sukarno period had come to an end. When he considered what had been achieved during his rule, as he did in his *Autobiography*, it is interesting to see the prominence that Sukarno gave to Jakarta:

Man does not live by bread alone. Although Djakarta's alleys are muddy and we lack roads, I have erected a brick-and-glass apartment building, a clover-leaf bridge, and our superhighway, the Djakarta Bypass, and I renamed the streets after our heroes: Djalan Diponegoro, Djalan Thamrin, Djalan Tjokroaminoto. I consider money for material symbols well spent. I must make Indonesians proud of themselves. They have cringed too long.[92]

But by late 1965 there was little to be proud of in Jakarta. Like the President's grandiose and ill-founded dreams, the skeletons of his unfinished monuments towered above slums and rotting refuse.

---

1. On Sukarno's life, see J. D. Legge, *Sukarno: A Political Biography*, Harmondsworth, Penguin, 1972, p. 77.

2. *Peringatan Ulang-Tahun ke-435 Kota Djakarta*, Djakarta, Pemerintah DKI, 1962, pp. 27, 30.

3. On Sukarno's relations with artists, see Soedarmadji J. H. Damais (editor), *Bung Karno dan Seni*, Jakarta, Yayasan Bung Karno, 1979.

4. For Sukarno's views on the Lapangan Merdeka, see *Republik Indonesia: Kotapradja Djakarta Raya*, p. 561.

5. Ngantung's official memoirs, like those of other Jakarta Mayors and Governors before 1966, are found in *Karya Jaya: Kenang-kenangan Lima Kepala Daerah Jakarta 1945-1966*, Jakarta, Pemerintah DKI, 1977, pp. 149-96.

6. *Djakarta Dalam Angka Tahun 1969*, Djakarta, Kantor Sensus dan Statistik, 1969, p. 7.

7. H. J. Heeren, 'The Urbanisation of Djakarta', *Ekonomi dan Keuangan Indonesia*, Vol. 8, No. 11, 1955.

8. On the rebels around Jakarta, see C. van Dijk, *Rebellion under the Banner of Islam*, The Hague, Nijhoff, 1981, pp. 102-7.

9. *Madjalah Kotapradja*, 30/2/1953.

10. Kenneth Watts, 'The Planning of Greater Djakarta: A Case Study of Regional Planning', *Ekistics*, No. 10, 1960, p. 402.

11. K. Watts, R. S. Danunagoro and L. O'Brien, *Rentjana Pendahuluan/ Outline Plan Djakarta Raya*, Djakarta, Kotapradja Djakarta Raja, 1957, p. 16.

12. S. Djauhari, 'The Capital City 1942-1967', *Masalah Bangunan*, Vol. 14, No. 1-2, 1969, p. 10.

13. Ayip Rosidi is cited in Burton Raffel, *The Development of Modern Indonesian Poetry*, New York, State University of New York Press, 1967, p. 257.

14. Official statistics on housing come from *Republik Indonesia*, p. 300; *Merdeka*, 25/10/1957; and Watts *et al.*, op. cit., pp. 13-14.

15. On fires in Jakarta, see *Madjalah Kotapradja*, 15/1/1953 and *Djakarta Dalam Angka Tahun 1969*.

16. On rubbish and sewage disposal, see *Madjalah Kotapradja*, 15/1/1953 and 28/2/1955.

17. On electricity and telephone services, see *Karya Jaya*, p. 65, and *Republik Indonesia*, p. 292.

18. Willard Hanna, *Bung Karno's Indonesia*, New York, American Universities Field Staff Report Series, 1961, letter of 29/10/1959.

19. Tjalie Robinson, *Piekerans van een Straatslijper*, p. 33.

20. On trams in Jakarta, see H. J. A. Duparc, *De Elektrische Stadstrams op Java*, pp. 26-8 and *Karya Jaya*, pp. 97-8.

21. Statistics on transport come from *Republik Indonesia*, p. 272; Watts *et al.*, op. cit., p. 18; and S. V. Sethuraman, *Jakarta, Urban Development and Employment*, Geneva, International Labour Organization, 1976, p. 23.

22. On urban government, see The Liang Gie, *Sedjarah Pemerintahan Kota Djakarta*, Chapter 9 and *Karya Jaya*.

23. Information on Jakarta finances comes from Djauhari, op. cit., p. 10 and *Karya Jaya*, p. 129.

24. Statistics on education come from *Djakarta Dewasa Ini*, Djakarta, Kotapradja Djakarta Raja, 1957, second edition, pp. 186-7; *Karya Jaya*, p. 262; *Sensus Penduduk 1961*, pp. 24-9; and *Djakarta Dewasa Ini*, p. 187.

25. Information on health comes from *Republik Indonesia*, pp. 401-8.

26. Watts *et al.*, op. cit., p. 30.

27. On Sumarno's health campaigns, see *Karya Jaya*, pp. 223-5.

28. Mortality statistics are from *Madjalah Kotapradja*, 30/4/1955 and Widjojo Nitisastro, *Population Trends in Indonesia*, p. 108.

29. R. Mochtar and R. Soedarjono, 'A General Public Health Survey within the Demonstration and Study Centre for Public Health and Preventive Medicine in Djakarta-City', *Madjalah Kedokteran Indonesia*, Vol. 7, No. 12, 1957, pp. 375–99.

30. J. W. Tesch, *The Hygiene Study Ward Centre at Batavia*.

31. Some information on Jakarta's privileged economic position is given in Willard Hanna, *Letters on Current Developments in Indonesia*, New York, American Universities Field Staff Reports Series, 1956, letter of 28/2/1957, p. 16.

32. Alisjahbana is cited in Herbert Feith and Lance Castles (editors), *Indonesian Political Thinking 1945–1965*, Ithaca, Cornell University Press, 1970, p. 322.

33. On the campaign to move the capital, see *Karya Jaya*, p. 94.

34. The section on Indonesianization of the economy is based on Ralph Anspach, 'Indonesia' in Frank H. Golay *et al.*, *Underdevelopment and Economic Nationalism in Southeast Asia*, Ithaca, Cornell University Press, 1969 and D. Sutter, *Indonesianisasi: Politics in a Changing Economy, 1940–1955*, Ithaca, 1959.

35. *Short Guide to Djakarta, Bogor, Bandung*, Djakarta, 1956, pp. 74–9.

36. Information on land ownership in Jakarta is from Sutter, op. cit., pp. 713–15 and *Republik Indonesia*, p. 330.

37. *Madjalah Kotapradja*, 15/10/1952.

38. Watts *et al.*, op. cit., p. 10.

39. The 1953–4 survey is Lembaga Penjelidikan Ekonomi dan Masjarakat, 'Penjelidikan Biaja Hidup di Djakarta', *Ekonomi dan Keuangan Indonesia*, Vol. 10, 1957, pp. 738–95. The 1937 survey was the Coolie Budget Survey in Batavia.

40. The Health Ministry reports are cited in Donald Hindley, *The Communist Party of Indonesia 1951–1963*, Berkeley, University of California Press, 1966, p. 16.

41. Information on inflation is from Herbert Feith, *The Decline of Constitutional Democracy in Indonesia*, Ithaca, Cornell University Press, 1962, pp. 377–8 and Anspach, op. cit., p. 198.

42. Lea Jellinek, 'The Birth and Death of a Jakarta Kampung', Ph.D. dissertation, Monash University, 1988.

43. On *sandang pandang* shops, see Rex Mortimer, *Indonesian Communism under Sukarno*, Ithaca, Cornell University Press, 1974, pp. 253–4.

44. Hanna, *Bung Karno's Indonesia*, letter of 25/9/1959.

45. On the Eurasians, see P. W. van der Veur, 'Eurasians of Indonesia: Castaways of Colonialism', *Pacific Affairs*, Vol. 27, 1954, pp. 124–37.

46. *Short Guide to Djakarta . . .*, p. 80.

47. *Sensus Penduduk 1961*, p. 9.

48. This section on the Chinese draws mainly on the following works: G. William Skinner, 'The Chinese Minority' in Ruth T. McVey (editor), *Indonesia*, New Haven, Hraf Press, 1967; Donald E. Willmott, *The National Status of the Chinese in Indonesia, 1900–1958*, Ithaca, Cornell University Press, 1961; and Mary F. Somers, *Peranakan Chinese Politics in Indonesia*, Ithaca, Cornell University Press, 1964.

49. Lance Castles, 'The Ethnic Profile of Djakarta', p. 175.

50. Biographical notes on the three Chinese Indonesians mentioned are found

in L. Suryadinata (editor), *Political Thinking of the Indonesian Chinese 1900–1977*, Singapore, Institute of Southeast Asian Studies, 1979 and *Madjalah Kotapradja*, Vol. 6, No. 11, 1957.

51. Feith, *Decline of Constitutional Democracy*, pp. 481–5.

52. On the Chinese press, see Charles A. Coppel, *Indonesian Chinese in Crisis*, Kuala Lumpur, Oxford University Press, 1983, p. 42.

53. The fate of Indonesian Chinese literature is discussed in John B. Kwee, 'Chinese Malay Literature of the Peranakan Chinese in Indonesia, 1880–1942', pp. 221–2.

54. *Djakarta Dewasa Ini*, p. 184.

55. C. Salmon and D. Lombard, *Les Chinois de Jakarta* pp. xxiv–xxv.

56. Lance Castles, 'The Ethnic Profile of Djakarta', p. 185.

57. On Betawi culture at this time, see *Djakarta Dewasa Ini*, pp. 182–4.

58. On the 'Senen Artists', see S. M. Ardan, 'In Memoriam: Sjuman Djaja (1934–1985)', *Indonesia*, No. 40, October 1985, pp. 123–6.

59. On migration to Jakarta, see Graeme J. Hugo, 'Population Mobility in West Java, Indonesia', Chapter 10.

60. On Minangkabau organizations in Jakarta, see Mochtar Naim, *Merantau. Pola Migrasi Suku Minangkabau*, Yogyakarta, Gadjah Mada University Press, 1979, p. 128, and on Batak organizations, Edward M. Bruner, 'Batak Ethnic Associations in Three Indonesian Cities', *Southwestern Journal of Anthropology*, Vol. 28, No. 3, 1972, pp. 207–29.

61. Dennis J. Cohen, 'Poverty and Development in Jakarta', Ph.D. dissertation, University of Wisconsin-Madison, 1975, pp. 124–30.

62. Tjalie Robinson, op. cit., pp. 21–5.

63. Pramudya Ananta Tur, 'Letter to a Friend from the Country', translated in *Quadrant*, September–October 1969, pp. 59–64.

64. Hatta is cited in Feith and Castles, op. cit., p. 289.

65. On the 'cross-boys', see *Merdeka*, 13/11/1957, 18/11/1957.

66. Cited in Raffel, op. cit., pp. 256–61.

67. Ayip Rosidi, *Djakarta Dalam Puisi Indonesia*, Djakarta, Dewan Kesenian Djakarta, 1972, p. 38.

68. A Western view of Jakarta is given in Hanna, *Letters on Current Developments in Indonesia*, letter of 24/9/1956 and Hanna, *Bung Karno's Indonesia*, letter of 29/10/1959.

69. Municipal action on land is discussed in *Karya Jaya*, p. 39.

70. *Madjalah Kotapradja*, 15/2/1953 and 15/3/1953.

71. References to land policies under Sumarno are from *Karya Jaya*, pp. 137, 139–41, 218–19.

72. References on *gelandangan* are from ibid., pp. 71–3, 177 and *Madjalah Kotapradja*, 15/2/1953.

73. On hawkers, see *Karya Jaya*, p. 142.

74. The case of *tanjidor* is given in *Madjalah Kotapradja*, 28/2/1955.

75. Sources used on the history of the Master Plan: G. H. Franklin, 'Assignment in Djakarta—a personal view of planning in Indonesia', *Royal Australian Planning Institute Journal*, Vol. 2, 1964, pp. 229–31; Watts, op. cit.; and Watts *et al.*, op. cit.

76. *Karya Jaya*, p. 117.

77. Ibid., p. 236.

214   JAKARTA: A HISTORY

78. Quoted in Ganis Harsono, *Recollections of an Indonesian Diplomat in the Sukarno Era*, St Lucia, University of Queensland Press, 1977, p. 266.

79. On resentment of Sudiro, see Feith, *Decline of Constitutional Democracy*, pp. 349–50.

80. Results of the 1955 and 1957 elections in Jakarta are to be found in Herbert Feith, *The Indonesian Elections of 1955*, Ithaca, Cornell University Press, 1957, p. 68 and *Harian Rakjat*, 10/7/1957.

81. *Karya Jaya*, p. 135.

82. Sudiro's organization of *kampung*-dwellers is described in *Madjalah Kotapradja*, 30/4/1955.

83. Ibid., 31/10/1957.

84. *Karya Jaya*, p. 107.

85. On the Krekot Bunder case, see ibid., p. 124 and *Notilen Dewan Perwakilan Kota Sementara Djakarta Raya*, minutes of meeting 17/3/1955.

86. Information on the events of 1952–7 comes from Feith, *Decline of Constitutional Democracy*, pp. 258–62, 508–9, 541–3 and 583.

87. Information on the administrations of Ngantung and Sumarno is from *Karya Jaya*.

88. For a description of Jakarta during the early 1960s, see ibid.; E. T. Pauker, 'Ganefo 1: Sports and Politics in Djakarta', *Asian Survey*, Vol. 5, 1965, pp. 171–85; Maslyn Williams, *Five Journeys from Jakarta*, Sydney, Collins, 1966; and Herbert Feith, 'The Dynamics of Guided Democracy' in McVey, *Indonesia*.

89. Williams, op. cit., pp. 23–4.

90. Information on the effect of politics on daily life comes from Feith, 'The Dynamics of Guided Democracy', pp. 368–72; *Karya Jaya*, p. 187; and Cohen, op. cit., pp. 142–4.

91. Description of events in Jakarta around the time of the coup is based on John Hughes, *Indonesian Upheaval*, New York, David McKay, 1967 and Harold Crouch, *The Army and Politics in Indonesia*, Ithaca, Cornell University Press, 1978.

92. Sukarno, *An Autobiography as told to Cindy Adams*, Hong Kong, Gunung Agung, 1966, p. 293.

6

Jakarta under Sadikin and His Successors: 1966–1985

Sadikin

ALI SADIKIN was Sukarno's parting gift to Jakarta. At the time of his appointment by Sukarno as Governor of Jakarta in April 1966, Major-General Ali Sadikin was thirty-nine years old and a former Minister of Marine Affairs in Sukarno's Cabinet. The odds seemed stacked against the city's new master. He was a Sukarno protégé, taking up his post in a period of rapid transition, when the President was under intense attack and the New Order Government of General Suharto was easing its way into office from a position of *de facto* control. Furthermore, Sadikin himself was not an army man but a marine, and the marines had a reputation of loyalty to Sukarno. Throughout 1966, big student demonstrations erupted in Jakarta, calling ever more impatiently for Sukarno's replacement. Anti-communist fervour mingled with indignation at the Government's economic mismanagement as prices of kerosene, bus fares, rice and other daily needs rose: the cost of living index in Jakarta increased more than tenfold over the period December 1965 to December 1967. The army collaborated with the student demonstrators, glad of assistance in discrediting Sukarno. By a series of steps, Sukarno was stripped of his powers, culminating in March 1967 when his lifetime presidency was revoked by parliament, and Suharto was declared Acting President—to be confirmed as full President a year later.

Despite this unpromising beginning, Sadikin settled in remarkably quickly and remained Governor until mid-1977, a far longer term of office than any previous incumbent. He was soon acknowledged to be the most successful governor Jakarta had had. Although his success was due in part to the rapid economic growth experienced under the New Order during his years of office, to some extent the personality and style of the man also contributed to his achievements.

A handsome, forceful man with a ready sense of the humorous and the dramatic, Sadikin was frequently described as charismatic. Certainly, when compared with President Suharto, he appeared vibrant and colourful. His rapport with people was immediate and his charm compelling, unlike the distant, pedestrian style of the President. Furthermore, Sadikin despised any semblance of feudalism, while Suharto favoured respect for harmony and status. The adjective 'hard' (keras) was often applied to Sadikin in recognition of his independent-mindedness and determination: he was quite prepared to meet conflict or criticism head on. His pious Muslim upbringing in West Java allowed him to feel at home with the religious leaders of Jakarta, but he prided himself also on his ability to enjoy modern dancing, modern art and the 'swinging' side of city life. Suharto must have tired of the continual invidious comparisons, the speculation that Sadikin might well follow—or even displace—him as president.

Comparison of Sadikin with Sukarno, on the other hand, reveals how inadequate it is to describe the former as charismatic. Sukarno depended heavily on pure charisma, defying all the restrictions of routine. With his armed forces training, Sadikin preferred order and good management, features of the rational, bureaucratic approach rather than the 'crash through' mentality of Sukarno. Efficiency was one of the qualities which he valued highly and towards which he tried to steer Jakarta.

Above all, Sadikin saw Jakarta as a Metropolitan City, in the English words (always with capital letters) so often used during these years. In many ways his vision was like Sukarno's: as the capital of a major nation, Jakarta was to be developed to become an equal of other great cities of the world. When asked about the standards which should be applied to the city, Sadikin replied that they were international: Jakarta should reach the level of Bangkok, Singapore or Manila.[1] The difference in approach between Sadikin and Sukarno lay in the fact that Sadikin saw this kind of development as necessary not merely for the sake of national pride but because Jakarta under the New Order was a centre of foreign investment. The city had to be able to offer foreign businessmen and tourists every convenience that they might find in Singapore or any other rival capital.

Pembangunan: The Era of Development

While inheriting many of Sukarno's dreams for Jakarta, Sadikin was much more fortunate in the economic conditions of his period of government. The New Order regime of President Suharto encouraged foreign investment at a time when world prices were rising rapidly for the country's main exports, notably minerals and timber. Foreign aid from the Western bloc was also available. Within only a few years, the technocrats of the New Order were able to turn the economy around. Inflation was checked and reduced to manageable proportions, and investment poured into the extraction of raw materials. As a major oil exporter, Indonesia profited from the jump in oil prices after 1973. Although the exports were produced mainly in Sumatra, Kalimantan and Irian Jaya, far from Jakarta, the city benefited indirectly from the massive increase in central government revenues from company taxes, and also from the fact that foreign investors set up offices in Jakarta, leading to a construction boom.

More than this, Jakarta attracted investment in its own right. Sadikin and the central government worked hard to promote the value of cheap labour and support services in the city. Over the period 1967 to 1971, Jakarta won 63 per cent of foreign investment projects in manufacturing (as distinct from extractive) enterprises, representing about half this kind of investment in Indonesia.[2]

With a greatly expanded tax base, it is not surprising that Jakarta's budgets grew dramatically during Sadikin's period as Governor. From Rp 1.2 billion in 1966–7, the municipal budget rose to Rp 89.5 billion in 1977–8.[3] Sadikin was operating under the most favourable financial conditions experienced by any ruler in Jakarta's history: if he could not create a prosperous city in a time of economic boom, when would it be possible?

The catchword of the New Order was *pembangunan* (development), which in Indonesia as in most countries seemed to be interpreted narrowly as construction and economic growth. It was the boom which enabled Sadikin to complete many of Sukarno's cherished projects and to begin new ones of his own. They transformed the face of the city. From a shabby sprawl relieved by a few scattered modern structures and a couple of pleasant

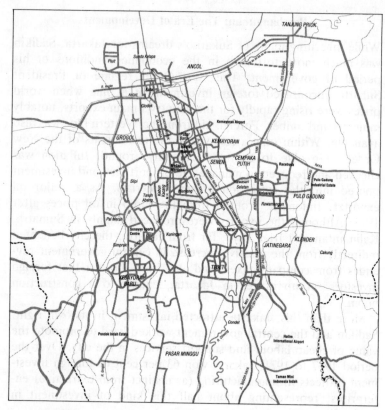

6.1 Jakarta in 1977 (Based on a map from Gunther W. Holtorf, *Falk Plan Jakarta*, Hamburg, Falk-Verlag, 1977)

residential areas, Jakarta became a reasonably well-regulated urban system with modern highways flanked by imposing buildings and several recreation centres. (See Map 6.1.)

Many of these projects had been planned by Sukarno, but it was Sadikin who found the funds and gained the credit for them. The gleaming white Istiqlal Mosque, overlooking the north-east corner of Medan Merdeka, was finally completed, as were the Ancol recreation complex, the parliament buildings at Senayan, and several new shopping centres which had received Sukarno's imprimatur. Sukarno's ideas were extended to cover further shopping centres and skyscrapers. Some projects bore Sadikin's personal stamp, like the cultural centre at Taman Ismail Marzuki, on the site of the old zoo which moved from Cikini to the southern outskirts of town. Another massive creation of the time, which was, however the conception of Mrs Suharto rather than of Sadikin, was the Taman Mini Indonesia Indah near the new international airport. When it was first announced, students attacked it as a waste of money; the final outcome was more modest than in the original plans and not as tasteless as many feared. It entertains visitors with representations of the different regions of the archipelago.

Apart from public investment, there was also considerable private construction during this period. Most spectacular were the multi-storey hotels which sprang up all over town, but principally along the Jalan Thamrin–Jalan Sudirman strip. The President Hotel, the Hilton and Kartika Plaza were joint ventures between Japanese or American capital and local entrepreneurs, which gave people with expense accounts accommodation of a standard to which international hotel chains had accustomed them. Less conspicuously, private companies found it profitable to build luxury housing for Jakarta's growing élite in salubrious new southern suburbs like Kuningan and Slipi.

Bricks, glass, concrete, and steel scaffolding provided part of what people admired in Sadikin's Jakarta. What was also appreciated was the smoother operation of city life as a result of his planning. Roads were repaired, widened, newly constructed and properly maintained, with traffic lights for better traffic flow. Public transport was greatly improved by the addition of hundreds of new buses, including minibuses from 1976 onwards, while a fleet of taxis and little motorized three-wheelers called *bajaj* also roamed the streets for custom.[4] Although still not able to keep pace with demand, the number of telephone installations and the supply of water and electricity grew remarkably during the Sadikin years. Television, begun in an experimental fashion in 1962, spread even into the *kampung*: in 1974, of the over 200,000 television sets registered in Indonesia, the capital had more than half.[5]

Sadikin strove to gain control of the city. In the municipal offices at Jalan Merdeka Selatan he put a large contingent of technocrats to work on planning Jakarta's development. A sleek twenty-storey glass building was erected to house them all. Never before had the city been so well researched, surveyed, analysed and tabulated. Plans rolled off the drawing-boards. The Jakarta Master Plan (1965–85), passed as law in 1967, aimed to tackle the city's problems in a systematic way and to plan future land use. It specified green belt areas to protect the environment, and centred modern industry in new zones, one south of the city on the road to Bogor and one in Pulo Gadung to the east, conveniently close to the harbour at Tanjung Priok. A plan for the greater Jakarta region predicted the spread of the metropolis into the surrounding provinces of Bogor, Tangerang and Bekasi and attempted to direct that growth.

Not only forward planning but also the financing of municipal development were challenges to which Sadikin responded in his usual dynamic way. When the central government failed to contribute to Jakarta on the scale he considered necessary and legitimate, he applied himself to better management of the city's own resources. Existing taxes were implemented more effectively and new ones were invented, earning Sadikin a reputation for financial originality. A lucrative new source of municipal revenue was found by legalizing and then taxing gambling (perhaps less new in reality in the light of colonial tax-farming). This made him unpopular not only with some military personnel who had previously profited from illegal gambling but also with the strong Muslim faction in the city, who considered his exploitation of vice as immoral. Under pressure, Sadikin abandoned one form of gambling (the Chinese game of Hwa Hwee) but persisted with others, challenging his critics to come up with some other way of funding the city's roads and hospitals. At its peak in 1968, revenue from gambling represented 29 per cent of Jakarta's budget.[6]

Hard-headed though he was, Sadikin did not look upon the city merely as a technocrat would: like Sukarno he also had an artist's eye. He, too, wanted Jakarta to be a place of beauty and culture. One welcome result was the effort put into tree-planting, which began to restore to some of the city's streets the shady comfort of old Batavia. The number of parks increased as he attempted to enforce the green belt areas of the Master Plan. Like Sukarno, he also enjoyed cultural pursuits, although his tastes were more catholic than the former President's. At the Taman Ismail Marzuki, old Betawi plays were revived alongside classical Javanese dance-dramas, foreign jazz bands and provocative works by modern Indonesian playwrights like W. S. Rendra. Exhibitions of batik painting alternated with avant-garde sculptures. A new art gallery (Balai Seni) was opened in the old Kota area in an urban conservation zone at Taman Fatahillah, where the restored Dutch town hall also reopened its doors as a museum of Jakarta.

Sadikin was the sponsor of culture, of urban conservation, of a more rational urban infrastructure, of grand new modern buildings: little wonder that he was extremely popular with Jakarta's growing middle classes, who could afford to appreciate the better things of life.

Managing Population Growth

Although Sadikin expressed confidence in the strength of the national culture when confronted with foreign influences,[7] he was far less certain of Jakarta's ability to survive as a Metropolitan City in the face of continuing waves of immigrants. While the economy grew, so did the city's population. Between 1966 and 1976 Jakarta grew from more than 3.6 million people to over 5.7 million, with only a negligible expansion of the municipal boundaries during that period. Between the censuses of 1961 and 1971, the annual increase was 4.5 per cent, giving Jakarta almost the fastest growth rate of any Indonesian city, exceeded only by two oil towns in the Outer Islands. Although the rate of growth from 1961 to 1971 was actually less than during the previous three decades, the sheer size of the population meant massive increases in absolute terms.[8]

Migration was now less important in Jakarta's growth than before. Whereas in 1961 less than half of the population was actually born in the city, by 1971 60 per cent was Jakarta-born. Like previous masters of Jakarta, Sadikin was concerned that most of the migrants from rural areas were out of place in a Metropolitan City. He even launched a campaign to 'Jakartanize Jakartans', by which he meant that Jakarta's citizens needed to adapt to metropolitan life.[9]

Population density was also rising to worrying levels in the inner city where from 400 to 700 people lived on each hectare in the early 1970s. In the same period, about 70,000 people squatted illegally on the city fringes or along canal banks and railway lines and around markets.[10] Most of the growing population, as usual, consisted of poor people without the wherewithal to participate in metropolitan life.

Sukarno had evaded the issue of Jakarta's poor, but Sadikin

attempted to deal with it. He tried several solutions, some of them new. One was to promote family planning as a means of cutting the birth rate, a notion rejected by Sukarno. Although sponsored enthusiastically by the New Order, the official pro- gramme began so late (1967) that it could not hope to make much impact in the short run; nor was it very popular among Jakartans.[11] Transmigration was explored as a policy alternative but never rigorously pursued, due partly to its expense. Not more than 3,000 transmigrants left the city in any year between 1971 and 1977: Sadikin insisted that transmigration was a responsibility of the central government.[12]

More spectacular as a solution was Sadikin's decision to de- clare Jakarta a 'closed city' for immigrants. In 1970, he decreed that all citizens must carry an identity card and only those who could thus prove that they were permanent residents would be permitted to live in Jakarta. Security teams were to conduct frequent raids to round up illegal immigrants who were to be returned to their place of origin. After the initial scare, it seems that this policy had little effect. Forging of identity cards was common, and many people sheltered new immigrants. Although the move had been hailed as a great new step in urban manage- ment, enforcement of the 'closed city' policy proved imposs- ible.[13]

Sadikin had to resign himself to a very large and growing population of urban poor. Interestingly, his main responses echoed those of the Dutch in Batavia of the 1920s and 1930s. He resorted to a combination of *kampung* improvement and the suppression of undesirable elements of the informal sector in which the urban poor were mainly engaged. Both had been tried on a small scale by the Dutch when the problem was much smaller.

Kampung improvement was the more positive solution. Sadikin was the first administrator since Dutch times to consider practical ways of improving the living conditions of the 60 to 80 per cent (estimates varied) of Jakarta's population who were *kampung*-dwellers. To his credit, he never seriously entertained Sukarno's fantasies of rehousing *kampung* people in blocks of multi-storey flats, a solution which would not have suited Jakarta's poor and which neither they nor the Jakarta Govern- ment could have afforded. He did experiment with 'site and services' housing on Jakarta's outskirts, aided by the World Bank which favoured that policy at the time. But relatively few poor people could pay for even that basic provision of serviced residential plots, and in any case the land was too far away from any likely source of work.[14] Like the Dutch, Sadikin also attempted to build special model housing for the poor but never managed to bring the cost down low enough. A sad example was the housing built at Muara Angke for fishermen in 1975. A year later it was reported that only 14 of the 360 simple houses were occupied, and those not by the fishermen who had formerly occupied the land but by relatively well-to-do boat owners and some civil servants. Unable to pay the deposit or the monthly instalments, ordinary fishermen squatted illegally nearby in much the same way as before the administration set out to rehouse them.[15]

The only effective way of improving the residential conditions of Jakarta's poor was through kampung improvement programmes of the kind which the Dutch had initiated, aimed at upgrading the physical environment of, and the services provided to, the kampung. Unlike the Dutch, the Jakarta Government under Sadikin tackled the kampung on a large scale, starting in 1969 and in 1974 gaining loans from the World Bank, which regarded the programme as 'an unparalleled socio-economic success'.[16] Appropriately, Sadikin named the scheme after Mohammed Husni Thamrin, the Orang Betawi who had so vehemently championed the cause of kampung-dwellers in the 1920s and 1930s. As in Dutch times, the programme was also a cheap one in terms of expenditure per head. Over the period 1969 to 1976, 166 kampung, comprising almost two million people, were upgraded at a cost of Rp 22,439,000,000 or about Rp 11,000 per head. Only in this way could as many people as possible share the benefits.[17]

As a result of the M. H. Thamrin Project, the appearance of kampung improved markedly. Admittedly, a visitor to some of the crowded inner kampung would find that hard to credit. For instance, in Kelurahan Tanah Sareal some lanes are unpaved and others could scarcely be narrower: house doors open directly onto passages about one metre wide. Kelurahan Duri contains many small factories which pollute the air and water. Further west, Kelurahan Angke makes a dismal impression: the canal here is very smelly, decorated every few metres with open privy-boxes balanced on stilts. People wash their clothes and even bathe in the same water, which is sluggish even in the rainy season.

Once the first adverse impressions have passed, however, one begins to notice the mark of the M. H. Thamrin Project in the form of weather-proofed paths and lined drains, and even more to the point, one begins to appreciate why the *kampung* are worth preserving from the point of view of the poor. For one thing, everyone here is not poverty-stricken. Flimsy timber and woven bamboo constructions stand next to solid brick two-storey newly painted houses with television antennas on their roofs. Small undistinguished buildings turn out to be *madrasah* (religious schools), prayer-houses and even mosques: the call to prayer, mercilessly amplified, sounds five times a day and the big drum is beaten for the Friday service. Even in these crowded precincts there is room for domestic animals: hens, ducks and goats wander in the lanes and over the rubbish heaps. These former villagers are also fond of pet birds, as can be seen from the occasional dovecot and the bird-cages which are hoisted aloft on poles to encourage their occupants to sing in the sunshine. Life in *kampung* is varied: they offer affordable shelter which is improved as people earn more.

Kampung themselves teem with opportunities for employment. *Pondok*, the boarding-houses first reported in the nineteenth century, are still to be found in the inner *kampung*. Sometimes just doss-houses, at other times they are centres of small enterprises. The owner may be a kerosene trader and his boarders, usually from the same village, fill the tins every morning, load them on each end of a shoulder-pole and sway off down the lanes, cawing: '*Minya-a-ak!*' Women sell goods and provide services from their homes while caring for children, and backyard workshops hum with the sounds of metalwork, carpentry and tailoring. By comparison with *kampung*, public housing is merely shelter, at a price which few of the poor can afford. The Kampung Improvement Programme represents a sensible choice to leave the *kampung* undisturbed and instead try to upgrade the environment.

The programme was judged so successful that it was extended in 1976 to Surabaya, Indonesia's second-largest city. Some of the details of the scheme were more debatable, and, to the Jakarta administration's credit, it altered the programme in later years to meet some criticisms. For instance, the fact that most money was spent in the first years on building roads was questioned on the grounds that most *kampung*-dwellers owned no vehicles but rather depended on footpaths within the *kampung*. Although the bulk of the budget continued to be spent on roads and footpaths, by 1975–6 the proportion spent on roads declined. Other services which were provided included lined drains, water hydrants, public laundry/toilet blocks and health clinics.[18]

The question of priorities continued to spark controversy. Although the programme declared that 'the worst should be improved first', it deliberately excluded the worst *kampung*: those built in illegal or unsafe areas, such as next to railway lines or canals. Indeed, houses in these areas were destined to be demolished. No solution at all was proposed for these people, the poorest in Jakarta. Observers were also puzzled by the low priority given to the provision of safe drinking water and disposal of rubbish and sewage. A World Bank consultant noted that almost half the residents of both improved and unimproved *kampung* were still buying water from vendors. Rubbish from *kampung* was inadequately collected (the head of the city Hygiene Department acknowledged in 1972 that only half of Jakarta's rubbish was being removed), and privies were too few and insanitary.[19] It is difficult to see the logic of providing health clinics while neglecting the very obvious environmental causes of common illnesses. Indeed, cholera continued to take its toll in Jakarta, although on a less alarming scale than in the nineteenth century.[20] On the other hand, some observers expressed surprise at how well *kampung* were provided with prayer-houses, mosques and local administration buildings under the programme.[21]

The trouble was that *kampung*-dwellers were not consulted about priorities.[22] Essentially the plans were imposed from above: only local heads, who were not directly elected by the people, were involved in planning. Lack of consultation also contributed to another problem, lack of maintenance. The planners considered their task ended once a *kampung* was 'improved'; maintenance of roads, drains and so on was the business of *kampung*-dwellers themselves. But few felt like maintaining what they had not chosen, more particularly in those cases where inappropriate services were provided, such as footpaths built well above ground level so they would not be flooded, and from which water ran off into the houses instead.[23]

On a broader front, the M. H. Thamrin Project looked strangely small compared with other expenditure in the city. A World Bank report questioned whether it was fair for only 15 to 20 per cent of the municipal budget to be spent on *kampung* where at least 60 per cent of the population lived.[24] Most of the rest of the budget went to services like roads, electricity and piped water which were mainly used by the more well-to-do. At the end of Sadikin's era, only 15 per cent of Jakartans could use piped water, yet this minority actually paid far less for water than did *kampung* residents.[25] Even education, which received a boost in Sadikin's budgets, could not reach the poorest: in 1971, just over half of the school-age children in Jakarta were attending school because there were simply not enough schools or teachers, and the costs of schooling were too high for many.[26] It also seemed strange that the Government provided heavily subsidized housing for public servants, who were far better paid than most *kampung*-dwellers. Raising these questions of equity in municipal expenditure brings a sense of *déjà vu*: from the colonial past comes the voice of a Jakartan who felt deeply on the subject—Mohammed Husni Thamrin himself.

It may seem churlish to scrutinize too closely a scheme which was a landmark in slum management in the Third World, yet the historical analogies are inescapable. It can be argued that, like the Dutch, the Jakarta administration chose the cheapest means of assisting the poor, so as not to jeopardize their concentration on building up the more visible parts of the city as a modern, international capital. And it was typical not only of the Sadikin regime but of the New Order Government in general that despite its best intentions of helping the poor, it did not feel obliged to consult them to find out what they needed most. It was enough to know that the capital had advanced greatly since Sukarno's time.

Land Clearance

While Sadikin was improving living conditions in the areas affected by the Kampung Improvement Programme, other policies were destroying the housing of many Jakartans without providing alternative accommodation.

The Master Plan specified areas which were either never to be built on (land set aside for roads, parks and so on) or which were to be cleared for special construction purposes such as industrial estates. Housing in these areas could be demolished when the land was thus required. A catch here was that, ostensibly in order to prevent land speculation, the details of the Plan were not made public, with the result that people could not be sure whether they were building on designated land. Nor was speculation deterred. Sadikin's era experienced a property boom which was fuelled partly by speculation on future development under the Master Plan. People with inside information bought up land before its future use was disclosed.[27]

In the 1970s, a series of land disputes received publicity in Jakarta. From time to time, the Governor ordered people in specified areas to leave, on pain of forcible removal. Usually they were offered removal expenses but no compensation, which, since most had no title to the land, they would have found difficult to claim. Ownership of only 35 per cent of Jakarta's plots of land was legally registered.[28] Most displaced Jakartans could claim compensation for property only, and because their housing (generally of timber and bamboo) could be dismantled, they were simply required to move it elsewhere. Rarely was an alternative site provided.

Land clearances were conducted like military operations. One of the worst occurred in November 1975 at Bendungan Hilir, an area which was intended to become a green belt zone. Security forces arrived at 10 p.m. and began demolishing houses. The inhabitants were caught by surprise. Although they had been warned to move, negotiations were still in progress over removal payments, and no date had been fixed for their departure. They watched as 250 houses were razed to the ground.[29]

Most victims of land clearance were too intimidated to do anything. Rarely did they protest, for very good reasons. In 1972, when the houses of 600 people in Kampung Rawasari Selatan were due to be demolished, a delegation of eight approached the mayor of the Central Jakarta district to make a written request to him. The eight were taken away by security police and questioned about their alleged relations with the banned Communist Party. The kampung inhabitants were given two weeks to demolish their own huts and leave the land, which was zoned as a green belt area. The mayor let it be known that the leader of the *kampung* delegation was a former political prisoner. That was quite sufficient to discredit the protest.[30]

The only recourse available to most people threatened with land clearance was the Legal Assistance Bureau, a body of lawyers established in Jakarta in 1970 by Adnan Buyung Nasution. A distinguished and eloquent Sumatran with an international reputation as a legal rights campaigner, Nasution was probably the best-known critic of the New Order. He was widely respected for his integrity, his expertise and his refusal to be silenced despite arrest and imprisonment. It is a credit to Governor Sadikin that he defended the work of the Bureau and even paid it a regular municipal subsidy although it was on occasions a gadfly to his administration. But there was relatively little that the Bureau could do in most disputes, since the cases were usually brought to it too late, after the demolition had occurred and the victims had been dispersed and demoralized. Because the municipal administration refused to take cases to court, the usual procedure was for the Legal Assistance Bureau to attempt to negotiate.[31]

One of the very few cases which reached a satisfactory conclusion in this fashion was that of Simpruk. A contracting company wanted to buy land in this district to build expensive houses, offering the occupants totally inadequate compensation. At the residents' request, the Legal Assistance Bureau intervened and was able to negotiate an agreement between the two parties. Not only did the company raise the land compensation considerably, but it also paid to move the people to a new area where alternative accommodation was provided. Although by the time the case was concluded many former residents had dispersed and were unable to receive compensation, at least some achieved satisfaction.

More typical was the case of Pondok Indah. Here also a company claimed an area of land for a complex which would include luxury housing, a shopping centre and a golf course on 300 hectares of land occupied by Orang Betawi farmers. Like the Simpruk scheme, it fitted the Master Plan and had official approval. When the owners of the land were offered a paltry sum for their property, they sought help from the Bureau. While negotiations were under way, a demolition squad moved in and tore down houses. Although the adverse publicity which followed shamed the company into offering further concessions to the owners, the latter were so numbed by the experience (one of them committed suicide) that they did not pursue the case with the Bureau. The victorious company, incidentally, had close connections with the ruling élite.

What was particularly unfair about so many of these land disputes was that no distinction was made between land seizure which might be justified by the public interest and that which was clearly for private profit, like the two cases just cited. It might be possible to persuade people to accept low compensation for land where a school was to be built, but not for luxury estates where developers made quick and handsome returns. And yet the apparatus of the city administration supported both kinds of demolition equally.

At the end of his term of office, Sadikin said that his heart almost failed him when he had to order a land clearance operation and that he never dared to witness one for fear that his resolve might weaken. Action was necessary, he said, in order that the public interest should be served. Unfortunately, it was not possible in most cases either to pay adequate compensation or to provide alternative housing sites: the municipality could not afford it. Nor could the administration allow these disputes to be fought out in court, since that would also waste both time and money.[32]

Street Clearance

If Sadikin had consulted *kampung*-dwellers he might have found what surveys in the Third World generally have shown about the urban poor, that what worries them most is not their environment but their inability to earn enough to support themselves.[33] It is a sad irony, then, that while living conditions were being improved in areas affected by the M. H. Thamrin Project, other policies were aimed at destroying the livelihood of many of the poor. In 1970, the year when Sadikin declared Jakarta a 'closed city', there also began a campaign against people who worked in various street-based occupations like *becak*-driving and street-vending.

There were two basic reasons for the municipal administrators' dislike of such occupations. Firstly, they harboured large numbers of migrants by offering an apparently endless variety of self-employed jobs for those with little skill or capital. If such work was discouraged, migration would diminish. Secondly, these workers did not suit the image of the new Metropolitan Jakarta. *Becak*-drivers cluttered up the streets, reducing the flow of motorized traffic and providing an embarrassing glimpse of the man-powered technology which lurked behind the thin facade of mechanization in Indonesia. A high-ranking municipal official said blandly that 'a characteristic of a metropolis is the disappearance of a variety of kinds of transport', as if that in itself was enough to condemn the *becak* to oblivion.[34] Similarly, hawkers congested the footpaths and created litter, like the abandoned banana-leaf plates around roadside foodstalls. This sort of eyesore could not be allowed in classy main streets like Jalan Thamrin, the so-called 'protocol areas' of Jakarta.

In 1970, there were 92,650 *becak* officially registered in Jakarta; unofficially their number was estimated at 150,000.[35] Propelled by at least two shifts a day, this would provide jobs for about 300,000 men, who could conservatively be expected to support another 900,000 people: altogether about 1,200,000 people were dependent on *becak*-driving. As a first step towards their gradual elimination, in 1970 Sadikin forbade the further manufacture of *becak*. In the following year he began restricting the areas in which they were permitted to operate. Police conducted raids on *becak* in prohibited areas and confiscated vehicles. Ali Sadikin commented, 'I really want to show newcomers that life in Jakarta isn't pleasant. It's like hell'.[36] In 1973 it was reported that the number of *becak* had fallen by one-third. To replace them, the *bajaj* was introduced—a little Indian-made passenger vehicle with a two-stroke engine.

Surveys indicated, however, that *becak* were not disappearing as fast as officially thought. Sadikin had underestimated two things. Firstly, the work continued because *becak*-drivers were determined to survive even if they had to compete in more restricted areas. They felt that they had no alternative. The driving licence and hiring fee required for *bajaj* were beyond most of them. Secondly, *becak* were popular with Jakartans. Bus transport was inadequate and operated only on main roads, far from the houses of most *kampung*-dwellers. Many small entrepreneurs relied on *becak* as a cheap way of carrying goods to and from markets. So *becak* persisted, under duress. They kept off main roads, where traffic was slowed down anyway by the rising tide of motor vehicles in Jakarta. Seven years after Sadikin had retired, officials estimated there were still 65,000 *becak* in the immediate region of Jakarta, indicating that most had moved to outer areas, where public transport was least satisfactory and police surveillance insignificant.[37]

In 1970, the authorities also began to clear pedlars off the pavements. As increasing numbers of new markets were built, the Government wished hawkers to move into them and stop cluttering up the streets. Hawkers complained that stall rents in the new multi-storey market buildings like those at Senen and Tanah Abang were too expensive. It was said that the new markets were dominated by Chinese and Arab traders. Moreover, as the authorities themselves admitted, there was simply not enough market space to accommodate all who wished to trade. Nevertheless, frequent raids were launched against pedlars, who were punished by fines and confiscation of goods. Policemen exploited the situation by demanding bribes to allow hawkers to continue their business. Although the authorities turned a blind eye to the overspill of pedlars onto streets around the new shopping centres, hawkers were evicted from the centre of town. A study of Kebun Kacang, a central city *kampung*, shows the hardship and frustration caused by the ban. With construction proceeding apace in the main street nearby, the people of Kebun Kacang enjoyed a thriving trade supplying small services and goods to building workers and the lower ranks of people employed in offices, banks and so on: those who could not afford to buy from bigger stores with high overheads, like the Sarinah Department Store where few came to buy but many entertained themselves on Jakarta's first escalator. Although the customers were there, Kebun Kacang hawkers were not permitted to serve them. After a short-lived boom, their incomes fell.[38]

Similar policies were pursued against prostitutes. The authorities reduced their numbers and concentrated them in special areas in the centre and north of the town, away from the better residential suburbs. On the other hand, 'modern-style' prostitution was acceptable: call-girls and massage parlours flourished.[39] Proving how 'swinging' he was, Sadikin also upgraded Jakarta's famous transvestites, the so-called *banci*: they were given a special go-go stand at the annual Jakarta Fair and even a charm contest at Taman Ismail Marzuki.[40] Like prostitutes, they became fashionable so long as they wore smart clothes, moved in the right circles and kept off the streets.

At the bottom of the heap were the *gelandangan*, those without a fixed abode.[41] According to the 1971 census there were 30,000 of them in Jakarta, but it was generally agreed that there were many more. They included the ubiquitous scavengers of Jakarta, who moved through the streets with fixed intent, plucking cigarette butts from the pavements with wooden tongs or rummaging in rubbish heaps for bottles, tins, paper: almost everything could be sold for recycling. In well-to-do suburbs like Kebayoran they circled in droves, with rattan baskets on their backs to carry the booty. Some *gelandangan* were beggars, of whom in 1977 there were still estimated to be about 5,000.[42] As in Sukarno's day but now more frequently, the *gelandangan* were hauled out of the makeshift shelters and underground drains where they made their homes and carted away to the outskirts of town. In 1975, there were two hundred such 'operations' against the *gelandangan*.[43] Some thousands were returned each year to their place of origin, at considerable public expense. In 1974, there occurred the first case of beggars being tried in court for contravening the law against begging: ninety-two were sentenced to a week in jail.[44]

For the many people eking out a living on the fringes of Jakarta society, it became ever harder to exist under Sadikin. From 1972, *becak*-drivers and petty traders were reporting sharply reduced incomes.[45] Questioned in 1977 about a possible replacement for Sadikin, a *becak*-driver said, 'I want a governor who can bring back a time like Sukarno gave us. We were free to make a living and to trade. Not like now: everywhere we're picked on.'[46] Efficiency was all very well for the better-off.

Rich and Poor

Sadikin's drive to rid the city of certain occupations would have been less callous if alternative employment had been created. The authorities certainly had this intention. According to the Master Plan for the city, one of the goals was the 'complete obliteration of unemployment by placing the unemployed into industry and other fields of occupation, including construction industry'.[47] Despite the construction boom and the new industrial zones, however, most Jakartans were not employed in the modern sector of the economy but continued to work mainly in the small-scale, undercapitalized and relatively unproductive enterprises of the kind which Sadikin was trying to discourage.[48] The modern industrial technology being imported into Jakarta could not provide large numbers of jobs. Indeed, local small entrepreneurs complained that the mass-manufactured goods from the new factories undermined their markets and thus reduced employment overall. Textile production was notorious in this respect. Competition for credit by foreign investors also forced up domestic interest rates, driving many local businesses to the wall.

The benefits of development in Jakarta were spread around very unequally. On the one hand, there is no doubt that the average Jakartan was much better off than other Indonesians: Jakarta was the wealthiest place in the country. Moreover, there seems to have been some improvement even in the lives of the poor during the Sadikin era. In the period 1970 to 1976 the expenditure of the lowest 40 per cent of the population increased by about 25 per cent in real terms. On the other hand, they were still very poor: low-income people were still spending more than half of their income on food. Moreover, the well-to-do did far better: in the same period 1970–6, the expenditure of the top 30 per cent increased by at least 50 per cent. The increasing gap between the rich and poor, found throughout Indonesia during this period, was seen in its most extreme form in Jakarta.[49].

Despite the Metropolitan City facade, it was impossible to ignore that gap. The most incongruous sight was the low mass of *kampung* which lapped at the feet of the skyscrapers of Jalan Thamrin and Jalan Sudirman. Although fences were built to hide these slums, no one was fooled. Standing on the terrace of the first floor of Sarinah Department Store, you could see across Jalan Thamrin the privies of Kampung Kebun Kacang perched precariously over the nearby canal. Jalan Thamrin itself impressed upon the pedestrian the planners' bias in favour of the well-to-do. Trudging down that hot and shadeless street, the footslogger soon realized that visitors were intended to sweep up to these banks, officers, hotels and embassies by car: even to cross the road was a major operation requiring the use of infrequent and steep overhead foot-bridges on which lurked crippled beggars.

The rich flaunted their wealth in all kinds of ways in Jakarta. About thirty night-clubs sprang up, some of them complete with casinos in which large amounts of money changed hands. This was one way of laundering 'hot' money, gained illegally through bribes and commissions.

Many of the newly rich were army men. The most famous corrupt general in Jakarta was Ibnu Sutowo, the director of the state oil company, Pertamina. For years he ran the organization as though it was his own personal empire, refusing to submit its accounts to public scrutiny. With considerable flair he built up a wide range of investments in many areas of the economy. Like any millionaire, he made generous public donations on behalf of Pertamina, among which in Jakarta were a hospital and a mosque. Sutowo's lavish life-style was the talk of Jakarta; for example, the town was agog at the wedding of his daughter in 1969, when almost the entire Jakarta élite was entertained in sumptuous fashion.[50] Finally, in 1975, a combination of Government efforts to gain control of Pertamina and the world economic recession undermined Pertamina's shaky international credit structure, forcing Sutowo to go into retirement. No one knew how much money he took with him, but some idea was gained in 1979 when it was revealed that a subordinate official in Pertamina named Thahir had died, leaving US$36,000,000 in just one of his bank accounts.[51]

It was difficult to see how public servants could become wealthy in legal ways considering how poorly they were paid. Those who reached the top and remained uncorrupted elicited special comment and suspicion from other members of the élite. A favourite Jakarta personality in this category was Hugeng Iman Santoso, chief of the national police. An engaging eccentric, Hugeng was best known for singing the falsetto lead in his Hawaiian music shows on radio and television; he was also fond of orang-utangs, which he kept as pets. But even more extraordinary in the Jakarta context, Hugeng was a hard-working and crime-hating policeman, whose pursuit of duty was his downfall. When he attempted to investigate car-smuggling activities at Tanjung Priok, he lost his job. His investigations were getting too close to people for whose influence and invulnerability he displayed too little respect.[52]

In some ways Ali Sadikin resembled Hugeng. During his term of office he whittled away the urban presence of the military.

They no longer controlled areas of Jakarta as they did in the late 1960s, when they interfered with traffic, took free bus rides and hung around on street corners casually nursing their weapons. Sadikin's conscientiousness and modest living was admired by the public and consequently distrusted by the national leadership. When he resigned as Governor in 1977 at the early age of fifty, Sadikin was replaced by an army man, General Cokropranolo, who was one of Suharto's personal advisers. No further public responsibilities were offered to Sadikin. Just as Hugeng had to content himself with his Hawaiian show, so Sadikin dwindled into being president of the Indonesian soccer federation.

Corrupt or not, the wealthy inhabited a different world from the majority of Jakarta's residents. Increasingly they adopted the trappings of international consumerism: Volvos or Mercedes Benz cars, supermarket shopping, American films in air-conditioned cinemas, horse-racing and games of golf. Beauty contests were the order of the day, as were pop bands thumping out the latest British or American hits. Women's magazines introduced Indonesian housewives to the world of Western feminine preoccupations: fashion, cuisine and marriage problems.

In this cosmopolitan culture, differences amongst the well-to-do tended to be submerged. The Chinese in particular continued to lose their distinctiveness, through choice or political pressure.[53] Now that the Government had banned their separate schools and press, many sought to assimilate as completely as possible by adopting Indonesian names and keeping the practice of traditional religion completely private, or abandoning it altogether in favour of Christianity or, to a lesser extent, Islam. Several prominent members of the Jakartan élite were Chinese who had changed their names, including Jusuf Wanandi (Lim Bian Kie), a leader of Golkar and an assistant to Major-General Ali Murtopo, and Arief Budiman (Soe Hok Djin), a student leader and intellectual.

The poor in Jakarta were more divided than the rich. Income differences in and between *kampung* grew. Some people and districts were better placed than others to profit from the construction boom and from factory jobs. For instance, the inner-city *kampung* of Kebun Kacang had ready access to building along nearby Jalan Thamrin: several of its members managed to succeed in the trading opportunities which resulted, leading to an awareness for the first time in the *kampung* of differences be-

tween the incomes of its inhabitants.[54] Ethnic divisions persisted
also, as new migrants sought compatriot communities and the
Orang Betawi in the outer *kampung* clung to their old culture,
insofar as they were not obliterated by land clearances or overwhelmed by newcomers.[55]

Yet some things drew the poor together. For one thing, almost
all of them spoke Bahasa Indonesia as their first language, a
remarkable fact considering that 40 per cent of the population
came from other linguistic regions. Secondly, a new kind of
popular culture began to emerge among the poorer sections of
society. Jakarta produced some trend-setting popular stars, including Benyamin S., Ellya, and Oma Irama.[56] A product of the
gambang kromong, clown style of Betawi theatre, Benyamin S.
sang and acted in comedy shows (and later films) with lyrics in
Jakartan dialect based on the everyday life of the *kampung*-
dweller and on themes from Betawi legends. Oma Irama and
Ellya rode to fame on the wave of *dangdut* music, a pulsating
rhythm which owed something to Malay pop and more to Hindi
film music. Many of their songs had a Betawi flavour. Flam-
boyantly dressed, Oma Irama made several musical films which
appealed to many traditional *kampung* values like attachment to
Islam. (He campaigned on behalf of the Muslim opposition in the
1977 and 1982 elections.) While the wealthy preferred pop songs
and films in the Western style, *kampung* people flocked to
shabby cinemas to see *dangdut* films and played the songs of
Oma Irama and Benyamin S. on the cheap cassette recorders
which were beginning to flood the markets. The Betawi cinematographer, Syuman Jaya, updated his earlier nostalgic film, *Si
Doel Anak Betawi*, with a new one, *Si Doel Anak Modern*, thus
sympathetically contrasting the Betawi experience of old and new
Jakarta.[57]

Despite the gulf between the rich and the poor, there were also
links between them in Jakarta. For instance, the poor were
accustomed to seeking patrons in the hope of finding a job or
gaining some small material benefit which would help to make
ends meet.[58] Young Jakartans all spoke Jakartan Malay, a dialect
of Bahasa Indonesia which borrowed from the old Betawi Malay
but had a distinctly modern, jazzy flavour. It was used by the
young as a lingua franca different from the native regional
languages of their parents or the stuffiness of the standard

Bahasa Indonesia used by authorities in school, work or in government.[59] The young were also united in their search for the Good Life. In the *kampung* as in the suburbs, consumerism spread: young people wanted not only radios and televisions, but also motor-cycles and smart clothes. To this extent, the ideal of the Metropolitan City had penetrated down to the lowest levels, whether or not it was within everyone's grasp.

Amongst intellectuals, the rush to buy revived the old debate about national identity and modern urban culture, although in a less vociferous way than during the Sukarno period. It was taken up most strongly by critics of the New Order like W. S. Rendra, who wrote the following verse in Jakarta in 1977:

We are dominated by the dream
of becoming other people.
We are strangers
in the land of our ancestors.
Dazed, the villagers chase dreams
and sell themselves to Jakarta.
Dazed, Jakartans chase dreams
and sell themselves to Japan,
Europe, and America.[60]

Politics in Abeyance

At Lubang Buaya on the southern outskirts of Jakarta, where the generals' bodies were thrown down a well during the attempted coup in 1965, a memorial was built in 1966. Dominated by a huge *garuda* with wings outstretched, it bears a frieze depicting events before and after the coup. 'Before' appears as a time of chaos, with men and women angrily gesticulating and debating. Then Suharto takes control—the symbol of reason and harmony. 'After' shows people quietly going about their business, under the protective eye of the military; women, significantly, are pictured only as gentle mothers. This was the ideological thrust of the New Order: stability and *pembangunan* and no politics—a complete reversal of the Sukarno period.

What this meant in Jakarta as elsewhere was that there were very few legal methods of expressing opposition to Government policies. Some parties, notably the PKI, had been banned; the remainder were soon forcibly merged into two uneasy groupings and the Government introduced its own political organization (which it insisted was not a party) called Golkar, made up of representatives of 'functional groups', including the army.

The results could be seen in the Jakarta regional assembly, the DPRD. Admittedly, Sukarno had already set the authoritarian tone when he introduced Guided Democracy, but the government of Jakarta in those days had been conducted in an atmosphere of political mobilization. Under Sadikin urban government was quiet and sedate. The Governor easily dominated meetings of the DPRD, where no open criticism of his policies was voiced. In 1977, the president of the assembly, a policeman, stated that differences of opinion were sorted out privately; if criticism was made public it 'could disrupt the peace and stability of society'.[61] Such words had historical overtones for those who remembered the colonial past.

True, the regime had begun in highly political circumstances. In 1966, Jakarta's streets had rung with the sounds of students demonstrating against Sukarno. These activities had been tolerated and even guided by the military because they had served a purpose at the time. As soon as Sukarno had been dislodged, students were instructed to return to their studies and to leave politics to their elders and betters. When disillusioned students attempted to criticize the Government for failing to curb corruption, they received short shrift. It was common practice for the Government to allow a certain level of dissent to build up in the columns of newspapers and in student meetings, and then suddenly to crack down with arrests and press closures, producing a period of inactivity.

There is no way of knowing how much political dissatisfaction lay dormant in Jakarta during the Sadikin years. Many people welcomed the relief from the constant politicking of the Sukarno era. Many others who benefited from economic advancement, including some *kampung*-dwellers, were content with the status quo. It should also be remembered that migrants to Jakarta, no matter how poor, felt that their conditions in the city were preferable to those in their place of origin.[62]

At the same time, dissent was dangerous. Memories of the aftermath of the 1965 coup—the arrests of communists and their sympathizers—hung over everyone. The employment prospects and even mobility of anyone at all tainted by involvement with the PKI were adversely affected, even assuming such a person was not already in prison. In a previous chapter mention was made of a community of railway workers which in the early 1960s was dominated by a Communist-led trade union. After 1965, this Jakarta *kampung* was described as subdued and intimidated. A vigorous anti-Communist had become the head of the *kampung*, which he controlled through a network of informers. At his behest the inhabitants contributed money for and built a prayer house to demonstrate that they were no longer associated with atheistic Communism.[63] Independent unionism ceased to exist.

Many of the frustrations of Jakartans were deflected away from the authorities. Sadly, those afflicted by Government moves against their livelihood sometimes responded by attacking other poor people. For instance, restrictions on *becak* resulted in some fierce clashes between *becak* men and the drivers of *bemo* and buses who inherited their lost passengers.[64] Sometimes the old scapegoats, the Chinese, were the main targets of criticism, especially during the early years of the New Order. In the wake of the coup, demonstrations raged against the communist Chinese Government for supporting the PKI. Although some Jakartan Chinese actually participated in the anti-Communist protests of 1966–7, in the eyes of most people the local Chinese were somehow linked with the People's Republic of China. It seemed to make no difference that in April 1966 a huge crowd of Indonesians of Chinese origin gathered in Jakarta to affirm their loyalty to Indonesia and to call for the breaking of diplomatic ties with Peking. In April 1967, there were heated disputes between Muslim youths and the Chinese: the former wrecked Chinese shops and beat up anyone who appeared Chinese. In attacks reminiscent of the events of 1740, Chinese were thrown into Jakarta's canals. On this occasion, fortunately, only a few deaths were recorded. As the new Government settled in, however, anti-Chinese feeling was brought under control. The military were too closely allied with Chinese businessmen to wish to brook much criticism of them. This meant, in the short run, greater security for the Chinese, although there were signs that too close an identification with government could carry its own risks, as the Chinese had already learnt from their relationship with the Dutch.[65]

That lesson was hammered home by the riots of January 1974, which broke the political lull in Jakarta. The riots were triggered off by the visit of the Japanese Prime Minister, Tanaka. Criticism of corruption and of the inequity inherent in the Government's development policies had been mounting in the months beforehand. Just before Tanaka's arrival, students in Jakarta met with Sadikin to raise fundamental questions about the future of the city. They argued that the city was being developed to serve the interests of foreigners and the rich, while the needs of the people at large were neglected. Sadikin made no reply.[66] Tanaka's visit focused attention on the conspicuous Japanese role in the Jakartan economy, especially the flood of Japanese consumer goods which were enjoyed by the more well-to-do. By extension, criticism of the Japanese also implied a protest against the Chinese who profited by selling Japanese goods, and against the élite who bought them. Political demonstrations by students greeted the Japanese Prime Minister, and the situation quickly deteriorated when unemployed *kampung* youths joined in and began burning and looting shops and cars. Significantly, the new Senen market complex which symbolized to many the displacement of small street-vendors by Chinese stall-owners, was badly damaged, as were night-clubs and car-yards. It was two days before the army gained the upper hand. In that time at least eleven people died and 137 were injured, while 522 cars and 117 buildings were damaged. The centres of disturbance were the main commercial areas of Glodok, Senen and Jalan Sudirman.[67]

Under Sadikin political dissent was never so clearly directed against the structure of society in Jakarta as it was in January 1974. Yet the undercurrents were there. Another straw in the wind was the way Jakartans voted in the 1971 and 1977 general elections.[68] As the seat of government, Jakarta was subjected to heavy propaganda from the Government political machine, Golkar, which won almost two-thirds of the national vote. Most Jakartans, however, gave their vote to opposition parties, especially to the Islamic parties, which contained the strongest critics of the Government. Perhaps this move against the national trend could be interpreted in part as an indication of the relative political freedom in Jakarta: the greater foreign presence in the city tended to reduce the overt pressure in favour of Golkar which affected voting elsewhere. In any case, the refusal to deliver a majority vote to the Government must also be seen as a sign of dissatisfaction with the New Order among many Jakartans. Significantly, even Ali Sadikin who, like all government officials, supported Golkar publicly, was noticeably un-enthusiastic about it in 1977.[69] Although many of his policies accorded with the thrust of New Order economic development, he did not identify completely with the Suharto élite: indeed, he was to turn against it in his retirement.

Sadikin's Dilemma

Sadikin represented the best example of New Order leadership at the urban level. The New Order encouraged entrepreneurship in the expectation that it would lead to economic growth, which would in turn provide benefits to the weak. Meanwhile, with the revenue earnings from the exploitation of natural resources, the Government would try to relieve the sufferings of the poor. Sadikin carried through this policy faithfully and efficiently in Jakarta, which experienced both rapid economic growth and a Kampung Improvement Programme.

There were, however, contradictions within the policy which Sadikin could not avoid. One of them was that the New Order was not whole-hearted about ensuring that the gains of the wealthy did 'trickle down' to the rest of society. Although Sadikin could point to certain hefty taxes on the wealthy, such as taxes on entertainment and car ownership, he was wary about introducing effective property taxation. A foreign taxation expert pointed out in 1972 that revenue in Jakarta from tax on land and buildings was on average only 2.5 to 4 per cent of all city revenue in previous years, whereas in other cities it was far higher: 24 per cent in Manila and 57 per cent in Calcutta. The same adviser estimated that the potential revenue from personal income tax in 1969–70 was Rp 189,000,000,000, but only 6 per cent of this amount was collected. Under pressure from the World Bank, the municipal administration began to tackle the question of taxation in the 1970s, yet for Sadikin it was obviously a political minefield. A high concentration of landholdings in Jakarta meant that the élite had strong vested interests in keeping property taxes low.[70]

Even more difficult for Sadikin was the knowledge that he could affect only the municipal scene, while the repercussions of national policies threatened to undo all his work. Immigrants swarmed into Jakarta because of insufficient employment in the countryside. The Green Revolution so enthusiastically promoted by the Government increased output but did not provide enough rural work to keep up with population growth. In fact, many of the wealthier farmers who profited from raised productivity used their earnings to introduce labour-saving methods like harvesting by sickle and rice-processing machines. Inequality grew in the countryside. Government public works schemes provided some additional employment, but still not enough. Under such conditions it was futile for Sadikin to declare Jakarta a closed city or to try to return homeless people to the villages.

Finally, Sadikin's own success in developing Jakarta was self-defeating. His dynamism and efficiency, aided by the Government's bias in favour of the city where most of them lived, made the city more attractive to investors and immigrants. Too much was concentrated in Jakarta: it took the lion's share of industrial investment, imports, upper ranks of the public service, and of registered vehicles, telephones and doctors. The gap between average incomes and expenditure in Jakarta and other towns, not to speak of that between Jakarta and rural areas, increased over the Sadikin period.[71] The pull of Jakarta grew, creating the overcrowding problems which so concerned Sadikin. If some of Jakarta's attractions had been spread more evenly over a number of other cities, the flood of immigrants would not have hit it so hard.

So long as there was continued economic growth which provided grounds for optimism and funds for government expenditure, it was not quite so difficult for Sadikin to keep at bay some of the ill-effects of inequality and overcrowding in Jakarta. But the bonanza could not last. The collapse of Pertamina in 1975 gave a foretaste of what was to come. When the oil company could not meet its financial commitments, many businesses in Jakarta struck severe financial trouble. For ordinary people this crisis and its impact on government finances meant a slowing-down in the construction and property boom and fewer commercial transactions. Workers were laid off.[72] Although foreign loans enabled Indonesia to recover from this setback, the question of what would happen when oil prices ceased to remain high was a daunting one, and the longer-term prospect of the exhaustion of oil reserves was virtually unthinkable. In the early 1980s OPEC was obliged to lower oil prices. Sadikin was fortunate to have retired in 1977 on a high note, before the economy turned sour.

Sadikin's Successors

After Sadikin, Jakarta had two governors up to 1986: Cokropranolo (1977–82) followed by Suprapto. Because neither made such a strong impact on the city as Sadikin did, little will be said about them here. Like Sadikin, both men came from the armed forces and from outside Jakarta.

Cokropranolo's term of office represented a slowing down of the pace of urban 'modernization' launched by Sadikin. Less favourable economic conditions undoubtedly contributed to this, but so also did the less dynamic style of Cokropranolo himself. Critics complained that 'development' flagged under his rule; others were grateful for his more lenient attitude towards the 'little people' of the city. He preferred to avoid confrontation and declared himself in favour of a 'social-religious' approach, which he claimed suited the values of Jakartans. As evidence of the new approach, he stated that he did not intend to make life harder for poor Jakartans but rather to help them work more productively. It is true that there were fewer evictions and land clearance under Cokropranolo, a source of dissatisfaction to those anxious for new construction opportunities. The authorities also seemed prepared to let street-traders and *becak*-drivers operate more freely than in Sadikin's time. Small-scale industry received some encouragement through the creation in 1979 of a Small Industry Region in Pulogadung and the provision of credit for home industries.[73]

On the other hand, there were several new urban developments under Cokropranolo which bore the Sadikin stamp, largely because most were first planned during the latter's term of office. For instance, in 1977 the Jakarta Export Processing Zone was occupied near Tanjung Priok, intended to be the first of several in Indonesia. Like such zones elsewhere in Asia, it contains factories producing garments and electronic goods exclusively for export by firms owned by foreign investors with some local equity. It introduced the new phenomenon of modern manufacturing jobs almost entirely for young women, although total employment is low (less the 8,000 in 1982).[74] Much smaller than its competitors overseas, the Jakarta Zone has the disadvantage of being a latecomer at a time when world trade is shrinking. Another innovation was the beginning of flat-building in Jakarta.

Starting as the provision of flats for the well-to-do, the movement spread until in 1978 the municipal construction company was planning blocks of cheap flats.[75] In 1980 four-storey blocks of flats were constructed in Kampung Kebun Kacang, ostensibly to house the former occupants of this inner-city *kampung*; however, most of them could not afford it and were forced to move elsewhere. As in earlier days, cheap public housing was still not cheap enough.[76]

The building of flats in the city centre was intended to check the depopulation of the centre and the relentless expansion of Jakarta. Planners considered that the city's continued southward thrust was jeopardizing the catchment areas for its water supply; it was therefore decided that denser growth should be encouraged.[77] In addition, Jakarta's planners were trying to tackle the city's growth on a wider regional basis. In 1977, the Jabotabek Metropolitan Development planning study was established with assistance from the World Bank to advise on the development of a Greater Jakarta Region which comprises the neighbouring areas of Jakarta, Bogor, Tangerang and Bekasi: hence the acronym Jabotabek. The intention is to relieve the pressure on Jakarta itself, but the outcome of this planning is uncertain. The Director of the Department of Public Works, which is responsible for urban planning, admitted in 1984 that the department was still unable to plan beyond immediate demands.[78]

As of 1986 it is difficult to assess the impact of Lieutenant-General Suprapto's governorship. An experienced administrator, he appears to share rather more of Sadikin's dash and decisiveness. Certainly he was not afraid to renew the crack-down on *becak*-drivers and illegal land occupation. Following a decree by him in February 1983, the number of *becak* in Jakarta fell significantly; in 1984, hundreds of homes were destroyed after forced evictions, and in late 1985, in the worst case of eviction in years, 5,000 squatters lost their shelter to make way for new luxury homes.[79]

'Modernization' of Jakarta continues along the lines set by Sadikin. Just as *becak* were intended to be abolished by decree, so from 1980 onwards the old *oplet* were phased out in favour of minibuses.[80] A fast new toll road from Jakarta to Tangerang was opened in 1984, and in the following year the international airport was moved from Halim to Cengkareng. Some spectacular plans have been drawn up to further improve urban infrastructure, but it is difficult to see how the heavy financial outlay entailed can be achieved or justified. For instance, the team charged with drafting a master plan for the Jabotabek region has advised that an adequate water supply for the capital would require investment equivalent to 60 per cent of all investment in water supply in Indonesia during the 1979–84 five-year plan. Similarly, the railway system designed for Jabotabek with Japanese assistance is estimated to cost over the period 1984–94 almost seven times the amount to be spent on all forms of public transport in Indonesia during the 1984–8 five-year plan.[81] Jakarta is only one (although much the biggest) of several large cities in Indonesia. Surabaya has two million inhabitants, and Bandung, Medan and Semarang each has more than one million. What would be left for them if such urban investment were to be lavished on the capital? And what of the 78 per cent of the Indonesian population who still live in rural areas?[82]

Efforts continue to be made to improve living conditions. The Kampung Improvement Programme, begun under Sadikin, has been further extended by his successors. Evaluations show that for *kampung*-dwellers the results of the programme, which is still restricted largely to roads,. drains and footpaths, are almost entirely beneficial.[83] The Kampung Improvement Programme has the great advantage of working with existing settlements; it is harder to find suitable accommodation for low-income people in newly developed sites. The National Housing Authority, created in 1974, attempts to provide public housing and sites-and-services projects to meet this need. These suffer from the perennial problem of the high price of land, which means that new housing closer to the centre is excessively dear, while the cheaper sites-and-services land at Klender, Cengkareng and Depok on the periphery is too far from employment for most people.[84] Flooding has been reduced by building the new Cakung and Cengkareng drains. But in 1984 urban authorities were obliged to admit that still only 30 per cent of the city's inhabitants were able to receive clean water; the rest simply could not afford it.[85] At the same time, the crime rate was reported to be rising.[86]

Larger forces beyond the control of municipal government are of some concern. As usual, population growth is a nagging problem. According to the 1980 census there were six and a half million people in Jakarta. This in fact represented a decline in growth: whereas between 1961 and 1971 the rate of increase had been 4.46 per cent per year, between 1971 and 1980 it had slowed to 3.93 per cent. The most recent increase cannot be accounted for by an expansion in municipal area, because the urban boundaries, after taking in about 10 per cent more space between 1961 and 1971, have not changed appreciably since then. Despite the falling growth rate, Jakarta's rulers are uncomfortably aware that the city is still predicted to reach at least 12 or possibly 15 million by the year 2000. By that time it is envisaged that the region of Jabotabek will comprise about 23 million people, or 30 million if growth fails to be controlled. The anticipated problems of administering that conurbation are immense.[87]

Apart from population growth, the other spectre which haunts Jakarta's planners is the economy. Since the oil boom of the 1970s, economic growth has slowed. As declining revenues from oil put pressure on the country's balance of payments, in 1983 the national Government was forced to cut back on public sector projects, including the building of roads and railways and the purchase of buses for Jakarta. In an attempt to make up for its own drop in investment, the Government has encouraged the private sector to boost its role in development. The trouble here has been that foreign investment generally has diminished, and the most active local private investment seems to be that of the Indonesian Chinese, which is politically embarrassing for a Government dedicated to promoting the 'economically weak' (i.e. indigenous) sector.[88]

The impact of slower economic growth has been felt by Jakartans. One piece of evidence is a study of construction workers' wages between 1979 and 1983 which showed some increase in real wages amongst most skilled employees, but little change for the majority of lower level workers.[89]

Recent Political Developments

Politically, Jakarta has been an eventful place in recent years, although the significance of those events for the city itself is harder to measure. As usual, the capital has been the arena for national skirmishes. Leading up to the 1982 general elections there was a remarkably agitated campaign in Jakarta. At two campaign meetings, in March and April, supporters of the Islamic Party PPP clashed with Golkar supporters, leading to violence and many arrests. When the subsequent election results showed that the Islamic party had lost its majority in the city for the first time under the New Order, observers speculated that voters had turned against the perceived violence of the PPP. Whatever the reason, however, the Islamic vote had dropped by only about 4 per cent, and Golkar, with 45 per cent of the vote, fell far short of its easy national majority of 64 per cent. Most voters in the capital still refused to endorse the Government's political organization.[90]

Jakarta's reputation of leaning away from the Government and towards Islamic politics has recently become a major irritant for the authorities. Ten years after the Malari affair of January 1974, Jakarta suffered another upheaval in 1984 which appeared to indicate deep-seated dissatisfaction among pious Muslims. On 12 September 1984, crowds of Islamic youths burned shops and vehicles and clashed with security forces in Tanjung Priok. They were dispersed by gunfire, and altogether at least 30 people were reported killed. In the following months, bomb explosions and mysterious fires in multi-storey buildings occurred in Jakarta. Most of these incidents were linked to criticisms of government connections with wealthy Indonesian Chinese businessmen.[91]

The Tanjung Priok affair resembled earlier cases of religious outbursts against authority: youths stormed out of a fiery Islamic prayer meeting to advance, unarmed but shouting anti-Government slogans, on security forces. The Government was shaken by the prospect of militant Islam playing a revolutionary role in the same way that it had done in Iran. Observers pointed to the special reasons why unrest was centred in the port area of Tanjung Priok. Living conditions there were especially difficult: on top of unhealthy housing and a shortage of drinking water, unemployment had grown as shipping in the port declined due to government restrictions on imports. Furthermore, the harbour population contains a high proportion of people from areas known to be strongly Muslim, notably the Sundanese, Buginese and Madurese. Finally, Islam is experiencing a resurgence, at least in part, because it is one of the few areas where independent organization is still accepted. It has become almost impossible to create political and industrial organizations free of government interference. Independent women's movements are also a thing of the past: now they are tied to the work of husbands and to government programmes.[92] The Islamic revivalist movement has taken on a populist strain worrying to the authorities.

The violence of 1984 led to wider political dissent because members of the so-called Group of 50 were alleged to have been implicated. Originating in 1980 with a petition to parliament calling for more representative and open government, the Group includes many influential people, including the well-known Jakarta personalities Ali Sadikin and former police chief, Hugeng Santoso, both now in retirement.[93] In 1985 and 1986, long-term jail sentences were imposed on two Group of 50 members, a former Government minister, H. M. Sanusi, and Lieutenant-General H. R. Dharsono, a former secretary-general of ASEAN. At the trial, one of the most eloquent witnesses in defence of Dharsono was Ali Sadikin.[94] From being a leading member of the New Order élite, Sadikin is now firmly identified with its critics.

Outbursts of violence in Jakarta seem likely to grow rather than diminish, given a number of current trends. The sluggish economy will fuel discontent, accompanied as it is by continuing population pressure on urban resources. The only area of employment for most people is still in the small-scale, under-capitalized economy, which suffers from restrictive policies and from competition with modern industry. An important political unknown is the character of the emerging population of second-generation Jakartans, who will soon make up the great majority in the city for the first time since the early twentieth century. Whereas immigrants are inclined to view Jakarta as an improvement on their poorer places of origin, their children may chafe at urban squalor. Finally, violence may be the only means by which Jakartans can express dissent. Sometimes, as in the past, this may involve the manipulation of crowds by opposing groups. As yet, however, there are few signs of widespread sustained disturbances; certainly nothing in Jakarta can compare, for instance, with recent events in Manila. The Indonesian Government still has the situation well in hand, and opposition is intimidated and disorganized.

1. *Tempo*, 31/5/1971.
2. S. V. Sethuraman, *Jakarta: Urban Development and Employment*, p. 20.

3. Ali Sadikin, *Gita Jaya*, Jakarta, Pemerintah DKI, 1977, p. 353.

4. On public transport in Jakarta, see Howard W. Dick, 'Urban Public Transport: Jakarta, Surabaya and Malang', *Bulletin of Indonesian Economic Studies*, Vol. 17, No. 1 and 2, March and July 1981.

5. On television, see Astrid Susanto, 'The Mass Communications System in Indonesia', in Karl D. Jackson and Lucian W. Pye (editors), *Political Power and Communications in Indonesia*, Berkeley, University of California Press, 1978, p. 232.

6. Dietrich Lerche, 'Membiayai Pembangunan Perkotaan: Kasus Pengetrapan Pajak Tanah dan Bangunan Secara Efektif', *Prisma*, Vol. 8, December 1972, p. 38.

7. Ali Sadikin, 'Saya Mendapat Kepuasan Batin', *Prisma*, Vol. 6, No. 5, May 1977, p. 52.

8. Sadikin, *Gita Jaya*, p. 97 gives information about population growth and municipal boundaries, as does Walter Mertens, 'Jakarta, a Country in a City', *Majalah Demografi Indonesia*, Vol. 2, No. 6, 1976.

9. On the 'Jakartanize Jakarta' campaign, see *Djakarta Membangun/Djakarta in Progress*, Djakarta, Pemerintah DCI, 1972, p. 72.

10. Planned Community Development Ltd., *Jakarta Urban Development Project*, New York, March 1974, mimeo., Annex 1.

11. On family planning in Jakarta, see T. H. Hull and I. B. Mantra, 'Indonesia's Changing Population', in Anne Booth and Peter McCawley (editors), *The Indonesian Economy During the Soeharto Era*, Kuala Lumpur, Oxford University Press, 1981, p. 270.

12. Sadikin, *Gita Jaya*, p. 201.

13. On the effect of the 'closed city' policy, see Suharso and A. Speare, 'Migration Trends', in Booth and McCawley, op. cit., pp. 310–11.

14. Robert L. Ayres, *Banking on the Poor. The World Bank and World Poverty*, Cambridge, MIT Press, 1983, p. 193 discusses the 'site-and-services' scheme.

15. *Tempo*, 7/8/1976.

16. The World Bank view of the Kampung Improvement Programme is given in *Laporan Peninjauan dari Rombongan Economic Development Institute Bank Dunia mengenai perbaikan Kampung (Proyek Moh. Husni Thamrin) di Jakarta*, Bappem Proyek MTH, DKI Jakarta, 1976, mimeo.

17. Costing on the scheme is given in Nick Devas, 'Indonesia's Kampung Improvement Program: An Evaluative Case Study', *Ekistics*, No. 286, January/February 1981, p. 28.

18. For the budgets of the Kampung Improvement Programme, see Sadikin, *Gita Jaya*, pp. 262–3

19. *Tempo*, 15/3/1972.

20. *Jakarta Dalam Angka 1978*, shows around 2,000 cases of cholera (and more than 100 deaths) in Jakarta annually in 1973–5.

21. Criticisms of the Kampung Improvement Programme were expressed in *Jakarta Urban Development Project, Laporan Peninjauan*, and Ayres, op. cit., p. 200.

22. Criticisms on lack of consultation and its consequences are to be found in Sidik Noormohamed, 'Housing the Poor in Jakarta', in J. J. Fox *et al.* (editors), *Indonesia: Australian Perspectives*, Canberra, Australian National University

Press, 1980, pp. 508–10; Devas, op. cit. and Ayres, op. cit., pp. 188–9.

23. The example of the inappropriate footpath is from Lea Jellinek, 'The Birth and Death of a Jakarta Kampung'.

24. *Laporan Peninjauan*, Group B report.

25. On water supply, see ibid., Group A report and Sadikin, *Gita Jaya*, p. 249.

26. *Sensus Penduduk 1971: Penduduk Jakarta Raya*, Jakarta, Kantor Sensus dan Statistik, 1974, p. 77.

27. On land speculation, see A. R. Saleh and M. Assegaf, 'Pembangunan dan pengorbanan: kasus pembebasan tanah di Jakarta', *Prisma*, Vol. 6, No. 3, March 1977, p. 57 and Adnan Buyung Nasution, 'Beberapa Aspek Hukum dalam Masalah Pertahanan dan Pemukiman di DKI Jakarta', Paper Lokakarya, 26–28 September 1978, 'Pemukiman bagi Penduduk Berpenghasilan Rendah di Jakarta', mimeo.

28. *Tempo*, 18/3/1972.

29. Ibid., 15/11/1975.

30. Ibid., 4/11/1972.

31. Information on cases defended by the Bureau comes from Saleh and Assegaf, op. cit., pp. 48–57, author's interview with A. B. Nasution, Jakarta, 2/4/1980, and *Tempo*, 15/9/1973 and 11/12/1976.

32. Ali Sadikin, *Menggusir dan Membangun*, Jakarta, Idayu Press, 1977, p. 25.

33. A survey conducted in 1972 among the poor of Jakarta showed that only 10 per cent were not satisfied with the area in which they lived, but they were all preoccupied with ways of increasing their barely adequate incomes. Gustaf F. Papanek, 'The Poor of Jakarta', *Economic Development and Cultural Change*, Vol. 24, No. 1, 1975, pp. 1–27.

34. *Tempo*, 29/11/1975.

35. Ibid., 29/1/1972.

36. Sadikin is quoted in ibid., 10/2/1973.

37. *Far Eastern Economic Review*, 8/3/1984.

38. Jellinek, 'The Birth and Death of a Jakarta Kampung'. See also by the same author, *The Life of a Jakarta Street Trader—Two Years Later*, Clayton, Monash University, 1978.

39. On prostitutes, see Hans-Dieter Evers, 'Subsistence Production and the Jakarta "Floating Mass"', *Prisma*, Vol. 17, June 1980, pp. 30–1.

40. Willard A. Hanna, *Pak Dikin's Djakarta*, American Universities Field Staff Reports Series, *Southeast Asia Series*, Vol. 17, No. 1, August 1969, p. 7.

41. On the *gelandangan* generally, see Parsudi Suparlan, 'The Gelandangan of Jakarta', *Indonesia*, No. 18, 1974, pp. 41–52.

42. *Kompas*, 19/12/1977.

43. *Tempo*, 3/7/1976.

44. Ibid., 23/11/1974.

45. Papanek, op. cit., p. 11.

46. *Tempo*, 10/6/1977.

47. *Rentjana Induk DCI Djakarta 1965–1985*, Djakarta, Pemerintah DCI, 1967, Part C.

48. Employment figures are given in Sethuraman, op. cit., pp. 12–13.

49. Information on incomes is from Anne Booth and R. M. Sundrum, 'Income

Distribution', in Booth and McCawley, op. cit., pp. 181–217 and Papanek, op. cit., p. 4.

50. Hanna, op. cit., pp. 2, 7–8.

51. *Asiaweek*, 28/3/1980, pp. 44–5.

52. On Hugeng, see *Express*, 11/1/1971.

53. On the Chinese under Sadikin, see Leo Suryadinata, *Eminent Indonesian Chinese: Biographical Sketches*, Singapore, Institute of Southeast Asian Studies, 1978, and Charles A. Coppel, *Indonesian Chinese in Crisis*.

54. Jellinek, 'The Birth and Death of a Jakarta Kampung'.

55. Differences between and within *kampung* are discussed in Gerald Hans Krausse, 'The Kampungs of Jakarta, Indonesia: A Study of Spatial Patterns in Urban Poverty', Ph.D. dissertation, University of Pittsburgh, 1975, and Papanek, op. cit.

56. On *dangdut* and Benyamin S., see *Tempo*, 22/3/1975 and 1/1/1977 and W. H. Frederick, 'Rhoma Irama and the Dangdut Style', *Indonesia*, No. 34, October 1982, pp. 103–30.

57. On Syuman Jaya, see Ardan, 'In Memoriam: Sjuman Djaja'.

58. On patronage in Jakarta, see Dennis Cohen, 'Poverty and Development in Jakarta', Ph.D. dissertation, University of Wisconsin-Madison, 1975, p. 320; Amir Karamoy and Achmad Sablie, 'The Communications Aspect and its Impact on the Youth of Poor Kampungs in the City of Jakarta', *Prisma*, Vol. 1, No. 1, May 1975, p. 62; and Evers, op. cit., p. 32.

59. On Jakartan Malay, see Stephen Wallace, 'The Linguistic Modernization of Jakarta' in Gloria Davis (editor), *What is Modern Indonesian Culture?*, Athens, Ohio University, 1979, pp. 69–88.

60. From the poem 'Song of a Bottle of Beer' by W. S. Rendra, trans. Harry Aveling, *State of Emergency*, Sydney, Wild and Woolley, 1980, p. 67.

61. Quoted in *Tempo*, 2/7/1977. Examination of some of the minutes of the DPRD meetings confirmed this view (*Risalah Rapat-Rapat Paripurna DPRD DKI Jakarta*, 1971–2).

62. Migrant views of Jakarta are given in Papanek, op. cit., p. 8.

63. Cohen, op. cit.

64. Examples of clashes between *becak* men and bus drivers are given in ibid., pp. 308–12 and *Tempo*, 15/4/1972.

65. See Coppel, *Indonesian Chinese in Crisis*.

66. *Tempo*, 12/1/1974.

67. For description and analysis of the January 1974 riots, see ibid., 26/1/1974 and R. William Liddle, 'Participation and the Political Parties' in Jackson and Pye, op. cit., pp. 185–7.

68. 1971 and 1977 election results are given in Sadikin, *Gita Jaya*, p. 159.

69. Sadikin's role in the 1977 election is discussed in *Far Eastern Economic Review*, 15/7/1977.

70. On property taxes, see Lerche, 'Membiayai Pembangunan Perkotaan', pp. 42–3 and by the same author, 'Efficiency of Taxation in Indonesia', *Bulletin of Indonesian Economic Studies*, Vol. 16, No. 1, 1980, pp. 39–40.

71. On Jakarta's dominance, see Booth and Sundrum, op. cit., pp. 195–200, and Graeme Hugo, 'Some Dimensions of Socio-Economic Inequality Associated with Urbanization and Urban Growth in Indonesia', paper presented at the

ASAA Conference, Brisbane, 1980, pp. 31–4.

72. The impact of Pertamina's collapse on Jakarta is discussed in *Tempo*, 22/11/1975.

73. On Cokropranolo, see articles in *Tempo*, 8/7/1978, 20/1/1979, 22/12/1979, 12/7/1980, 2/10/1982.

74. Peter G. Warr, 'The Jakarta Export Processing Zone: Benefits and Costs', *Bulletin of Indonesian Economic Studies*, Vol. 19, No. 3, December 1983, pp. 28–49.

75. Plans for flat-building are reported in *Tempo*, 27/5/1978.

76. Lea Jellinek describes flat-building at Kebun Kacang in 'The Birth and Death of a Jakarta Kampung'.

77. For evidence of the depopulation of central Jakarta between 1971 and 1980, see Jeremy Evans, 'The Growth of Urban Centres in Java since 1961', *Bulletin of Indonesian Economic Studies*, Vol. 20, No. 1, 1984, p. 45. Discussion of the need for central blocks of flats is found in Simandjuntak, 'Pembangunan Perumahan Maju Pesat Dikhawatirkan Tumbuh Slum Baru', *Prisma*, Vol. 12, No. 4, 1983, pp. 70–88, and *Tempo*, 18/10/1980.

78. Soenarjono Danoedjo, 'Everyone using urban facilities must pay for them', *Prisma*, Vol. 32, June 1984, p. 57.

79. On Suprapto, see *Tempo*, 2/10/1982. For reports of evictions under his governorship, see *Tempo*, 8/12/1984 and 14/12/1985.

80. *Tempo*, 21/7/1979 and 20/9/1980.

81. Estimates of costs of water supply and railway plans are given in *Far Eastern Economic Review*, 29/3/1984.

82. Population statistics are from 1980 census.

83. Recent evaluations of the Kampung Improvement Programme are John Lewis Taylor, 'An Evaluation of Selected Impacts of Jakarta's Kampung Improvement Programme', Ph.D. dissertation, University of California, 1983, and Amir Karamoy, 'The Kampung Improvement Program: Hope and Reality', *Prisma*, Vol. 32, June 1984, pp. 19–36.

84. On alternative methods of providing low-cost housing in Jakarta, see Colin Rosser, 'The Evolving Role of a National Agency for Housing and Urban Development in Indonesia', *Habitat International*, Vol. 7, No. 5/6, 1983, pp. 137–49.

85. Soenarjono Danoedjo, op. cit.

86. Reports on crime in Jakarta are given in *Tempo*, 20/9/1980 and 29/1/1983.

87. Figures on Jakarta's population growth and expansion of municipal area are from Evans, op. cit. Estimates of the growth of Jakarta and Jabotabek are given by Hariri Hadi, Deputy for Regional Planning, in 'Kecamatan Towns can Stem the Invasion of Large Cities', *Prisma*, Vol. 32, June 1984, p. 50.

88. Discussion of the Indonesian economy in recent years is found in *Far Eastern Economic Review*, 18/8/1983, 26/1/1984 and 16/1/1986. For an example of Indonesian Chinese business initiative, see the article on Liem investors, ibid., 7/4/1983. This group has been involved in considerable property development in Jakarta.

89. The study of construction workers' wages is reported by Hal Hill, 'Survey of Recent Developments', *Bulletin of Indonesian Economic Studies*, Vol. 20, No. 2, August 1984, p. 36.

90. For discussion of the election campaign and voting, see Robert Cribb, 'Elections in Jakarta', *Asian Survey*, Vol. 24, No. 6, June 1984, pp. 655–64.

91. Reports on the Tanjung Priok affair and subsequent disruptions in Jakarta come from *Tempo*, 22/9/1984, 13/10/1984, 27/10/1984, 3/11/1984, 24/11/1984 and *Far Eastern Economic Review*, 27/9/1984.

92. Women's organizations have complained publicly about restrictions imposed on them: see *Tempo*, 8/9/1984.

93. For discussion of the Group of 50, see David Jenkins, *Suharto and His Generals: Indonesian Military Politics 1975–1983*, Ithaca, Cornell University Press, 1984.

94. *Far Eastern Economic Review*, 14/11/1985.

Conclusion

THE two main themes pursued in this book have been those which preoccupy all historians: continuity and change. For residents of Jakarta, change is more obvious than continuity, but a longer-term view discloses persistent elements in the city's history.

Since its inception, the nature of the city's society has shifted dramatically. The Dutch began the process by evicting the original inhabitants of the old Indonesian town in order to create their own synthetic Batavian population, consisting of Europeans, Chinese and slaves from outside Java. By the nineteenth century, the intermingling of different ethnic groups and a changing balance of immigrants had produced a new Batavian society: in addition to immigrant European, Chinese, Arab and Indian minorities there was a new indigenous Betawi category resulting from an amalgam of Indonesian groups. This community, like the *Peranakan* variants of the Chinese and European groups, spoke a local version of Malay and evolved its own urban culture, greatly influenced by the cosmopolitan environment of Batavia. Despite extensive cultural exchanges, however, Batavia remained a highly stratified society, in which the Europeans held the dominant position, followed by the Chinese and lastly by the Indonesians. These social differences were reflected in the economy: Europeans occupied the top administrative positions and ran the harbour and international business houses; the Chinese held the intermediate rungs of trade and manufacturing and were skilled craftsmen; while Indonesians took the lowest positions in administration, provided the labour on the wharves and construction sites and in the warehouses, worked as domestic servants and created their own employment. In keeping with their different incomes and pursuits, the Chinese and Europeans lived in distinct areas of the city and Indonesians occupied the districts away from the main roads, in their own *kampung*.

Political and demographic upheavals have changed the face of the city in the twentieth century. Already by 1930 an influx of immigrants had overwhelmed the relatively closely knit, slowly growing urban society of the nineteenth century, challenging the *Peranakan* and Betawi cultures with more exclusive European, Chinese and Indonesian values. Ethnic groups again became more distinct and mutually suspicious, as in the early days of Batavia, with the difference that the Indonesian groups were now being welded together by a consciousness of Indonesian nationhood. Political antagonism emerged not only at an underground level, but openly in the People's Council and the Municipal Council, in the press and in public gatherings. A rising new Indonesian Western-educated élite challenged Dutch colonial supremacy, albeit without making much impression on it.

The Japanese overthrew Dutch rule, replacing it temporarily with their own form of imperialism. During the Occupation, Indonesians gained governmental, administrative and military experience, and were ready to defy the attempted reimposition of Dutch rule in 1945. In the years 1941–9, Jakarta deteriorated physically as political and military objectives led to the neglect of strictly urban needs.

When the Dutch finally left in 1949, the new Jakarta struggled to adjust to its position as capital of an independent Indonesian republic. Some steps were relatively easy: the Indonesian élite moved into the positions and houses of the departing Europeans, and many landmarks of European domination like statues and clubs were destroyed or transformed. The situation of the Chinese was a difficult one. Over the years they were required to play down their cultural difference. Although they continued to hold a key position in the economy and in fact worked closely with members of the Indonesian élite in a business capacity, they were subjected to constant criticism and occasional violence from groups which felt neglected by the government. The concentration of Chinese in the commercial areas of the city made them easy targets for attack.

Since 1949, the city's population has exploded. Waves of Indonesian immigration have relegated the old Orang Betawi to the position of a threatened minority, forced out of their *kampung* by urban growth. As Jakarta has become the focus for 'modern' urban life, Betawi culture has been cast aside as irrelevant. The inner city experienced overcrowding and then, in the late 1970s, gradual depopulation as massive new construction works replaced residential areas with highways, office and shopping blocks and hotels. Markets have lost much of their magic to 'modernization'. In the multi-storey glass shopping centre at Glodok, Chinese vendors in little booths display electric fans and plastic wares rather than the silks and ceramics which delighted early visitors to Batavia. Senen Market has been shorn of most of the seedy, racy atmosphere of the past, when stolen goods changed hands in the maze of stalls, prostitutes pestered and pickpockets fleeced the passer-by, and gangs of youths of various ethnic origins (Chinese, Batak, Ambonese) fought with knives in the alleys.

The built-up area spread, gobbling up rural land. Highways, freeways and toll-roads have destroyed the former sleepiness of many areas. In the 1970s, new manufacturing zones were created, where modern jobs became available, although never quickly enough to sustain the rapidly growing population. As the numbers of the wealthy have grown, élite residential areas, once limited to Menteng and Kebayoran Baru, have proliferated, and now include such suburbs as Kuningan and Cempaka Putih. The atmosphere of these streets is less friendly than in the *kampung*: people surround their houses with high walls and fences which are often topped by barbed wire and spikes.

Despite the transformation of Jakarta, a closer look reveals that some things have remained remarkably similar over the years. Some physical features persist. The site remains difficult: its low level makes flooding a hazard during the rainy season and provides a challenge for urban planners and architects. To the north-east, near Tanjung Priok, fish are still farmed in ponds: the *bandeng* raised there are eaten as a delicacy at Chinese New Year. Between the port and the old part of town, the main road passes large marshy tracts where huts seem to float on the water, connected by raised paths or narrow wooden bridges. Climatically, Jakarta is still a tropical city where most people, apart from the privileged few who can afford to live in air-conditioned surroundings, have to contend with uncongenially moist or hot conditions. The River Ciliwung still meanders brownly through the city, disciplined in its final stretch by canals that run through the northern districts and the harbour of Sunda Kelapa, although river traffic has now all but disappeared except for rafts of bamboo floated down from the rural interior. And while many new landmarks have emerged in recent years, the vast central square has remained virtually untouched since the eighteenth century, apart from the erection of Sukarno's National Monument.

Jakarta remains a port city. Although sea transport is less significant today than in previous centuries, inter-island trade and international shipping still tie up at Sunda Kelapa and Tanjung Priok and contribute to the city's and the nation's economy. And as the centre of government, Jakarta retains the aura of power created by the Dutch in colonial times. The authority of the President is comparable with that of the previous Governors-General, although by now the resources and administrative apparatus of government have increased so enormously that Jakarta has even more potential to influence the nation than Batavia once had. So the city's magnetism for power-seekers and clients has grown, and even ordinary Jakartans seem to derive some vicarious pleasure from being close to the source of all rumours.

The growth of the city in recent years has been so rapid that the old buildings and streets have often been swept away or dwarfed by new construction. Yet the determined observer can find large areas which have survived remarkably well. The best example is Kota, the old northern section of the city. Although efforts have recently been made to preserve a few notable old buildings like the former Town Hall, neglect by both colonial and Republican governments has been the most powerful force for conservation, allowing many structures to retain their original purposes as dwellings, shop-houses and places of worship. The neglect is all too obvious in peeling paintwork and huge piles of rubbish. Some canals are so choked that homeless people have built makeshift shelters on the debris. Except for Glodok, which has been disrupted by redevelopment of commercial areas, most of the new urban construction has occurred elsewhere in the city. Nineteenth-century European buildings have clung on, too, in Gambir, and early twentieth-century Menteng has been protected by conservation regulations.

Vestiges of the city's cultural past persist. Despite the social upheaval of the last century, the city retains a colourful mixture of ethnic groups, held together by a common language and a sense of belonging to a vibrant modern city.

Although dimmed over time, Jakarta's Chinese culture is still distinctive and can be glimpsed in the *kampung* of the northern city, where, for instance, delicate red and gold paper funeral ornaments are made in home workshops to the accompaniment of Chinese music from cassette-players. Chinese festivals are more unobtrusive now. New Year celebrations are limited to the lighting of enormous red candles in the temples and reunions of families and friends. At the Pu-Du festival, food offerings are no longer fought over by beggars but are distributed more decorously by allotting tickets to people in a queue. Chinese characters have disappeared from signs in Glodok, but many shadowy *toko* (shop-houses) remain, and in Chinese restaurants one may glimpse a Chinese businessman deep in conversation with his business partner: European, Japanese or Indonesian as the case may be.

Similarly, Betawi culture clings to the fringes of the city, precariously preserved in the orchard district of Condet to the south. There *salak* groves almost hide the houses, some of them decorated with carvings and stylized patterns in the old Betawi fashion. Since it was declared a cultural preservation zone in 1976, Condet's inhabitants have complained about the regulations which are intended to hold back the waves of development lapping around them.[1]

The Dutch presence lingers in places like Pasar Baru, the narrow market street to the north-east of what was Weltevreden. Blue Band margarine is advertised as in colonial times and the occasional Dutch shop name catches the eye: the Tropen bookshop stands out amidst the many Chinese *toko* and Indian textile stores (Hassaram's, Chotirmall's, Gehirmall's, Bombay Silk Store). And although Europeans may no longer be present in significant numbers, Western culture continues to have high status in Jakarta, which is still the most Westernized city in the archipelago forty years after the declaration of independence. To put it differently, Jakarta remains a cosmopolitan city, open to foreign influences: just as in the colonial period, it is not tied down by its past but accepts and adapts new ideas. *Dangdut* music is as much a result of cultural exchange today as *kroncong* once was. The mingling of many ethnic groups in the city continues to spark new cultural variants.

Despite the frenzied din of the traffic and the spread of buildings, some reminders linger of the carefree, spacious days of pre-war Batavia when Si Doel and Tjalie Robinson and their friends flew kites in the open fields and sailed their raft down the

Ciliwung. Their spirit lives on in Jakarta's youngsters. At the end of every rainy season, children fly their flimsy kites in the cool breeze, and on the pavement of Jalan Thamrin itself, next to the stream of Toyotas and Volvos, squat small boys who could have come straight out of Tjalie Robinson's books: with great concentration they lower a line through a broken grating and fish in the storm drains beneath.

A visit to any night-market shows the spirit which Tjalie so admired in Jakarta: the willingness to sample everything. At this *warung* one can eat *ayam Semarang*, at that one *soto kaki kambing*, and at another *nasi rames*, while a nearby cart glitters with bottles of multi-coloured syrups ready to mix Jakarta's favourite crushed ice drinks. Adjacent restaurants offer Chinese or spicy Minangkabau dishes, and even the latest imported fast foods. Jakartans are enterprising eaters.

The ingenuity of Jakartans continues to be seen not only in their culture but in the urban economy. Because there is still relatively little modern employment, most people find and create their own work in the ways they have done in the past. Although there are now many more modern factories, offices, shops and transport, the flood of newcomers has mainly had to earn a living in the same unskilled and underpaid types of occupations as before. A visit to a new market block like Tanah Abang proves how inadequate these buildings are to house the sea of hawkers. The sheer specialization of their wares is breath-taking: a dozen pedlars line the pavement with second-hand door-handles; two dozen have spare parts for every conceivable model and vintage of car; others display strings of nicely graduated old keys. Demands meet with a quick response from people anxious to create a niche for themselves. Just as the *becak* was a clever local invention that first satisfied the transport needs of Jakartans in the 1940s, so other Jakartans were quick to turn the packaging boom of the 1960s to their advantage by rapidly expanding the recycling business. Backyard workshops turn out commodities to meet every need, from batteries to ice creams.

Discussion of *becak*-driving and street-vending inevitably leads us to another recurring theme in Jakarta's history: the clash of interests between urban policy-makers and the mass of the city's inhabitants. Ever since the Dutch founded Batavia in 1619, municipal authorities have adopted a vision of the city which has failed to accommodate the needs of most of its inhabitants. The

Dutch envisaged Batavia as a European enclave which would serve as a port centre for their residence, administration and trade. The Chinese were tolerated as useful in the urban economy. Indonesians were admitted to be necessary as manual labour, but they were always treated as peripheral. It did not matter that Europeans (even including Eurasians) were never more than a small minority of the urban population: it was still their city and it was to be administered for their convenience. Such government revenue as was available for urban infrastructure was devoted to making the areas of town where Europeans lived and worked as efficient and pleasant as possible. The neglect of Indonesian *kampung* was justified on the grounds that Indonesians contributed almost nothing towards the municipal revenue, and if they were not able to maintain themselves in town they should return to the countryside where they belonged.

Since Indonesia's independence, Jakarta's new rulers have had their own image of the capital which, although differing from that of the Dutch, has had similar consequences for the majority of the city's inhabitants. National pride led Sukarno to try to turn the capital into the show-piece of Indonesia, full of magnificent structures which would win the admiration of foreigners and build Indonesian self-confidence. Unfortunately the country's resources would not allow the total transformation of the capital, merely the commencement of isolated projects. Meanwhile, the city's population grew so rapidly that Sukarno's pet schemes threw into relief the decrepitude in which most people were forced to live and work. Urban policies were not evolved to cope with the masses, whom Sukarno loved to exhort but upon whom he looked with some impatience when they disfigured his city.

Urban policies since Sukarno have been far more realistic and devoted more to productive projects than to a search for urban prestige and pride, although that trend of thinking is still discernible. For instance, in 1979 the Minister for Home Affairs declared: 'Because the centre of government is in Jakarta, so Jakarta must be able to make greater efforts to raise the level and standard and prestige of the state, nation and people of Indonesia compared with other regions.'[2] The aim is still to build a modern city of the kind which can stand comparison with other world metropolises. The motivation may be economic—the desire to attract foreign investment—as much as nationalistic, but the outcome is even more repressive towards the millions who cannot find a living in the modern sector. Sadikin and his successors have been much more efficient than governors of Sukarno's day, partly because they have had more resources at their disposal in an oil-fed economy. Efficiency in pursuit of the Metropolitan City is far more to be feared by Jakarta's 'little people' than Sukarno's half-baked megalomania. A city in which wide roads are laid down and kept clear for cars, trucks and taxis, where pavements along the main streets are stripped of anything deemed to detract from urban beauty, where vast expanses of land are cleared for new hotels, office blocks, department stores and well-serviced residential suburbs: this is the city which Jakarta's planners and the burgeoning middle classes want and which has no room for the majority of the poor, who cannot afford motor transport apart from buses, who live in largely unserviced, 'substandard' *kampung* on land to which they usually have no title, and who will never have well-paid regular jobs.

Any government of an overcrowded city whose inhabitants cannot find remunerative employment has a very difficult task on its hands. Its situation is not unique: many Third World countries experience the same thing. There are no easy solutions, but tackling the problem may be made more difficult by the way in which it is perceived. In the case of Jakarta, throughout its history governments have tended to regard the 'superfluous people' as the ones with the problem: they must change their attitudes or go back to the countryside. The bulk of government efforts and resources has always been devoted to building up the modern sector of the city, regardless of the fact that this sector has largely served a minority. Since Sukarno, this has been justified in terms of economic growth: if there is no growth then no benefits can filter down to the growing population. Although it is clear that a minority does very well by this kind of policy, it is often hard to see how it benefits the majority of Jakartans. Meanwhile, the authorities claim that it is impossible to provide for the needs of the bulk of the city's population for the simple reason that they cannot afford to pay for services. In 1984, the Director of the department responsible for urban planning stated: '... [T]he task of city government is not just to serve, but rather it must also obtain revenue in order to be able to serve the community. In the end it is this which brings about the situation in which those who can pay get the services.'[3]

The central fallacy which has persisted from 1619 to the present is that it is possible to create a city for the privileged few, cut off from the countryside of the majority poor. South Africa's governments have tried to do this and have succeeded only temporarily and at the price of massive repression. In a poor country, so long as people are free to move in the way that they are not in South Africa, the influx of poor people will always subvert the myth of a city for the modern élite. In any case, the poor are needed in the city, despite the disdain of the authorities: it is the cheap services which they provide and the presence of their surplus labour which keeps wages low in domestic service and even in the modern sector.

Does the study of Jakarta's history have any significance beyond helping one to appreciate and understand a diverse and complex city? It must have, because of the importance of Jakarta in the history of Indonesia's cities generally, and because of the lessons which can be learned from it for the study of Third World cities.

Jakarta has been regarded since colonial times as the country's foremost city, which sets the tone for others to follow. Many urban experiments have originated there before being applied elsewhere. For instance, Batavia/Jakarta was the first Indonesian city to get a municipal council, the first to have a Kampung Improvement Programme, the first to restrict the operation of *becak*. Indonesians also look to Jakarta as a pace-setter in modern urban culture. The capital is the media centre of the nation. What goes on in Jakarta therefore has reverberations elsewhere in the archipelago.

What can other Third World cities learn from Jakarta's history? There is no doubt that in recent years the Jakartan experience has aroused interest. Here is a very large, predominantly poor city in a country which has the fortune to have more lucrative resources at its disposal than many, due to its possession of large oil reserves. There has been rapid and impressive expansion of the modern part of the city as a result of unprecedented investment, both foreign and domestic. But what has been done to assist the urban poor, the city's majority? The main negative lessons are the futility of trying to suppress the small-scale sector of the economy, in which most people are engaged, and of trying to deal with the city in isolation from the overcrowded countryside. The positive lesson has been the modest success of the Kampung Improvement Programme, which has shown how to improve people's surroundings without disrupting their communities and livelihood.

Jakarta does not offer nightmarish portents for the future of cities in the way that Calcutta does. The narrow lanes of its slums do not plumb such depths of human degradation. Fortunately, the economic foundations of Jakarta are not crumbling away as Calcutta's have been doing for decades, although both cities draw upon similarly over-populated and poor rural hinterlands, where deep-seated problems remain to be solved. Jakarta reeks not so much of decay as of bad faith. Over the centuries, its rulers have built an enclave for themselves and neglected the needs of the vast majority of city-dwellers. They have not gone quite as far as the rich of Manila, who have surrounded a whole suburb with security walls as protection against the implied threat of the city's poor. (Many individual houses in Jakarta's wealthy areas, however, are heavily fortified.) Nevertheless, the division of the city into fragments of modern metropolis enjoyed by the well-to-do, and the vast maze of jerry-built *kampung* is clear to anyone. Judging from the urban and national policies pursued so far, there seems no prospect that the gap between those divergent sections of the city, or the gap between Jakarta and the rest of the country, is likely to be narrowed.

1. For comments on Condet as a conservation zone, see *Tempo*, 19/1/1980.

2. Reported in *Tempo*, 10/2/1979.

3. Soenarjono Danoedjo, 'Everyone using urban facilities must pay for them', p. 59.

Glossary

ayam Semarang—chicken cooked in the Semarang style.
Badan Perjuangan—Struggle Organizations: groups formed to further the cause of the Revolution of 1945–9.
bajaj—small Indian-made motorized passenger vehicle.
banci—transvestite.
barongsai—dragon-like creature, part of Chinese festivals.
becak—trishaw or pedicab.
bendy—two-wheeled light horse-drawn conveyance.
benedenstad—'lower city': in this case the old northern part of Batavia.
Budi Utomo—Javanese organization founded in 1908.
Capgomeh—carnival at the end of the Chinese New Year celebrations, held on the fifteenth day of the New Year.
cokek—Jakartan song and dance performed by women wearing Chinese-style costumes and accompanied by *gambang kromong*.
dangdut—type of Indonesian pop music.
deleman—two-wheeled horse-drawn carriage.
DPRD—Dewan Perwakilan Rakyat Daerah: Municipal Assembly.
dukun—healer.
gado-gado—Indonesian mixed vegetable dish with spicy peanut sauce.
gambang kromong—Jakarta-style *gamelan* or orchestra and singing, influenced by Chinese.
gambus—music featuring the Arab lute.
garuda—mythical bird resembling an eagle, part of Indonesia's national emblem.
gelandangan—people with no fixed address.
Golkar—acronym from Golongan Karya, the organization of functional groups which supports the New Order Government.
IEV—Indo-Europeesch Verbond: Eurasian League, founded in 1919.
jago—champion, *kampung* leader.
kampung—literally 'village'; in the urban context, an unplanned, unserviced area inhabited by an Indonesian community.
Kaum Betawi—organization of Orang Betawi, founded in 1923.
kebaya—long-sleeved blouse worn by women.
kris—Javanese dagger.

kroncong—small guitar, giving its name to a style of European-influenced popular music.

langgar—Islamic prayer-house.

lenong—Jakartan folk theatre.

lurah—*kampung* chief.

Mardijker—Asian Christians originally from Portuguese-held territories in Asia.

Masyumi—Modernist Islamic party, founded in 1943.

merdeka—freedom, independence.

Moor—name given to Indian Muslims during the Dutch period.

mylord—form of horse-drawn carriage.

Nahdatul Ulama—orthodox Islamic party, founded in 1926.

nasi rames—rice with side dishes.

nyai—female housekeeper; Indonesian unofficial wife of a foreigner.

oplet—motor vehicle (usually a converted Morris) carrying eight passengers on a fixed route.

Orang Betawi—Jakarta-born Indonesians of specifically Jakartan culture: characteristics include being Muslim, speaking Jakartan Malay. (Sometimes also called Betawi Asli, Anak Betawi or Jakarta Asli.)

palanquin—closed four-wheeled horse-drawn carriage.

Pecun—Chinese festival which involves a boat race; held in June.

pembangunan—development.

pemuda—youth.

pencak—Indonesian martial art.

Peranakan—born in the Indies or Indonesia; usually applied to Indonesian Chinese.

perjuangan—armed struggle.

Peta—Pembela Tanah Air (Protectors of the Fatherland): Indonesian volunteer army created by the Japanese in 1943.

petak—one-roomed *kampung* apartments opening onto a shared verandah.

PKI—Partai Komunis Indonesia: Indonesian Communist Party, founded in 1920.

PNI—Partai Nasional Indonesia: Indonesian National Party, founded in 1927.

pondok—doss-house or boarding-house. Also a Muslim boarding school.

PPP—Partai Persatuan Pembangunan (Unity Development Party): current opposition party consisting of a coalition of Islamic parties.

prau—Indonesian boat.

Pu-du—Chinese festival to appease wandering souls; held in August–September.

PUTERA—acronym from Pusat Tenaga Rakyat (Centre of People's Power): political organization formed by the Japanese in 1943.

Rebutan—Indonesian name for Pu-du.

Regent—Dutch name for *bupati*, the highest-ranking Javanese official.

rijsttafel—'rice-table': Dutch version of an Indonesian meal consisting of rice and many side-dishes.

romusha—'economic soldier': Indonesian recruited by the Japanese to work as a labourer.

ronggeng—itinerant Indonesian dancing-girl.

sado—two-wheeled horse-drawn vehicle in which passengers sit back to back (*dos-à-dos*).

said—Arab hereditary title.

salak—kind of fruit with shiny brown skin.

sambal—spicy Indonesian side-dish.

Sarekat Islam—Islamic League, formed in 1912.

semangat—spirit.

sheikh—Arab hereditary title.

sirih—chewing mixture of areca-nut, gambier and lime wrapped in betel leaf.

soto kaki kambing—goat's foot soup.

STOVIA—School tot opleiding van inlandsche artsen (School for training native doctors): a 1900 upgrading of the old *doctor-Djawa* school in Batavia.

tanjidor—Jakartan orchestra using European brass band instruments.

THHK—Tiong Hoa Hwee Koan: neo-Confucianist Chinese organization, founded in 1900.

toko—Chinese shop-house.

topeng—Indonesian mask-dance.

totok—full-blood: usually used by the Dutch to refer to Europeans.

trekker—transient: used by the Dutch to denote a European who had come to the Indies to work but not to live permanently.

Vaderlandsche Club—Patriots Club, established by Europeans in 1929.

VOC—Vereenigde Oost-Indische Compagnie: Dutch East India Company, founded in 1602.

warung—small shop or stall.

wayang—theatrical performance.

Select Bibliography

Primary Sources

Books

Alisjahbana, S. Takdir, *Indonesia in the Modern World*, New Delhi, Congress for Cultural Freedom, 1961; reprinted as *Indonesia: Social and Cultural Revolution*, Kuala Lumpur, Oxford University Press, 1966, and Singapore, Oxford University Press, 1984.

Angelino, P. de Kat, *Batikrapport*, Vol. 1, Weltevreden, Landsdrukkerij, 1930.

Anwar, Chairil (editor), *The Complete Poetry and Prose of Chairil Anwar*, trans. Burton Raffel, Albany, State University of New York Press, 1970.

Bastin, John and Brommer, Bea, *Nineteenth Century Prints and Illustrated Books of Indonesia*, Utrecht, Het Spectrum, 1979.

Batavia, de Hoofdstad van Nederlands Oost Indien, in derzelver Gelegenheid, Opkomst, Voortreffelijke Gebouwen, Hooge en Laage Regeering, Geschiedenissen, Kerkzaamheden, Koophandel, Zeden, Luchtsgesteldheid, Zeikten, Dieren en Gewassen, bechreven met Plaatsen, Amsterdam, Petrus Conradi, 1782.

Batavia als Handels-, Industrie- en Woonstad/Batavia as a Commercial, Industrial and Residential Centre, Batavia, Kolff, 1937.

'Bengal Civilian' (Charles Walter Kinloch), *Rambles in Java and the Straits in 1852*, Simpkin, Marshall and Co., 1853; reprinted Singapore, Oxford University Press, 1987.

Biervillas, Innigo de, *Voyage d'Innigo de Biervillas, Portugais, à la cote de Malabar, Goa, Batavia et autres lieux des Indes Orientales*, Paris, Dupuis, 1736.

Bousquet, G. H., *A French View of the Netherlands Indies*, London, Oxford University Press, 1940.

Brugmans, I. J. *et al.* (editors), *Nederlandsch-Indie onder Japanse Bezetting: Gegevens en documenten over de jaren 1942–1945*, Franeker, Wever, second edition, 1960.

Cook, James, *Captain Cook's Journal 1768–1771*, Adelaide, Libraries Board of South Australia, 1968.

Cornelia, Nonna, *Kokki Bitja*, Batavia, ninth edition, 1881.

Couperus, Louis, *The Hidden Force*, trans. A. Teixeira de Mattos, London, Cape, 1921.

Dagh-Register gehouden int Casteel Batavia, 1674, J. A. van der Chijs (editor), 's-Gravenhage, Nijhoff, 1902.

Daum, P. A., *Hoe Hij Raad van Indie Werd*, 's-Gravenhage, J. C. Opmeer, 1888.

Delden, Emile van, *De Particuliere Landerijen op Java*, Leiden, S. C. van Doesburgh, 1911.

Djajadiningrat, P. A. A., *Herinneringen*, Amsterdam, Batavia, Kolff, 1936.

Djakarta Dewasa Ini, Djakarta, Djapenko, second edition, 1957.

Djakarta Membangun/Djakarta in Progress, Djakarta, Pemerintah DCI, 1972.

Djojohadikusumo, Margono, *Herinneringen uit 3 Tijdperken*, Jakarta, Indira, 1969.

Doren, J. B. J. van, *Reis naar Nederlands Oost Indie*, 's-Gravenhage, J. and H. van Langenhuysen, 1851.

Eggink, E. J., *Na 25 Jaar. Beknopt Gedenkschrift ter Gelegenheid van het 25-jarig bestaan der Gemeente Batavia*, Batavia, Indonesische Drukkerij, 1930.

Excursiegids voor Oud-Batavia, Batavia, 1947.

Fabricius, Johan, *Hoe Ik Indie Terugvond*, Den Haag, Leopoldus, 1947.

Feith, Herbert and Castles, Lance (editors), *Indonesian Political Thinking 1945–1965*, Ithaca, Cornell University Press, 1970.

Ferguson, Margaretha, *Mammie ik ga dood. Aanteekeningen uit de Japanse tijd op Java 1942–1945*, Den Haag, Leopold, 1976.

———, *Elias in Batavia en Jakarta*, Den Haag, Leopold, 1977.

Fryke, Christopher and Schweitzer, Christopher, *Voyages to the East Indies*, London, Cassell, 1929, first edition 1700.

Gani, M., *Surat Kabar Indonesia pada Tiga Zaman*, Jakarta, Departemen Penerangan, 1978.

Gent-Detelle, Njonja E. van, *Boekoe Obat-obat voor Orang Toea dan Anak-anak*, Djocdja, fourth edition, 1880.

Gorkom, W. J. van, *Ongezond Batavia, Vroeger en Nu*, Batavia, Javasche Boekhandel, 1913.

Graaf, H. J. de, *Batavia in Oude Ansichten*, Zaltbommel, 1970.

Graaff, Nicolaus de, *Oost-Indise Spiegel*, Hoorn, Warnsinck, 1707.

Hanifah, Abu, *Tales of a Revolution*, Sydney, Angus and Robertson, 1972.

Hanna, Willard A., *Letters on Current Developments in Indonesia*, New York, American Universities Field Staff Reports Series, 1956.

———, *Bung Karno's Indonesia*, New York, American Universities Field Staff Reports Series, 1961.

———, *Pak Dikin's Djakarta*, New York, American Universities Field

Staff Reports Series, 1969.

Harsono, Ganis, *Recollections of an Indonesian Diplomat in the Sukarno Era*, St Lucia, University of Queensland Press, 1977.

Hogendorp, C. S. W. de, *Coup d'Oeil sur l'Isle de Java et les Autres Possessions Neerlandaises dans l'Archipel des Indes*, Bruxelles, 1830.

Ido, Victor (Hans van der Wall), *De Paupers*, 's-Gravenhage, J. C. Opmeer, 1912; reissued 's-Gravenhage, Thomas en Eras, 1978.

Idrus, *Dari Ave Maria ke Jalan Lain ke Roma*, Jakarta, Balai Pustaka, 1978.

Het Indische Staatsbeeld Voorheen en Thans, Bandoeng, Stichting Technisch Tijdschrift, 1939.

The Indonesian Town. Studies in Urban Sociology, The Hague, Van Hoeve, 1958.

Johanna, Njonja, *Boekoe Masakan Baroe*, Batavia, 1897.

Karya Jaya: Kenang-kenangan Lima Kepala Daerah Jakarta 1945–1966, Jakarta, Pemerintah DKI, 1977.

Keuchenius, W. M., *Beschrijving der Bataviasche Jurisdictie, en Onderzoek naar de Oorzaken der Meerdere Ongezondheid van Batavia en Deszelfs Rhee* (1st ed. 1807), Batavia, 1875.

Kol, H. van, *Uit Onze Kolonien*, Leiden, A. W. Sijthoff, 1903.

Kotapradja Djakarta Raya, Djakarta, Kementerian Penerangan Republik Indonesia, n.d. (1952?).

Kwee Kek Beng, *Doea Poeloe Lima Tahun Sebagai Wartawan*, Batavia, Kuo, 1948.

Leclerq, Jules, *Un Sejour dans l'Ile de Java*, second edition, Paris, Plon, 1898.

Loos-Haaxman, *Johannes Rach en Zijn Werk*, Batavia, 1928.

Lubis, Mochtar, *Twilight in Djakarta*, trans. Claire Holt, London, 1963.

Marre, J. de, *Batavia, Begrepen in Zes Boeken*, Amsterdam, A. Wor en de Erve G. onder de Linden, 1740.

Mihardja, Achdiat K., *Polemik Kebudayaan*, Jakarta, Pustaka Jaya, third edition, 1977.

Nederlandsch-Indisch Plakaatboek, 1602–1811, ed. J. A. van der Chijs, Batavia, Nijhoff, 1889.

Nieuhof, Johan, *Voyages and Travels to the East Indies 1653–1670*, with an Introduction by Anthony Reid, Singapore, Oxford University Press, 1988 (reprinted from *A Collection of Voyages and Travels*, London, 1732).

Nieuwenhuys, R. (E. Breton de Nijs), *Vergeelde Portretten. Uit een Indisch Familiealbum*, Amsterdam, 1954.

_____, *Tempo Doeloe*, Amsterdam, Querido 1961.

_____, *Batavia: Koningin van het Oosten*, 's-Gravenhage, Thomas en Eras, 1976.

_____ (editor), *Wie Verre Reizen Doet*, Amsterdam, Querido, 1975.

_____, *Een Beetje Oorlog*, Amsterdam, Querido, 1979.

Nio Joe Lan, *Riwàjat 40 Taon dari Tiong Hoa Hwe Koan-Batavia (1900–1939)*, Batavia, 1940.

Olivier, Johannes, *Land- en Zeetogten in Nederlands Indie*, Amsterdam, Sulpke, 1827–30.

Ong-Tae-Hae, *The Chinaman Abroad; or a desultory account of the Malay Archipelago, particularly of Java* (trans. W. H. Medhurst), Shanghae, no publisher, 1849.

Pakpahan, G., *1261 Hari di bawah Sinar Matahari Terbit*, Jakarta, no publisher, second edition, 1979.

Peringatan Ulang-Tahun ke-435 Kota Djakarta, Djakarta, Pemerintah DKI, 1962.

Perron, Edgar du, *Indies Memorandum*, Amsterdam, Bezige Bij, 1946.

——, *Het Land van Herkomst*, Amsterdam, G. A. van Oorschot, 1978 (first published 1935).

Pers, A. van, *Nederlandsch Oost Indische Typen*, 's-Gravenhage, 185?.

Pijper, G. F., *Fragmenta Islamica*, Leiden, Brill, 1934.

Ponder, H. W., *Java Pageant*, Seeley Service Co., London, 1934; reprinted as *Java Pageant: Impressions of the 1930s*, Singapore, Oxford University Press, 1988.

Preservation in Jakarta, Jakarta, Jakarta Capital City Government, 1975.

Raffles, T. S., *The History of Java*, first edition, London, 1817; reissued Kuala Lumpur, Oxford University Press, 1965, and Singapore, Oxford University Press, 1988 (with an Introduction by John Bastin).

Rees, W. A. van en J. C. Rappard, *Neerlands Indie*. Batavia, Leiden, A. W. Sijthoff, 1881.

Reiden, B. van der, *Rapport betreffende eene gehouden enquete naar de arbeidtoestanden in de Industrie van Stootjes en Inheemsche Sigaretten op Java*, Deel I. West Java, Bandoeng, Landsdrukkerij, 1934.

Rendra, W. S., *State of Emergency*, trans. Harry Aveling, Sydney, Wild and Woolley, 1980.

Ritter, W. L. and Hardouin, E., *Java. Tooneelen uit het Leven, Karakterschetsen en Kleederdrachten van Java's Bewoners*, Leiden, 1872.

Robinson, Tjalie (Jan Boon), *Piekerans van een Straatslijper*, Den Haag, Tong Tong, 1976, first edition, 1953.

Roorda van Eysinga, Ph. P., *Verschillende Reizen en Lotgevallen*, Amsterdam, Johannes van der Hey, 1830–2.

Rosidi, Ayip, *Djakarta dalam Puisi Indonesia*, Djakarta, Dewan Kesenian Djakarta, 1972.

Rosihan Anwar, H., *Kisah-Kisah Jakarta Setelah Proklamasi*, Jakarta, Pustaka Jaya, 1977.

——, *Kisah-Kisah Zaman Revolusi: Kenang-kenangan seorang wartawan, 1946–1949*, Jakarta, Pustaka Jaya, 1979.

Sadikin, H. Ali, *Gita Jaya*, Jakarta, Pemerintah DKI, 1977.

——, *Menggusir dan Membangun*, Jakarta, Idayu Press, 1977.

Sarekat Islam Lokal, Jakarta, Arsip Nasional Republik Indonesia, 1975.

Scidmore, E. R., *Java, the Garden of the East*, The Century Co., New York, 1899; reprinted Singapore, Oxford University Press, 1984.

Selberg, Eduard, *Reis naar Java en Bezoek op het Eiland Madura*, trans. W. L. de Sturler, Amsterdam, Oldenburg, 1846.

Short Guide to Djakarta, Bogor, Bandung, Djakarta, Ministry of Information, fourth edition, 1956.

Sjahrir, Soetan, *Out of Exile*, New York, Greenwood, 1949.

Smit, J. (editor), *De Volledige Briefwisseling van E. J. Potgieter en Cd. Busken Huet*, Groningen, 1972.

Soemarno Sosroatmodjo, H., *Dari Rimba Raya ke Jakarta Raya. Sebuah Otobiografi*, Jakarta, Gunung Agung, 1981.

Stavorinus, Johan Splinter, *Voyages to the East Indies*, trans. S. H. Wilcocke, London, 1798.

Stockdale, J. J., *Sketches, Civil and Military of the Island of Java and its Immediate Dependencies* ..., London, Stockdale, second edition, 1812.

Sukarno, *An Autobiography as told to Cindy Adams*, Hong Kong, Gunung Agung, 1966.

Tan Malaka, *Dari Pendjara ke Pendjara*, Jogjakarta, Pustaka Purba, n.d.

Teenstra, J. H. W., *Diogenes in de Tropen*, Amsterdam, Vrij Nederland, 1947.

Teenstra, M. D., *De Vruchten mijner werkzaamheden gedurende mijner reize over de Kaap de Goede Hoop naar Java en terug* ..., Groningen, H. Eeckhof, 1828–9.

Tesch, J. W., *The Hygiene Study Ward Centre at Batavia: Planning and Preliminary Results 1937–1941*, Leiden, University of Leiden, 1948.

Thorn, William, *Memoir of the Conquest of Java*, London, T. Egerton, 1815.

25 Jaren Decentralisatie in Nederlandsch-Indie, 1905–1930, Semarang, Vereeniging voor Locale Belangen, 1930.

Valentijn, Francois, *Oud en Nieuw Oost Indien*, Amsterdam, S. Keizer, 1862, first edition, 1724–6.

Veer, W. de, *Particuliere Landerijen en de Openbare Veiligheid in de Residentie Batavia*, Batavia, 1904.

Verslag van de Vereeniging 'Dorcas' te Batavia over 1908–1909, Batavia, 1909.

Veth, Bas, *Het Leven in Nederlandsch Indie*, 's-Gravenhage, J. C. Opmeer, 1900.

50 Jaren 1885–1935 Bataviaasch Nieuwsblad, Batavia, Kolff, 1935.

Vries, J. J. de, *Jaarboek van Batavia en Omstreken*, Weltevreden, 1927.

Wal, S. L. van der, *De Volksraad en de Staatkundige Ontwikkeling van Nederlands-Indie*, Groningen, J. B. Wolters, 1964.

_____ (editor), *Officiele Bescheiden Betreffende de Nederlands-*

Indonesische Betrekkingen, 1945–1950, Vol. 1, 's-Gravenhage, Nijhoff, 1971.

Wall, V. I. van de, *Oude Hollandsche Buitenplaatsen van Batavia*, Deventer, 1943.

Wehl, David, *The Birth of Indonesia*, London, Allen and Unwin, 1948.

Weitzel, A. W. P., *Batavia in 1858*, Gorinchem, J. Noordvijn, 1860.

Williams, Maslyn, *Five Journeys from Jakarta*, Sydney, Collins, 1966.

Wit, Augusta de, *Java: Facts and Fancies*, W. P. van Stockum, The Hague, 1912; reprinted Singapore, Oxford University Press, 1984.

Wright, A. and Breakspear, O. T. (editors), *Twentieth Century Impressions of Netherlands India*, London, Lloyds Greater Britain Publishing Co., 1909.

Zee, D. van der, *Batavia. De Koningin van het Oosten/The Queen of the East*, Rotterdam, Dr Gustav Schueler, 1926.

Articles

Balfas, M., 'A Child of the Revolution', *Indonesia*, No. 17, April 1974, pp. 43–50.

Bleeker, P., 'Bijdragen tot de Medische Topographie van Batavia', *Tijdschrift voor Nederlandsch-Indie*, Vol. 5, No. 2, 1843, pp. 281–332, 640–58.

———, 'Bijdragen tot de Geneeskundige Topographie van Batavia. IV Bevolking', *Tijdschrift voor Nederlandsch-Indie*, Vol. 8, No. 2, 1846.

———, 'Bijdrage tot de Statistiek der Bevolking van Java', *Tijdschrift voor Nederlandsch-Indie*, Vol. 9, No. 4, 1847.

———, 'Nieuwe Bijdragen tot de kennis der Bevolkingstatistiek van Java', *Bijdragen tot de Taal-, Land- en Volkenkunde van Nederlandsch Indie*, Vol. 3, No. 4, 1869.

Brandt, W., 'Sterfte te Batavia 1929–1931', *Geneeskundige Tijdschrift voor Nederlands-Indie*, Vol. 80, 1940, pp. 1470–7.

'Chronologische Gescheidenis van Batavia, geschreven door een Chinees', *Tijdschrift voor Neerlands-Indie*, Vol. II, 1840, pp. 1–114.

Cordes, J. H. W., 'Flora en Pomona te Batavia', *De Indische Gids*, Vol. 11, No. 1, 1889.

Franklin, G. H., 'Assignment in Djakarta—a personal view of planning in Indonesia', *Royal Australian Planning Institute Journal*, Vol. 2, 1964, pp. 229–36.

Greiner, Dr, 'Over Land en Zee: van Rio Janeiro naar Java', *Tijdschrift voor Nederlandsch Indie*, nieuwe serie, Vol. 2, No. 2, 1873, pp. 341–83.

Grijns, C. D., 'Lenong in the Environs of Jakarta: a report', *Archipel*, No. 12, 1976, pp. 175–202.

Gunning, H. C. H., 'Het Woningvraagstuk', *Koloniale Studien*, Vol. 2, No. 1, 1908, pp. 109–26.

Haas, J. H. de, 'Zuigelingensterfte in Batavia', *Geneeskundige Tijdschrift voor Nederlandsch-Indie*, Vol. 78, 1938, pp. 1467–512.

_____, 'Sterfte naar Leeftijdsgroepen in Batavia, in bijzonder op den kinderleeftijd', *Geneeskundige Tijdschrift voor Nederlandsch-Indie*, Vol. 79, 1939, pp. 707–26.

'De haven te Tanjong-Priok Batavia', *Tijdschrift voor Nederlandsch-Indie*, nieuwe serie, Vol. 6, Part 1, 1877, pp. 99–116.

Heeren, H. J., 'The Urbanisation of Djakarta', *Ekonomi dan Keuangan Indonesia*, Vol. 8, No. 11, 1955, pp. 696–736.

Hooyman, Jan, 'Verhandeling over den Tegenwoordigen Staat van den Land-bouw in de Ommelanden van Batavia', *Verhandelingen van het Bataviaasch Genootschap*, Vol. 1, 1781, pp. 173–262.

'Ibukota dan Ali Sadikin', *Progres*, Vol. 120, June 1977, pp. 25–47.

Mochtar, R. and Soedarjono, R., 'A General Public Health Survey within the Demonstration and Study Centre for Public Health and Preventive Medicine in Djakarta-City', *Madjalah Kedokteran Indonesia*, Vol. 7, No. 12, 1957, pp. 375–99.

Nes, J. F. W. van, 'De Chinezen op Java', *Tijdschrift voor Nederlandsch-Indie*, Vol. 13, No. 1, 1851, pp. 239–53, 292–313.

Ouwehand, C. D., 'Mortaliteit te Batavia', *Geneeskundige Tijdschrift voor Nederlandsch-Indie*, Vol. 52, 1912, pp. 296–309.

'Penjelidikin Biaja Hidup di Djakarta', *Ekonomi dan Keuangan Indonesia*, Vol. 10, 1957, pp. 738–95.

Pramudya Ananta Tur, 'Letter to a Friend from the Country', *Quadrant*, September–October 1969, pp. 59–64.

Sadikin, Ali, 'Saya Mendapat Kepuasan Batin', *Prisma*, Vol. 6, No. 5, May 1977.

Sajono, 'Infant Mortality in Djakarta', *Paediatrica Indonesica*, Vol. 4, No. 4, 1964, pp. 236–47.

Salmon, Claudine and Lombard, Denys, 'Le Poème en Maleis d'un Peranakan sur la Visite du Roi Chulalongkorn à Batavia en 1871', *Archipel*, No. 22, 1981, pp. 133–66.

Satyawati Suleiman, 'The Last Days of Batavia', *Indonesia*, No. 28, October 1979, pp. 55–64.

Simandjuntak, 'Pembangunan Perumahan Maju Pesat Dikhawatirkan Tumbuh Slum Baru', *Prisma*, Vol. 12, No. 4, 1983, pp. 70–88.

Soenarjono Danoedjo, 'Everyone using urban facilities must pay for them', *Prisma*, Vol. 32, June 1984.

Teisseire, Andries, 'Beschrijving van een Gedeelte der Omme- en Bovenlanden dezer Hoofdstad', *Verhandelingen van het Bataviaasch Genootschap*, Vol. VI, 1792, pp. 1–107.

Watts, Kenneth, 'The Planning of Greater Djakarta: A Case Study of Regional Planning', *Ekistics*, No. 10, 1960, pp. 401–5.

Wetering, F. H. van der, 'Kampongverbetering', *Koloniale Studien*, Vol. 23, 1939, pp. 307–25.

Published Official Records

Gemeenteblad van Batavia, Weltevreden, Batavia Gemeenteraad.

Indisch Verslag, Batavia, Landsdrukkerij.

Jakarta Dalam Angka/Statistical Yearbook of Jakarta, Jakarta, Kantor Sensus dan Statistik.

Java Government Gazette, Batavia.

Koloniaal Verslag, Batavia, Landsdrukkerij.

Maandverslagen omtrent de Werkzaamheden aan den Bouw der Haven-werken van Batavia, 1877–1885, Batavia, Landsdrukkerij, 1877–85.

Madjallah Kotapradja, Mingguan Resmi Kotapradja Djakarta Raya, 1950–7.

Notilen Dewan Perwakilan Kota Sementara Djakarta Raya, Djakarta, Pemerintah DKI, 1955.

Notulen der Vergadering van de Gemeenteraad van Batavia, Batavia, Gemeenteraad, 1917–1941.

Rapport der Kommissie ingesteld bij Gouvernementsbesluit...met het doel om de kwestie omtrent de geschikste plaats waar Eene Zeehaven voor Batavia kan worden daargesteld, te beoordeelen, Batavia, Landsdrukkerij, 1874.

Rentjana Induk DCI Djakarta 1965–1985, Djakarta, Pemerintah DCI, 1967.

Rentjana Pendahuluan untuk Kota Djakarta/Outline Plan for the City of Djakarta, Djakarta, Djawatan Pekerdjaan Umum Kotapradja Djakarta Raya, 1957.

Risalah Rapat-Rapat Paripurna DPRD DKI Jakarta, Jakarta, Pemerintah DKI, 1971–2.

Sensus Penduduk 1961 DCI Djakarta Raya, Jakarta, Biro Pusat Statistik, 1963.

Sensus Penduduk 1971: Penduduk Jakarta Raya, Jakarta, Kantor Sensus dan Statistik, 1974.

Verslag van de Commissie tot Bestudeering van Staatsrechtelijke Hervormingen (Visman-Commissie), Batavia. Landsdrukkerij, 1941.

Verslag van de Toestand der Gemeente Batavia over 1912, Weltevreden, Batavia, Gemeenteraad, 1912.

Verslag van de Toestand der Gemeente Batavia over 1917, Weltevreden, Landsdrukkerij, 1919.

Volkstelling 1930/Census of 1930 in Netherlands Indies, Batavia, Landsdrukkerij, 1933–6.

Zestiende Verslag va de Arbeidsinspectie, Batavia, Landsdrukkerij, 1937.

Newspapers and Periodicals

Api

Asia Raya

Asiaweek
Bataviaasch Nieuwsblad
Berita Kaoem Betawi
Bintang Barat
Expres
Java-Bode
Kompas
Merdeka
Neratja
Pemandangan
Pembrita Betawi
Sin Po
Sinar Terang
Tempo

Unpublished Sources

Hoek, L. G. C. A. van der, 'Memorie van overgave van Batavia 1931–1934', *Mailrapport* 1320/1934, Ministry of Colonies Archives, Den Haag.

Hogendorp, C. S. W. van, 'Algemeen Jaarlijksch Verslag van de Staat der Residentie Batavia over 1824', Collectie van Hogendorp nr. 83, Algemeen Rijksarchief, Den Haag.

International Bank for Reconstruction and Development, *Greater Djakarta, the Capital City of Indonesia*, New York, 1971.

Laporan Peninjauan dari Rombongan Economic Development Institute Bank Dunia Mengenai Perbaikan Kampung (Proyek Moh, Husni Thamrin) di Jakarta, Bappem Proyek MHT, DKI Jakarta, 1976, mimeo.

Moir, Hasel V. J. and Soetjipto Wirosardjono, 'The Informal Sector in Jakarta', Report to the ILO, Geneva; Jakarta, LIPI-LEKNAS and Kantor Sensus dan Statistik, 1977.

Planned Community Development Ltd., *Jakarta Urban Development Project*, New York, March 1974, mimeo.

Secondary Sources

Books

Abdurrachman Surjomihardjo (editor), *Beberapa Segi Sejarah Masyarakat-Budaya Jakarta*, Jakarta, Pemerintah DKI Jakarta, 1977.

_____, *Pemekaran Kota/The Growth of Jakarta*, Jakarta, Djambatan, 1977.

Abeyasekere, Susan, *One Hand Clapping: Indonesian Nationalists and the Dutch, 1939–1942*, Clayton, Monash University, 1976.

Ali, R. Mohammad and Bodmer, F., *Djakarta Through the Ages*, Djakarta, Government of the Capital City of Djakarta, 1969.

Anderson, Benedict R. O'G., *Java in a Time of Revolution: Occupation and Resistance, 1944–1946*, Ithaca, Cornell University Press, 1972.

Ayres, Robert L., *Banking on the Poor. The World Bank and World Poverty*, Cambridge, MIT Press, 1983.

Benda, Harry J., *The Crescent and the Rising Sun: Indonesian Islam under the Japanese Occupation, 1942–1945*, The Hague and Bandung, Van Hoeve, 1958.

Bianpoen, *Research and Development for Urban Management: Case Jakarta*, Rotterdam, Erasmus Universiteit, 1983.

Blumberger, J. Th. Petrus, *Politieke Partijen en Stroomingen in Nederlandsch-Indie*, Leiden, Leidsche Uitgeversmaatschappij, 1934.

——, *De Indo-Europeesche Beweging in Nederlandsch Indie*, Haarlem, Tjeenk Willink, 1939.

Blusse, Leonard, *Strange Company: Chinese settlers, mestizo women and the Dutch in VOC Batavia*, Dordrecht, Foris Publications, 1986.

Booth, Anne and McCawley, Peter (editors), *The Indonesian Economy During the Soeharto Era*, Kuala Lumpur, Oxford University Press, 1981.

Breuning, H. A., *Het Voormalige Batavia, Een Hollandsche Stedestichting in de Tropen*, Amsterdam, Albert de Lange, 1954.

Budiaman, *Folklor Betawi*, Jakarta, Pustaka Jaya, 1979.

Colenbrander, H. T., *Jan Pietersz. Coen: Levensbeschrijving*, 's-Gravenhage, Nijhoff, 1934.

Conference on Modern Indonesian History, July 18–19, 1975, Centre for Southeast Asian Studies, University of Wisconsin, 1975.

Coppel, Charles A., *Indonesian Chinese in Crisis*, Kuala Lumpur, Oxford University Press, 1983.

Critchfield, Richard, *The Golden Bowl Be Broken. Peasant Life in Four Cultures*, Bloomington, Indiana University Press, 1973.

Crouch, Harold, *The Army and Politics in Indonesia*, Ithaca, Cornell University Press, 1978.

Damais, Soedarmadji J. H. (editor), *Bung Karno dan Seni*, Jakarta, Yayasan Bung Karno, 1979.

Davis, Gloria (editor), *What is Modern Indonesian Culture?*, Athens, Ohio University, 1979.

Dijk, C. van, *Rebellion Under the Banner of Islam*, The Hague, Nijhoff, 1981.

Dorleans, Bernard, *Etude Geographique de Trois Kampung a Djakarta*, Paris, Universite de Paris-Sorbonne, 1976.

Duparc, H. J. A., *De Elektrische Stadstrams op Java*, Rotterdam, Wyt, 1972.

Encyclopaedie van Nederlandsch Oost-Indie, 's-Gravenhage, Nijhoff, 1918.

Feith, Herbert, *The Indonesian Elections of 1955*, Ithaca, Cornell University Press, 1957.

_____, *The Decline of Constitutional Democracy in Indonesia*, Ithaca, Cornell University Press, 1962.

Fox, J. J. *et al.* (editors), *Indonesia: Australian Perspectives*, Canberra, Australian National University Press, 1980.

Golay, Frank *et al.*, *Underdevelopment and Economic Nationalism in Southeast Asia*, Ithaca, Cornell University Press, 1969.

Haan, F. de, *De Priangan*, Batavia, Kolff, 1910.

_____, *Oud Batavia*, Batavia, Kolff, 1922.

Hadisutjipto, S. Z., *Bara dan Njala Revolusi Phisik di Djakarta*, Djakarta, Pemerintah DCI Djakarta, 1971.

_____, *Sekitar 200 Tahun Sejarah Jakarta (1750–1945)*, Jakarta, Pemerintah DKI Jakarta, 1979.

Heuken, Adolf, *Historical Sites of Jakarta*, Jakarta, Cipta Loka Caraka, 1982.

Hindley, Donald, *The Communist Party of Indonesia 1951–1963*, Berkeley, University of California Press, 1966.

Holt, Claire, *Art in Indonesia*, Ithaca, Cornell University Press, 1967.

Hughes, John, *Indonesian Upheaval*, New York, David McKay, 1967.

Hugo, Graeme J., *Population Mobility in West Java*, Yogyakarta, Gadjah Mada University Press, 1978.

Ingleson, John, *In Search of Justice: Workers and Unions in Colonial Java, 1908–1926*, Singapore, Oxford University Press, 1986.

Jackson, Karl D. and Pye, Lucien W. (editors), *Political Power and Communications in Indonesia*, Berkeley, University of California Press, 1978.

Janssen, J. G., *Grondregistratie Jacatra, Batavia, Djakarta*, no publisher, no place, n.d. (1951?).

Jellinek, Lea, *The Life of a Jakarta Street Trader*, Clayton, Monash University, 1976.

_____, *The Life of the Poor in Indonesian Cities*, Clayton, Monash University, 1978.

_____, *The Life of a Jakarta Street Trader—Two Years Later*, Clayton, Monash University, 1978.

Jenkins, David, *Suharto and His Generals. Indonesian Military Politics 1975–1983*, Ithaca, Cornell University Press, 1984.

Joel, H. F., *Honderd Jaar Java Bode*, Djakarta, Koninklijke Drukkerij de Unie, 1952.

Kahin, G. McT., *Nationalism and Revolution in Indonesia*, Ithaca, Cornell University Press, 1952.

Kalff, S., *De Slavernij in Oost-Indie*, Baarn, Hollandia-drukkerij, 1920.

Kartodirdjo, Sartono, *Protest Movements in Rural Java*, Singapore, Oxford University Press, 1973.

Koentjaraningrat, *Masyarakat Desa di Selatan Jakarta*, Jakarta, LIPI, 1975.

Koks, J. Th., *De Indo*, Amsterdam, H. J. Paris, 1931.

Kongres Wanita Indonesia, *Sejarah Setengah Abad Pergerakan Wanita Indonesia*, Jakarta, Balai Pustaka, 1978.

Kumar, Ann, *Surapati, Man and Legend*, Leiden, Brill, 1976.

Kwee Tek Hoay, *The Origins of the Modern Chinese Movement in Indonesia*, Ithaca, Cornell University Press, 1969.

Lea, J. P. and Courtney, J. M. (editors), *Cities in Conflict: Studies in the Planning and Management of Asian Cities*, Washington, World Bank, 1985.

Legge, J. D., *Sukarno: A Political Biography*, Harmondsworth, Penguin, 1972.

McCoy, Alfred W. (editor), *Southeast Asia under Japanese Occupation*, New Haven, Yale University Press, 1980.

McVey, Ruth T., *The Rise of Indonesian Communism*, Ithaca, Cornell University Press, 1965.

—— (editor), *Indonesia*, New Haven, Hraf Press, 1967.

Mackie, J. A. C. (editor), *The Chinese in Indonesia*, Melbourne, Nelson, 1976.

Manderson, Lenore (editor), *Women's Work and Women's Roles*, Canberra, Australian National University Press, 1983.

Meilink-Roelofsz, M. A. P., *Asian Trade and European Influence in the Indonesian Archipelago between 1500 and 1630*, The Hague, Nijhoff, 1962.

Milone, Pauline Dublin, *Urban Areas in Indonesia: Administrative and Census Concepts*, Berkeley, University of California, 1966.

Mona, Matu, *Riwajat Penghidupan dan Perdjuangan M. Husni Thamrin*, (first edition 1941), Medan, 1952.

Mortimer, Rex, *Indonesian Communism under Sukarno*, Ithaca, Cornell University Press, 1974.

Muliakusuma, Sutarsih, *Perkawinan dan Perceraian pada Masyarakat Betawi*, Yogyakarta, Gadjah Mada University Press, 1982.

Naim, Mochtar, *Merantau. Pola Migrasi Suku Minangkabau*, Yogyakarta, Gadjah Mada University Press, 1979.

Nieuwenhuys, Rob, *Oost-Indische Spiegel*, Amsterdam, Querido, 1973.

Noer, Deliar, *The Modernist Muslim Movement in Indonesia, 1900–1942*, Kuala Lumpur, Oxford University Press, 1973.

Owen, Norman (editor), *Death and Disease in Southeast Asian History*, Singapore, Oxford University Press, 1987.

Rahardjo, Julfita *et al.*, *Wanita Kota Jakarta: kehidupan keluarga dan keluarga berencana*, Yogyakarta, Gadjah Mada University Press, 1980.

Papers of the Dutch–Indonesian Historical Conference held at Noorwijkerhout, the Netherlands, 19–22 May 1976, Leiden, Bureau of Indonesian Studies, 1978.

Papers of the Dutch Indonesian Historical Conference held at Lage Vuursche, Netherlands, June 1980, Leiden, Bureau of Indonesian Studies, 1982.

Raffel, Burton, *The Development of Modern Indonesian Poetry*, New York, State University of New York Press, 1967.

Reid, A. J. S. (editor), *Slavery, Bondage and Dependency in Southeast Asia*, St Lucia, University of Queensland Press, 1983.

———, *Indonesian National Revolution 1945–1950*, Melbourne, Longmans, 1974.

Republik Indonesia: Kotapradja Djakarta Raja, Djakarta, Kementerian Penerangan, n.d.

Safwan, Mardanas, *Peranan Gedung Menteng Raya 31 dalam Perjuangan Kemerdekaan*, Jakarta, Pemerintah Kota Jakarta, 1973.

———, *Peranan Gedung Kramat Raya 106 dalam Melahirkan Sumpah Pemuda*, Jakarta, Pemerintah Kota Jakarta, 1979.

Salmon, Claudine and Lombard, Denys, *Les Chinois de Jakarta, Temples et Vie Collective*, Paris, Cahier d'Archipel, 1977.

Sethuraman, S. V., *Jakarta, Urban Development and Employment*, Geneva, International Labour Organization, 1976.

——— (editor), *The Urban Informal Sector in Developing Countries*, Geneva, International Labour Organization, 1981.

Soekanto, S. A., *Matahari Jakarta: Lukisan Kehidupan M. Husni Thamrin*, Jakarta, Pustaka Jaya, 1973.

Somers, Mary F., *Peranakan Chinese Politics in Indonesia*, Ithaca, Cornell University Press, 1964.

Suryadinata, Leo, *Prominent Indonesian Chinese in the Twentieth Century: A Preliminary Survey*, Athens, Ohio, 1972.

———, *Peranakan Chinese Politics in Java, 1917–1942*, Singapore, Institute of Southeast Asian Studies, 1976.

———, *Eminent Indonesian Chinese: Biographical Sketches*, Singapore, Institute of Southeast Asian Studies, 1978.

——— (editor), *Political Thinking of the Indonesian Chinese, 1900–1977*, Singapore, Institute of Southeast Asian Studies, 1979.

Sutter, D., *Indonesianisasi: Politics in a Changing Economy, 1940–1955*, Ithaca, Cornell University Press, 1959.

Taylor, Jean, *The Social World of Batavia: European and Eurasian in Dutch Asia*, Madison, University of Wisconsin Press, 1983.

The Liang Gie, *Sedjarah Pemerintahan Kota Djakarta*, Djakarta, Kotapradja Djakarta Raya, 1958.

Tjandrasasmita, Uka, *Sejarah Jakarta*, Jakarta, Pemerintah DKI Jakarta, 1977.

Van Niel, Robert, *The Emergence of the Modern Indonesian Elite*, The Hague and Bandung, Van Hoeve, 1960.

Vermeulen, J. T., *De Chineezen te Batavia en de Troebelen van 1740*, Leiden, E. Ijdo, 1938.

Verster, J. F. L. de Balbian and Zeggelen, M. C. Kooy-van, *Ons Mooi Indie: Batavia Oud en Nieuw*, Amsterdam, Meulenhoff, 1921.

Wall, V. I. van der, *The Influence of Olivia Mariamne Raffles on*

European Society in Java (1812–1814), no publisher, n.d.

Widjojo Nitisastro, *Population Trends in Indonesia*, Ithaca, Cornell University Press, 1970.

Wijaya, Hussein (editor), *Seni-Budaya Betawi*, Jakarta, Pustaka Jaya, 1976.

Williams, Lea E., *Overseas Chinese Nationalism: The Genesis of the Pan-Chinese Movement in Indonesia 1900–1916*, Glencoe, Free Press, 1960.

Willmott, Donald E., *The National Status of the Chinese in Indonesia, 1900–1958*, Ithaca, Cornell University Press, 1961.

Articles

Abdurachman, Paramita R., ' "Portuguese" Presence in Jakarta', *Masyarakat Indonesia*, Vol. II, No. 1, 1975, pp. 89–103.

Abeyasekere, Susan, 'Colonial Urban Politics: The Municipal Council of Batavia', *Kabar Seberang*, Vol. 13–14, 1984, pp. 17–24.

Ardan, S. M., 'In Memoriam: Sjuman Djaja (1934–1985)', *Indonesia*, No. 40, October 1985, pp. 123–6.

Blusse, Leonard, 'Chinese Trade to Batavia during the Days of the V.O.C.', *Archipel*, No. 18, 1979.

———, 'Batavia, 1619–1740: the Rise and Fall of a Chinese Colonial Town', *Journal of Southeast Asian Studies*, Vol. XII, No. 1, March 1981.

———, 'The Caryatids of Batavia: Reproduction, Religion and Acculturation under the V.O.C.', *Itinerario*, Vol. VII, No. 1, 1983, pp. 57–85.

Bruner, E. M., 'Batak Ethnic Associations in Three Indonesian Cities', *Southwestern Journal of Anthropology*, Vol. 28, No. 3, 1972, pp. 207–29.

Budiman, Arief, 'Ali Sadikin: One-Man Revolt', *Quadrant*, September–October 1969, pp. 75–7.

Canter Visscher, J. Th., 'De Waarheid over 22 Mei 1848', *Tijdschrift voor Nederlandsch-Indie*, Vol. 10, No. 2, 1881, pp. 401–34.

Castles, Lance, 'The Ethnic Profile of Jakarta', *Indonesia*, Vol. 1, April 1967, pp. 153–204.

Chambert-Loir, H. en J. Dumarcay, 'Le Langgar Tinggi de Pekojan, Jakarta', *Archipel*, No. 30, 1985, pp. 47–56.

Cobban, James L., 'The Ephemeral Historic District in Jakarta', *Geographical Review*, Vol. 75, No. 3, 1985.

Cohen, Dennis, 'The People Who Get in the Way: Poverty and Development in Jakarta', *Politics* (Australia), Vol. 9, No. 1, May 1974, pp. 1–9.

Cribb, Robert, 'Political Dimensions of the Currency Question 1945–1947', *Indonesia*, Vol. 31, April 1981, pp. 113–36.

———, 'Elections in Jakarta', *Asian Survey*, Vol. 24, No. 6, June 1984.

Critchfield, Richard, 'The Plight of the Cities: Djakarta—the First to "Close"', *Columbia Journal of World Business*, Vol. 6, 1971, pp. 89–93.

Devas, Nick, 'Indonesia's Kampung Improvement Program: An Evaluative Case Study', *Ekistics*, No. 286, January/February 1981.

_____, 'Financing Urban Land Development for Low Income Housing: An analysis with particular reference to Jakarta, Indonesia', *Third World Planning Review*, Vol. 5, No. 1, August 1983.

Dick, Howard, 'Urban Public Transport: Jakarta, Surabaya and Malang', *Bulletin of Indonesian Economic Studies*, Vol. 17, Nos. 1 and 2, March and July 1981.

'Djakarta's Satellite Town', *Asian Review*, No. 51, January 1955, pp. 82–4.

Djauhari, S., 'The Capital City 1942–1967', *Masalah Bangunan*, Vol. 14, Nos. 1–2, 1969, pp. 8–12.

Dorodjatun, K. Jakti, 'The Bang Ali Era and the Development of Jakarta', *Prisma*, No. 8, December 1977, pp. 75–8.

'Dossier Cinema', *Archipel*, No. 5, 1973, pp. 54–230.

Evans, Jeremy, 'The Growth of Urban Centres in Java since 1961', *Bulletin of Indonesian Economic Studies*, Vol. 20, No. 1, 1984, pp. 44–57.

Evers, Hans-Dieter, 'Subsistence Production and the Jakarta "Floating Mass"', *Prisma*, Vol. 17, June 1980, pp. 27–35.

_____, 'The Contribution of Urban Subsistence Production to Incomes in Jakarta', *Bulletin of Indonesian Economic Studies*, Vol. 17, No. 2, 1981, pp. 89–96.

Faille, P. de Roo de la, 'De Chineesche Raad te Batavia en het door dit college beheerde fonds', *Bijdragen van de Koninklijke Instituut*, Vol. 80, 1924, pp. 302–24.

Frederick, W. H., 'Rhoma Irama and the Dangdut Style', *Indonesia*, No. 34, October 1982, pp. 103–30.

Grijns, C. D., 'A la Recherche du "Melayu Betawi" ou parler Malais de Batavia', *Archipel*, No. 17, 1979, pp. 135–58.

Haan, F. de, 'De Laatste der Mardijkers', *Bijdragen tot de Taal-, Land- en Volkenkunde*, Vol. 73, 1917, pp. 219–54.

Hoetink, B., 'Chineesche Officieren te Batavia onder de Compagnie', *Bijdragen tot de Taal-, Land- en Volkenkunde*, Vol. 78, 1922, pp. 1–136.

Hugo, Graeme, 'Circular Migration', *Bulletin of Indonesian Economic Studies*, Vol. 13, No. 3, 1977, pp. 57–66.

Jellinek, Lea, 'The Pondok of Jakarta', *Bulletin of Indonesian Economic Studies*, Vol. 13, No. 3, November 1977, pp. 67–71.

Jobst E., 'Stedebouwkundige Ontwikkeling van Batavia', *Indisch Bouwkundig Tijdschrift*, No. 5, 1926, pp. 71–6 and No. 6, 1926, pp. 89–94.

Karamoy, Amir, 'The Kampung Improvement Program: Hope and

Reality', *Prisma*, Vol. 32, June 1984, pp. 19–36.

Karamoy, Amir and Sablie, Achmad, 'The Communication Aspect and its Impact on the Youth of Poor Kampungs in the City of Jakarta', *Prisma*, Vol. 1, No. 1, May 1975, pp. 62–8.

Krausse, Gerald, 'Economic Adjustments of Migrants in the City: the Jakarta Experience', *International Migration Review*, Vol. 13, Part 45, 1978, pp. 46–70.

——, 'Intra-urban variations in Kampung settlements in Jakarta', *Journal of Tropical Geography*, Vol. 46, 1987, pp. 11–26.

Lekkerkerker, C., 'De Baliers van Batavia', *De Indische Gids*, Vol. 40, No. 1, 1918.

Lerche, Dietrich, 'Membiayai Pembangunan Perkotaan: Kasus Pengetrapan Pajak Tanah dan Bangunan secara Efektif', *Prisma*, Vol. 8, December 1972, pp. 37–46.

——, 'Efficiency of Taxation in Indonesia', *Bulletin of Indonesian Economic Studies*, Vol. 16, No. 1, 1980, pp. 34–51.

Logsdon, Martha G., 'Neighborhood Organisation in Jakarta', *Indonesia*, No. 18, 1974, pp. 53–70.

Lombard, Denys, 'A Travers le Vieux Djakarta. 1. La Mosquée des Balinais', *Archipel*, No. 3, 1972, pp. 97–101.

Lubis, Mochtar, 'Jakarta kota penuh kontras', *Prisma*, Vol. 6, No. 5, May 1977, pp. 32–44.

Masmimar Mangiang, 'The Economics of Scavenging', *Prisma*, Vol. 13, 1979, pp. 36–45.

Mertens, Walter, 'Jakarta, a Country in a City', *Majalah Demografi Indonesia*, Vol. 2, No. 6, 1976, pp. 50–109.

Ming, Hanneke, 'Barracks-Concubinage in the Indies, 1887–1920', *Indonesia*, No. 35, April 1983.

Muhadjir, 'Dialek Jakarta', *Majalah Ilmu-Ilmu Sastra Indonesia*, Vol. 2, 1964, pp. 25–52.

Oey, Mayling, 'Jakarta dibangun kaum pendatang', *Prisma*, Vol. 6, No. 5, May 1977, pp. 63–70.

Papanek, Gustaf F., 'The Poor of Jakarta', *Economic Development and Cultural Change*, Vol. 24, No. 1, October 1975, pp. 1–27.

Papanek, H., 'Wanita di Jakarta', *Masyarakat Indonesia*, Vol. 5, No. 2, 1978.

Pauker, E. T., 'Ganefo 1: Sports and Politics in Djakarta', *Asian Survey*, Vol. 5, 1965, pp. 171–85.

Pringgodigdo, Soewarni, 'Over du Perron en zijn invloed op de Indonesische intellectuelen (1936–1939)', *Cultureel Nieuws*, Vol. 2, No. 16, January 1952, pp. 135–49.

Rahardjo, S., 'Tjara membeli tanah dan membangun di Djakarta', *Mahkota*, Vol. 1, No. 1, May 1972, pp. 11–18.

Rosser, Colin, 'The Evolving Role of a National Agency for Housing and Urban Development in Indonesia', *Habitat International*, Vol. 7, No. 5/6, 1983, pp. 137–49.

Saleh, A. R. and Assegaf, M., 'Pembangunan dan pengorbanan: kasus pembebasan tanah di Jakarta', *Prisma*, Vol. 6, No. 3, March 1977, pp. 48–59.

Sjahrir, Kartini, 'Asosiasi Klan Orang Batak di Jakarta', *Prisma*, Vol. 12, No. 1, 1983, pp. 75–81.

Skinner, G. W., 'Java's Chinese Minority: Continuity and Change', *Journal of Asian Studies*, Vol. 20, No. 3, May 1961, pp. 353–62.

Smith, T. M. and Smith, R. S., 'Municipal Finance', *Bulletin of Indonesian Economic Studies*, Vol. 7, No. 1, March 1971, pp. 114–31.

Soemargono F., 'Les Chansons de Benjamin: un corpus du Jakartanais', *Archipel*, No. 7, 1974, pp. 69–92.

Soemarno Sosroatmodjo, 'Jakarta bukan hanya bagi yang berduit', *Prisma*, Vol. 6, No. 5, May 1977, pp. 53–5.

Soetjipto Wirosardjono, 'The meaning, limitations and problems of the informal sector', *Prisma*, No. 32, June 1984, pp. 78–83.

Suharso, 'Migration and education in Jakarta', *Masyarakat Indonesia*, Vol. 4, Nos. 1–2, June 1977, pp. 1–28.

Sundrum, R. M., 'Household income patterns', *Bulletin of Indonesian Economic Studies*, Vol. 10, No. 1, March 1974, pp. 82–105.

_____, 'Changes in consumption patterns in urban Java, 1970–1976', *Bulletin of Indonesian Economic Studies*, Vol. 13, No. 2, July 1977, pp. 102–16.

Suparlan, Parsudi, 'The Gelandangan of Jakarta', *Indonesia*, No. 18, 1974, pp. 41–52.

Supranto, J., 'Hasil survey kampung-kampung DKI yang terkena Proyek M. Husni Thamrin', *Prisma*, Vol. 2, No. 5, October 1973, pp. 80–8.

Sutherland, Heather, 'Pudjangga Baru: Aspects of Indonesian Intellectual Life in the 1930s', *Indonesia*, No. 6, October 1968, pp. 106–27.

Temple, G., 'Migration to Jakarta', *Bulletin of Indonesian Economic Studies*, Vol. 11, No. 1, March 1975, pp. 76–81.

Thalib, Dahlan, 'The government and finances of Djakarta', *Bulletin of Indonesian Economic Studies*, October 1968, pp. 90–8.

Van der Veur, Paul, 'The Eurasians of Indonesia: A Problem and Challenge in Colonial History', *Journal of Southeast Asian History*, Vol. 9, No. 2, September 1968, pp. 191–207.

_____, 'Race and Color in Colonial Society', *Indonesia*, No. 8, 1969, pp. 69–79.

Wal, S. L. van der, 'De Nationaal-Socialistische Beweging in Nederlands-Indie', *Bijdragen en Mededeelingen van het Historisch Genootschap*, Vol. 82, 1968, pp. 35–56.

Warr, Peter G., 'The Jakarta Export Processing Zone: Benefits and Costs', *Bulletin of Indonesian Economic Studies*, Vol. 19, No. 3, December 1983, pp. 28–49.

Zwier, Jac., 'De Opzet van het Bestuur van de Satellietstad Kebayoran nabij Djakarta (1948–1950)', *Indonesie*, No. 4, 1950–51, pp. 419–41.

Unpublished Sources

Cohen, Dennis, 'Poverty and Development in Jakarta', Ph.D. dissertation, University of Wisconsin-Madison, 1975.

Cobban, James, 'The City on Java: an essay in historical geography', Ph.D. dissertation, University of California, 1970.

Cribb, Robert, 'Kota Diplomasi? Jakarta in the early Revolution', paper presented at the AAS Annual Meeting, Toronto, 14 March 1981.

_____, 'Jakarta in the Indonesian Revolution, 1945–1949', Ph.D. dissertation, University of London, School of Oriental and African Studies, 1983.

Hugo, Graeme John, 'Population Mobility in West Java, Indonesia', Ph.D. dissertation, Australian National University, 1975.

_____, 'Some Dimensions of Socio-Economic Inequality Associated with Urbanization and Urban Growth in Indonesia', paper presented at the ASAA Conference, Brisbane, 1980.

Jellinek, Lea O., 'The Birth and Death of a Jakarta Kampung', Ph.D. dissertation, Monash University, 1988.

Krausse, Gerald Hans, 'The Kampungs of Jakarta, Indonesia: a Study of Spatial Patterns in Urban Poverty', Ph.D. dissertation, University of Pittsburgh, 1975.

Kwee, John B., 'Chinese Malay Literature of the Peranakan Chinese in Indonesia 1880–1942', Ph.D. dissertation, University of Auckland, 1978.

Logsdon, Martha Gay, 'Leaders and Followers in Urban Neighborhoods: An Exploratory Study in Djakarta, Indonesia', Ph.D. dissertation, Yale University, 1975.

Milone, Pauline D., 'Queen City of the East: the Metamorphosis of a Colonial Capital', Ph.D. dissertation, University of California, 1966.

Nasution, Adnan Buyung, 'Beberapa Aspek Hukum dalam Masalah Pertahanan dan Pemukiman di DKI Jakarta', Paper Lokakarya 26–28 September 1978, 'Pemukiman bagi Penduduk Berpenghasilan Rendah di Jakarta'.

Rush, James Robert, 'Opium Farms in Nineteenth Century Java', Ph.D. dissertation, Yale University, 1977.

Taylor, John Lewis, 'An Evaluation of Selected Impacts of Jakarta's Kampung Improvement Programme', Ph.D. dissertation, University of California, 1983.

Wallace, Stephen, 'Linguistic and Social Dimensions of Phonological Variations in Jakarta Malay', Ph.D. dissertation, Cornell University, 1976.

Index

ABDULLAH, BASUKI, 144
Abendanon, J. H., 105
Affandi, 144, 160
Agriculture: in Batavia region in seventeenth and eighteenth centuries, 23–9, 38, 41–3; Cultivation System, 52–3, 82; Chinese farmers in Batavia region during nineteenth century, 61, 62; in West Java in nineteenth century, 81; in Batavia Residency during Depression, 102; and Green Revolution, 241–2
Airport, 90, 126, 244
Al-Aidrus, Said Husain Abu Bakar, 40
Al-Habashi, Said 'Ali bin 'Abd-al-Rahman, 93
Alatas family, 63–4
Alisjahbana, Takdir, 92, 97, 182
Anwar, Rosihan, 144
Ambon, 8, 28
Ambonese in Batavia, 29, 64, 97–8, 150
Ancol, 34, 170, 198, 218
Angke, 35, 173
Anwar, Chairil, 144–5, 159–60
Aquarium, 92
Arabs: in Batavia under VOC, 22, 40; in nineteenth-century Batavia, 53, 63–4; in early twentieth-century Batavia, 93, 106, 109, 120; Arab shopkeepers and Japanese, 140; Arab traders in markets, 231
Architecture: in eighteenth-century Batavia, 17–19, 25, 36–7; in nineteenth-century Batavia, 54–7, 64–5; in early twentieth-century Batavia, 91–2, 115; and Sukarno,

168–9, 201–2; and Sadikin, 219; see also under Housing
Archives, National, 36–7
Ardan, S. M., 192
Army: of VOC, 20, 29, 31; in nineteenth-century Batavia, 55–6, 80; and nyai, 77, 115; Dutch army withdraws from Batavia, 126; Japanese army arrives in Batavia, 134–5; British forces in Jakarta, 133, 148–9; Dutch army in 'police actions', 133, 157, 161; guerrilla resistance by Republicans, 133, 149–61; Republican army, 138, 146, 151, 159, 161; rebel groups after 1949, 172; during 1950s, 187, 205; and Guided Democracy, 205–9; and 1965 coup, 209–10; since 1965, 215, 220, 234–5
Army Commander's Office (Gedung Pancasila), 55
Arnowo, Dul, 183
Art: during Japanese Occupation, 143–4; during Revolution, 160; Sukarno's patronage of, 168–70, 190; in 1950s and early 1960s, 195; promotion by Sadikin, 220
Asia Raya, 135, 143
Asian Games, 170, 178, 198, 201, 207
Asrama Indonesia Merdeka, 145
Asrama Menteng 31, 146–7

BADAN PERJUANGAN, 149, 151
Bajaj, 219, 230
Balai Seni, 220
Balinese: in Batavia under VOC, 20, 21, 23, 29, 34, 35; in nineteenth-

century Batavia, 64; in Jakarta in 1961, 191

Banci, 92, 231–2

Bandanese, in Batavia, 29

Bandung, 82–3, 98, 100, 106, 172, 245

Bangsawan, 192

Banten, 6, 8–13, 71, 81–2, 100, 107

Baperki, 189

Barongsai, 63, 72

Batavia: origin of, 12; besieged in seventeenth century, 12–13; origins of population in seventeenth century, 13–14; fort, 15; development of walled town, 15, 17; housing and architecture in during eighteenth century, 17–19; municipal administration in during eighteenth century, 19; population in 1673, 19–20; Eurasians in during seventeenth and eighteenth centuries, 20–1; slaves in, 21–3; Chinese in during seventeenth and eighteenth centuries, 23–8; Mardijkers in, 28; other ethnic groups in Batavia under the VOC, 29–30; and *kampung*, 30–1; language in, 31, 33; women in, 33–4; religion in, 34–5; Europeans in during eighteenth century, 35–7; population in 1730, 38; known as 'Queen of the East', 3, 39, 48, 57, 123, 141; health in under VOC, 39–40; spread of settlement, 40–1; population in 1730, 40; population in 1779, 41; decline of old walled town, 41–3; and hinterland, '42, 43; seat of government moved to Weltevreden, 44; European view of Batavia in nineteenth century, 48–57, 60; building of Tanjung Priok, 49, 82; size and population in nineteenth century, 52; urban economy in nineteenth century, 52–3; spread of European settlement in nineteenth century, 54–7; European society in nineteenth century, 57–61; Chinese society in nineteenth century, 61–3; Arabs in nineteenth century, 63–4; Indonesians in nineteenth century,

64–7; divisive forces in nineteenth-century society, 68–71; health in nineteenth century, 71–5; women and culture in nineteenth century, 75–80; compared with Surabaya, 81; as centre of colonial administration, 83; comparison of in 1900 and in 1940, 88–94; education in early twentieth century, 94–9; Indonesian nationalism in early twentieth century, 98–9, 101–8; labour organization in, 101–2; Depression in, 102–3; Sarekat Islam in, 104–6; communism in, 106–7; developments in Arab and Chinese communities in early twentieth century, 109–14; Europeans in early twentieth century, 114–17; Municipal Council, 118–24; *kampung* improvement in, 120–3; European view in early twentieth century, 123–4; attacked by Japanese, 126; name changed, 133–4; Dutch resume rule in, 133, 157–9; transfer of sovereignty in, 161

Batavia, Residency, 59, 65, 67, 96, 102–4, 134, 136

Bataviaasch Nieuwsblad, 116

Batik, industry in Batavia, 66–7, 158

Becak: introduction of, 91, 124; numbers of and employment in, 141, 176, 229–30; policies towards, 124, 228–32, 243–4; reaction of *becak*-drivers, 232, 239

Beggars, 142, 196, 198, 232–3

Bekasi, 62, 141, 220, 244

Bemo, 239

Bencon, Captain, *see under* So Bing Kong

Bendungan Hilir, 227

Benyamin S., 236

Bicycles, 91, 92, 141, 176

Biervillas, Innigo de, 18

Bogor, 173, 220, 244; *see also* Buitenzorg

Bousquet, G. H., 117

British: rivalry with VOC, 7–12, 42; rule in Java, 55–8; army in Jakarta,

133, 148–57; Embassy attacked, 205, 207

Budi Utomo, 98

Budiman, Arief, 235

Buitenzorg, 43, 55, 82–3, 100; *see also* Bogor

Buses, 156, 176, 219, 239; minibuses, 219, 244

Busken Huet, Conrad, 59, 117

CAKUNG, 104, 245

Calcutta, 75, 241, 263

Canals: in Batavia under VOC, 15, 17, 18, 36, 39, 41; in nineteenth-century Batavia, 49, 53, 63, 71, 74; in twentieth-century, 90, 93, 196, 223–4, 233, 256

Capgomeh, 62–3, 93, 190, 199, 258

Cars, 90, 115, 141, 176, 235

Cempaka Putih, 256

Cengkareng, 180, 244–5

Children: in Chinese theatre and festivals, 17, 63; in *kampung*, 66, 93; upbringing of, 76–8, 113; infant mortality, 74, 94, 181; and Revolution, 159; of immigrants, 192; orphanages, 19, 24, 35, 198; *see also* Education; *Pemuda*; Students

China, 23–5, 62, 109–13, 159, 188–9, 239

Chinese: in Jayakarta, 6; early trade, 7, 9; in Batavia under VOC, 14, 17, 19, 22–30, 33–5, 37–8; in nineteenth-century Batavia, 53, 61–3, 67–9, 72–80; in early twentieth-century Batavia, 94, 104–7, 109–14, 118–23, 126; during Japanese Occupation, 139–40; during 1945–9, 150–1, 156, 158–9; in Jakarta during 1950s and early 1960s, 173, 181, 183–4, 188–91; in Jakarta since 1965, 235, 239–40, 246–7, 257–8; economic role of, 22–5, 38, 61–2, 67, 80, 104, 106–7, 158, 183–4, 231, 239; officer system, 25, 27, 62, 111; religion of, 25, 38, 68, 110, 189, 235; living conditions of, 24–5, 69, 72–4, 94, 181; relations with governments, 25–8, 68–9, 79–80, 110–12, 139–40, 146–7, 158–9, 188–90; numbers of, 19, 25–6, 27, 61, 111–12, 188; culture of, 25, 34, 62–3, 76–80, 109–14, 188–91, 235, 257–8; anti-Chinese feeling, 26–7, 104, 150–1, 189–90, 199, 239–40, 247

Cholera, 72, 94, 123, 225

Christianity, 6, 19, 20, 28, 31, 38, 61, 68, 188, 189, 192, 235; *see also* Churches

Churches: first in Batavia, 15; Portuguese Church (Gereja Sion), 31; Willemskerk, 56, 61; Catholic cathedral, 56

Cikini, 57, 66, 115, 205, 218

Ciliwung River, *see under* Rivers

Cinema, 56, 91–2, 106, 113–15, 174, 183, 192, 194, 195, 235–6

Cirebon, 42, 101

Civil service, 59, 68, 80, 83, 96, 100, 121, 136, 171, 173, 185, 208, 226, 234

Clubs: Harmonie, 54–5, 60, 68; Concordia, 55; sporting, 93; nightclubs, 234

Coen, Jan Pieterszoon: and Jayakarta, 9–12; and sieges of Batavia, 12–13; death of, 13; and European colonization, 13, 14; and Chinese, 23; statue removed by Japanese, 134

Cokropranolo, Lt.-Gen., 235, 243–4

Communism, *see under* Partai Komunis Indonesia

Coffee, 42, 43, 52–3

Condet, 258

Conservation, 220–1, 257–8

Cook, Captain James, 40

Coolies, 23, 25–6, 29, 39, 66, 71, 82, 94, 100, 107

Cornelis Senen, 29

Corruption: by Dutch, 27, 41–2, 80; in 1950s, 187, 196; under Guided Democracy, 208; in 1970s, 234, 238

Council, Municipal: in early twentieth-century Batavia, 98, 106, 108, 112, 118–24, 255; re-established by

Dutch, 158; during 1950s, 177, 188, 196–9, 202–13; restructured by Sukarno, 206; under Sadikin, 238

Council, People's, 98, 103, 106, 108, 112, 116, 118, 121, 255

Couperus, Louis, 76

Crime, 67, 93, 156, 172–3, 234, 245

'Cross-boys', 194

Crush Malaysia Campaign, 202, 207

Culture: Jakarta as melting-pot of, 254–5, 257–9; of Chinese in Batavia under VOC, 17, 22, 24–5, 34; of Europeans in Batavia under VOC, 17–20, 22, 33–7; of Europeans in nineteenth-century Batavia, 54–61; of Chinese in nineteenth-century Batavia, 61–3; of Indonesians in nineteenth-century Batavia, 65–7; emergence of distinctive Batavian culture, 75–80; in early twentieth-century Batavia, 92, 95–7, 108, 110–17; during Japanese Occupation, 135, 143–5; and Revolution, 160; in Jakarta in 1950s and 1960s, 168–70, 188–90, 192–6, 199–200; under Sadikin, 220–1, 224, 235–7

DAENDELS, H. W., 44, 55–6

Daendels' Palace (Finance Department), 55

Dahler, P. F., 139

Dance, 30, 58, 60, 63, 76, 79, 80, 144, 192, 194–5

Dangdut, 236, 258

Darul Islam, 160–1, 172

Daum, P. A., 59, 72

Deleman, 49, 176

Dendang, 79

Department of Justice (Mahkamah Agung), 55

Depression of 1930s in Batavia, 93–4, 102–3, 116, 122

Dharsono, General H. R., 248

Dukuh Atas, 197

Duri, 223

Dutch: for Dutch activities in South-East Asia and Batavia in seventeenth and eighteenth centuries, *see*

under VOC; Europeans; for Dutch life and policies in nineteenth and early twentieth centuries, *see under* Europeans; return to Jakarta in 1945, 149–51; regain control of Batavia, 152–61; relinquish control, 161, 255; and urban economy in 1950s, 183–4; numbers in Jakarta in 1956 and 1961, 187–8; campaign against by Sukarno, 207; reminders of in Jakarta today, 258

Dutch East India Company, *see under* VOC

ECONOMY: of Batavia under VOC, 15, 22–4, 27, 38, 41–3; in nineteenth-century Batavia, 52, 53, 62, 68, 82–3; in early twentieth-century Batavia, 100–3; of Jakarta during Japanese Occupation, 140–1; of Jakarta in 1945–9, 154–5, 158–9; of Jakarta in 1950s, 181–7; of Jakarta in 1965–7, 215; of Jakarta under Sadikin, 217–20, 242; of Jakarta since Sadikin, 243, 246, 248, 259

Education: under VOC, 35; in nineteenth-century Batavia, 59, 61, 65, 76; in early twentieth-century Batavia, 91, 92, 94–9, 101, 110–13, 116, 123; during Japanese Occupation, 135, 145; during 1945–9, 156–7, 159; in Jakarta in 1950s, 174, 179–80, 188–9; in 1971, 226

Elections: for Batavia Municipal Council, 118; in 1950s, 177, 202–3; in 1971 and 1977, 240–1; in 1982, 246–7

Electricity, 90, 115, 175, 219

Ellya, 236

Entertainment: in Batavia under the VOC, 17, 22, 28–30, 37; in the nineteenth century, 54–8, 65, 77–80; in early twentieth century, 91–3, 113–16; in 1950s and early 1960s, 192, 194–5, 199–200; under Sadikin, 218–19, 231, 235–7; *see also* Cinema; Clubs; Dance; Festivals; Gambling; Literature; Music; Sport; Theatre

Erbervelt, Pieter, 21
Estates: private, sale of, 41; in nineteenth century, 62, 67, 80; in early twentieth century, 104-7, 121; expropriated by Japanese, 140; unrest on in 1945-6, 151; bought by government in 1950s, 184
Ethical Policy: impact in Batavia, 94-7, 105, 118; and 'Association Idea', 95, 98, 114, 119; and Chinese, 110-11; and Europeans, 114
Eurasians: under VOC, 19-21; in nineteenth-century Batavia, 53, 57, 60-1, 75-80; life in early twentieth-century Batavia, 116, 119; during Japanese Occupation, 139-42; after independence, 187-8; see also Europeans
Europeans: entry into early South-East Asia, 5-7; rivalry amongst, 7-12; in Batavia in seventeenth century, 13-14, 17-20; slave ownership, 22, 23; and Chinese, 26-7; life in eighteenth-century Batavia, 33, 35-42; view of Batavia in nineteenth century, 48-57; life in nineteenth-century Batavia, 54, 56-61, 75-9; trekkers, 60, 75; health of in nineteenth-century Batavia, 71-4; and tempo doeloe, 83; life in early twentieth-century Batavia, 94-5, 98, 114-17; in Municipal Council, 118-24; and coming of war, 125-6; internment by Japanese, 134, 138-9; in 1945-9, 150-1, 158; after 1949, 183-4, 187-8, 191, 254

FAMILY PLANNING IN JAKARTA, 222
Fatahillah, 6, 221
Festivals: Governor-General's birthday, 30; Chinese, 62-3, 79, 93, 256, 258; Lebaran, Mi'raj, Maulud, 93, 173; Pasar Gambir, 93; Queen's birthday, 97, 135; Japanese, 135
Finances, municipal: under VOC, 19; in early twentieth century, 119-23; in 1950s, 178, 182; foreign aid and, 201; under Sadikin, 217, 220, 226,

241; since 1977, 245, 261
Fires, 71, 121, 175
Floods: in nineteenth century, 69, 71, 74; in early twentieth century, 90, 122; since 1949, 181, 198, 245, 256
Food: in nineteenth-century Batavian culture, 75, 78-9; selling, 93, 100-1, 230, 259; price of, 106; shortage of during Japanese Occupation, 139, 141-3; struggle for control over during 1945-9, 155, 159; as part of cost of living, 186-7, 207, 215; as part of Jakartan culture, 193, 256, 259
Fort of Batavia, 11-12, 15, 30, 43-4
Franklin, George, 200-1
Fryke, Christopher, 18, 30

GALUR, 174
Gambang kromong, 76, 77, 144, 190, 236
Gambir, 169, 179, 257; see also Weltevreden
Gambling, 27, 79, 110, 220, 234
Gambus, 79, 144
Gang Kenari Hall, 98
Gas, 57
Gedung Pola, 170
Gelandangan, 197-8, 232
Glodok, 25, 27, 69, 134, 190, 256-8
Golkar, 235, 238, 240-1
Gondangdia, 90, 115, 124
Government, Municipal: of Batavia under VOC, 19; in nineteenth century, 74-5; in early twentieth-century Batavia, 96, 104, 118-24; under Japanese Occupation, 136, 142-3; in 1945-9, 149-51, 154; relations of and central government, 169-70, 177-8; under Sukarno, 196-205, 208; since 1966, 217-32, 238, 241, 243-5, 260-3
Governor of Jakarta: origin of position, 169; powers of, 177-8, 206-7; see also Cokropranolo; Ngantung; Sadikin; Sumarno; Suprapto
Governor-General, in Batavia: under VOC, 15, 19, 27, 30, 35-6, 43; in

nineteenth century, 55, 59–60, 83; see also Coen; Daendels
Governor-General's palace, 55, 68, 161; see also Istana Merdeka
Group of 50, 248
Guided Democracy, 167, 177–8, 194–5, 198, 200, 202, 205–6, 208

HALIM, 209, 244
Han Swie Tik, 190
Hanifah, Abu, 136, 144
Harbour: of Pajajaran, 5; of Jayakarta, 6; of Batavia, 15, 17, 41, 48–9, 52; importance of today, 256; see also Tanjung Priok; Sunda Kalapa
Harian Rakjat, 209
Harmonie Club, see under Clubs
Hatta, Mohammad, 137, 145–9, 194
Hawkers: in eighteenth-century Batavia, 29; in nineteenth-century Batavia, 53; in early twentieth-century Batavia, 93, 100–1, 103, 124; during Japanese Occupation, 141–2; since 1949, 198–9, 229–31, 243, 259
Health: in eighteenth-century Batavia, 18, 40; in nineteenth-century Batavia, 66, 71–5; in early twentieth-century Batavia, 73–5, 94, 123; during 1950s, 180–1, 186; in kampung in 1970s, 225; see also Hospitals
Hoevell, W. H. van, 59–61
Hospitals: in Batavia under the VOC, 24, 35; Military Hospital, 55, 74; Cikini Hospital, 66; in early twentieth century, 91; Jakarta General Hospital, 136, 154; gift of Sutowo, 234
Hotels: in Batavia in nineteenth century, 54; Hotel des Indes, 54, 156; Hotel Borobudur, 55; Hotel Indonesia, 167, 170, 178, 201; used for housing after 1949, 174; Western criticism of, 195; President Hotel, 219; Hilton Hotel, 219; Kartika Plaza, 219; spread of under Sadikin, 219
Housing: in Batavia under VOC, 17, 18, 24, 36, 40, 41; in nineteenth-

century Batavia, 54, 56–7, 64–5, 69; in early twentieth-century Batavia, 92, 94, 115; as issue in Municipal Council, 121–3; in 1945–9, 157–8; in 1950s, 173–5, 181, 193, 200–2; since 1966, 219, 222–3, 227–9, 243–5, 247; see also under Squatters; Kampung
Hugeng Iman Santoso, 234–5, 248
Hurgronje, Christiaan Snouck, 95–6

IDRUS, 142, 143, 160
Indians: in Batavia during VOC period, 19, 21, 22, 28, 31; in Batavia in nineteenth century, 53, 63, 254; in Pasar Baru, 258
Indo-Europeesch Verbond, 116, 119, 188
Indonesians: in Batavia under the VOC, 22, 26, 35; in nineteenth-century Batavia, 64–9, 72–9; life in early twentieth-century Batavia, 93–5, 99–80; impact of Western education on, 95–9; emergence of nationalism amongst, 98–100; work in early twentieth-century Batavia, 100–3; political activity of in early twentieth-century Batavia, 103–8; relations with Europeans in early twentieth-century Batavia, 114–17; in Municipal Council, 118–24; attitude to coming of war, 134; attitudes towards Japan during Occupation, 136–7; culture during Occupation, 143–4; in Jakarta 1945–9, 154, 159; 'Indonesianization' of economy, 183–4; see also Javanese; Orang Betawi; Slaves
Industry: under VOC, 23, 25, 38, 41; in nineteenth-century Batavia, 66–7, 82; in early twentieth-century Batavia, 93, 100–2; in 1945–9 period, 158; in 1950s, 183–5; under Sadikin, 217, 220, 232–3, 256; since 1977, 243
Inflation, 106, 141, 186, 207–8
Informal sector, policies towards, 124, 199, 222, 229–32, 243, 248, 259, 262;

see also Becak; Hawkers; Prostitutes
Investment in Jakarta, 182, 216–17, 233, 242, 246
Islam: rise as force in South-East Asia, 6; in Batavia under VOC, 34–6, 40; in nineteenth-century Batavia, 63, 65, 69–70, 72, 78; in early twentieth-century Batavia, 93, 97, 103–6, 109; and Japanese, 137; in 1950s, 160–1, 189, 203; in Jakarta since 1966, 220, 224–5, 235, 239–40, 246–7; *see also* Mosques
Istana Merdeka, 55, 168; *see also* Governor-General's palace

Jago, 67, 144
Jakarta: attractions of, 257; culture in, 254, 258–9; impact on Indonesia, 262; origin of name, 6, 134; name first used during Japanese Occupation, 133–4; life in city under Japanese, 135–45; becomes capital of Indonesian Republic, 133, 147, 161; population of in 1945, 140–1; as Kota Proklamasi, 147; under British control, 148–57; as Kota Diplomasi, 152; returns to Dutch control, 157–60; Dutch relinquish, 161; Sukarno's vision of, 167–71; population growth in 1950s, 171–2; housing in 1950s, 173–5; transport in 1950s, 176; urban government in 1950s, 177–8, 197–9; education in 1950s, 179; health in 1950s, 180–1; urban economy in 1950s, 182–7; Europeans in after 1949, 187–8; Chinese in 1950s, 188–91; urban culture in 1950s and early 1960s, 191–6; urban planning under Sukarno, 200–2; politics in Jakarta under Sukarno, 202–10; Sadikin's achievements in Jakarta, 215–21, 241–2; efforts to restrain growth of Jakarta's population, 221–2; housing policies under Sadikin, 222–6; land clearance in Jakarta in the 1970s, 227–9; informal sector in, 229–32; wealth and poverty in Jakarta in

1970s, 232–7; politics in Jakarta under Sadikin, 237–41; policies in Jakarta since 1977, 243–5; political developments since 1977, 246–8; review of changes in Jakarta's history, 254–6; review of continuity in Jakarta's history, 256–60; lessons to be learned from Jakarta's history, *see* Batavia; *see also* Batavia; Jayakarta; Sunda Kalapa
Jakarta Export Processing Zone, 243–4
Jalan Thamrin, 169–70, 197, 201–2, 230, 233, 235, 259
Japan: Dutch attitude towards before Pearl Harbor, 125; and start of Pacific War, 126; division of archipelago into regions, 133, 135; policy towards Indonesian nationalism, 133–8; and Islam, 137; and culture in Jakarta, 143–4; and *pemuda* in Jakarta, 144–8; and declaration of independence, 146–8; surrender of, 133, 148; Japanese attacked on Jakarta's outskirts after surrender, 150–1; aid to Jakarta, 201, 245; investment, 219; anti-Japanese riots, 239–40
Jatinegara, 190; *see also* Meester Cornelis
Java, Central and East: early trade of, 7; sugar industry in, 82, 103; people from in Batavia in 1930, 100; migration from, 171, 193; *see also* Javanese; Mataram
Java, West: early kingdoms, 4–6; pepper production of, 7; in seventeenth century, 8–13; in eighteenth century, 29, 42–3; in nineteenth century, 52–3, 64, 66, 71, 75, 81–2; Sundanese in Batavia in 1930, 99–100; communism in, 106–7; Dutch control in 1947–9, 157, 160; Darul Islam movement in, 160–1, 172; migration from, 171; Sundanese in Jakarta, 191, 192, 193, 247
Java-Bode, 117
Javanese: traders in seventeenth cen-

tury, 9; besiege Batavia, 12, 13; not permitted to live within Batavia's walls, 13; in Batavia under VOC, 19, 29, 39–40; in nineteenth-century Batavia, 53, 64; in early twentieth-century Batavia, 97–100; in Jakarta in 1961, 191; see also Java, Central and East

Jaya, Otto, 144

Jaya, Syuman, 192, 236

Jayadiningrat, P. A. Achmad, 95–6, 98, 107

Jayakarta: origins, 6; description of, 6–7; Dutch interest in, 8–9; rivalry with Banten, 9; siege of Dutch fort in, 11–12; town razed by VOC, 12

Jembatan Lima, 114

KAMPUNG: origins in Batavia, 30–1; in nineteenth-century Batavia, 60, 66–7, 69–71; in early twentieth-century Batavia, 90, 92, 94, 107; as issue in Municipal Council, 120–4; during Japanese Occupation, 141, 143; during 1945–9, 151; during 1950s, 174–5, 179–81, 186, 201, 203–5; railway workshop kampung, 193, 204, 208, 239; political activity in, 203, 208, 240; improvement programme, 222–6, 245, 262; and demolition, 227–9, 244; differentiation in during 1970s, 235, 237

Kampung Bali, 31

Kampung Bandan, 31

Kampung Bugis, 31, 64

Kampung Kebun Kacang, 186, 231, 233, 235, 244

Kampung Krekot Bunder, 175, 204–5

Kan, H. H., 112

K'ang Yu Wei, 109, 111

Kaum Betawi, 98

Kebayoran Baru, 158, 169, 173, 175, 179, 197, 232, 256

Kebon Sayur, 197

Kebon Sirih, 57, 145

Kemayoran, 61, 106, 126

Khaerun, Haji Akhmad, 150

Khouw family, 62, 80

Klender, 245

Koningsplein, 41, 56, 93, 106; see also Lapangan (Medan) Merdeka

Kota, 175, 220–1, 257; see also Batavia

Kramat, 57, 63

Krawang, 141, 154–5

Kroncong, 28, 64, 76, 79, 80, 93, 116, 144, 258

Kuningan, 219, 256

Kwee Kek Beng, 112

Kwitang, 66, 106

LAND: clearance in Batavia in early twentieth century, 106, 122; clearance under Sukarno, 198, 202; clearance under Sadikin, 227–9; clearance since 1977, 243–4; registration, 197, 227; speculation, 178, 227

Language: Indonesian as main in Jakarta, 254; Portuguese in Batavia, 28, 33; emergence of Malay as lingua franca in Batavia, 31, 33; in nineteenth-century Batavia, 61, 65, 75–8; in early twentieth-century Batavia, 99, 108, 110–12; Japanese policy on, 134–5; foreign languages in Jakarta, 188–90; adaptation by immigrants, 192–3; as unifying force, 236–7, 257; Jakartan Malay, 236–7

Lapangan Banteng, 170; see also Waterlooplein

Lapangan (Medan) Merdeka, 168–9, 257; see also Koningsplein

Law: under VOC, 21, 22, 28; as divisive force in nineteenth-century Batavia, 69; marriage law, 20, 69; and the Chinese, 112; Law School, 98, 136; citizenship law, 159, 188

Lee Man Fong, 190

Legal Assistance Bureau, 228–9

Lenong, 192

Lie Hok Thay, 190

Literature: novels in nineteenth-century Batavia, 58, 59, 72, 76, 79; of Peranakan Chinese, 68, 76, 113, 190; Nyai Dasima, 77–8; Indonesian

in early twentieth century, 92, 108; during 1942-9, 160; since 1949, 195-6, 237
Luar Batang, 40
Lubang Buaya, 237
Lubis, Mochtar, 196

MAEDA, ADMIRAL, 145, 147
Malacca, 5-7
Malaria: in Batavia under VOC, 40; in nineteenth-century Batavia, 71, 72, 74; in twentieth-century Batavia, 94, 180
Malays, 20, 64, 191
Manggadua, 105
Manggarai, 139
Manila, 241, 248, 263
Mardijkers, 19, 28, 29, 31, 64
Markets: tax farming of, 27; descriptions of by Europeans, 30, 60; as focal points for growth, 41; during Japanese Occupation, 142; since 1949, 170, 199, 218, 231; supermarkets, 235; and 1974 riots, 240; and modernization, 256; see also Tanah Abang; Pasar Baru; Pasar Senen
Marre, Jan de, 18
Marunda, 67
Marzuki, Ismail, 144
Masyumi, 203, 206
Mataram, 9, 10, 12, 13
Mayor: of Batavia arrested by Japanese, 134; during 1942-9, 134, 136, 150-1, 154, 157; power of mayor of Jakarta, 169, 177; in 1950s, 198-9, 201, 202-4
Meester Cornelis, 29, 57, 88, 104, 107, 117; see also Jatinegara
Menteng, 90, 106, 115, 121, 146-7, 154, 158, 175, 256-7
Michiels, Augustijn, 28-9
Migration: to Batavia under VOC, 13-14, 20-1, 23-9, 31-2; to Batavia in nineteenth century, 57, 61-5, 74-6, 80-1; in early twentieth century, 88-90, 99-101, 109, 111, 114-15; during 1942-9, 140-1; to

Jakarta 1948-65, 171-3; attitudes of and adaptation by migrants, 185, 192-3, 196, 238; in 1960s, 221; from Jakarta, 198, 222; and 'closed city' policy, 222, 229; and informal sector, 229-30; from Javanese countryside, 241-2; in twentieth century, 255; see also Population
Miss Tjitjih's, 192
Molenvliet, 41, 53-4
Mook, H. van, 150
Mook, Mevrouw van, 139
Moors, see under Indians
Mortality: in Batavia under VOC, 31, 39-40; in nineteenth-century Batavia, 71, 73; in early twentieth-century Batavia, 73-5, 81, 94, 123; in 1950s, 181; see also Health; Population
Mosques: Mesjid Angke (Jami Al-anwar), 36; Lubang Buaya, 40; in kampung, 93, 224-5; Pekojan, 93; attendance and Sarekat Islam, 104; Japanese and, 137; Istiqlal, 170, 218; gift of Sutowo, 234; see also Islam
Muara Angke, 90, 223
Muis, Abdul, 105-6, 124
Municipal offices, 219
Museums: Central, 56; Tekstil, 64; Jakarta Municipal, 221; Bahari (Maritime), 15
Music: by slaves, 29; in nineteenth-century Batavia, 56, 65, 76, 77, 79; in early twentieth-century Batavia, 93, 116; during Japanese Occupation, 144; since 1949 in Jakarta, 190, 199-200, 220, 235, 236, 253, 258

NAHDATUL ULAMA, 203, 205
Nasution, Adnan Buyung, 228-9
National Monument (Monas), 167-9, 257
Nationalism: and Western education, 95; emergence of Indonesian, 98-9; spread of in Batavia in early twentieth century, 101, 108; and Sarekat Islam, 104-6; and communism, 106-7; Chinese attitudes to Indone-

sian, 112–13; in Municipal Council, 118–25; Indonesian and approach of war, 125; Indonesian nationalists and the Japanese, 134–8, 143–8; Indonesian nationalists declare independence, 133, 146–7; Indonesian nationalists and Dutch return, 149–51; and culture, 160, 195; *see also Pemuda*; Partai Komunis Indonesia; Sarekat Islam; Sukarno

New Order regime: origins of, 215; policies of, 217, 226, 237, 241–2; critics of, 237, 240–1, 248; relations with Chinese, 239, 246; support for in Jakarta, 240–1

Ngantung, Henk, 169–70, 198, 206–7

Nijs, Breton de (pseudonym of Rob Nieuwenhuys), 79

Noordwijk, 54

Nusa Tenggara Timur, people from in Batavia/Jakarta, 21, 64, 191

Nyai, 20, 34, 77–8, 104, 114, 115

OEI TIANG TJOE, 139

Oma Irama, 236

Ong-Tae-Hae, 37–8

Opium, 27, 60, 80, 110

Oplet, 176, 244

Orang Betawi: origins and characteristics of, 65–7, 254; women, 76–9; on private estates, 80; outnumbered by immigrants, 99–100; involvement in 1924 uprising, 105; in Municipal Council, 96, 98, 120; and Japanese Occupation, 140; and Kebayoran Baru, 158; education level of, 180; survival since 1949, 191–2, 220, 236, 255, 258

PAK KODOK (pseudonym of Tjian Hok San), 190

Pane, Armijn, 92

Parapatan, 57

Parks, under Sadikin, 220; *see also* Koningsplein; Lapangan Merdeka

Partai Komunis Indonesia: in Batavia, 103, 106–7; Madiun revolt, 161; in 1950s in Jakarta, 195, 203–4; and

Guided Democracy, 205–6, 208–9; and 1965 coup, 209–10; New Order attitudes towards, 238–9

Partai Nasionalis Indonesia, 203, 205

Pasar Baru, 63, 69, 258

Pasar Minggu, 180, 192

Pasar Senen, 69, 170, 190, 192, 231, 240, 256

Pegangsaan, 57

Pekojan, 31, 63, 64, 93

Pemuda: during Japanese Occupation, 144–8; and declaration of independence, 146–8; operations in Jakarta in 1945–9, 149–61, 205; and 'cross-boys', 194

Perron, Edgar du, 117

Pertamina, 234, 242

Petojo, 31, 139

Planetarium, 170

Planning, urban: under VOC, 14–17, 27; by Daendels, 44, 55; during nineteenth century, 49, 57, 71, 74–5; in early twentieth century, 90, 121–3; of Kebayoran Baru, 158; and Sukarno, 167–71, 196–202; under Sadikin, 219–20, 225–7, 232; since 1977, 244–5

Plas, Ch. O. van der, 140–1, 150

Pluit flood control scheme, 181, 198

Police, 154, 227, 231, 234

Political unrest: among Chinese in eighteenth century, 26; in nineteenth-century Batavia, 59–60, 62, 80; in early twentieth-century Batavia, 101, 103, 105, 107; party infighting in 1950s, 202–3; violence in 1950s, 205–6; coup of 1965, 209–10; under Sadikin, 238–40; 1984 riots and aftermath, 247

Pondok, 71, 74, 92, 94, 224

Pondok Indah, 228

Population: mix in Jakarta, 254, 257–8; in seventeenth-century Batavia, 14, 19–21, 26; in eighteenth-century Batavia, 26, 30–1, 38, 40–1; in nineteenth-century Batavia, 52, 57, 61, 64–5, 69, 75, 81; in early twentieth-century Batavia, 88, 99,

109, 111, 114–15; in 1945, 140–1; in 1948, 171; in 1950s, 174–5, 181, 187–8; since 1950s, 191, 221, 245–6, 248

Portuguese, 5–7, 28, 31, 33

Poverty: in Batavia under VOC, 20, 44; in nineteenth-century Batavia, 61, 65, 67, 69, 71–5; in early twentieth-century Batavia, 92–4, 101–3, 106–7, 120, 122, 124; in 1942–9, 139–42, 150, 155; in Jakarta in 1950s and early 1960s, 173–5, 186–7, 192, 198, 205; in Jakarta in 1970s, 222–36, 239, 242; in Jakarta since 1977, 243–5, 248, 261–3

Press: in nineteenth-century Batavia, 59, 76; in early twentieth-century Batavia, 108, 112, 116–17; during Japanese Occupation, 135, 142; during 1946–7, 154, 157; since 1949, 189–90, 208, 238

Priangan, 42, 43, 81

Pringgodigdo, Suwarni, 159

Prison, 15, 19, 134, 138–9, 210, 232, 238–9

Prostitution, 77, 93, 103, 142, 185, 231–2

Pulo Gadung, 180, 220, 243

PUTERA, 137

RACH, JOHANNES, 36

Radio, 149, 190, 209, 237

Raffles, Olivia Mariamne (wife of Lt.-Gen. Raffles), 57

Rawasari Selatan, 257

Rebana, 65

Recreation, see under Entertainment

Religion: before the seventeenth century, 4–6; in Batavia under VOC, 17, 19, 20, 25, 28, 31, 34–5, 38, 40; in nineteenth-century Batavia, 61, 62–3, 65, 68–70, 72, 78; in early twentieth-century Batavia, 93, 103–6, 109–10; during Japanese Occupation, 137; in Jakarta since 1949, 160–1, 189, 192, 220, 224–5, 235, 239, 247–8; see also Christianity; Churches; Islam; Mosques;

Temples

Rendra, W. S., 220, 237

Republic, Indonesian: declared in Jakarta, 133, 146–8; relations with British, 149–57; resists Dutch reimposition of power, 133, 148–61; makes Yogyakarta capital, 133, 151; transfer of sovereignty to, 133, 161; policy towards Chinese in 1946, 159; armed rebellion against after 1949, 172, 182, 206

Revolution of 1945–9, 151, 160, 167, 202

Rijswijk, 54, 58

Rivers of Jakarta region, Ciliwung, 4, 18, 39, 40, 256; Angke, 4, 63; Cisadane, 4; Bekasi, 4; Citarum, 4

Roads: in Batavia under VOC, 18, 35, 36, 41; in nineteenth-century Batavia, 53–4, 62; in early twentieth-century Batavia, 90, 93, 119, 122, 123; during Japanese Occupation, 134, 142; under Sukarno, 167–70, 178, 197–201, 204; under Sadikin, 218–20, 225–6; since 1977, 244, 256

Robinson, Tjalie (pseudonym of Jan Boon), 91, 176, 188, 193, 258–9

Romusha, 136, 140, 146

Ronggeng, 30, 60, 80, 144

Roorda van Eysinga, Ph. P., 53, 72

Rosidi, Ayip, 174, 195

Rubbish disposal, 39, 71, 122, 175, 186, 200, 206–7, 225, 232, 257

SADIKIN, LT.-GEN. ALI: appointed Governor of Jakarta, 215; character and vision of, 216; and development of Jakarta, 217–21; and population growth, 221–2; and kampung improvement, 223–6; and land clearance, 226–9; and policies towards informal sector, 229–32; and army, 234–5; resignation of, 235, 242; and 1974 riots, 240; and taxation, 241; and New Order, 240, 248; impact on Jakarta, 261

Sado, 49, 66, 91, 176

Saleh, Raden, 66

Salemba, 57, 61, 98, 139, 175, 179
Sapi-ie, 120, 122
Sarekat Islam, in Batavia, 103–6
Sarinah department store, 167, 170, 231, 233
Sawah Besar, 174, 190
School of Arts, 98
Schools, *see under* Education
Schouwburg (Gedung Kesenian), 56
Semarang, 100, 101, 106–7, 245
Senayan, 167, 170, 207, 218
Senen, *see under* Pasar Senen
Senen artists, 192
Servants, domestic, 58, 60, 78, 100, 185
Sewage disposal, 39, 66, 71, 94, 122, 175, 196, 223–4
Shipping: under VOC, 23, 40; in nineteenth century, 49, 82; in twentieth century, 102, 184, 257
Si Pitung, 67
Siauw Giok Tjhan, 189
Simanjuntak, Cornel, 144
Simpruk, 228
Sin Po, 112, 190
Singapore, 49, 82, 202, 216
Slaves: in Batavia under VOC, 14, 20–3, 28–9, 31, 254; in nineteenth-century Batavia, 52, 64, 78
Slipi, 219
So Bing Kong, 23
Sport: in early twentieth-century Batavia, 92, 93, 115; during Japanese Occupation, 144; under Sukarno, 170, 178, 198, 201, 207; under Sadikin, 235
Squatters, 124, 173, 197–8, 221, 223, 243
Stambul, 76, 77, 114, 116, 192
Statues and monuments, 55, 134, 167–70, 237
Stavorinus, J. S., 41
STOVIA, 98–9, 105
Strikes in Batavia, 101–2
Students: Indonesian students in early twentieth-century Batavia, 97–9; and Japanese Occupation, 145–6; and anti-Sukarno demonstrations,

215; and New Order regime, 219, 235, 238, 240
Sudiro, 199, 201, 202–4
Sugar industry, 23, 25, 29, 38, 41, 82, 103
Suharto, General, 209–10, 215, 216, 237; *see also* New Order regime
Sukarno: before 1942, 98, 107; and Japan, 125, 137–8; during 1945–9, 145–50, 154; vision of Jakarta, 167–71, 201–2; and trams, 176; and political change in Jakarta, 177, 205–8; and Chinese, 190; and culture, 194–5; interference with planning, 200–2; downfall, 209–10, 215; *Autobiography*, 210; and Sadikin, 215–16; impact on Jakarta, 232, 260
Sukarno's house at Pegangsaan Timur 56, 147, 156
Sulawesi, people from in Batavia/ Jakarta, 21, 29, 31, 64, 191, 247
Sumarno, Dr, 180, 198, 206
Sumatra: Sumatrans in Batavia/ Jakarta, 97, 182, 191–3; migration to, 198; rebellion in, 182, 206
Sunda Kalapa, 4–5, 6, 256–7
Sundanese, *see under* Java, West
Sung Chung-Ch'uan, 189
Suprapto, Lt.-Gen., 244–5
Supratman, W. R., 99, 112
Surabaya, 75, 81, 82, 90, 100, 101, 106–7, 149, 224, 245
Surapati, 23
Sutarjo Kartohadikusumo, 116, 136
Sutowo, Ibnu, 234
Suwiryo, 150, 151, 154, 156–7
Swimming pools, 92, 115
Syahrir, Sutan, 145, 154
Syamsurijal, 198

Tabrani, Mohamad, 183
Taman Ismail Marzuki, 200, 218, 220, 232
Taman Mini Indonesia Indah, 219
Tan In Hok, 189
Tan Tjeng Bok, 114
Tanah Abang, 41, 64, 175, 231, 259

Tanah Sareal, 223

Tanah Tinggi, 105, 175, 181

Tangerang, 61, 62, 100, 105, 107, 150, 220, 244

Tanjidor, 199–200

Tanjung Priok: site of archaeological excavations, 4; building of harbour, 48–9, 52, 70, 82; in early twentieth century, 100, 102; bombed by Japanese, 126; education levels at, 180; scandal at, 187; under New Order, 220, 234; riots at, 247

Taxation: tax-farming by Chinese, 27, 41, 80, 110; municipal taxes in early twentieth century, 120; by Japanese, 140; municipal since 1949, 178, 217, 220, 241

Taxis, 219

Telephone, 91, 154, 175, 208, 219

Television, 219, 224, 237

Temples, Chinese: in Batavia/Jakarta, Wihara Dewi Samudera, 17; Klenteng Gunung Sari (Sentiong), 25; Wihara Dharma Bhakti, 25; Ancol temple, 34–5; building of, 68, 110, 190

Thamrin, Mohammad Husni: personal background, 96; stages of his political development, 98, 108; in Municipal and People's Councils, 119–24; and Japanese, 125–6; death of, 125–6; *kampung* improvement programme named after him, 223–6

Theatre, Chinese in eighteenth-century Batavia, 17; in nineteenth-century Batavia, 62, 76, 79; during Japanese Occupation, 144; in 1950s, 192; promotion by Sadikin, 220; in 1970s, 236

Tijn, B. van, 158

Tiong Hoa Hwee Koan, 110–21

Tirtoadisuryo, 104

Town Hall, 19, 26, 151, 154, 157, 221, 257

Trade: spice, 5–7, 43; under VOC, 14, 15, 17, 23–4, 42–3; in nineteenth century, 52–3, 62, 63, 66, 68; in early twentieth-century, 100, 103–4,

111; impact of Japanese Occupation, 140; Dutch policies in 1947–9, 158; since 1949, 183–4, 217; *see also* Hawkers

Trade unions, 101–2, 204, 208, 239

Trains: railway building in nineteenth century, 49, 53; during Japanese Occupation, 141, 147; Republican control in 1946, 156; commuters in 1957, 173; plans for Jabotabek railway system, 245

Trams, 52–3, 147, 149, 156, 176

Transport, under VOC, 17, 30, 36, 41, 43; in nineteenth-century Batavia, 49, 52–3, 66, 81–2; in early twentieth-century Batavia, 90, 91, 100, 115, 124; during Japanese Occupation, 141; in 1945–9, 147, 156; during 1950s, 173, 176, 200; disrupted in early 1960s, 207–8; under Sadikin, 215, 219, 230, 237, 239; since 1977, 244, 245, 256

Tur, Pramudya Ananta, 160, 194

United Nations, 152, 160–71, 200

United States, 152, 160–1, 194–5, 201, 219

University of Indonesia, 179, 208

Usmar Ismail, 144

Vaderlandsche Club, 116–17, 119

Valentijn, Francois, 18, 24–5

Veth, Bas, 58–9, 117

VOC (Vereenigde Oost-Indische Compagnie): origins, 7–8; and Coen, 9, 11; in Jayakarta, 11, 12; trade in Asia, 13; and European colonization, 14; in Batavia, 15, 19, 20; policy towards Eurasians, 20–1; and slaves, 21–2; and Chinese, 23, 25–6; organization of ethnic groups, 30; decline of, 38, 41, 42; development of coffee cultivation, 42, 43; charter expires, 43

Wanandi, Jusuf, 235

War, Second World: response in Indonesia to outbreak, 125–6; experience of in Jakarta, 134–46; end of, 148

Water, drinking: under VOC, 39–40; in nineteenth-century Batavia, 69, 71, 74; in early twentieth-century Batavia, 119, 122, 123; in 1950s, 175, 180–1; in 1970s, 225–6; since 1977, 245, 247

Waterlooplein, 54, 55, 134; see also Lapangan Merdeka

Watts, Kenneth, 200

Wealth: in Batavia under VOC, 18, 22, 25, 33–8, 41–2; in nineteenth-century Batavia, 58, 62–4, 68, 77–8, 80; in early twentieth-century Batavia, 112, 115, 120; during Japanese Occupation, 140; in Jakarta since 1949, 181–2, 187, 233–5, 241, 256

Weltevreden, 41, 44, 54–7, 115; see also Gambir

West New Guinea/West Irian, 161, 207

Williams, Maslyn, 207–8

Women: in Batavia under VOC, 14, 20, 22, 30, 33–4; in nineteenth-

century Batavia, 57–8, 60–1, 66–7, 75–80, 82; in early twentieth-century Batavia, 92, 96, 100–1, 105, 108, 113–15; during Japanese Occupation, 139, 142–3, 145; during 1945–9, 156, 159; in Jakarta in 1950s and 1960s, 179, 184–5, 204, 207; under New Order, 224, 235, 237, 243, 247

Work: in Batavia under VOC, 22–4, 28–9; in nineteenth-century Batavia, 58, 64, 66–7, 74, 82; in early twentieth-century Batavia, 94, 96–7, 100–3; in 1960s, 171, 184–5, 203–4; under Sadikin, 224, 229–33, 248, 259; since 1977, 246, 248, 259

World Bank, 222–3, 226, 241, 244

YOGYAKARTA, 133, 151, 152, 154, 161

Youth Oath Building, 98–9, 108

ZAALBERG, F. H. K., 116

Zentgraaf, H. C., 117

Zoo, 37, 66

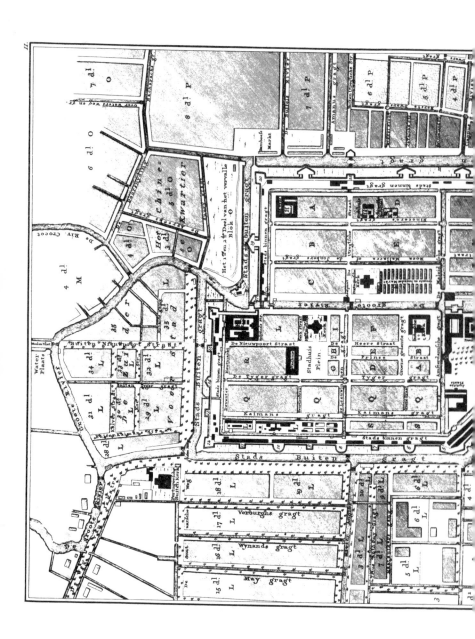